Sunset

NEW EASY BASICS

COOKBOOK

EDITED BY JERRY ANNE DI VECCHIO

SUNSET BOOKS INC. • MENLO PARK • CALIFORNIA

SUNSET BOOKS INC.
President/Chief Executive Officer: *Stephen J. Seabolt*
VP, Chief Financial Officer: *James E. Mitchell*
VP, Manufacturing Director: *Lorinda B. Reichert*
Director, Sales & Marketing: *Richard A. Smeby*
Editorial Director: *Bob Doyle*
Director of Finance: *Lawrence J. Diamond*
Production Director: *Lory Day*
Retail Sales Development Manager: *Becky Ellis*
Art Director: *Vasken Guiragossian*

New Easy Basics was produced in conjunction with
Rebus, Inc., New York, NY.

Editor and Publisher: *Rodney M. Friedman*
Associate Publisher: *Barbara Maxwell O'Neill*
Editor in Chief: *Charles L. Mee, Jr.*
Executive Editor: *Marya Dalrymple*

Staff for this Book
Editor: *Jerry Anne Di Vecchio*
Developmental Editor: *Linda J. Selden*
Art Director: *Timothy Jeffs*
Computer Production: *Sara Bowman*
Writers: *Mary B. Johnson, Bonnie J. Slotnick*
Illustrations: *Dorothy Reinhardt, Sally Shimizu, Timothy Jeffs*
Photography: *Thom DeSanto*
Photography Assistant: *John Vitollo*
Food Stylist: *Diane Simone Vezza*
Food Styling Assistant: *Tracy Donovan*
Prop Stylist: *Valorie Fisher*
Test Kitchen: *Sandra Rose Gluck, Ellie Ritt, Miriam Rubin, Tracey Seaman, Helen Taylor Jones*
Nutritional Analysis: *Hill Nutrition Associates, Inc.*
Editorial Assistant: *James W. Brown, Jr.*
Production Coordinator: *Patricia S. Williams*

Front cover: Fudge Brownies (page 163). Design by
Robin Weiss. Photography by Ed Carey. Food styling by
Sandra Cook.

Welcome to good cooking . . .

The best can be so simple. Being simple is so
basic. And the basics can be so easy. This is
why Sunset's *New Easy Basics* is such a great
cookbook, why it's in my kitchen, and why it
should be in yours, too.

True, I'm hardly the beginner this book is
designed to serve. But I still have to look up
how long it takes to roast an 18-pound turkey,
steep a chicken breast, or boil an artichoke.
These invaluable facts, plus hundreds of tips
and techniques, are easily accessed in *New
Easy Basics*. They are the stepping stones to
success that brings culinary confidence.

So welcome to this book. Let the recipes
and directions on these pages help you create
memorable meals and inspire you to stretch
your wings. You will be working with information that is straight to the point, helpful in a
pinch, and always there to guide you to delicious results.

Every recipe is accompanied by a nutritional analysis (see page 12) prepared by Hill
Nutrition Associates, Inc., of Florida. We are
grateful to Lynne Hill, R.D., for her advice and
expertise.

All of the recipes were developed in the
Sunset test kitchens. If you have comments or
suggestions, please let us hear from you. Write
to us at:

Sunset Books
Cookbook Editorial
80 Willow Road
Menlo Park, CA 94025

If you would like to order additional
copies of any of our books, call us at 1 (800)
643-8030, ext. 544, or check with your local
bookstore.

Cheers,

Jerry Di Vecchio

Jerry Di Vecchio

CONTENTS

GETTING STARTED

Welcome to the kitchen, where the family relaxes and regroups as promising aromas fill the air; where party guests gather as if drawn by a magnet; where shelling peas, kneading dough, and cutting out cookies are shared pleasures. The kitchen—equal parts classroom, laboratory, and artist's studio—is a place in which to learn and grow, to create and to teach. Ideally, cooking is a rewarding challenge, never a chore—or a bore.

With this book as a guide, you are about to embrace a pastime that is both work and play—about to embark on creative adventures that will bring you a lifetime of satisfaction (and torrents of praise) while accomplishing the day-to-day goal of feeding family and friends.

This is no armchair book; it's one to experience as you read. With recipes serving as detailed lessons, the text spells out all the fundamentals of good cooking. You'll find—thoroughly explained—the basic techniques you need to establish yourself as an accomplished cook. Moreover, these skills will prepare you to cook from other books besides this one, to try recipes given to you by friends, and even to experiment with original concoctions. As you travel the path to kitchen expertise, some dishes will be singled out as family favorites, while others will become your signature specialities for entertaining.

By doing and tasting, you'll come to know the principles of good cooking. You'll learn which aspects of cooking allow freedom to bend the rules, and which techniques depend on scientific precision. Some recipes include variations that will inspire you, showing you just how easy it is to be innovative within familiar guidelines.

Even if you've never ventured much beyond heating a frozen dinner, this book can lead you to attempt recipes you've always thought intimidating or impossible—a perfectly puffed cheese soufflé, for ex-ample, or a fragrant, crusty loaf of yeast bread, or a holiday turkey, plump with savory stuffing and roasted to a golden, juicy turn.

Novice cooks often worry that this sort of "from-scratch" goodness will mean armloads of hard-to-find ingredients, hours of steamy toil, and stacks of dishes in the sink. You can forget any such qualms. We've streamlined our material to suit the busy schedule of today's cook who, as likely as not, works at a job until 5 P.M. (or later) on weekdays. You will see that the recipes call for only widely available ingredients, and our shopping lists are short. Time-consuming, labor-intensive dishes are omitted—there are plenty of other sources that offer such recipes.

And, besides, expert cooks tend to agree that the best-tasting dishes are often the simplest ones, prepared with fresh ingredients and an eye on fat content, and cooked using classic, basic techniques. Follow our directions with care and you needn't fear disappointment or failure; each recipe will yield a solid success.

Throughout the book you will find step-by-step photographs illustrating some of the more useful or complicated techniques. You'll also discover tips and shortcuts and, to help you orchestrate the full show, there is advice on how to devise interesting and healthy menus, get organized, shop wisely, and store food to keep it at its best. In addition, every one of our recipes is accompanied by a nutritional analysis.

The upcoming pages include information on the good cook's basic equipment; instructions on how to measure accurately; and a glossary of cooking terms used in the book. Just as it's important to know that you need to buy the freshest ingredients, you must also be knowledgeable about these aspects of cooking to achieve great results.

So—dive in and have fun developing your new reputation as the best cook in town.

MEASURING

There's no getting around it—measurement is critical. If you want to achieve consistent results each time you prepare a recipe, you must measure the ingredients accurately. Measure liquids in standard glass or plastic measuring cups designed for that purpose. Set the cup on a counter, bend down to check it at eye level, and adjust accordingly. Measure dry or solid ingredients in a set of cups made to hold an exact capacity. Don't shake or pack dry ingredients down unless a recipe specifies doing so. Stir a dry ingredient, such as flour, spoon gently into the specific-size cup (piling it high), then scrape the top to level.

Measuring equipment

Standard cups for liquid measuring come in 1-, 2-, and 4-cup (240-, 470-, and 950-ml) sizes with a pouring spout. Measurement marks are on the sides.

Standard cups for dry measuring come in sets that include ¼ cup, ⅓ cup, ½ cup, and 1 cup.

Standard measuring spoons in sets of four include ¼-, ½-, and 1-teaspoon measures, plus 1 tablespoon. Use for liquid and dry ingredients.

How to measure ingredients

Liquid. For accurate measuring, place cup on level surface, pour in ingredient, and read markings on cup at eye level.

Brown sugar. With fingers, pack firmly into cup until even with rim. When inverted, brown sugar will hold its shape.

Dry. Gently spoon ingredient into cup, piling high; level off with metal spatula or straight-sided knife.

Solid vegetable shortening. With spatula, pack into cup; run spatula through to release air; pack again and level off.

Butter or margarine. Cut desired amount following markings on stick; or spoon out and level tub margarine (*not whipped*).

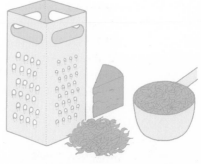

Shredded cheese. Lightly put shreds in dry measuring cup until even with rim; don't pack unless recipe says to do so.

SELECTING COOKWARE

A cook's fundamental armory of pots and pans does not have to be as extensive as the gleaming displays in the kitchenware shops suggest. In fact, it's wiser to purchase high-quality utensils one at a time, rather than invest in an inexpensive but seemingly complete set that turns out not to meet your needs. Start with the most-used pans: 1-, 2-, 3-, and 5- to 6-quart (950 ml, 1.9-, 2.8-, and 5- to 6-liter) pans with lids; a stockpot; a wide (10- to 12-inch/25- to 30-cm) plain or nonstick frying pan with a lid; a medium-size (7- to 8-inch/18- to 20-cm) omelet pan; a shallow baking or roasting pan with a rack; a 10- by 15-inch (25- by 38-cm) rimmed baking pan; a 14- to 16-inch (35.5- to 40-cm) wok (nonstick woks are available); and a double boiler.

No matter what its purpose, a pan should have a thick bottom and a sturdy handle (or handles). Make sure your pans are so well balanced that, empty or full, they will stand squarely on burners with the lid on or off. Choose pans with tight-fitting lids as well as firmly mounted, insulated handles and knobs. The interior sides should be straight, curving gently to meet the bottom so that there are no "corners" inaccessible to a spoon or whisk.

What follows is a brief survey of cookware materials, and a discussion of the advantages and disadvantages of each. If you are uncertain about what to buy or how to use your cookware, consult a knowledgeable salesperson at a housewares store, or call the manufacturer's helpline.

Aluminum. This metal is a quick, even heat conductor, so it's ideal for pans used for browning and sautéing. For best results, be sure that the aluminum is heavy cast, not thin. Be aware that aluminum can react with acidic foods (such as tomatoes or wine), and salt or chemicals used to purify water may cause surface pitting and darkening. Aluminum pans that are treated, coated, or lined (on the inside) with a durable, nonreactive material such as stainless steel resist these changes best.

Cast iron. Cast-iron pans absorb, distribute, and retain heat effectively. However, they're very heavy and need special care. At one time, all cast iron required "seasoning" before use, but many pans now come preseasoned; you can also buy cast-iron cookware with a colorful enamel coating inside and out, as well as pans with nonstick linings. Uncoated cast iron must be dried thoroughly and stored without

lids in a dry place to prevent rust. Pots made of this material are extremely durable and relatively inexpensive, although the special coatings add considerably to the price.

Copper. This material is a superb heat conductor. However, copper cookware can be prohibitively expensive (a pan may cost upwards of $100). Also, copper is chemically reactive with many foods, producing off flavors and discoloration. For this reason, copper pots are always lined—often with tin or stainless steel—and the lining must be treated with care and reapplied if it gets scratched or worn. Copper does, however, have a place in medium-price cookware: It is layered into, or applied onto, the bottoms of stainless-steel or aluminum pans to improve their heat conductivity.

Glass and ceramic (heatproof). These relatively inexpensive materials absorb heat more slowly than metal but retain the heat longer. Glass and ceramic bakeware manufactured to resist extreme temperatures can go directly from freezer to oven, and some of the bakeware is even stovetop-safe. However, many types of glass cookware will break with sudden temperature changes, contact with stovetop elements, or under the broiler.

Nonstick. Nonporous, nontoxic plastic coatings or finishes permit cooking with a minimum amount of fat and also make cleaning easy. Some coatings deteriorate at high temperature, and some should not be used in the oven; only those specially made for broiling should be used under a direct heat. Metal tools and abrasive cleaners can scratch some coatings (use wooden or plastic tools with nonstick-coated cookware), and not all are dishwasher-safe. Price is determined by the quality of the pan and the coating or finish.

Porcelain enamel. Often called "enamel," this glassy surface can be bonded to iron, aluminum, steel, or stainless steel. Porcelain bonded to iron does the best job distributing heat, but when bonded to aluminum or steel, conduction is spotty. Porcelain is nonreactive and is easy to clean. However, the finish chips easily, so handle with care, especially when storing. Prices vary.

Stainless steel. Solid stainless steel conducts heat unevenly, and therefore is best used around an aluminum, copper, or carbon-steel core. Nonreactive, it doesn't spot or stain readily. The cost of stainless-steel cookware varies according to its "gauge" (thickness), finish, and core.

BAKEWARE & BAKING ACCESSORIES

Always use the right-size pan or dish for the recipe. If the size isn't marked on the utensil, measure the dimensions from the inside top edges, or check its capacity by measuring the amount of water it holds. A standard 8-inch (20-cm) square pan holds about 1½ quarts (1.4 liters); a 9-inch (23-cm) square or 7- by 11-inch (18- by 28-cm) pan holds about 2 quarts (1.9 liters); and a 9- by 13-inch (23- by 33-cm) pan holds about 3 quarts (2.8 liters).

For cakes and cookies, use baking sheets with smooth seams (for ease in cleaning). For pies and breads, use metal, glass, or ceramic pans.

Bakeware

Plain tube pan

5- by 9-inch (12.5- by 23-cm) loaf pan

9-inch (23-cm) round cake pan

9- by 13-inch (23- by 33-cm) baking pan

Removable-rim pan

10- by 15-inch (25- by 38-cm) rimmed baking pan

Pie pan

Muffin pan

Baking sheet

8-inch (20-cm) square pan

Tart pans

Fluted tube pan

Baking Accessories

Soufflé dish

Custard cups

Biscuit cutter

Racks

Pastry Tools

Pastry blender

Pastry bag and tips

Pastry brushes

Slicing wheel

Pastry wheel

Rolling pins

ABOUT KNIVES

It's surprising how often a kitchen is well equipped in almost every respect except for knives—yet you will rarely make a meal without using one. The quality and condition of your knives will determine, to a great extent, your efficiency as a cook.

A knife's performance depends on the quality of its steel and the excellence of its "grind" (cutting edge). To take and hold a keen edge, a blade must be made of a high-carbon-content steel. Carbon content determines the hardness of a blade—and hardness is essential for a sharp edge.

A carbon-steel knife, therefore, would seem to be the best choice, but there are disadvantages—this material can darken and discolor, and it will rust if you don't dry it carefully after washing. Stainless steel, a combination of carbon steel and chromium, has noncorrosive properties, so it stays shiny. But stainless steel with a low carbon content will not keep a sharp edge. High-carbon stainless, which takes a good edge, requires a little more effort to sharpen, but it is worth it.

The pros and cons of carbon and stainless balance each other fairly well—you'll probably put as much effort into keeping a carbon-steel knife clean as you would put into keeping a low-carbon stainless-steel knife sharp, and, if frequently honed on a steel (shown bottom right), the stainless gives just as good a cutting edge as the carbon.

Chrome-plated knives look similar to stainless-steel knives, but they don't give the same service. In time, the chromium finish wears off, and the edge is likely to rust.

Look for quality. Usually a knife's price is related to its quality. But there are other tests. Grip the handle to be sure the knife is well balanced, with the center of gravity near the handle (especially important in large knives). Look for a "full tang"—an extension of the blade that runs the full length of the handle. This metal extension may not be visible, but three rivets in the handle usually indicate a full tang (don't be fooled by knives with fake rivets hiding a tang of only 2 in./5 cm or so). The best knives taper from the heel to the tip, and from the top of the blade to the cutting edge. The exception: A good high-carbon stainless-steel Asian cleaver. The bolster protects the grip hand from the blade.

Proper care of knives. Keep your knives in their own protected place—not in a drawer where contact with other kitchen tools may dull their edges. Hang them on a magnetic rack or keep them in a slotted block of wood specially designed for knife storage. To preserve their handles, never soak knives in water or wash them in a dishwasher. If you do, the wooden handles will dry and warp, loosening the tang. Simply wash and dry knives immediately. It's safe to scour carbon knives with abrasives.

Basic knives. Shown below are seven knife types that can handle virtually any kitchen cutting job: *paring knife*, for peeling, seeding, and pitting; *utility knife*, for slicing tomatoes and fruit; *boning knife*, for boning meat, fish, or chicken; *slicing knife*, for carving large cuts of meat into thin slices; *butcher knife*, for cutting up raw meat or poultry and large foods like watermelon; *chef's knife* (also known as a French knife), for chopping and mincing vegetables and for many other uses; and a *serrated knife*, for slicing bread or such baked goods as angel food cakes. A *steel* keeps your knives sharp (see page 96).

Paring knife

Utility knife

Boning knife

Slicing knife

Butcher knife

Chef's (French) knife

Serrated knife (bread knife)

Steel (see page 96 for how to use)

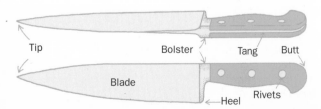

Tip   Bolster   Tang   Butt

Blade

Heel   Rivets

USEFUL KITCHEN EQUIPMENT

Once you've made the more difficult and expensive kitchen purchases, like pots, pans, and knives, the real fun can begin—the fascinating job of selecting the smaller tools that are indispensable for all sorts of special tasks. These items can be inexpensive, but you should resist the urge to economize here. Consider it an investment that will pay off in efficiency and in the longevity of the tool itself.

Customize your choice of tools according to the kinds of cooking you do. And keep in mind the type of finish on your pots and pans (nonstick and other less-durable surfaces call for nonmetal spatulas and spoons).

Be sure to look for quality construction. Multi-part implements should be solidly riveted together, with good-size handles made of heatproof material. Wooden utensils should be made of dense, smooth wood that won't break or splinter in use. Bowls and colanders should be well balanced and not "tippy."

Learn to care for your tools—follow the manufacturer's advice for washing and drying to prevent damage and rust. If you rely on a dishwasher, make sure that your kitchen tools are dishwasher-safe.

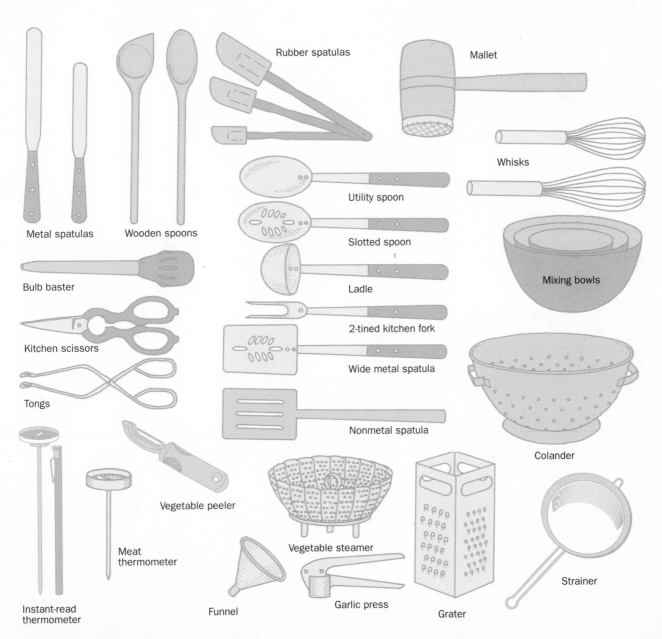

Metal spatulas

Wooden spoons

Rubber spatulas

Mallet

Whisks

Utility spoon

Slotted spoon

Ladle

Mixing bowls

Bulb baster

Kitchen scissors

2-tined kitchen fork

Wide metal spatula

Tongs

Nonmetal spatula

Colander

Vegetable peeler

Meat thermometer

Vegetable steamer

Instant-read thermometer

Funnel

Garlic press

Grater

Strainer

A GLOSSARY OF COOKING TERMS

Al dente: An Italian term used to describe any type of pasta that is cooked until tender but slightly firm to the bite.

Bake: To cook, covered or uncovered, by dry heat (usually in an oven). When applied to meats and poultry cooked uncovered, the process is often called roasting.

Bake blind: To bake a pastry shell empty, without a filling. See page 167 for more information on how to bake blind.

Baking powder: A chemical leavening agent produced in three forms, all activated when combined with liquid. Tartrate acts instantly. Phosphate is activated partially by liquid, partially by heat. Double-acting is activated mainly by heat, releasing most of its carbon dioxide in the baking process. (The recipes in this book were tested with double-acting baking powder.)

Baking soda: A leavening agent that releases gas only when mixed with an acid agent, such as buttermilk, yogurt, or lemon juice.

Baste: To brush or spoon pan drippings or other fat or liquid over food as it cooks to keep the surface moist and to add flavor.

Batter: A liquid mixture (containing flour and other ingredients) that can be stirred.

Beat: To stir or mix rapidly with a spoon, whisk, or an electric mixer, adding air to make a mixture smooth, lighter, or fluffier.

Blanch: To immerse food briefly in boiling water, either to help loosen the skin or to cook briefly to set color and flavor. See page 123.

Blend: To thoroughly combine two or more ingredients until smooth and uniform in texture, color, and flavor.

Boil: To heat liquid hot enough for bubbles to constantly rise and break on the surface. To cook food in boiling liquid.

Boned, rolled, and tied: Meat cuts that are boned, then rolled into a compact shape and tied to secure.

Bouquet garni: A cluster of herbs that is tied together and used for flavoring.

Braise: To cook gently in a small amount of liquid in a covered pan. Food may or may not be browned first.

Braise-Deglaze: A way to cook foods in a small amount of liquid until liquid evaporates and foods brown. More liquid is then added and mixture is stirred to release browned particles.

Bread: To coat with bread or cracker crumbs before cooking, usually after first dipping food into beaten egg or other liquid so crumbs will adhere.

Broil: To cook by direct heat under a broiler.

Broth: Liquid in which meat, poultry, fish, or vegetables, or a combination, are cooked; also called stock.

Brown: To cook in a small amount of fat until browned on all sides, giving food an appetizing color.

Caramelize: To melt sugar without scorching, until it turns golden brown and develops characteristic flavor. To cook onions and other vegetables until sweet and golden.

Chop: To cut food into small pieces.

Coat: To cover a food with another ingredient, such as egg or flour, by sprinkling, dipping, or rolling.

Coat a spoon: The stage reached by a thickened liquid mixture when it leaves an even film on the back of a metal spoon.

Combine: To stir together two or more ingredients until blended.

Core: To remove the seeded center of a fruit or vegetable.

Cream: To beat until soft, smooth, and fluffy, as for butter and sugar.

Crimp: To seal the edges of two pieces of pastry together by pressing with fingers or fork tines.

Cube: To cut into small cubes (usually a specific size). "Cubed" meats are mechanically tenderized or pounded to break up muscle fibers.

Curdled: Separated into a liquid containing small solid particles (caused by overcooking or too much heat or agitation).

Cut in: To distribute solid fat into dry ingredients with a pastry blender (or two table knives, scissors fashion) until particles are desired size.

Dash: A very small amount, less than 1/8 teaspoon.

Deglaze: To loosen browned particles from bottom of a pan by adding wine, broth, or other liquid.

Degrease: To skim fat from surface of a liquid.

Dice: To cut into very small pieces (usually 1/8 to 1/4 in./3 to 6 mm).

Dot: To scatter bits of an ingredient, such as butter, over surface of food.

Dough: A thick, pliable mixture of flour and liquid ingredients, firm enough to be kneaded or shaped with the hands.

Dredge: To coat or cover food lightly but completely with flour, sugar, or other fine substance, shaking off excess.

Drippings: Melted fat and juices given off by meat or poultry as it cooks, usually by frying or roasting.

Drizzle: To pour oil, melted fat, sugar syrup, icing, or other liquid in a fine stream, making a pattern over food surface.

Dust: To sprinkle lightly with flour or sugar, shaking off excess.

Emulsion: A mixture, such as mayonnaise, in which fatty particles are suspended in a liquid.

Fat: Generic term for fats that are solid at room temperature, such as butter, margarine, lard, vegetable shortening, and the rendered drippings of meat and fowl.

Fillet: The boneless tenderloin of meat or poultry; a boneless piece or slice of meat or fish; filleting is the process of removing bones.

Flake: To lightly break foods into small, thin pieces, usually with the tines of a fork.

Floweret: A small flower, one of a cluster of composite flowers, of broccoli or cauliflower.

Flute: To make decorative indentations around the edge of pastry, vegetables, or fruit.

Fold in: To gently combine a light, delicate, aerated substance, such as whipped cream or beaten egg whites, into a heavier mixture by lifting mixture up and over with each stroke.

Freeze: To get cold enough to become solid.

Fry: To cook in hot fat. To pan-fry, use a small amount of fat. To deep-fry, immerse foods in fat.

Garnish: To decorate a completed dish, making it more attractive.

Gel: To congeal.

Glaze: To coat with a substance or mixture that gives food a sheen.

Gluten: Protein part of wheat flour that is essential in bread-making.

Grate: To rub solid food against a metal object that has sharp-edged holes, reducing food to thin shreds.

Grease: To rub fat or oil on the surface of a bowl, pan, or other utensil to prevent food from sticking.

Grill: To cook on a rack over direct heat—gas, electricity, or charcoal.

Grind: To run food through a food chopper or food processor until of very fine texture.

Hull: To remove stems or outer husks (as from strawberries or nuts).

Julienne: Matchstick pieces of vegetables, fruits, or cooked meats; or a technique for cutting foods into matchstick pieces.

Knead: To work dough with hands in a fold-and-press motion.

Lemon-vinegar water: Water to which lemon juice or vinegar has been added to prevent discoloration or darkening of foods, such as apples or artichokes. Add ½ to 1 tablespoon (15 ml) lemon juice or vinegar for each quart (950 ml) of water.

Line: To cover inside or bottom of a baking dish or pan with parchment or wax paper.

Marinade: A seasoned liquid, usually containing an acid, such as vinegar, lemon juice, or wine, in which meat, poultry, or seafood soaks to enhance its flavor.

Marinate: To soak in a marinade.

Mash: To crush to a soft mass.

Mask: To cover completely, as with a sauce, aspic, mayonnaise, or cream.

Meringue: Egg whites that have been beaten with sugar to form a thick, stiff foam.

Mince: To cut or chop into very fine pieces.

Pan-broil: To cook, uncovered, in an ungreased or lightly greased frying pan, pouring off fat as it accumulates.

Pan-fry: To cook in a frying pan in a small amount of fat.

Parboil: To boil until partially cooked; remainder of cooking is done by another method.

Pare: To cut away outer skin using a small knife or vegetable peeler.

Peel: To strip, cut off, or pull away skin or rind.

Pit: To remove the seed from whole fruits such as apricots, avocados, and cherries.

Poach: To gently cook in a simmering liquid so food retains its shape.

Pot roasting: To cook a large piece of meat by braising.

Punch down: To expel air from a risen yeast dough by pushing it down with fists or a mixing with a dough hook.

Purée: To rub food through a strainer, or to whirl food in a blender or a food processor, to a smooth mixture.

Reduce: To decrease quantity and concentrate flavor of a liquid by rapid boiling in an uncovered pan.

Render: To melt fat by heating in a pan on the stove or in the oven.

Roast: To cook meat or poultry, uncovered, by dry heat (usually in an oven); also, a cut of meat cooked by this method.

Roux: Mixture of melted fat and flour, cooked until bubbly to remove the raw, starchy taste of flour; used to thicken soups and sauces.

Salad oil: Oil made from vegetables or seeds, such as corn or sunflower.

Sauté: To cook in a small amount of fat over high heat.

Scald: To heat milk to just below the boiling point (when tiny bubbles appear around edge of pan).

Score: To cut shallow grooves or slits through surface or outer layer of food to speed cooking, to prevent edge fat of meat from curling, or to make decorative pattern.

Sear: To brown meat on all sides over high heat.

Shortening, solid: A solid fat made from refined vegetable oil that has been partially hydrogenated and whipped.

Shred: To cut, tear, or grate into thin, irregular strips.

Shuck: To remove an outer covering, such as the husks and silk of corn or the shells of oysters.

Sift: To lighten or remove lumps from dry ingredients, such as flour or powdered sugar, by passing them through a fine strainer or sifter.

Simmer: To cook in liquid close to the boiling point (bubbles form slowly and burst before reaching surface).

Skim: To remove fat or scum from the surface of a liquid with a spoon or bulb baster.

Steam: To cook in water vapors, on a rack or in a steam basket, in a covered pan above boiling water.

Steep: A way of cooking food with the residual heat of hot liquid.

Stew: To cook food gently in simmering liquid, often in a covered pan.

Stir: Using a spoon or whisk in a broad, circular motion, to mix ingredients without beating in air, or to prevent them from sticking.

Stir-fry: To cook small food pieces of food quickly in a small amount of fat over high heat in a wide pan or wok, stirring constantly.

Strain: To separate solids from liquid by passing them through a strainer or colander.

Tart: A shallow open-face savory or sweet pie, or similarly shaped dessert.

Tender-crisp: A test for doneness of vegetables where they are cooked through but are still slightly crunchy.

Tent: To cover meat or poultry loosely with a piece of foil.

Toss: To mix lightly but rapidly by lifting and turning ingredients with two forks or spoons.

Truss: To secure wings or legs close to poultry with skewers or string.

Whip: To beat rapidly with a whisk, or electric mixer, incorporating air to lighten a mixture and increase its volume.

Whisk: To beat with a whisk; a tool with a multiple thin-wire base.

Yeast: A microscopic, single-cell organism that converts its food into alcohol and carbon dioxide through a process known as fermentation. See page 147 for more information.

Zest: Colored outer layer of the peel of citrus fruits.

PUTTING IT ALL TOGETHER

"Is dinner ready? I'm starved!" "That smells great!" "This is delicious!" Enthusiastic eaters fire a cook's passion and creativity. Frequent offerings of family favorites balanced by new or slightly exotic offerings can perk up the weekly round of meals. With time at a premium, getting a meal on the table may pose enough of a challenge. But memorable mealtimes (and efficient cooking) require planning and organization. For some, this begins with putting a week's worth of menus on paper. And, if recipes are also selected, you can make a single, complete shopping list for the basics—and a master plan for a week of good eating. Advance planning can become second nature, and with increased experience, the basic cooking tasks will go more quickly and smoothly.

Sizing up your week

The thought of being so organized may either thrill or terrify you. What if you forget something? But this strategy will save you time—and money—in the long run. And should you forget something, pick it up when you select the fresh fish or produce you want to use that day.

About Our Nutritional Data

For each recipe, we provide a nutritional analysis stating calorie count; grams of total fat and saturated fat; milligrams of cholesterol and sodium; grams of carbohydrates, fiber, and protein; and milligrams of calcium and iron. Generally, the analysis applies to a single serving, based on the number of servings given for each recipe and the amount of each ingredient. If a range is given for the number of servings and/or the amount of an ingredient, the analysis is based on the average of the figures given.

The nutritional analysis does not include optional ingredients or those for which no specific amount is stated. If an ingredient is listed with a substitution, the information was calculated using the first choice.

Sit down (when you're not hungry or hurried) with your calendar and your favorite recipes. Think about the week ahead: Will you be home earlier or later than usual on some days? Does the family have activities and obligations that mean they'll be rushing off after (or during) dinner? Will friends be in town? Begin your meal planning with the main courses in mind, since you can often build meals from leftovers of a roast or casserole. Take stock of staples in your pantry and freezer. A supply of back-up items, such as canned tuna or frozen corn, will allow you some flexibility and peace of mind.

Healthful meals are just as easy to fix as those that aren't good for you. Using recipes that have been nutritionally analyzed, like those in this book, helps you keep track of your intake of fat, sodium, and cholesterol. Keep in mind the basic nutritional standards recommended by health experts: Your daily diet should include six to eleven servings from the bread and cereal group (a serving equals 1 slice enriched or whole grain bread, ½ cup pasta, rice, or cooked cereals, or ¾ cup ready-to-eat cereal); two to three servings (about 3 oz./85 g each) from the meat group (meats, fish, poultry, eggs, dried beans, peas, and nuts); three to five servings from the vegetable group (including dark green and yellow vegetables); two to four servings from the fruit group, including one citrus; and two to three servings from the milk group, which includes yogurt and cheese.

Planning your menus

As you choose the components of a meal, keep in mind the need for variety in color, flavor, temperature, and texture. The most appetizing meals pose contrasts: crisp against smooth, spicy against mild, soothingly warm against refreshingly chilled. An extreme example of what *not* to serve at one meal is cream of cauliflower soup followed by macaroni and cheese, with tapioca pudding for dessert. But here's a model for a tempting meal: To start, a crisp green salad with a vinaigrette dressing; followed by robustly seasoned chili and warm flour tortillas; and for dessert, chocolate frozen yogurt.

Make dessert choices that contrast with the type of meal they follow. After a hearty beef stew, fruit tastes refreshing. But you can end a light meal, such as soup and salad, with something outrageously rich—like a frosted chocolate layer cake. Balance is the prime objective.

Selecting your recipes

It's easy to wind up with a three-ring circus on your hands at serving time if you fail to carefully select and read your recipes in advance. Indeed, a poorly planned meal can set you up for a juggling act—pan-frying veal cutlets, mashing potatoes, and whisking a vinaigrette all at once. And while it may seem like using two oven-cooked recipes in a menu is fuel efficient, that's only true if both bake at the same temperature. If you have just one oven, don't plan to serve a cheese-topped vegetable side dish that cooks at 350°F (175°C) along with biscuits that bake at 425°F (220°C).

When you're entertaining, streamline your schedule by choosing some dishes that can be made ahead of time. Salads and desserts are good candidates for advance preparation. Don't create a menu of recipes that demand an hour or more each of preparation, constant watching, or hands-on attention. Instead, lavish your time on a complicated entrée and complete the meal with simple side dishes. And don't feel guilty if it's easier to purchase dessert at the bakery.

Most cooks find it's safest to try no more than one new recipe at a time. If you're eager to serve something new when your boss (or mother) is coming to dinner, you may want to give the recipe a "dress rehearsal" at a family meal first.

Organizing your time

Scheduling a meal for smooth serving—with everything ready at once—can be tricky, especially for the novice cook. But freedom from last-minute panic is well worth the planning.

Base your "game plan" on the time you would like to serve the meal, and then work backward to the initial preparation of ingredients, creating a step-by-step scenario in 10-minute increments. Take into account that many tasks can be dovetailed. You may toss the salad while the rolls heat in the oven, or mash the potatoes while the turkey stands until carving time.

Estimate the time that the work will take based on your level of experience. As you become more proficient, the time you need for tasks like onion-chopping will decrease. The same is true for unfamiliar recipes; when you've cooked a dish a few times, and are comfortable with the techniques required, the whole process will go more quickly. And, finally, be sure to say yes when guests ask, "Can I help?"

Emergency Substitutions

Emergency	Substitution
1 cup (109 g) cake flour	1 cup (125 g) all-purpose flour minus 2 tablespoons
1 teaspoon baking powder	¼ teaspoon baking soda plus ½ teaspoon cream of tartar
1 package (1¾ teaspoons) active dry yeast	1 compressed yeast cake, crumbled
1 tablespoon cornstarch (used for thickening)	2 tablespoons all-purpose flour
1 cup (240 ml) buttermilk or sour milk	1 cup (240 ml) plain yogurt or 1 tablespoon (15 ml) white vinegar or lemon juice stirred into 1 cup (240 ml) milk and allowed to stand for 5 minutes
1 cup (240 ml) corn syrup	1 cup (200 g) granulated sugar plus ¼ cup (60 ml) liquid*
1 cup (240 ml) honey	1¼ cups (250 g) granulated sugar plus ¼ cup (60 ml) liquid*
2 egg yolks (used for thickening)	1 whole egg
1 square (1 oz./30 g) unsweetened chocolate	3 tablespoons unsweetened cocoa powder plus 1 tablespoon (15 ml) melted butter or margarine
1 ounce semisweet baking chocolate	1 ounce unsweetened chocolate plus 1 tablespoon sugar
1 can (about 1 lb./455 g) tomatoes	2½ cups (323 g) chopped, peeled, fresh tomatoes, simmered for about 10 minutes
1 cup (240 ml) catsup or tomato-based chili sauce	1 can (8 oz./240 ml) tomato sauce plus ½ cup (100 g) granulated sugar and 2 tablespoons (30 ml) white vinegar
1 teaspoon dry mustard	1 teaspoon prepared mustard
½ teaspoon grated fresh ginger	¼ teaspoon ground ginger
½ cup (50 g) sliced leeks	½ cup (80 g) sliced shallots or ½ cup (50 g) green onions

*Use a liquid called for in recipe. Equivalence is based on how product functions in recipe, not on sweetness.

SOUPS

To banish the chill of a rainy day, to satisfy a ravenous January hunger, to warm up friends beside a crackling fire . . . what more comforting fare than a mug or bowl of homemade soup? And in the steamy days of summer, when appetites flag, soup, again, is just the thing—this time iced, and vibrant with seasonal produce.

Soup-making used to be a labor-intensive, all-day task. You'd start from scratch, making broth with meat or poultry bones, plus water and chopped or sliced vegetables. The broth needed to be seasoned and skimmed, then allowed to simmer for hours. Today, you may still choose to make your own broth (see pages 18 and 19), but you can also save time by using *canned* broths—beef, chicken, or vegetable—which are flavorful bases to which all sorts of ingredients can be added. And some soups, such as our zesty gazpacho and thick, tangy borscht, are made without broth.

Soup-making skills

Many soup recipes do require ingredients to be neatly chopped, diced, or cubed, but apart from the cutting, few specialized cooking techniques are needed. For soups that will be puréed, vegetables do not have to be a uniform size. They are cut up simply to shorten their cooking time and to release their flavors.

You can purée soup in a blender or food processor. Some cooks prefer to use a handheld immersion blender. This ingenious little appliance lets you create a velvety purée right in the pot, or thicken a soup by puréeing some but not all of the solids.

Taste before serving

Mysterious transformations take place in the soup pot. Flavors blend and mellow; some seasonings intensify, while others (such as salt) seemingly disappear. It is important to taste your soup just before serving, and then adjust the seasonings accordingly.

Flavors change with chilling, too, so cold soups also need a last-minute check. An herb that was assertive when the soup was hot may have less flavor after chilling.

In addition, chilling thickens soups, especially puréed soups. So be sure to stir a cold soup before serving it; then, if necessary, thin it with additional broth, water, or milk.

FIRST-COURSE SOUPS

What follows is a mouth-watering selection of hot and cold soups, and a few that taste delicious prepared either way. As a first course or as a hearty companion for a salad or sandwich, about 1 cup (240 ml) of soup makes a satisfying serving.

Consider the ingredients and flavors in your soup and avoid repeating them in the main course and side dishes. Also, take into account how filling a first-course soup can be—you don't want to fill up your guests so much that they aren't hungry for the rest of the meal.

If it's more convenient, you can make these soups ahead. Reheat soup in an uncovered pan, stirring, just until it's hot.

Creamy Tomato Soup

  1 tablespoon butter or margarine
  1 small carrot, finely chopped
  1 small onion, finely chopped
  2 tablespoons all-purpose flour
  ¾ teaspoon dried basil
  ¾ teaspoon dried thyme
  ½ teaspoon salt
  ½ teaspoon pepper
  1½ cups (360 ml) 2% milk
  1 large can (about 28 oz./795 g) crushed tomatoes
  ¼ cup (10 g) chopped fresh basil or parsley
    Grated Parmesan cheese

Melt butter in a 4-quart (3.8-liter) nonstick pan over medium-low heat. Add carrot and onion; cook, stirring frequently, until onion is soft (about 3 minutes); remove from heat.

Stir in flour, dried basil, thyme, salt, and pepper. Gradually pour in milk, stirring constantly, and cook over medium-low heat, continuing to stir, until boiling and slightly thickened (about 5 minutes). Gradually whisk in tomatoes and their liquid. Reduce heat and simmer, uncovered, stirring often, until full-flavored (about 15 minutes). Sprinkle each serving with chopped fresh basil and a little grated Parmesan cheese. *Makes 4 servings*

PER SERVING: *145 calories, 5 g total fat, 3 g saturated fat, 15 mg cholesterol, 678 mg sodium, 20 g carbohydrates, 3 g fiber, 6 g protein, 196 mg calcium, 2 mg iron*

Potato Bisque

  2 teaspoons olive oil
  1 large onion, halved and thinly sliced
  1 cup (120 g) thinly sliced celery (including some tops)
  2 large potatoes (about 1 lb./455 g total), peeled and thinly sliced
  2 cups (470 ml) reduced-sodium chicken broth or Homemade Chicken Broth (page 18)
  1¼ teaspoons salt
  ¾ teaspoon pepper
  ½ teaspoon ground sage
  ½ teaspoon dried thyme
  2 tablespoons cornstarch mixed with 3 tablespoons (45 ml) water
  2 cups (470 ml) 2% milk
  2 tablespoons (30 ml) lemon juice
  ¼ cup (10 g) chopped fresh dill

Heat oil in a 4- to 5-quart (3.8- to 5-liter) nonstick pan over medium heat. Add onion and celery; cover and cook, stirring frequently, until onion is soft (about 5 minutes). Add potatoes, broth, salt, pepper, sage, and thyme. Bring to a boil; cover, reduce heat to medium-low, and simmer until potatoes are very tender when pierced (about 25 minutes). Transfer mixture to a food processor; whirl until smoothly puréed, then return to pan.

Stir cornstarch mixture and add with milk to purée. Cook over medium heat, stirring frequently, until soup boils and thickens slightly (about 10 minutes). Remove pan from heat and stir in lemon juice and dill. *Makes 4 to 6 servings*

PER SERVING: *166 calories, 5 g total fat, 2 g saturated fat, 8 mg cholesterol, 798 mg sodium, 26 g carbohydrates, 2 g fiber, 6 g protein, 163 mg calcium, 1 mg iron*

Mushroom & Potato Bisque

Prepare *Potato Bisque*, but stir in 4 ounces (115 g) sliced *mushrooms* when you add chicken broth. Eliminate lemon juice and dill.

Shrimp Bisque

Prepare *Potato Bisque*, but add 8 ounces (230 g) *small cooked shelled shrimp* or 1 package (12 oz./340 g) frozen, cooked shrimp, thawed, just before adding cornstarch mixture.

Icy Gazpacho

 1 slice firm white bread, crumbled (about 1 cup/45 g)

 3 tablespoons (45 ml) olive oil

 2 tablespoons (30 ml) red wine vinegar

 6 large tomatoes, peeled and seeded (about 3 lbs./1.35 kg total)

 1 large cucumber (about 12 oz./340 g), peeled

 1 large red bell pepper (about 8 oz./230 g), seeded

 1 small red onion (about 4 oz./115 g)

 ½ medium-size avocado (about 10 oz./285 g whole), pitted and peeled

 1 cup (240 ml) reduced-sodium tomato-vegetable juice

 ¾ teaspoon salt

 ½ teaspoon dried oregano

    Ice cubes (optional)

In a large bowl, combine bread crumbs, oil, and vinegar; set aside.

Cut tomatoes, cucumber, bell pepper, onion, and avocado into large chunks; place in a large bowl and mix. Working in batches, transfer vegetables to a food processor and pulse just until coarsely chopped.

Add vegetables to bread crumb mixture, then stir in tomato-vegetable juice, salt, and oregano. To serve, ladle soup into bowls and add 1 or 2 ice cubes to each bowl, if desired. Or, cover and chill for up to 6 hours.   *Makes 6 to 8 servings*

PER SERVING: *153 calories, 9 g total fat, 1 g saturated fat, 0 mg cholesterol, 329 mg sodium, 18 g carbohydrates, 4 g fiber, 3 g protein, 37 mg calcium, 2 mg iron*

Vegetable Borscht

 2 medium-size potatoes (about 12 oz./340 g total)

 1 quart (950 ml) water

 2 medium-size beets (about 12 oz./340 g total)

 1 can (about 15 oz./425 g) tomatoes

 ¼ cup (60 ml) cider vinegar

 2 tablespoons sugar

 ¼ cup (60 ml) plain lowfat yogurt

    Thinly sliced green onions

    Salt and pepper

Peel potatoes and beets, rinse, and coarsely chop. In a 2- to 3-quart (1.9- to 2.8-liter) pan over high heat, bring potatoes, beets, and water to a boil. Reduce

heat and simmer, covered, until potatoes mash easily when pressed (15 to 18 minutes). Add tomatoes, vinegar, and sugar; simmer for 5 more minutes. Working in batches, transfer mixture to a food processor or blender; whirl until smoothly puréed. If necessary, reheat soup in pan. Pour into 6 bowls.

Place yogurt in a small zip-seal plastic bag; snip off one corner to make an ⅛-inch (3-mm) hole. Squeeze a 1-inch (2.5-cm) diameter round of yogurt onto each soup; draw a knife tip a few times through center of each round to form a sunburst. Sprinkle with green onions. Offer salt and pepper to taste.

Makes 6 servings

PER SERVING: *96 calories, 0.5 g total fat, 0.1 g saturated fat, 0.6 mg cholesterol, 155 mg sodium, 22 g carbohydrates, 2 g fiber, 3 g protein, 43 mg calcium, 1 mg iron*

Chilled Zucchini Soup

 4 cups (about 1 lb./455 g) sliced zucchini or crookneck squash

 2 cups (470 ml) reduced-sodium chicken broth or Homemade Chicken Broth (page 18)

 1 medium-size red onion (about 6 oz./170 g), thinly sliced

 ⅓ cup (80 ml) reduced-fat sour cream

 ¼ cup (60 ml) plain lowfat yogurt

 ½ cup (20 g) snipped fresh dill

 ¾ teaspoon salt

 ¼ teaspoon black pepper

 ⅛ teaspoon ground red pepper (cayenne)

    Shelled sunflower seeds (optional)

Combine squash, broth, and onion in a 2-quart (1.9-liter) pan. Bring to a boil; cover, reduce heat, and simmer until vegetables are very tender (about 30 minutes).

Working in batches, transfer mixture to a food processor or blender; whirl until smoothly puréed. Transfer purée to a large bowl; whisk in sour cream, yogurt, dill, salt, black pepper, and ground red pepper. Let cool, then cover and refrigerate until cold (at least 4 hours). Serve cold, garnished with sunflower seeds, if desired.   *Makes 4 servings*

PER SERVING: *92 calories, 4 g total fat, 2 g saturated fat, 8 mg cholesterol, 658 mg sodium, 11 g carbohydrates, 1 g fiber, 5 g protein, 86 mg calcium, 2 mg iron*

FULL-MEAL SOUPS

Though most of the preceding soups can serve as a light supper, these meal-in-a-bowl recipes are hearty enough to star in a dinner for family or friends. Crusty French bread or a hot quick bread from the chapter on breads (see page 158) would round out a comfortably informal country-style supper. You might start with a green salad, or follow the soup with fruit and cheese, or offer both.

Meatball Minestrone

 1 package (10 oz./285 g) frozen chopped spinach, thawed and squeezed dry
 1½ pounds (680 g) ground lean beef
 ⅓ cup (33 g) fine dry bread crumbs
 ¼ cup (60 ml) 2% milk
 1 large egg
 1 teaspoon salt
 ¼ teaspoon pepper
 1 tablespoon (15 ml) olive oil
 1 large onion, coarsely chopped
 1 cup (130 g) sliced carrots
 3 cloves garlic, minced or pressed
 8 cups (1.9 liters) reduced-sodium chicken broth
 1 can (about 1 lb./455 g) no-salt-added tomatoes
 1 can (about 15 oz./425 g) kidney beans, drained and rinsed
 ¾ teaspoon dried basil
 ¾ teaspoon dried oregano
 1 cup (115 g) rotelle or elbow macaroni
   Grated Parmesan cheese

In a large bowl, combine spinach, beef, bread crumbs, milk, egg, salt, and pepper. Shape into thirty-six 1-inch (2.5-cm) meatballs.

Heat oil in a 5- to 6-quart (5- to 6-liter) nonstick pan over medium heat. Working in batches, add meatballs; cook, turning, until browned on all sides (about 4 minutes). With a slotted spoon, remove meatballs from pan, leaving drippings. Repeat until all meatballs are browned. Set meatballs aside.

Add onion, carrots, and garlic to drippings, and cook over medium heat, stirring occasionally, until soft (about 5 minutes). Stir in broth, tomatoes (break up with a spoon) and their liquid, beans, basil, and oregano. Cover, reduce heat, and simmer until richly flavored (about 20 minutes).

Stir in pasta and meatballs; cover and simmer until pasta is just tender to bite (about 10 minutes). Add Parmesan cheese to taste.   *Makes 6 servings*

PER SERVING: *568 calories, 30 g total fat, 11 g saturated fat, 121 mg cholesterol, 1,228 mg sodium, 40 g carbohydrates, 6 g fiber, 33 g protein, 155 mg calcium, 6 mg iron*

Vegetable Basil Soup

 1 tablespoon (15 ml) olive oil
 1 large carrot, thinly sliced
 1 large stalk celery, thinly sliced
 1 large onion, chopped
 4 cloves garlic, minced or pressed
 4 cups (950 ml) reduced-sodium chicken broth or Homemade Chicken Broth (page 18)
 1 large potato (about 8 oz./230 g), cut into ¼-inch (6-mm) cubes
 ¾ teaspoon salt
 1½ teaspoons pepper
 ½ small head cauliflower (about 9 oz./255 g), cut into small flowerets
 2 large tomatoes (about 1 lb./455 g total), peeled and diced
 2 small zucchini or yellow squash (about 8 oz./230 g total), halved lengthwise and sliced crosswise ¼ inch (6 mm) thick
 1 cup (110 g) frozen tiny peas
 ½ cup (20 g) chopped fresh basil
   Grated Parmesan cheese

Heat oil in a 4- to 5-quart (3.8- to 5-liter) nonstick pan over medium heat. Add carrot, celery, onion, and garlic; cook, stirring occasionally, until onion is soft (about 5 minutes). Add broth, potato, salt, and pepper. Bring to a boil; cover, reduce heat, and simmer until potatoes are tender when pierced (about 15 minutes).

Add cauliflower, tomatoes, and zucchini; return to a boil. Cover, reduce heat, and simmer until cauliflower is tender when pierced (about 15 minutes).

Add peas and basil; simmer, uncovered, until peas are hot (about 5 minutes). Add Parmesan cheese to taste.   *Makes 6 servings*

PER SERVING: *154 calories, 4 g total fat, 0.7 g saturated fat, 0 mg cholesterol, 641 mg sodium, 25 g carbohydrates, 6 g fiber, 6 g protein, 63 mg calcium, 2 mg iron*

Soothing Chicken Soup

1 chicken (3½ to 4 lbs./1.6 to 1.8 kg), rinsed
3 large stalks celery, sliced
3 medium-size carrots, sliced
1 large onion, thinly sliced
3 cloves garlic, minced or pressed
4 parsley sprigs (about 5 in./12.5 cm each)
2 bay leaves
2 teaspoons dried thyme
1 teaspoon coriander seeds
½ teaspoon black peppercorns
½ teaspoon whole allspice
2 quarts (1.9 liters) water
4 ounces (115 g) wide egg noodles
1 package (10 oz./285 g) frozen tiny peas
  Salt

Remove and discard skin and fat from chicken. Place chicken in a 6- to 8-quart (6- to 8-liter) pan. Add celery, carrots, onion, garlic, parsley, bay leaves, thyme, coriander, peppercorns, allspice, and water. Cover and bring to a boil over high heat; reduce heat and simmer gently, skimming scum, until chicken is no longer pink at thigh bone; cut to test (about 1 hour total).

Remove pan from heat; lift out chicken and transfer to a plate. Discard parsley. Skim fat from broth. (At this point, you may chill the broth until cold or for up to 3 days. The fat hardens and can be lifted off if you chill the broth first.)

When chicken is cool, pull meat from bones. Discard bones and any skin. Tear meat into bite-size pieces. (At this point, you may cover and chill meat for up to 3 days.)

Cover soup and bring to a boil over high heat. Add noodles; cook until tender to bite (6 to 8 minutes). Stir in peas and chicken, and heat through (3 to 4 minutes). Add salt to taste.   *Makes 6 servings*

Per serving: *305 calories, 5 g total fat, 1 g saturated fat, 113 mg cholesterol, 204 mg sodium, 28 g carbohydrates, 5 g fiber, 35 g protein, 77 mg calcium, 4 mg iron*

Homemade Chicken Broth
PICTURED ON FACING PAGE

Follow recipe for *Soothing Chicken Soup* up to point of skimming fat. If you want to use broth immediately, skim and discard fat. If chilling, strain broth into a 2-quart (1.9-liter) pan; discard vegetables and reserve meat for another use. After chilling (for up to 3 days), lift off fat. If you plan to freeze broth, reheat it briefly to reliquefy it, then pour into freezer containers. Broth may be frozen for up to 3 months.
Makes about 1½ quarts (1.4 liters) broth

New England Clam Chowder

4 slices bacon (about 2¼ oz./63 g), diced
1 large onion, chopped
1 medium-size carrot, chopped
1 medium-size stalk celery with leaves, chopped
3 large potatoes (about 1 lb./455 g total), scrubbed and cut into ¼-inch (6-mm) cubes
1½ cups (360 ml) water
½ teaspoon salt
½ teaspoon pepper
½ teaspoon dried thyme
  About 6 drops liquid hot pepper seasoning (or to taste)
2 cups (470 ml) 2% milk
¼ cup (60 ml) half-and-half (light cream)
3 cans (6½ oz./185 g each) chopped or minced clams

In a 3- to 4-quart (2.8- to 3.8-liter) nonstick pan over medium heat, cook bacon, stirring occasionally, until crisp (5 to 7 minutes). Remove bacon and drain on paper towels. Spoon out all but 2 tablespoons (30 ml) of the drippings.

To remaining drippings, add onion, carrot, and celery; cook over medium heat, stirring frequently, until onion is soft (4 to 5 minutes). Add potatoes, water, salt, pepper, thyme, and hot pepper seasoning; increase heat and bring to a boil. Reduce heat, cover, and simmer until potatoes are very tender when pierced (18 to 20 minutes). Stir in milk, half-and-half, clams and their liquid, and reserved bacon. Heat just until piping hot; do not boil.
Makes 6 servings

Per serving: *251 calories, 9 g total fat, 3 g saturated fat, 48 mg cholesterol, 369 mg sodium, 24 g carbohydrates, 3 g fiber, 19 g protein, 187 mg calcium, 15 mg iron*

MAKING HOMEMADE CHICKEN BROTH

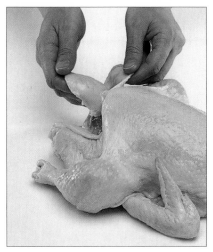

1 Before starting to cook broth, remove skin and any excess fat from chicken. A chicken weighing 3½ to 4 pounds (1.6 to 1.8 kg) is good for broth-making.

2 As chicken cooks, foamy scum will rise to the surface. Skim off scum periodically to ensure a clear, appetizing broth. Rinse spoon each time you skim broth.

3 Remove chicken from large pan and set aside. Pour broth into a large strainer or colander placed over a 2-quart (1.9-liter) pan. Reserve chicken for another use.

4 When broth is chilled, fat will congeal in a solid layer on top. Use a large spoon to lift fat from surface, then discard.

5 Before placing broth in freezer containers, heat it briefly to liquefy it and make it pourable. If you use broth in small amounts for recipes, freeze it in ice cube trays; when frozen, pop cubes into heavy-duty plastic bags and freeze for up to 3 months.

SALADS & DRESSINGS

Salad, these days, has status. Carefully composed or casually mixed, a salad can start a meal or end it, accompany the entrée, or—served with some crusty bread or rolls—make a light repast in itself. Best of all, salads are packed with vitamins, minerals, and fiber, and are filling and often low in fat.

The marriage of salad ingredients and dressing is judged by its balance of flavors, textures, and colors. Think of a Caesar salad, in which the sweet romaine lettuce serves as a foil for crunchy croutons and piquant Parmesan; or of an Asian-style salad, in which soy-and-sesame-flavored noodles are accented with bright, crisp vegetable slivers.

Bottled dressings are convenient, of course. But, for delicious variety, choose from our well-rounded repertoire of vinaigrettes and mayonnaise-based dressings. Seasoned with lemon juice, herbs, Dijon mustard, balsamic vinegar, or walnut oil, they enhance fresh vegetables.

To spark your own creativity, look at the salad greens assembled on page 22. Although some may not be your everyday garden varieties, they can be found in most supermarket produce sections. There, too, you may find many special salad mixtures of different types of lettuces, chicories, mustards, and other greens, as well as herbs and edible flowers. When setting out to shop for salad fixings, include a visit to your local farmers' market or farmstand, sources of the freshest seasonal produce. And explore our heartier salad options of pasta, beans, and potatoes, too.

Choosing & handling greens

Keep freshness in mind as you select greens. Look for untarnished leaves, tender or crisp as suits the variety. Yellowed, wilted, dry, or curled outer leaves are signs that greens are over the hill.

Always handle greens gently because they bruise easily. Wash them and shake off as much water as possible; then drain on paper towels until barely damp. Wrap leaves loosely in a clean kitchen towel or paper towels, slip them into a plastic bag, and refrigerate for no more than a few days. When you're ready to use the greens, pat off any excess moisture and tear—don't cut—them into bite-size pieces. Or whirl greens in a salad spinner if using at once.

SALADS

Caesar Salad

- 1 clove garlic, peeled
- 6 anchovy fillets, blotted dry
- 2 tablespoons grated Parmesan cheese
- 3 tablespoons (45 ml) reduced-calorie mayonnaise
- 2 tablespoons (30 ml) lemon juice
- 1 tablespoon (15 ml) olive oil
- ¼ teaspoon salt
- ¼ teaspoon pepper
- 1 large head romaine lettuce (about 1¼ lbs./565 g), torn into bite-size pieces
- 1 cup (1 oz./30 g) plain croutons

In a blender or food processor, whirl garlic, anchovies, 1 tablespoon of the cheese, the mayonnaise, lemon juice, oil, salt, and pepper until smooth.

To serve, place dressing in a large salad bowl, add romaine, and mix to coat. Add croutons and remaining 1 tablespoon cheese, and mix gently. Serve immediately.   *Makes 4 servings*

PER SERVING: *141 calories, 9 g total fat, 2 g saturated fat, 9 mg cholesterol, 528 mg sodium, 11 g carbohydrates, 3 g fiber, 6 g protein, 109 mg calcium, 2 mg iron*

Main-Course Caesar

Prepare *Caesar Salad* and add 12 ounces (340 g) grilled, broiled, or boiled shelled *shrimp*, or 12 ounces (340 g) cooked *chicken* pieces to the greens.

Spinach & Shrimp Salad with Warm Mustard Dressing

- 12 cups (about 12 oz./340 g) firmly packed, rinsed, and drained spinach leaves
- 12 ounces (340 g) shelled cooked tiny shrimp
- 1 tablespoon sugar
- 1 teaspoon cornstarch
- ⅓ cup (80 ml) Dijon mustard
- ¼ cup (60 ml) reduced-sodium chicken broth or water
- 1 tablespoon (15 ml) rice vinegar
- 2 tablespoons minced fresh dill or 1½ teaspoons dried dill weed

Cut spinach into strips about ⅜ inch (9 mm) wide. Place spinach in a wide, shallow bowl; top with shrimp. (At this point, you may chill airtight for up to 4 hours.)

In a 1-quart (950-ml) pan, combine sugar and cornstarch. Whisk in mustard, broth, and vinegar. Cook over high heat, stirring constantly, until dressing boils; stir in dill. Pour dressing over salad. Mix well and serve at once.   *Makes 6 to 8 servings*

PER SERVING: *80 calories, 0.7 g total fat, 0.2 g saturated fat, 95 mg cholesterol, 435 mg sodium, 4 g carbohydrates, 1 g fiber, 12 g protein, 71 mg calcium, 3 mg iron*

Cobb Salad

- ¼ cup (60 ml) olive oil
- 3 tablespoons chopped chives
- 3 tablespoons (45 ml) white wine vinegar
- 1 tablespoon (15 ml) balsamic vinegar
- 1 teaspoon grainy Dijon mustard
- ½ teaspoon salt
- ½ teaspoon pepper
- 1 medium-size head iceberg lettuce (about 15 oz./425 g), shredded
- 1 large tomato (about 8 oz./230 g), chopped
- 1½ cups (6 oz./170 g) diced cooked chicken
- 1 large avocado (about 12 oz./340 g), pitted, peeled, and diced
- 2 large hard-cooked eggs (page 107), chopped
- 4 ounces (115 g) sliced bacon, crisply cooked, drained, and crumbled
- 2 ounces (55 g) blue-veined cheese, finely crumbled

In a food processor or blender, combine oil, chives, wine vinegar, balsamic vinegar, mustard, salt, and pepper; whirl until smooth. Place lettuce in a large, wide salad bowl. Pour two thirds of dressing over lettuce and mix well; then spread out lettuce in an even layer. Arrange tomato, chicken, avocado, eggs, bacon, and cheese separately on top of lettuce. Drizzle salad with remaining dressing. Mix to serve. *Makes 4 servings*

PER SERVING: *471 calories, 37 g total fat, 9 g saturated fat, 162 mg cholesterol, 717 mg sodium, 12 g carbohydrates, 3 g fiber, 24 g protein, 182 mg calcium, 4 mg iron*

iceberg

butter
(Boston)

romaine

escarole

red leaf

radicchio

chicory

spinach

Belgian
endive

frisée

mizuna

arugula

oakleaf

watercress

mâche
(corn salad,
lamb's tongue)

dandelion
greens

baby mustard

Summer Greens Salad with Mustard-Tarragon Vinaigrette

PICTURED ON PAGE 27

¼ cup (60 ml) white wine vinegar

1½ tablespoons (23 ml) Dijon mustard

1 clove garlic, pressed or minced

1 teaspoon dried tarragon

¼ cup (60 ml) olive oil

12 cups (¾ to 1 lb./340 to 455 g) baby salad leaves, rinsed and crisped, or any mixed greens, rinsed, crisped, and torn
Salt and pepper
Nasturtium flowers or other edible flowers (optional)

To make vinaigrette, in a small bowl, whisk together vinegar, mustard, garlic, and tarragon. Whisking constantly, pour in oil in a steady stream.

In a large bowl, combine salad greens and vinaigrette; mix, then add salt and pepper to taste. Garnish with edible flowers, if desired.
Makes 6 to 8 servings

PER SERVING: *80 calories, 8 g total fat, 1 g saturated fat, 0 mg cholesterol, 84 mg sodium, 2 g carbohydrates, 0.6 g fiber, 0.6 g protein, 28 mg calcium, 0.4 mg iron*

Carrot Salad

4 large carrots, peeled and cut into matchstick-size pieces

¼ cup (60 ml) olive oil

2 tablespoons chopped fresh tarragon or ½ teaspoon dried tarragon

2 tablespoons (30 ml) lemon juice

2 tablespoons drained canned green peppercorns
Salt and pepper

In a 5- to 6-quart (5- to 6-liter) pan, bring 6 cups (1.4 liters) water to a boil. Add carrots, and cook, uncovered, until just barely tender to bite (about 2 minutes). Drain at once in a colander and immediately immerse in ice water to stop cooking. When cool, drain again.

Place carrots in a serving dish or bowl and mix gently with oil, tarragon, lemon juice, and green peppercorns. (At this point you may cover and chill up until next day.)

Season carrots with salt and pepper to taste, and serve at room temperature.   *Makes 4 servings*

PER SERVING: *165 calories, 14 g total fat, 2 g saturated fat, 0 mg cholesterol, 187 mg sodium, 11 g carbohydrates, 3 g fiber, 1 g protein, 30 mg calcium, 0.6 mg iron*

Potato-Avocado Salad with Ginger-Lime Dressing

2 pounds (905 g) small red thin-skinned potatoes (about 1½-in./3.5-cm diameter), scrubbed

½ cup (50 g) thinly sliced green onions

6 tablespoons (90 ml) lime juice

1 to 2 fresh jalapeño chiles, stemmed, seeded, and minced

1 tablespoon chopped cilantro

2 teaspoons minced fresh ginger

½ teaspoon sugar

1 small (8 oz./230 g) firm-ripe avocado
Salt

In a 4- to 5-quart (3.8- to 5-liter) pan, bring 2 quarts (1.9 liters) water to a boil over high heat. Add potatoes; cover and simmer until tender when pierced (15 to 20 minutes). Drain and let stand until cool enough to touch. Cut potatoes into quarters.

In a large bowl, mix potatoes, green onions, lime juice, chiles, cilantro, ginger, and sugar. (At this point, you may cover and let stand, or chill for up to 3 hours.) Halve, pit, and peel avocado; cut into ½-inch (1-cm) cubes. Add avocado to potatoes and stir gently until mixed. Season to taste with salt.
Makes 4 servings

PER SERVING: *265 calories, 7 g total fat, 1 g saturated fat, 0 mg cholesterol, 28 mg sodium, 48 g carbohydrates, 5 g fiber, 6 g protein, 18 mg calcium, 2 mg iron*

Edible Flowers

What better garnish for a salad than edible flowers? They're available at farmers' markets and some supermarkets. Chive flowers, nasturtium flowers (and leaves), rose petals, squash blossoms, and violets are some we like for their subtle flavor and fragrance. Just rinse the flowers gently and pat dry before using.

◄ *An Assortment of Salad Greens*

Roasted Pepper & Tomato Salad

- 4 medium-size green or red bell peppers (about 1½ lbs./680 g total) or a combination of both, halved and seeded
- 4 medium-size tomatoes (about 1½ lbs./680 g total), peeled and cut into bite-size chunks
- ⅓ cup (45 g) ripe olives, such as calamata, pitted and coarsely chopped
- ¼ cup (10 g) chopped fresh basil
- 3 tablespoons (45 ml) olive oil
- 2 tablespoons (30 ml) balsamic vinegar
- 2 cloves garlic, crushed and peeled
- 1 teaspoon dried oregano
- ½ teaspoon salt
- ¼ teaspoon pepper
- 6 cups (about 6 oz./170 g) mixed salad greens

To roast peppers, place, cut side down, on a rimmed baking pan and place under broiler about 6 inches (15 cm) from heat. Broil until peppers are well blistered and charred (about 10 minutes). Cover pan with foil (see page 124) and let peppers steam to loosen skins (15 to 20 minutes). Peel and discard skins.

Cut roasted peppers into thin strips and place in a bowl. Stir in tomatoes and olives.

In a cup, combine basil, oil, vinegar, garlic, oregano, salt, and pepper; stir into bell pepper mixture. Cover and let stand at room temperature for about 1 hour, or refrigerate until the next day, but bring to room temperature before serving. To serve, discard garlic. Line individual plates with greens and mound pepper mixture on top.   *Makes 4 servings*

PER SERVING: *151 calories, 12 g total fat, 2 g saturated fat, 0 mg cholesterol, 389 mg sodium, 11 g carbohydrates, 3 g fiber, 2 g protein, 60 mg calcium, 2 mg iron*

Soba Noodle Salad

- 2 tablespoons (30 ml) lemon juice
- 2 tablespoons (30 ml) oyster sauce
- 2 tablespoons (30 ml) reduced-sodium soy sauce
- 1 teaspoon Oriental sesame oil
- 8 ounces (230 g) soba noodles or capellini
- 1½ cups (120 g) julienne slivers green or red bell peppers
- ½ cup (60 g) thinly sliced celery
- ½ cup (50 g) thinly sliced green onions
- ½ cup (65 g) roasted, salted cashews

To prepare dressing, in a small bowl, mix together lemon juice, oyster sauce, soy sauce, and oil. Set aside.

In a 5- to 6-quart (5- to 6-liter) pan, bring about 3 quarts (2.8 ml) water to a boil over high heat. Add noodles and cook, uncovered, just until barely tender to bite (about 5 minutes for soba; 2 to 3 minutes for capellini). Drain noodles and rinse with cold water until cool; drain again.

In a serving bowl, mix noodles, bell peppers, celery, green onions, and reserved dressing; sprinkle with cashews.   *Makes 4 servings*

PER SERVING: *331 calories, 10 g total fat, 2 g saturated fat, 0 mg cholesterol, 1,233 mg sodium, 55 g carbohydrates, 4 g fiber, 13 g protein, 51 mg calcium, 3 mg iron*

New Mexican Chili Bean Salad

- ¼ cup (60 ml) red wine vinegar
- 2 tablespoons (30 ml) olive oil
- 1 teaspoon chili powder
- 1 teaspoon ground cumin
- 1 teaspoon dried oregano
- ¼ teaspoon pepper
- 1 can (about 15 oz./425 g) garbanzos
- 1 can (about 15 oz./425 g) kidney beans
- 1 can (about 15 oz./425 g) pinto beans
- 1 can (about 15 oz./425 g) whole-kernel corn
- 1 large (about 8 oz./230 g) red bell pepper, stemmed, seeded, and coarsely chopped
- ½ cup (50 g) chopped green onions
- ⅓ cup (15 g) chopped cilantro
- 1 can (about 4 oz./115 g) diced green chiles

To prepare dressing, in a small bowl, combine vinegar, oil, chili powder, cumin, oregano, and pepper. Set aside.

In a colander, rinse garbanzos, kidney beans, pinto beans, and corn; drain well. In a large bowl, mix bean and corn mixture with bell pepper, green onions, cilantro, chiles, and reserved dressing. Cover and chill for at least 1 hour or up until the next day, stirring occasionally.   *Makes 8 servings*

PER SERVING: *191 calories, 5 g total fat, 0.6 g saturated fat, 0 mg cholesterol, 447 mg sodium, 30 g carbohydrates, 7 g fiber, 8 g protein, 50 mg calcium, 3 mg iron*

DRESSINGS

MAYONNAISE & MAYONNAISE-BASED DRESSINGS

You may think that mayonnaise is tricky to make, but it's a snap once you understand the simple technique. And mayonnaise can be made with your choice of flavorful oils and vinegars. Mayonnaise serves as a base for other dressings; we offer recipes for five of them.

Since it is considered potentially harmful to eat foods made with raw eggs (due to the risk of salmonella poisoning), our recipe uses an egg white that has been acidified for at least 48 hours.

Mayonnaise

    1   large egg white
        At least 3 tablespoons (45 ml) lemon juice or vinegar
    2   tablespoons (30 ml) water
    2   tablespoons (30 ml) Dijon mustard
    1   cup (120 ml) vegetable oil or olive oil
        Salt

In a small bowl, combine egg white and 3 tablespoons (45 ml) of the lemon juice or vinegar. Stir just to mix, then cover airtight and refrigerate for at least 48 hours or for up to 4 days (upon longer standing, the egg white begins to solidify).

Put egg mixture in a blender, food processor, or deep bowl of an electric mixer. Add water and mustard. Whirling, or beating mixture at high speed, add oil in a slow, steady stream until mixture starts to thicken, then add oil faster, incorporating until smooth. Season mayonnaise to taste with more lemon juice or vinegar and salt. Serve, or cover and refrigerate for up to 1 week.   *Makes 1½ cups (240 ml)*

PER TABLESPOON: *83 calories, 9 g total fat, 1 g saturated fat, 0 mg cholesterol, 33 mg sodium, 0.1 g carbohydrates, 0 g fiber, 0.1 g protein, 0.3 mg calcium, 0 mg iron*

Green Herbed Mayonnaise

In a blender or food processor, place ¼ cup (15 g) lightly packed chopped *parsley*; ⅓ cup (35 g) chopped *chives*; 1 *green onion* (including top), chopped; ¼ to ½ teaspoon *dried dill weed*; and 2 teaspoons *lemon juice*. Whirl until finely chopped. Stir into ½ cup (120 ml) *mayonnaise*. (At this point, you may cover and refrigerate.)   *Makes about 1 cup (240 ml)*

Thousand Island Dressing

In a medium-size bowl, stir together 1 cup (240 ml) *mayonnaise*; ¼ cup (60 ml) *tomato-based chili sauce*; 1 tablespoon chopped *green bell pepper*; 1 *green onion* (including top), chopped; 2 tablespoons *sweet pickle relish*; and a dash of *paprika*. Stir well to blend. (At this point, you may cover and refrigerate.) *Makes about 1½ cups (360 ml)*

Green Goddess Dressing

In a blender or food processor, place 1 clove *garlic*, minced or pressed; ¼ cup each coarsely chopped *parsley* (15 g), *green onions*, including tops (25 g), and *watercress* (15 g); ½ teaspoon *salt*; 1 teaspoon *dried tarragon*; 1 teaspoon *anchovy paste* or finely chopped anchovy fillets; and 2 teaspoons *lemon juice*. Whirl until smoothly puréed. Stir into 1 cup (240 ml) *mayonnaise*. (At this point, you may cover and refrigerate.)   *Makes about 1½ cups (360 ml)*

Chutney Dressing

In a medium-size bowl, stir together ½ cup (120 ml) each *mayonnaise* and *sour cream*, and 2 to 4 tablespoons (30 to 60 ml) finely chopped *chutney*. (At this point, you may cover and refrigerate.) *Makes 1 to 1¼ cups (240 to 300 ml)*

Herbed Buttermilk Dressing

In a medium-size bowl, combine 1 cup (240 ml) *buttermilk*; 2 tablespoons each minced fresh *parsley*, *dill*, and *mint*; 2 tablespoons *onion*; ¼ teaspoon each *dried basil*, *oregano*, and *rosemary*; and 1 clove minced *garlic*. Let stand for 5 minutes. Stir in 1 cup (240 ml) *mayonnaise*, and, if desired, 4 ounces (115 g) crumbled *blue-veined cheese*. Add *salt* and *pepper* to taste.   *Makes about 2 cups (470 ml)*

VINAIGRETTE DRESSINGS

The perfect salad dressing is both vibrant and discreet, adding flavor accents while allowing the salad components to speak for themselves. The basic vinaigrette and the variations that follow make use of different oils and vinegars. The possibilities for fresh combinations are endless. You can even reduce the fat in dressings by substituting fruit purées or juices for some or all of the oil. The lowfat dressings will still coat the greens nicely, and the sweetness of the fruit will balance the sharpness of the vinegar.

Oils

Keep all oils tightly closed and in a cool, dark place to preserve quality for the maximum amount of time. Do not refrigerate oils. If you do, they solidify and get rancid faster.

Olive oil. Paired with wine vinegar, olive oil forms the classic vinaigrette. Offered in many grades, the highest-quality, most flavorful oil comes from the first light pressing of the olives and is graded "extra virgin." Virgin and other oils of subsequent pressings are increasingly neutral in taste. Keep olive oils tightly closed to retain freshness for months.

Vegetable oils. Pressed from the seeds of plants (corn, cotton, peanut, safflower), these all-purpose oils are mild to neutral in flavor.

Nut oils. These oils are pressed from raw or roasted walnuts, almonds, or hazelnuts (filberts). To dress greens or fruit salads, use 1 to 3 parts walnut or almond oil to 1 part lemon juice or wine vinegar; toasted hazelnut oil is more potent—use only 1 to 2 parts oil to 1 part lemon juice.

Flavored oils. Oils reach new heights when infused with fresh herbs, lemon, or garlic—to name some stellar seasonings. Store oils in a dark, cool place. Once opened, their flavor potency begins to decline.

Vinegars

Cider vinegar. Golden in color, this vinegar is made from apple cider. Its flavor and aroma are quite sharp.

Distilled white vinegar. This colorless vinegar is made from grain alcohol. It also has a sharp aroma and taste.

Fruit vinegars. With their pronounced fruit flavors and colors, these pair well with mild vegetable oils on mixed greens or fresh fruit salads.

Wine vinegars. These vinegars are produced from both red and white wines, and sherry. Their flavors are complex, and they complement olive oil or vegetable oil.

Balsamic vinegar. Made from aged grape juice rather than wine, balsamic vinegar has a unique sweetness and gets its dark color from aging in wooden casks.

Basic Vinaigrette

- ½ cup (120 ml) red or white wine vinegar
- 1 teaspoon salt
  Pinch of pepper
- 1½ cups (360 ml) olive oil or vegetable oil, or a combination of both

In a small bowl, combine vinegar, salt, and pepper. Whisking constantly, pour in oil in a steady stream. (At this point, you may cover and let stand at room temperature; mix again before using.)
Makes 2 cups (470 ml)

PER TABLESPOON: *90 calories, 10 g total fat, 1 g saturated fat, 0 mg cholesterol, 69 mg sodium, 0.1 g carbohydrates, 0 g fiber, 0 g protein, 0.5 mg calcium, 0 mg iron*

Mustard Vinaigrette

Prepare *Basic Vinaigrette*, but add 2 tablespoons (30 ml) *Dijon* or other prepared mustard before whisking in the oil. See page 23 for a Mustard-Tarragon Vinaigrette recipe and facing page for how to make it.

Lemon Vinaigrette

Prepare *Basic Vinaigrette*, but substitute ½ cup (120 ml) *lemon juice* for vinegar and decrease oil to ½ cup (120 ml).

Balsamic-Shallot Vinaigrette

Prepare *Basic Vinaigrette* using *balsamic vinegar*. Add ¼ cup (40 g) minced *shallots*.

HOW TO MAKE MUSTARD-TARRAGON VINAIGRETTE

1 With a variety of oils and vinegars on your kitchen shelves, you can mix and match to make lots of different dressings. Some vinegar choices, from left to right: tarragon, ginger-chile, balsamic, and red wine. And some oils you might consider: lemon-pepper, extra-virgin olive, walnut, and virgin olive.

2 In a small bowl, whisk together vinegar, mustard, garlic, and tarragon. You can create a vinaigrette to complement a specific salad by varying your choice of herbs. Mustard adds a rich, piquant note to a vinaigrette and thickens the dressing, too.

3 Whisk dressing as oil is added in a steady stream to make a temporary emulsion. On standing, the dressing separates. Stir to recombine ingredients.

4 Mustard-Tarragon Vinaigrette is the ideal dressing for Summer Greens Salad (see page 23), made with a mix of tender baby salad leaves and edible flowers. Add the dressing and mix the salad just before serving so that the vinaigrette does not wilt the delicate greens.

POULTRY

Infinitely adaptable, poultry can star at a traditional Sunday dinner, a festive holiday table, or a casual weekday meal. Seasoned simply with herbs or bursting with a savory stuffing, poultry offers succulent goodness that appeals to a variety of tastes.

Types of poultry

Here's a brief glossary of poultry varieties:

Chicken. The most common size for a young chicken is 2½ to 5 pounds (1.15 to 2.3 kg). Such birds can be cooked by almost any method. At one time, smaller birds were called broilers and larger ones, fryers. Now the term "broiler-fryer" covers the whole range.

A chicken weighing 5 to 7 pounds (2.3 to 3.1 kg), however, is properly called a roaster because it is best cooked in this fashion. Its scale makes a big impression at a dinner party, and ensures leftovers for family meals.

Older fowl, often sold as stewing chickens, are best simmered for broth. The meat will not be as succulent as that from a younger bird, but it's fine for salads or sandwiches.

Capon. This is a young male chicken neutered to increase its ratio of meat to bone, especially in the breast. It is usually 4 to 8 months old and weighs 4 to 7 pounds (1.8 to 3.1 kg). Capons are ideal for roasting.

Rock Cornish game hen. Delicately flavored, this young hybrid chicken weighs from 1 to 2 pounds (455 to 905 g). Cook it whole for an individual serving or split a large one in half to serve two.

Turkey. Today's young turkeys, which range from about 10 to 30 pounds (4.5 to 8.5 kg), turn out tender and moist if properly roasted; it's very important to avoid overcooking. For best results, refer to the chart on page 29 rather than relying on the wrapper for oven temperatures and cooking times.

Buying, storing & handling

When buying fresh poultry, note the "pull date" and safe-handling instructions on the label, and make sure the package isn't torn or leaking. Keep poultry in its wrapping until ready to use. Store poultry in the refrigerator and cook within 2 days (cooked poultry keeps for 3 days). Thaw frozen poultry in the refrigerator; remove the giblets as soon as possible.

After preparing raw poultry, wash your hands, counters, cutting boards, and utensils—anything that the raw poultry has touched—with hot, soapy water, then rinse.

Basic Poultry Roasting Time & Temperature Chart

The most accurate measurement of doneness for poultry is the internal temperature at a specific location on the bird as registered on a meat thermometer, either the conventional model or the instant-read type. This method of testing is best because the shape, age, and tenderness of poultry influences how fast it cooks and so does the oven temperature.

A conventional thermometer is inserted in poultry before roasting. For a turkey, the thermometer stem is placed through the thickest part of the breast meat to the bone, or, for a boneless breast, in the middle of the thickest part of the meat. For a whole chicken, the thermometer is inserted into the thickest part of the thigh (on the breast side) to the bone.

To use an instant-read thermometer, as you approach the end of cooking time, insert the stem of the thermometer through the thickest part of the breast or the thigh (on the breast side) to the bone. It will take about 15 seconds to get an accurate reading. The meat should register the temperature indicated in the chart below. A stuffed chicken may take a few minutes longer than the time given in the chart; a large stuffed turkey may take up to 50 minutes longer. To be safe, take a separate reading for the stuffing; it should register at least 140°F (60°C).

There are several other ways to judge the degree of doneness for poultry. For a whole bird, the skin color should be a rich, golden brown and the leg should jiggle easily. Breast meat is done when white at the bone (or in the center of a boneless piece); a leg or thigh should not be pink at the bone.

The chart below is a guideline for plain roasted poultry. However, some recipes in this chapter include additional steps and ingredients, and may vary from these basic guidelines.

Tips for perfect roasting

For a whole bird, place breast side up on a V-shaped rack in a shallow pan. If desired, smear with softened butter or olive oil, or follow the instructions in your recipe. For extra moistness and flavor, you may baste chicken and game hens with pan juices every 15 minutes and turkey every 30 minutes. If a bird appears to be browning too much before it is done, place foil loosely over the dark areas.

Allow whole chickens to stand in a warm place for 10 to 15 minutes and turkeys for 15 to 30 minutes before carving to allow the meat juices to settle.

Type of poultry	Oven temperature	Weight	Doneness	Roasting time
Turkey				
breast, bone-in	350°F (175°C)	4–6 lbs. (1.8–2.7 kg)	165°F (74°C)*	1–1½ hrs.
breast, boned & tied	350°F (175°C)	4–5 lbs. (1.8–2.3 kg)	165°F (74°C)**	1–1½ hrs.
thigh	375°F (190°C)	½–1½ lbs. (230–680 g)	180°F (82°C)***	¾–1¼ hrs.
whole, unstuffed	350°F (175°C)	10–13 lbs. (4.5–5.9 kg)	160°F (71°C)*	1½–2¼ hrs.
whole, unstuffed	325°F (165°C)	14–23 lbs. (6.3–10.4 kg)	160°F (71°C)*	2–3 hrs.
whole, unstuffed	325°F (165°C)	24–27 lbs. (10.8–12.3 kg)	160°F (71°C)*	3–3¾ hrs.
whole, unstuffed	325°F (165°C)	28–30 lbs. (12.6–13.6 kg)	160°F (71°C)*	3½–4½ hrs.
Chicken				
breast halves, boned & skinned	450°F (230°C)	4–5 oz. (115–140 g)	white in center	12–15 mins.
whole breast, bone-in	450°F (230°C)	1 lb. (455 g)	white in center	15–20 mins.
legs & thighs, attached or apart	400°F (205°C)	10 oz. (285 g)	not pink at thigh bone	40–45 mins.
whole, unstuffed	375°F (190°C)	3½–5 lbs. (1.6–2.3 kg)	180°F (82°C)***	1–1¼ hrs.
whole, unstuffed	375°F (190°C)	5–7 lbs. (2.3–3.1 kg)	180°F (82°C)***	1¼–1½ hrs.
Rock Cornish Game Hen				
whole, unstuffed	450°F (230°C)	1–2 lbs. (455–905 g)	not pink at thigh bone	30–40 mins.

*Insert meat thermometer through thickest part of breast to bone
**Insert meat thermometer into center of thickest part of breast
***Insert meat thermometer through thickest part of thigh to bone

MAKING OVEN-FRIED CHICKEN

1 For the coating, combine the bread crumbs, Parmesan, salt, and pepper in a pie pan or other wide, shallow dish; stir until well mixed.

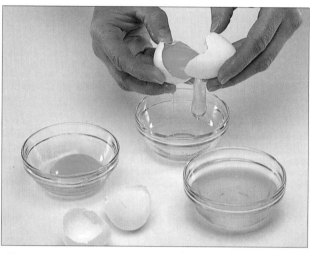

2 To separate an egg, strike eggshell gently on edge of a bowl; as egg breaks, hold shell halves upright to catch yolk. Let most of egg white drain into bowl, then carefully pass yolk from one shell-half to the other until all white is in bowl. Drop yolk into second bowl. (If whites are to be beaten, pour into a third bowl before separating another egg.) You will not need yolks for this recipe.

3 Dip each piece of chicken in the egg mixture, then roll in the seasoned crumbs, taking care to coat completely. Place all chicken pieces (except breasts), skin side up, in a rimmed baking pan. Be sure to leave some space between chicken pieces; crust will not be crisp at points where pieces touch or overlap. And leave space to add breasts to pan later.

4 Coleslaw (flecked with bright strands of carrot) and hot homemade biscuits (see page 153) are perfect accompaniments for the crispy chicken.

CHICKEN

FRYING

What makes fried chicken truly finger-licking good? Southerners add flavor by soaking chicken in buttermilk first. And sizzling-hot fat makes a crust that's crisp but not greasy tasting.

For those who want to cut down on fat and still enjoy crispy-crusted chicken, try "oven-frying." This method requires no added fat—you just bake the crumb-coated pieces until golden brown.

Southern Fried Chicken with Milk Gravy

    1 broiler-fryer chicken (about 3 lbs./1.35 kg), cut into pieces
    1 cup (240 ml) buttermilk
    1 cup (125 g) all-purpose flour
    1 teaspoon salt plus additional to taste
    ½ teaspoon pepper plus additional to taste
       Solid vegetable shortening
  2½ cups (590 ml) 2% milk

Place chicken in a medium-size bowl and pour buttermilk over it; set aside for 30 minutes. In a pie pan, combine ¾ cup (95 g) of the flour, 1 teaspoon of the salt, and ½ teaspoon of the pepper. Coat chicken pieces, one at a time, in the flour, shaking off excess; reserve excess flour. Place chicken pieces slightly apart on a rack and refrigerate, uncovered, for 1 hour.

Melt enough shortening in a heavy-bottomed, wide frying pan over medium-high heat to reach a depth of ¼ inch (6 mm). Meanwhile, recoat chicken with reserved flour, shaking off excess.

To test temperature of fat, drop a pinch of flour into pan; flour should float and sizzle. (If flour sinks and disperses, fat is not hot enough for frying.)

When fat is hot, add chicken pieces, skin side down. Allow enough space between pieces for fat to sizzle; this assures even cooking and browning.

Cook chicken pieces for 10 minutes; reduce heat to medium. With tongs, turn pieces over and continue cooking until meat is no longer pink; cut to test (about 10 minutes for breast meat, 15 minutes for remaining pieces.) Drain chicken pieces on paper towels; keep warm.

Pour off and reserve drippings, leaving browned particles on bottom of pan. Return ¼ cup (60 ml) drippings to pan; scrape browned particles free. Blend in the remaining ¼ cup (30 g) flour and cook, stirring, over medium-high heat until bubbly. Gradually whisk in milk and continue cooking and stirring until sauce boils and thickens (about 5 minutes). Season to taste with salt and pepper. Serve chicken with gravy. *Makes 4 servings*

PER SERVING: *712 calories, 47 g total fat, 14 g saturated fat, 151 mg cholesterol, 413 mg sodium, 21 g carbohydrates, 0.5 g fiber, 49 g protein, 249 mg calcium, 3 mg iron*

Oven-Fried Chicken

PICTURED ON FACING PAGE

  1¼ cups (125 g) plain fine dry bread crumbs
   ¾ cup (about 2¼ oz./60 g) grated Parmesan cheese
   ½ teaspoon salt
   ¼ teaspoon pepper
    2 large egg whites
    2 tablespoons (30 ml) water
    1 broiler-fryer chicken (2½ to 3 lbs./1.15 to 1.35 kg), cut into pieces

In a pie pan, combine bread crumbs, Parmesan cheese, salt, and pepper. In another pie pan, beat egg whites and water just until blended.

Dip chicken pieces in egg mixture, then roll in crumb mixture; set aside breast pieces. Place remaining chicken pieces, skin side up, without touching, in a 10- by- 15-inch (25- by 38-cm) rimmed baking pan. Bake, uncovered, in a 375°F (190°C) oven for 25 minutes, then add breast pieces to pan. Continue to bake until the crust is crisp and browned and meat is no longer pink at thigh bone; cut to test (about 20 more minutes). *Makes 4 servings*

PER SERVING: *597 calories, 31 g total fat, 10 g saturated fat, 138 mg cholesterol, 984 mg sodium, 25 g carbohydrates, 1 g fiber, 50 g protein, 307 mg calcium, 4 mg iron*

Herbed Oven-Fried Chicken

Follow recipe for *Oven-Fried Chicken*, but stir 1½ teaspoons dried *oregano* or basil into the crumb mixture.

CHICKEN *continued*

ROASTING

There are many ways to dress up a basic roast chicken, none of them requiring much fuss. Flavor the bird to your taste, and stuff, baste, or glaze it. Seasoning can start from within—stuff an onion, whole garlic cloves, a handful of fresh herbs, strips of citrus peel, or half a lemon into the cavity. Or try either of the stuffings on page 49. For extra flavor, you can also spread or rub seasonings such as herbed butter, mustard mixtures, pesto, or mashed garlic under the skin. Basting the bird with pan drippings or melted butter as it cooks enhances flavoring. For flavor and a shiny finish, brush melted marmalade or a honey-and-soy-sauce glaze over the bird during the last 10 minutes of roasting.

Basic Roast Chicken

  1 *chicken (about 4 lbs./1.8 kg)*
  ½ *teaspoon salt*
  2 *tablespoons butter or margarine*
     About 2½ cups (250 g) stuffing (optional, see page 49)

Remove giblets from chicken and reserve for other uses. Pull off and discard lumps of fat from chicken. Rinse bird inside and out and pat dry.

Rub cavity with salt. Ease your fingers under the chicken breast skin from the front and the back of the chicken to loosen, but leave in place. Mash the butter to soften, then rub it evenly over the breast, under the skin.

Stuff body cavities with stuffing, if using. Use metal skewers to pin skin over body cavity and pin neck skin to back (see How to Stuff a Turkey, page 51; this method applies to chickens as well).

Place chicken, breast side up, on a V-shaped rack in a 9- by 13-inch (23- by 33-cm) baking pan.

Roast, uncovered, in a 375° (190°C) oven until a meat thermometer inserted through thickest part of thigh to the bone registers 180°F/82°C (1 to 1½ hours). Baste with pan drippings every 15 minutes during last half of cooking time. Transfer bird to a platter. Remove skewers. Let stand for 10 minutes before carving. *Makes 4 servings*

PER SERVING: *560 calories, 36 g total fat, 11 g saturated fat, 189 mg cholesterol, 488 mg sodium, 0 g carbohydrates, 0 g fiber, 56 g protein, 31 mg calcium, 3 mg iron*

Mustard Roast Chicken

  1 *chicken (about 4 lbs./1.8 kg)*
  5 *tablespoons (75 ml) grainy or regular Dijon mustard*
  1 *teaspoon dried thyme*
  ½ *teaspoon ground nutmeg*
  6 *tablespoons (90 ml) whipping cream*
  12 *ounces (340 g) mushrooms (caps about 1 in./2.5 cm wide)*
  1 *tablespoon butter or margarine*
  1 *tablespoon (15 ml) lemon juice*
  1½ *teaspoons dried or drained canned pink or green peppercorns*
     Salt and pepper

Remove giblets from chicken and reserve for other uses. Pull off and discard lumps of fat from chicken. Rinse bird inside and out and pat dry. Place chicken, breast side up, on a V-shaped rack in a 9- by 13-inch (23- by 33-cm) baking pan.

Mix 3 tablespoons (45 ml) of the mustard with the thyme and nutmeg. Ease your fingers under the chicken breast skin from the front and the back of the chicken to loosen, but leave in place. Smear about half of the mustard mixture evenly over breast, under the skin. Stir 2 tablespoons (30 ml) of the cream into the remaining mustard mixture.

Roast chicken, uncovered, in a 400°F (205°C) oven. After 30 minutes, spoon the remaining mustard mixture onto legs and wings. Continue to cook until bird is richly browned (25 to 30 minutes) and meat thermometer inserted through thickest part of thigh to the bone registers 180°F (82°C).

Clean mushrooms; remove discolored stem ends. Cut mushrooms in half vertically through stems. Place in a wide nonstick frying pan with butter, lemon juice, and peppercorns. Cook over high heat, stirring often, until liquid evaporates and mushrooms are lightly browned (4 to 5 minutes). Keep warm.

Tilt chicken to drain its juices into baking pan. Transfer chicken to a platter and spoon mushrooms alongside; keep warm.

Skim fat from pan drippings. Add remaining 4 tablespoons (60 ml) cream and remaining 2 tablespoons (30 ml) mustard to drippings. Stirring constantly, bring to a rolling boil over high heat. Tilt chicken platter and drain juices into the sauce. Offer sauce on the side. *Makes 4 servings*

PER SERVING: *656 calories, 42 g total fat, 15 g saturated fat, 210 mg cholesterol, 700 mg sodium, 5 g carbohydrates, 1 g fiber, 58 g protein, 56 mg calcium, 4 mg iron*

Roast Chicken with Herbs

1 chicken (about 4 lbs./1.8 kg)
3 cloves garlic, peeled and halved
2 bay leaves
2 tablespoons butter or margarine
½ teaspoon salt
½ teaspoon pepper
¼ teaspoon ground sage
¼ teaspoon dried thyme

Remove giblets from chicken and reserve for other uses. Pull off and discard lumps of fat from chicken. Rinse bird inside and out and pat dry. Rub skin of chicken with 1 cut clove garlic; then put all garlic and bay leaves into body cavity.

In a small bowl, mash butter with salt, pepper, sage, and thyme. Spoon 2 teaspoons of the butter mixture into body cavity.

Ease your fingers under chicken breast skin from the front and the back of the chicken to loosen, but leave in place. Rub the remaining butter mixture evenly under the skin. Place chicken, breast side up, on a V-shaped rack in a 9- by 13-inch (23- by 33-cm) baking pan. Roast, uncovered, in a 375°F (190°C) oven until a meat thermometer inserted through thickest part of thigh to the bone registers 180°F/82°C (1 to 1½ hours). Baste occasionally with pan drippings during the last 30 minutes of roasting. Transfer bird to a platter. Let stand for 10 minutes before carving.   *Makes 4 servings*

PER SERVING: *578 calories, 37 g total fat, 12 g saturated fat, 193 mg cholesterol, 503 mg sodium, 1 g carbohydrates, 0.1 g fiber, 56 g protein, 43 mg calcium, 3 mg iron*

BRAISING

A moist-heat method used to tenderize tough cuts of meat, braising plays a different role with chicken. Today's plump chickens arrive at the market naturally moist and tender, so we braise them only to effect delicious flavor variations. With each change of braising liquid and seasoning, chicken turns into an exciting new experience. As a bonus, the braising liquid can become a base for a flavorful sauce, a marvelous enhancement for noodles or rice. To keep the sauce lean, remove excess fat from the chicken and skin before cooking. If made ahead, braised chicken is best reheated in a covered pan over low heat.

Coq au Vin

3 slices bacon (about 2 oz./55 g), coarsely chopped
1 broiler-fryer chicken (about 2½ lbs./1.15 kg), cut into pieces
8 to 10 small white onions (about 1 lb./455 g total)
8 ounces (230 g) small mushrooms, stem ends trimmed
1 cup (240 ml) dry red wine
2 cups (470 ml) reduced-sodium beef broth
2 tablespoons (30 ml) Dijon mustard
2 tablespoons chopped parsley
2 teaspoons cornstarch mixed with 1 tablespoon (15 ml) water

In a wide nonstick frying pan over medium heat, cook bacon, stirring frequently, until crisp (about 6 minutes). Remove with a slotted spoon, drain, and set aside; discard drippings.

Add chicken to pan, skin side down; increase heat to medium-high and cook, turning, until browned on all sides (about 10 minutes). Remove chicken and set aside. Add onions to pan, reduce heat to medium, and cook, stirring frequently, until soft (about 4 minutes). Remove onions and set aside. Stir in mushrooms and cook, stirring frequently, until soft (about 3 minutes); remove mushrooms and set aside.

Add wine to pan and bring to a boil over high heat, scraping browned particles free from pan. Boil until reduced to about ¾ cup/180 ml (about 3 minutes). Add broth, then whisk in mustard. Return chicken, onions, and mushrooms to pan. Bring to a boil; cover, reduce heat to medium-low, and simmer until chicken is no longer pink at thigh bone; cut to test (about 30 minutes).

With a slotted spoon, lift out chicken and vegetables; arrange on a platter and keep warm. Skim off and discard fat from pan juices. Stir bacon, parsley, and cornstarch mixture into pan juices; cook, stirring, until sauce boils and thickens slightly (about 3 minutes). Pour over chicken and vegetables.
Makes 4 servings

PER SERVING: *466 calories, 25 g total fat, 7 g saturated fat, 118 mg cholesterol, 659 mg sodium, 8 g carbohydrates, 1 g fiber, 39 g protein, 38 mg calcium, 3 mg iron*

CHICKEN *continued*

Yogurt-Orange Chicken

　4　chicken legs and thighs, split (about 2 lbs./905 g total)
　½　teaspoon salt
　¼　teaspoon pepper
　1　teaspoon olive oil
　1　large onion, chopped
　2　cloves garlic, minced or pressed
　¾　teaspoon grated orange peel
　¾　cup (180 ml) orange juice
　½　cup (120 ml) reduced-sodium chicken broth
　1　teaspoon sugar
　½　teaspoon ground coriander
　½　teaspoon ground cumin
　1　tablespoon all-purpose flour mixed with ¾ cup (180 ml) plain lowfat yogurt

Sprinkle chicken lightly with ¼ teaspoon of the salt and the pepper. Heat oil in a wide nonstick frying pan over medium-high heat. Add chicken and cook, turning, until browned on all sides (about 10 minutes). Remove chicken and set aside. Pour all but 1 tablespoon (15 ml) fat from pan.

Add onion and garlic to pan, reduce heat to medium, and cook, stirring, until onion is soft (about 2 minutes). Return chicken to pan; add orange peel, orange juice, broth, sugar, coriander, cumin, and the remaining ¼ teaspoon salt. Bring to a boil, then return chicken to pan; cover, reduce heat, and simmer until meat is no longer pink at thigh bone; cut to test (about 25 minutes).

With a slotted spoon, lift chicken onto a platter and keep warm. Stir flour-yogurt mixture into pan juices and cook, stirring, over high heat until sauce boils and thickens slightly (about 3 minutes). Pour sauce over chicken.　*Makes 4 servings*

PER SERVING: *387 calories, 20 g total fat, 6g saturated fat, 109 mg cholesterol, 458 mg sodium, 16 g carbohydrates, 1 g fiber, 33 g protein, 116 mg calcium, 2 mg iron*

Braised Chicken with Dried Cranberries

PICTURED ON FACING PAGE

　8　chicken thighs (about 2 lbs./905 g total)
　3¾　cups (890 ml) reduced-sodium chicken broth
　1　cup (240 ml) dry white wine
　4　cloves garlic, minced or pressed
　2　tablespoons minced fresh ginger
　1　tablespoon grated lemon peel
　1　cup (90 g) dried cranberries
　2　teaspoons butter or margarine
　2　tablespoons (30 ml) water
　1½　cups (275 g) couscous
　1½　tablespoons cornstarch mixed with 3 tablespoons (45 ml) water

In a wide nonstick frying pan over high heat, brown chicken, turning often (15 to 20 minutes); do not crowd. Remove pieces as browned. Discard fat in pan, wipe clean, and return chicken to pan. Add 1½ cups (360 ml) of the broth, the wine, garlic, ginger, and peel. Cover and bring to a boil over high heat; reduce heat and simmer until meat is no longer pink at thigh bone; cut to test (about 25 minutes).

Meanwhile, combine cranberries, butter, and water in a medium-size nonstick frying pan. Bring to a boil over high heat, stirring often, and boil until water evaporates and cranberries are glazed (about 3 minutes). Set aside.

To prepare couscous, in a 1½-quart (1.4-liter) pan, bring remaining 2¼ cups (530 ml) broth to a boil over high heat. Stir in couscous. Cover pan, remove from heat, and let stand for 5 to 10 minutes. Fluff with a fork before serving.

With a slotted spoon, transfer cooked chicken to a platter; keep warm. Spoon off and discard fat from pan juices. Boil juices over high heat, uncovered, until reduced to 1½ cups (360 ml). Whisk cornstarch mixture into sauce and whisk until boiling resumes. Add half the cranberry mixture to sauce. Pour sauce into a small pitcher. Spoon couscous onto platter with chicken. Top chicken with remaining cranberry mixture. Accompany chicken and couscous with sauce. Add salt to taste.　*Makes 4 servings*

PER SERVING: *699 calories, 22 g total fat, 7 g saturated fat, 114 mg cholesterol, 532 mg sodium, 81 g carbohydrates, 4 g fiber, 39 g protein, 45 mg calcium, 3 mg iron*

BRAISED CHICKEN WITH DRIED CRANBERRIES

1 Brown chicken thighs in batches, if necessary, to avoid crowding them in the pan. Rather than turning chicken with a fork, use a spatula or tongs so that you don't lose juices.

2 Return all browned chicken pieces to pan and add broth, wine, garlic, ginger, and lemon peel. Cover pan, bring liquid to a simmer, and cook until chicken is no longer pink at thigh bone. Be sure to keep liquid simmering rather than at a full boil.

3 When chicken is done, remove from pan. Skim fat from pan juices; bring to a boil, uncovered, and cook over high heat until reduced to 1½ cups (360 ml). Whisk cornstarch mixture into pan, whisking constantly until mixture returns to a boil (mixing cornstarch with cold water before adding it to hot liquid helps prevent a lumpy sauce).

4 The chicken thighs, topped with some of the glazed cranberries, make a most appealing meal when served with couscous and Brussels sprouts; asparagus or green beans would be good, too. Pour the sauce into a pitcher to add to individual portions.

CHICKEN *continued*

Garlic Chicken

 4   *slices bacon (about 2¼ oz./63 g)*
 8   *chicken thighs (about 2 lbs./905 g total)*
 2   *medium-size onions, chopped*
 8   *cloves garlic, minced or pressed*
 1¼ *cups (300 ml) dry white wine*
 1   *teaspoon dried basil*
 1   *teaspoon poultry seasoning*
 ½   *teaspoon salt*
 ¼   *teaspoon pepper*
 1   *teaspoon cornstarch mixed with 1 tablespoon (15 ml) water*

In a wide nonstick frying pan over medium heat, cook bacon until crisp (about 6 minutes). Remove bacon from pan, drain, crumble, and set aside. Discard drippings.

Add chicken to pan, skin side down; increase heat to medium-high. Cook, turning, until browned on all sides (about 10 minutes). Remove chicken and set aside. Remove and discard all but 1 tablespoon (15 ml) fat from the pan.

Add onions and garlic to pan; reduce heat to medium and cook, stirring frequently, until onions are soft (about 5 minutes). Return chicken and bacon to pan. Add wine, basil, poultry seasoning, salt, and pepper. Bring to a boil; cover, reduce heat, and simmer until chicken is no longer pink at thigh bone; cut to test (about 20 minutes).

With a slotted spoon, lift out chicken; arrange on a platter and keep warm. Stir cornstarch mixture into pan juices and cook over high heat, stirring, until sauce boils and thickens slightly (about 2 minutes). Spoon sauce over chicken to taste.
Makes 4 servings

PER SERVING: *439 calories, 24 g total fat, 7 g saturated fat, 115 mg cholesterol, 450 mg sodium, 11 g carbohydrates, 2 g fiber, 32 g protein, 62 mg calcium, 2 mg iron*

Cutting Up a Whole Bird

To remove leg and thigh, grasp leg and pull away from body. Cut through skin, exposing joint. Bend thigh back from body; cut close to body through hip joint. Repeat with other leg.

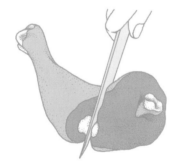

To separate leg from thigh, cut through skin between joints. Then bend leg back from thigh to expose joint; cut through joint and bottom skin.

To remove wing, pull away from body. Cut through skin to expose shoulder joint; sever at joint. To remove wing tip, cut at joint. Repeat with other wing.

To separate back from breast, cut along each side of backbone between rib joints.

Bend back piece in half at joint (natural break); cut to separate.

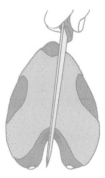

To split breast, place breast skin side up; cut through skin and meat along one side of breastbone. (To bone breast, see page 40.)

STEEPING

Steeping is the name given to the technique for cooking without heat from beneath the pan. It makes the subtle process of poaching lean, delicate-textured poultry and seafood more controllable. Surprisingly, this gentle method cooks certain foods as quickly as simmering does. Steeped at lower temperatures, foods retain more of their natural juices and cook more evenly.

Adapted from a classic Chinese cooking method, steeping involves immersing food in a pan of boiling water that has just been removed from the heat. Then the pan is covered tightly and the food is left in the hot water to finish cooking. Unlike traditional poaching, in simmering water, steeping uses only the heat retained in the hot water.

To establish the amount of water needed, place ½ to 2 pounds (230 to 905 g) bone-in or boneless chicken breast halves in a pan large enough to hold the pieces in a single layer (the pieces can overlap slightly, but water needs to flow between them). The pan must also be deep enough so that the water can cover the chicken by 1 to 2 inches (2.5 to 5 cm). Add the water, then lift out the chicken. At this point, add any desired seasonings (such as lemon slices, fresh ginger, onion, or herbs) to the water. This method also works for fish steaks or small whole fish.

To steep, cover the pan and bring the water and seasonings to a rolling boil over high heat. Remove from the heat and quickly immerse chicken (or fish) in the water. Cover the pan tightly and let stand. Do not open the lid until it's time to check for doneness.

For chicken, allow 16 to 18 minutes for bone-in breasts that weigh about 8 ounces (230 g). To check doneness, cut into the thickest part; it should no longer be pink. If not done, return to hot water, cover, and let steep slightly longer. (For fish, let steep 6 to 8 minutes per in./2.5 cm of thickness, or less time if you are cooking no more than 8 oz./230 g total. To check doneness, lift out and cut into the thickest part; it should look just opaque but still moist.)

Drain chicken (or fish) and serve hot, or plunge into ice water to cool quickly; drain and serve cold. If made ahead, cover and chill. If desired, boil seasoned cooking water, uncovered, to make a concentrated broth for use in soups and sauces.

Steeped Chicken with Basil Dressing

 4 skinless, boneless chicken breast halves (about 1¼ lbs./565 g total)
   About ½ cup (20 g) chopped fresh basil
   Parsley sprigs
 ½ cup (120 ml) olive oil
 ¼ cup (60 ml) white wine vinegar
 2 tablespoons grated Parmesan cheese
 2 cloves garlic
 ⅛ teaspoon pepper
   Lettuce leaves
 3 large tomatoes (about 1½ lbs./680 g total), thinly sliced
   Fresh basil leaves (optional)

Steep chicken according to directions at left, adding some fresh basil and fresh parsley sprigs to steeping liquid. Refrigerate if desired. Cut chicken across the grain into slices about ½ inch (1 cm) wide.

To prepare basil dressing, in a blender or food processor, combine ½ cup (20 g) of the chopped basil, the oil, vinegar, Parmesan cheese, garlic, and pepper; whirl until smoothly puréed.

Line a serving plate with lettuce leaves; arrange tomato slices on top. Place chicken slices on tomatoes, then drizzle with a little of the basil dressing. Serve remaining dressing in a bowl to add to taste. Garnish with basil leaves, if desired.   *Makes 4 servings*

PER SERVING: *512 calories, 31 g total fat, 5 g saturated fat, 117 mg cholesterol, 192 mg sodium, 10 g carbohydrates, 3 g fiber, 49 g protein, 84 mg calcium, 3 mg iron*

Steeped Chicken with Tonnato Sauce

Steep chicken according to directions at left, adding a few teaspoons dried or fresh *tarragon* to steeping liquid. Chicken may be served hot, cool, or chilled with the sauce.

To prepare *Tonnato Sauce*, place 1 can (3 oz./85 g) drained *water-packed tuna*; ½ cup (50 g) chopped *green onions* (including tops); ¼ cup (15 g) packed chopped *parsley*; 2 drained canned *anchovy fillets*; ½ teaspoon *dried tarragon*; 2 teaspoons *Dijon mustard*; 2 tablespoons (30 ml) *lemon juice*; and 2 tablespoons (30 ml) plain *nonfat yogurt* in blender or food processor. Whirl until smooth; scrape container sides often. Stir in ¼ cup (60 ml) more plain nonfat yogurt.

PREPARING EASY BAKED CHICKEN KIEV

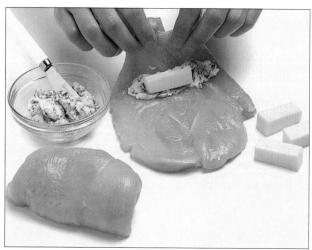

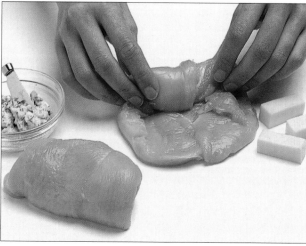

1 Spread some of the herb-butter mixture on each pounded chicken breast half, about 1 inch (2.5 cm) from lower edge. Lay a piece of cheese on top of the butter. Fold lower edge of breast over filling.

2 Fold in sides of breast toward center, then continue to roll up filled cutlet to form a neat bundle.

3 Using your fingers to help hold bundle closed, dip each bundle in egg mixture and let excess drain for a moment; then carefully roll bundle in bread crumb mixture, coating it evenly and completely. Place bundles, seam side down, in a baking dish, leaving a little space between them.

4 For a pretty presentation, cut each chicken bundle crosswise into four or five slices and fan them on the plate. Keep the side dishes simple—steamed green beans, along with white rice dotted with diced carrots and green onions, are good choices.

CHICKEN *continued*

BAKING

Pop a panful of chicken pieces into the oven, set the timer, and you're home free. In fact, many baked chicken recipes are that easy, and they can be doubled to accommodate a hungry crowd. For extra flavor, try marinating, stuffing, coating, or glazing the poultry pieces.

When you plan to bake bone-in chicken pieces—or cook them by any of the other methods detailed in this chapter—you'll find that you can save money if you buy a whole bird and cut it up yourself. With the step-by-step instructions illustrated on page 36, you can learn to cut up a chicken quickly. If whole fresh chickens are on sale, consider buying several to cut up yourself. That way you'll have enough legs and thighs for one meal and enough breasts for another.

Easy Baked Chicken Kiev

PICTURED ON FACING PAGE

- 8 skinless, boneless chicken breast halves (about 2½ lbs./ 1.15 kg total)
- ½ cup (50 g) fine dry bread crumbs
- ½ cup (about 1½ oz./40 g) grated Parmesan cheese
- 1½ teaspoons dried oregano
- ½ teaspoon salt
- ¼ teaspoon pepper
- 4 tablespoons (2 oz./55 g) butter or margarine
- 1 tablespoon chopped parsley
- 4 ounces (115 g) jack cheese, cut into eight pieces ½ inch by 1½ inch (1 cm by 3.5 cm)
- 2 large eggs beaten with 2 tablespoons (30 ml) water

Place breast halves, one at a time, between 2 sheets of plastic wrap. With flat side of a mallet or with a small frying pan, gently pound breasts until each is about ¼ inch (6 mm) thick; set aside.

In a pie pan, combine bread crumbs, Parmesan cheese, 1 teaspoon of the oregano, the salt, and pepper; set aside. In a small bowl, mash butter with parsley and remaining ½ teaspoon oregano.

Spread about ½ tablespoon of the herb-butter mixture on each breast about 1 inch (2.5 cm) from lower edge; lay a piece of jack cheese on butter mixture. Fold lower edge of breast over filling, then fold in sides and roll up to enclose filling.

Roll each bundle in egg mixture and drain briefly; then roll in bread crumb mixture until evenly coated. Place bundles, seam side down, without touching, in a 9- by 13-inch (23- by 33-cm) baking pan. Cover and refrigerate for at least 4 hours or overnight.

Bake, uncovered, in a 425°F (220°C) oven until chicken is no longer pink in center; cut to test (about 30 minutes).   *Makes 8 servings*

PER SERVING: *329 calories, 15 g total fat, 8 g saturated fat, 170 mg cholesterol, 531 mg sodium, 6 g carbohydrates, 0.3 g fiber, 41 g protein, 220 mg calcium, 2 mg iron*

Teriyaki Chicken

- 4 chicken legs and thighs (about 1¾ lbs./795 g total)
- ⅓ cup (80 ml) reduced-sodium soy sauce
- ¼ cup (60 ml) vegetable oil
- 2½ tablespoons (38 ml) honey
- 2 tablespoons (30 ml) dry sherry
- 2 green onions (including tops), thinly sliced
- 1 teaspoon grated fresh ginger or ½ teaspoon ground ginger
- 1 clove garlic, minced or pressed

Place chicken in a zip-seal plastic bag. In a small bowl, combine soy sauce, oil, honey, sherry, green onions, ginger, and garlic; pour over chicken in bag. Seal bag and turn several times to coat chicken. Set bag in a shallow pan and refrigerate for 4 hours or until next day, turning occasionally.

Pour off and discard marinade. Place chicken, skin side up, on a rack in a 9- by 13-inch (23- by 33-cm) baking pan. Bake, uncovered, in a 350°F (175°C) oven until chicken is no longer pink at thigh bone; cut to test (about 45 minutes).   *Makes 4 servings*

PER SERVING: *271 calories, 17 g total fat, 4 g saturated fat, 90 mg cholesterol, 278 mg sodium, 4 g carbohydrates, 0.1 g fiber, 26 g protein, 15 mg calcium, 1 mg iron*

CHICKEN *continued*

Lemon Rosemary Chicken

1¼ *cups (56 g) soft whole-wheat bread crumbs (2 to 3 bread slices whirled in a blender or food processor)*

2 *tablespoons minced fresh rosemary or 2 teaspoons dried rosemary, crumbled*

1 *tablespoon minced parsley*

1 *teaspoon grated lemon peel*

½ *teaspoon pepper*

6 *skinless, boneless chicken breast halves (about 2 lbs./ 905 g total)*

1 *tablespoon (15 ml) lemon juice*

Lemon wedges (optional)

Salt

In a medium-size bowl, combine bread crumbs, rosemary, parsley, lemon peel, and pepper. Arrange chicken breasts slightly apart in an oiled 10- by 15-inch (25- by 38-cm) rimmed baking pan. Moisten top of chicken with lemon juice, then press an equal amount of bread crumb mixture over the surface of each piece, covering evenly.

Bake chicken, uncovered, in a 400°F (205°C) oven until crumb topping is browned and meat is no longer pink in the thickest part; cut to test (18 to 25 minutes). Accompany chicken with lemon wedges, if desired, and salt to taste. *Makes 6 servings*

PER SERVING: *199 calories, 3 g total fat, 0.7 g saturated fat, 88 mg cholesterol, 149 mg sodium, 5 g carbohydrates, 0.7 g fiber, 36 g protein, 30 mg calcium, 2 mg iron*

How to Bone a Chicken Breast

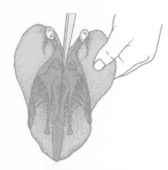

Place breast skin side down; run a sharp knife down center to sever thin membrane and expose keel bone (dark spoon-shaped bone) and thick white cartilage.

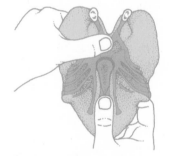

Placing one thumb on tip end of keel bone and other at base of rib cage, grasp breast firmly in both hands. Bend breast back with both hands until keel bone breaks through.

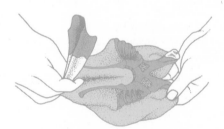

Run finger under edge of keel bone and thick cartilage, then pull out and discard.

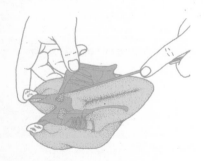

Insert knife under long first rib. Pressing knife along bones, cut meat free. Cut rib away, and sever and remove shoulder joint. Repeat with other side of breast.

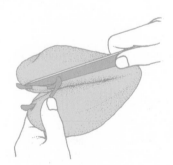

With fingers, locate wishbone. Cutting close to bone, remove wishbone.

Lay breast meat flat on a cutting board and cut breast in half; remove white tendon from bottom side of each half. Pull off skin, if suggested in recipe.

STIR-FRYING

There are many good reasons to fire up the wok (or frying pan) and serve one of these dishes: They're high in protein and low in fat (stir-fries require very little oil, especially if a nonstick pan is used), and you can tailor the vivid flavors to any taste.

Because stir-frying is a rapid process, the ingredients must all be cut and measured before you start. But you can buy some ingredients prepared and ready to go into the pan. Chicken is now sold boned, skinned, and cut up—even marinated. You can also buy cut-up vegetables at salad bars and supermarkets. And rice—the standard accompaniment for stir-fries—cooks so quickly that the timing works out perfectly. (For a cross-cultural experience, serve a stir-fry in a tortilla—as we did in the recipe below.)

Stir-Fried Chicken & Chile Tacos

      2   medium-size red bell peppers (about 12 oz./340 g total)
      2   fresh Anaheim (California or New Mexico) green chiles (2 oz./55 g total) or 1 large green bell pepper (about 8 oz./230 g)
      4   or 5 fresh jalapeño chiles (about 4 oz./115 g total)
    1⅓   pounds (605 g) skinless, boneless chicken breasts
      1   tablespoon (15 ml) vegetable oil
      1   large onion, thinly sliced
      3   cloves garlic, minced
      1   tablespoon cumin seeds
      ½   cup (20 g) chopped cilantro
      3   tablespoons (45 ml) lime juice
          Salt and pepper
     12   warm corn or flour tortillas (6- or 7-in./15- or 18-cm diameter)
          Lime wedges
          Salsa
          Plain nonfat yogurt

Stem and seed bell peppers and Anaheim and jalapeño chiles. Cut bell peppers and chiles into thin slivers about 3 inches (8 cm) long. Cut chicken crosswise into thin slices about 3 inches (8 cm) long.

Heat 2 teaspoons of the oil in a nonstick wok or wide nonstick frying pan over high heat until hot but not smoking. Add chicken and stir-fry until chicken is no longer pink; cut to test (4 to 5 minutes). Remove chicken from pan.

Return pan to high heat. Add remaining 1 teaspoon oil, the onion, garlic, and cumin; stir-fry for 1 minute. Add bell peppers and chiles. Stir-fry until they are limp (about 2 minutes). Return cooked chicken to the pan. Add cilantro and lime juice, and salt and pepper to taste. Pour into a large bowl.

To assemble each taco, fill a tortilla with chicken mixture. Squeeze a lime wedge over the filling. Add salsa and yogurt to taste. Fold tortilla to enclose filling.   *Makes 4 to 6 servings*

PER SERVING: *352 calories, 6 g total fat, 0.9 g saturated fat, 70 mg cholesterol, 185 mg sodium, 42 g carbohydrates, 6 g fiber, 34 g protein, 158 mg calcium, 4 mg iron*

Kung Pao Chicken

      ¼   cup (60 ml) reduced-sodium chicken broth
      2   tablespoons (30 ml) reduced-sodium soy sauce
      2   tablespoons (30 ml) dry sherry
      1   teaspoon cornstarch
      1   teaspoon Oriental sesame oil
     12   ounces (340 g) skinless, boneless chicken breasts, cut into ¼- by 2-inch (6-mm by 5-cm) pieces
      3   cloves garlic, chopped or slivered
      ¼   to ¾ teaspoon crushed red pepper flakes
          About 1 tablespoon (15 ml) vegetable oil
     10   green onions, ends trimmed (6 cut into 1½-in./3.5-cm pieces; 4 reserved for garnish)
      ⅓   cup (42 g) unsalted dry-roasted peanuts
          About 4 cups (520 g) hot cooked rice

In a small bowl, mix broth, soy sauce, sherry, cornstarch, and sesame oil; set aside. In a medium-size bowl, mix chicken with garlic and red pepper flakes.

Heat 2 teaspoons of the vegetable oil in a nonstick wok or wide nonstick frying pan over high heat until hot but not smoking. Add half the chicken mixture and stir-fry until chicken is golden brown and no longer pink in thickest part; cut to test (about 3 minutes). Transfer to a plate. Repeat with remaining chicken, adding oil as needed.

Return cooked chicken to pan; stir in reserved sauce, green onion pieces, and nuts. Cook, stirring, until sauce bubbles and thickens (about 1 minute). Serve with rice; add green onion garnish.
Makes 4 servings

PER SERVING: *503 calories, 12 g total fat, 2 g saturated fat, 49 mg cholesterol, 394 mg sodium, 65 g carbohydrates, 3 g fiber, 29 g protein, 72 mg calcium, 4 mg iron*

CHICKEN *continued*

GRILLING & BROILING

Cooking chicken directly under or over a heat source requires a watchful eye and a ready hand with the tongs. But the resulting irresistible flavors— enhanced by marinades, spice rubs, or basting sauces—will more than reward the attention.

Poultry pieces grill more quickly and evenly than whole birds, unless a spit is used. First, oil the grill rack or broiler-pan rack. Start the poultry pieces, skin side down, under the broiler (or, skin side up, on the grill), then turn and cook the second side to golden.

Grilled Chicken Legs with Olives

PICTURED ON FACING PAGE

- 4 *whole chicken legs (drumsticks with thighs attached, 6 to 8 oz./170 to 230 g each)*
- ½ *cup (70 g) pimento-stuffed olives, chopped*
- 1 *clove garlic, minced or pressed*
- 1 *teaspoon minced fresh rosemary or ½ teaspoon dried rosemary, crumbled*
- 1 *large eggplant (about 1½ lbs./680 g), stemmed and cut crosswise into rounds ¾ inch (2 cm) thick*
- 2 *tablespoons (30 ml) olive oil*
- 2 *tablespoons (30 ml) orange juice*
- 2 *teaspoons honey*

Rinse chicken and pat dry. Slide your fingers beneath skin to separate it from thigh and drumstick meat, but leave skin in place. In a small bowl, combine olives, garlic, and rosemary. Tuck one fourth of the olive mixture under skin on top side of each leg, pushing to distribute equally.

Brush both sides of eggplant with oil. In a small bowl, mix orange juice and honey; set aside. Place chicken on a grill 4 to 6 inches (10 to 15 cm) above a solid bed of medium coals (you can hold your hand at grill level only 4 to 5 seconds). Cook for 20 minutes, turning often to avoid burning.

Add eggplant to grill. Turn chicken and eggplant to brown evenly (15 to 25 more minutes). Brush both with honey mixture. Cook, turning and basting often, until eggplant is very soft when pressed and chicken is no longer pink at thigh bone; cut to test (about 5 more minutes). *Makes 4 servings*

PER SERVING: *367 calories, 22 g total fat, 5 g saturated fat, 90 mg cholesterol, 500 mg sodium, 15 g carbohydrates, 3 g fiber, 28 g protein, 87 mg calcium, 3 mg iron*

Chicken Kebabs Shanghai

- ¾ *teaspoon grated orange peel*
- ⅓ *cup (80 ml) orange juice*
- 3 *tablespoons firmly packed brown sugar*
- 2 *tablespoons (30 ml) soy sauce*
- 4 *teaspoons minced fresh ginger*
- 4 *teaspoons (20 ml) wine vinegar*
- 1 *tablespoon (15 ml) Oriental sesame oil or vegetable oil*
- ½ *teaspoon ground coriander*
- 1½ *pounds (680 g) skinless, boneless chicken breasts*
- 8 *ounces (230 g) peeled and cored pineapple*

In a large bowl, combine orange peel, orange juice, sugar, soy sauce, ginger, vinegar, oil, and coriander. Cut chicken into 1½-inch (3.5-cm) chunks and stir into orange juice mixture. Cover and chill for at least 30 minutes or up to 2 hours. Cut pineapple into about 1-inch (2.5-cm) chunks.

On thin skewers, thread chicken and pineapple, alternating 2 pieces chicken with 1 piece pineapple. Brush remaining marinade over pineapple. Place skewers on a broiler-pan rack. Broil about 4 inches (10 cm) from heat, turning once, until chicken is no longer pink in thickest part; cut to test (12 to 14 minutes). *Makes 4 servings*

PER SERVING: *300 calories, 6 g total fat, 1 g saturated fat, 99 mg cholesterol, 630 mg sodium, 21 g carbohydrates, 0.7 g fiber, 40 g protein, 36 mg calcium, 2 mg iron*

Smoking with Hardwoods

Smoldering hardwood chunks and chips impart a special flavor and aroma to grilled foods. First, soak the wood in water for about 30 minutes (for an average fire, use about 4 oz./115 g of wood) and put it on the coals or in a foil pan on lava rocks. Add chunks at the start of cooking, and chips throughout the cooking since they burn quickly. Cover to capture smoke flavors.

Bags of various "flavors" of wood, such as hickory, mesquite, oak, and alder, are available at gourmet food stores and through catalogs. Experiment to discover which woods complement your favorite grilling recipes.

GRILLED CHICKEN LEGS WITH OLIVES

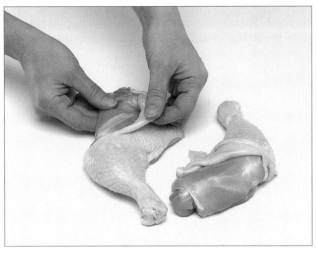

1 To create pockets for olive mixture, use your fingers to loosen skin from flesh of chicken legs; be careful not to detach skin completely.

2 If using fresh rosemary, you'll need to remove leaves from stems. Hold stem tightly with one hand and slide thumb and forefinger of other hand down stem to strip off leaves. Mince leaves with a chef's knife—they're quite tough.

3 With your fingers, push olive mixture into pocket between skin and flesh of chicken legs. Replace skin, then pat gently to distribute olive mixture evenly under skin. Grill over medium coals until meat is no longer pink at thigh bone.

4 Along with the chicken and eggplant, you might like to grill some bell peppers—yellow, red, or green—as a colorful accompaniment.

GAME HENS

These plump little chickens make marvelous company fare. Their delicate flavor is enhanced by almost any seasoning, and they can be grilled, roasted, or broiled. For easy handling and fast cooking, first split the hens lengthwise with kitchen scissors. Keep garnishes to scale: Mixed baby salad greens, grape or currant clusters, lady apples, and kumquats are perfect additions to the platter or plate that holds these mini-hens.

Grilled Game Hens with Cilantro Marinade

- ⅔ cup (30 g) minced cilantro
- ¼ cup (60 ml) marsala or apple juice
- 3 tablespoons (45 ml) honey
- 2 tablespoons (30 ml) reduced-sodium soy sauce
- 4 cloves garlic, minced or pressed
- 1 teaspoon dry mustard
- 4 Rock Cornish game hens (about 1½ lbs./680 g each)

In a 1-quart (950-ml) pan, combine ½ cup (20 g) of the cilantro, the marsala, honey, soy sauce, garlic, and mustard. Bring to a boil over high heat. Remove pan from heat and let mixture cool.

Meanwhile, reserve necks and giblets for another use. With kitchen scissors, split birds lengthwise through breastbones. Rinse hens and pat dry. Open hens; press, skin side up, to crack bones so birds lie flat. Place hens and marinade in a large zip-seal plastic bag. Seal bag and turn several times to coat hens; set in a shallow pan. Chill for 1 hour or up until next day, turning occasionally.

Place hens, skin side up, on a grill 4 to 6 inches (10 to 15 cm) above a solid bed of medium coals (you can hold your hand at grill level only 4 to 5 seconds). Cook, turning to brown evenly, for 20 minutes. Baste with marinade and turn often until hens are no longer pink at thigh bone; cut to test (15 to 20 more minutes). Sprinkle with remaining cilantro.
Makes 4 servings

PER SERVING: *641 calories, 39 g total fat, 11 g saturated fat, 281 mg cholesterol, 441 mg sodium, 17 g carbohydrates, 0.2 g fiber, 49 g protein, 41 mg calcium, 2 mg iron*

Game Hens with Spinach-Rice Stuffing

PICTURED ON FACING PAGE

- 1 teaspoon olive oil
- 4 green onions (including tops), sliced
- 1 large stalk celery, finely chopped
- 12 ounces (340 g) spinach leaves, cut into strips ¼ inch (6 mm) wide, or 1 package (10 oz./285 g) frozen chopped spinach, thawed and drained well
- ⅓ cup (20 g) finely chopped parsley
- 2 cups (260 g) cold cooked rice
- 1¼ teaspoons salt
- ¾ teaspoon pepper
- ¾ teaspoon dried rosemary, crumbled
- 3 Rock Cornish game hens (about 1½ lbs./680 g each)
- 2 tablespoons butter or margarine
- 1 tablespoon (15 ml) lemon juice
- ½ teaspoon dried fines herbes

Heat oil in a wide nonstick frying pan over medium heat until hot but not smoking. Add green onions and celery; cook, stirring frequently, until soft (about 5 minutes). Reduce heat to medium-low. Add spinach and ¼ cup (15 g) of the parsley; cover and cook, stirring occasionally, until wilted (about 2 minutes). Remove pan from heat and stir in rice, 1 teaspoon of the salt, ½ teaspoon of the pepper, and the rosemary. Place stuffing in a bowl; set aside until cool enough to handle.

With kitchen scissors, cut hens in half lengthwise along breastbone and backbone. Rinse and pat dry. Press scant equal portion of stuffing onto cut side of each hen half. Holding stuffing in place with your hand, flip hens and arrange, skin side up, in an oiled 10- by 15-inch (25- by 38-cm) baking pan.

Melt butter in a 1-quart (950-ml) pan over low heat. Stir in remaining parsley, salt, and pepper, and the lemon juice and fines herbes. Brush over hens. Bake, uncovered, in a 375°F (190°C) oven until hens are no longer pink at thigh bone; cut to test (45 to 60 minutes). During last 30 minutes, baste occasionally with pan drippings.   *Makes 6 servings*

PER SERVING: *488 calories, 31 g total fat, 10 g saturated fat, 198 mg cholesterol, 644 mg sodium, 16 g carbohydrates, 2 g fiber, 35 g protein, 102 mg calcium, 4 mg iron*

PREPARING GAME HENS WITH SPINACH-RICE STUFFING

1 For stuffing, add spinach and parsley to pan after green onions and celery have softened. Cover pan and cook until spinach is wilted (about 2 minutes), stirring occasionally. Remove from heat and uncover pan to cool mixture.

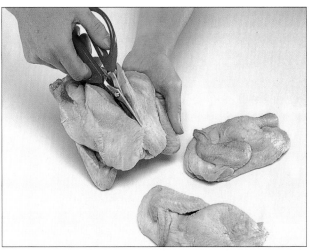

2 Use sturdy kitchen scissors or poultry shears to halve game hens along breastbone, then along backbone. Rinse and dry hen halves; remove any large pieces of fat from inside cavities of hens.

3 Pack equal portions of the rice stuffing into cavity of each hen half. Hold stuffing in place with your hand as you turn hen half over, then place it in a baking pan lightly coated with oil.

4 Use a wide metal spatula (two, if necessary) to remove the hens from the pan. The stuffing serves as a starchy side dish, so you need to add only a vegetable, such as colorful baby carrots.

TURKEY

Once only appearing annually, turkey has turned into a year-round staple. Now turkey parts, from breast cutlets to ground turkey, work perfectly in recipes traditionally made with other meats. Devotees of chili, meatloaf, and burgers have embraced ground turkey as a healthful alternative to red meat. Strips of turkey tenderloin are just as delectable as pork when stir-fried with soy sauce and ginger. And we've turned to turkey for lower-fat cold cuts, bacon, and sausage.

The gobbler still rules the roost on the holiday platter. Inside the traditional roast turkey, however, there may be innovative stuffings that enhance both the white and the dark meat: Additions such as fruits, fresh herbs and mushrooms, ethnic sausages, spices, and hearty grains promise a lifetime of festive occasions when the turkey is the center of attention. (See page 49 for stuffing recipes and page 51 for how to stuff a turkey.) And to carve that splendid bird with skill and economy, see the simple carving directions on page 50.

Grilled Turkey & Zucchini Kebabs

  3 tablespoons capers with liquid
 ½ cup (120 ml) lemon juice
  2 tablespoons (30 ml) olive oil
 ¼ teaspoon pepper
  2 pounds (905 g) skinless, boneless turkey breast, cut into 1-inch (2.5-cm) cubes
  4 medium-size zucchini (about 1½ lbs./680 g total)
     Lemon wedges

To make marinade, drain caper liquid into a shallow pan or dish; cover drained capers and refrigerate. Stir lemon juice, oil, and pepper into caper liquid; reserve ¼ cup (60 ml) of the marinade. Add turkey to remaining marinade and stir. Cover and refrigerate for at least 30 minutes or up to 2 hours.

Lift turkey from marinade and drain briefly (discard marinade). Thread turkey equally onto 6 metal skewers. Cut each zucchini in half lengthwise; coat zucchini with reserved marinade.

Place turkey and zucchini on a lightly oiled grill 4 to 6 inches (10 to 15 cm) above a solid bed of medium coals (you can hold your hand at grill level only 4 to 5 seconds). Cook, turning as needed and basting several times with reserved marinade, until turkey is no longer pink in thickest part; cut to test (about 15 minutes). Sprinkle with drained capers; offer lemon wedges to squeeze over meat.
Makes 6 servings

PER SERVING: *231 calories, 6 g total fat, 0.9 g saturated fat, 94 mg cholesterol, 272 mg sodium, 5 g carbohydrates, 0.6 g fiber, 39 g protein, 35 mg calcium, 2 mg iron*

Ground Turkey Chili Mole

  1 medium-size onion, chopped
 ¾ cup (180 ml) water
  1 pound (455 g) ground turkey
  2 cloves garlic, minced or pressed
  1 can (about 15 oz./425 g) kidney beans, drained and rinsed
  1 can (15 oz./425 g) stewed tomatoes
  1 can (8 oz./230 g) tomato sauce
  1 tablespoon unsweetened cocoa powder
  1 tablespoon (15 ml) molasses
  1 teaspoon ground cumin
  1 teaspoon paprika
 ½ teaspoon dried basil
 ½ teaspoon dried oregano
 ¼ teaspoon liquid hot pepper seasoning
     Tortilla or corn chips

In a 4- to 5-quart (3.8- to 5-liter) pan over high heat, combine onion and ½ cup (120 ml) of the water. Boil, uncovered, until liquid evaporates and onion begins to stick. Add another ¼ cup (60 ml) water, stir to free browned bits, and boil dry again.

Add turkey and garlic; stir, crumbling meat and cooking until juices have cooked away and turkey is no longer pink.

Stir in beans, tomatoes, tomato sauce, cocoa, molasses, cumin, paprika, basil, oregano, and hot pepper seasoning. Bring to a boil; reduce heat, cover, and simmer until flavors blend (about 30 minutes). Spoon into bowls; serve with tortilla chips.
Makes 4 servings

PER SERVING: *321 calories, 10 g total fat, 2 g saturated fat, 83 mg cholesterol, 865 mg sodium, 32 g carbohydrates, 9 g fiber, 28 g protein, 117 mg calcium, 5 mg iron*

Greek Turkey Burgers

2 cups (470 ml) plain nonfat yogurt

¾ cup (180 ml) white wine vinegar or sherry vinegar

2 tablespoons dried dill weed

2 medium-size red onions (about 12 oz./340 g total)

2 teaspoons vegetable oil

1 pound (455 g) ground turkey

1 teaspoon ground cumin
   Pepper

½ cup (120 ml) water

4 whole-wheat pita breads (about 6-in./15-cm diameter)

2 small cucumbers (about 12 oz./340 g total), peeled and thinly sliced

4 small tomatoes (about 1 lb./455 g total), sliced

To prepare yogurt sauce, in a small bowl, stir together yogurt, ½ cup (120 ml) of the vinegar, and the dill weed; set aside.

Chop 1 onion. Thinly slice the other onion and separate into rings; set aside.

Heat oil in a wide nonstick frying pan over medium-high heat. Add chopped onion and cook, stirring often until onion is soft (about 5 minutes). Transfer to a large bowl; let cool slightly. Add turkey, cumin, and a generous sprinkling of pepper to onion; stir to combine. Shape turkey mixture into 4 patties, about ½ inch (1 cm) thick.

Place patties in same frying pan and cook over medium-high heat to brown both sides (about 8 minutes total); turn once. Drain and discard fat. Add water and remaining ¼ cup (60 ml) vinegar. Reduce heat, cover, and simmer until almost all liquid has evaporated and patties are no longer pink in center; cut to test (about 7 minutes).

Meanwhile, wrap pita breads in foil and place in a 250°F (120°C) oven until hot (about 15 minutes). In a medium-size bowl, mix together cucumbers, onion rings, tomatoes, and half the yogurt sauce.

Offer turkey patties with pita breads, cucumber mixture, and remaining yogurt sauce; assemble elements into sandwiches. *Makes 4 servings*

PER SERVING: *519 calories, 15 g total fat, 4 g saturated fat, 59 mg cholesterol, 504 mg sodium, 60 g carbohydrates, 4 g fiber, 35 g protein, 373 mg calcium, 6 mg iron*

Turkey-Spinach Stir-Fry

¼ cup (60 ml) reduced-sodium chicken broth

2 teaspoons cornstarch

1 teaspoon crushed red pepper flakes
   About 2 tablespoons (30 ml) reduced-sodium soy sauce

1 tablespoon (15 ml) sake or dry sherry

1 teaspoon Oriental sesame oil

1½ pounds (680 g) spinach, roots and wilted leaves discarded, leaves rinsed and drained

2 teaspoons vegetable oil

8 ounces (230 g) mushrooms, sliced

¾ to 1 pound (340 to 455 g) skinless, boneless turkey breast, cut into slices ⅛ inch (3 mm) thick

4 teaspoons minced fresh ginger

3 green onions (including tops), thinly sliced
   Hot cooked rice

In a small bowl, mix broth and cornstarch until smooth, then add red pepper flakes, 2 tablespoons (30 ml) of the soy sauce, the sake, and sesame oil.

Place a nonstick wok or wide nonstick frying pan over high heat. When pan is hot, add spinach. Cover and cook, stirring often, just until leaves wilt (2 to 3 minutes). If pan is crowded, add half the spinach; when it wilts, add remainder and cook until it wilts. Pour spinach into a colander and let drain.

Return pan to heat and add vegetable oil. When oil is hot but not smoking, add sliced mushrooms and stir often until liquid evaporates and mushrooms are lightly browned (3 to 5 minutes).

Add turkey and ginger. Stir-fry until turkey is no longer pink; cut to test (about 3 minutes).

Stir cornstarch mixture to recombine. Add to turkey mixture and stir until sauce boils. Stir in green onions and spinach, and cook just to heat through (about 30 seconds). Spoon onto plates; accompany with hot rice and soy sauce to taste.
Makes 4 servings

PER SERVING: *203 calories, 5 g total fat, 0.8 g saturated fat, 61 mg cholesterol, 477 mg sodium, 11 g carbohydrates, 4 g fiber, 30 g protein, 145 mg calcium, 6 mg iron*

TURKEY continued

Turkey Jambalaya

1 large onion, chopped

1 medium-size (about 4 oz./115 g) green bell pepper, stemmed, seeded, and chopped

¼ cup (30 g) diced celery

1 teaspoon minced or pressed garlic

½ cup (120 ml) plus 2 tablespoons (30 ml) water

4 ounces (115 g) turkey sausage, thinly sliced

4 ounces (115 g) turkey ham, cut into ½-inch (1-cm) cubes

2 slices (1½ oz./45 g total) turkey bacon, diced

3 cups (710 ml) reduced-sodium chicken broth

1 can (about 1 lb./455 g) crushed tomatoes

1 cup (185 g) long-grain white rice

¼ cup (15 g) chopped parsley

½ teaspoon dried basil

½ teaspoon dried thyme

½ teaspoon pepper

¼ teaspoon ground red pepper (cayenne)

1 bay leaf

1 jar (10 oz./285 g) shucked fresh small oysters

1 pound (455 g) medium-size shrimp, shelled and deveined
   Salt

In a 5- to 6-quart (5- to 6-liter) pan over high heat, combine onion, bell pepper, celery, garlic, and ½ cup (120 ml) of the water. Stir frequently until moisture evaporates and vegetables begin to stick to pan (about 10 minutes). Stir free with the remaining 2 tablespoons (30 ml) water. Add turkey sausage, ham, and bacon; stir frequently until mixture begins to brown (8 to 10 minutes).

Stir in broth, tomatoes, rice, parsley, basil, thyme, black pepper, ground red pepper, bay leaf, and juices drained from oysters. Bring to a boil over high heat; cover, reduce heat, and simmer until rice is tender to bite (30 to 40 minutes). Stir occasionally.

Add shrimp and oysters (cut in half if large). Cook, uncovered, just until shrimp turn pink (about 8 minutes); stir often. Discard bay leaf. Season to taste with salt. *Makes 8 servings*

PER SERVING: *249 calories, 6 g total fat, 2 g saturated fat, 110 mg cholesterol, 674 mg sodium, 27 g carbohydrates, 2 g fiber, 21 g protein, 83 mg calcium, 6 mg iron*

Raspberry-Glazed Turkey Tenderloins

½ cup (144 g) seedless raspberry jam

6 tablespoons (90 ml) raspberry vinegar

¼ cup (60 ml) Dijon mustard

1 teaspoon grated orange peel

½ teaspoon dried thyme

4 turkey breast tenderloins (about 2¼ lbs./1.15 kg total)

In a 2- to 3-quart (1.9- to 2.8-liter) pan, whisk together jam, vinegar, mustard, orange peel, and thyme. Bring to a boil over high heat and cook, stirring, until reduced by about one fourth (2 to 3 minutes). Reserving about ½ cup (120 ml) of the glaze, coat turkey with some of the remaining glaze.

Set turkey on a broiler-pan rack. Broil about 4 inches (10 cm) below heat, turning and basting once with some of remaining glaze, until turkey is no longer pink in thickest part; cut to test (8 to 10 minutes). Slice turkey crosswise and arrange on plates. Accompany with reserved glaze.   *Makes 4 to 6 servings*

PER SERVING: *319 calories, 1 g total fat, 0.4 g saturated fat, 127 mg cholesterol, 401 mg sodium, 21 g carbohydrates, 0.4 g fiber, 51 g protein, 30 mg calcium, 3 mg iron*

Turkey Tenderloin Tips

The whole muscle lying inside the center of the turkey breast against the bone is called the tenderloin. Skinless and boneless, this sizable portion of white meat is ready to use in almost any recipe calling for chicken, veal, pork, or beef. At less than 1 gram of fat per cooked ounce, turkey tenderloin is one of the leanest protein choices available. Take a look at its versatility:

• *Pounded, it becomes a scaloppine stand-in.*

• *Cut into chunks, it's perfect for kebabs or stew.*

• *Ground in a food processor, it's leaner than other ground turkey, which often includes skin. Try it in meatballs.*

• *Thinly sliced into strips, it will work well in a stir-fry, pasta sauce, burrito, or stroganoff.*

STUFFINGS FOR TURKEY, CHICKEN & GAME HEN

Stuffing transforms a simple roast bird into a feast. You can prepare the stuffing up to a day in advance, then cover and refrigerate it. But to guard against food poisoning, do not stuff the bird until just before roasting. And after the bird is cooked, spoon out all the stuffing and refrigerate leftovers.

As the bird cooks, the stuffing may expand, so pack it into the cavities with a light hand. Place any stuffing that doesn't fit into the bird in a lightly greased baking dish; cover and cook it alongside the bird during the last hour of roasting.

Whether you're roasting game hens, chicken, or turkey, allow ½ cup (90 g) to 1 cup (180 g) of stuffing per pound (455 g) of poultry.

For the Old-Fashioned Bread Stuffing, below, use day-old bread—stuffing made with soft, fresh bread becomes mushy with cooking. If you have only fresh bread on hand, place slices in a 150°F (66°C) oven until dried throughout.

Old-Fashioned Bread Stuffing

> 5 tablespoons (72 g) butter or margarine
> 3 large onions, chopped
> 2 cups (246 g) chopped celery
> 1½ teaspoons dried marjoram
> ¾ teaspoon pepper
> ¾ teaspoon ground sage
> ¾ teaspoon dried thyme
> 12 cups (about 15 oz./425 g) day-old whole wheat or white bread (or a mixture of both), cut into ½-inch (1-cm) cubes
> ½ cup (30 g) chopped parsley
> 1⅓ cups (320 ml) reduced-sodium chicken broth
> Salt

Melt 1 tablespoon of the butter in a wide nonstick frying pan over medium heat. Add onions and celery; cook, stirring occasionally, until golden (about 15 minutes). Add remaining 4 tablespoons (57 g) butter, the marjoram, pepper, sage, and thyme; heat until melted (about 2 minutes). Remove from heat.

In a large bowl, combine bread cubes, parsley, and broth; add onion mixture. With 2 spoons, mix until bread cubes are moistened. Season to taste with salt. (At this point, you may cover and refrigerate for up to 1 day; let stand at room temperature for about 20 minutes before stuffing poultry.)
Makes about 14 cups (about 1.35 kg)

PER SERVING: *141 calories, 6 g total fat, 3 g saturated fat, 11 mg cholesterol, 271 mg sodium, 20 g carbohydrates, 3 g fiber, 4 g protein, 48 mg calcium, 2 mg iron*

Barley-Corn Stuffing with Sausage

> 1¾ cups (about 12 oz./340 g) quick-cooking pearl barley, rinsed
> 6 cups (1.4 liters) reduced-sodium chicken broth
> 12 ounces (340 g) bulk pork sausage
> 1 tablespoon (15 ml) olive oil or vegetable oil
> 1 tablespoon butter or margarine
> 2 to 3 large onions, chopped
> 1 tablespoon minced fresh sage or 1½ teaspoons ground sage
> ½ teaspoon pepper
> 4 cups (665 g) fresh corn kernels (cut from about 5 medium-size ears), or 2 packages (10 oz./285 g each) frozen corn kernels
> Fresh sage leaves (optional)
> Salt

Bring barley and broth to a boil in a 4- to 5-quart (3.8- to 5-liter) pan over high heat; cover and simmer until barley is tender to bite (about 10 minutes). Drain, reserving broth. Set broth and barley aside. Rinse and dry pan. Chop or crumble sausage and add to pan. Cook over medium-high heat, stirring often until richly browned (about 10 minutes). Spoon meat onto paper towels to drain.

Add oil, butter, onions, sage, and pepper to pan. Stir often until onion is tinged with brown and sweet-tasting (about 40 minutes). Add corn and stir often for 5 minutes; add barley and sausage. Pour stuffing into a shallow 9- by 13-inch (23- by 33-cm) baking dish and add 1 cup (240 ml) of the reserved broth (save extra broth for other uses). Cover dish snugly with foil. (At this point, you may chill until next day.) Bake in a 350°F (175°C) oven until hot in center (about 40 minutes or 1 hour if cold). Uncover and garnish with sage leaves. Add salt to taste.

Note: You can stuff a turkey, chicken, or game hen rather than baking in the pan.   *Makes 12 servings*

PER SERVING: *283 calories, 15 g total fat, 5 g saturated fat, 22 mg cholesterol, 351 mg sodium, 30 g carbohydrates, 5 g fiber, 8 g protein, 22 mg calcium, 1 mg iron*

ROAST TURKEY WITH GIBLET GRAVY

The size of the turkey you roast depends on your guest list and on your fondness for leftovers. Generally, figure on about 1 pound (455 g) of turkey (bone-in) per person.

Preparing the turkey. Remove neck and giblets and reserve for giblet gravy (see information at right). Rinse bird inside and out; pat dry with paper towels.

To roast without stuffing, rub inside of turkey with salt and roast according to the chart on page 29.

To stuff the turkey, see recipes on page 49. Do not stuff turkey until just before roasting. Place turkey breast side down. Lightly stuff neck cavity. Bring neck skin up and over cavity to enclose stuffing. With a metal skewer, fasten neck skin to back, threading the skewer in and out several times.

Turn bird over and lightly stuff body cavity. Use 2 or 3 metal skewers to close cavity, threading the skewers in and out 3 or 4 times.

Because the breast of a turkey (or chicken) cooks more quickly than the meat at the thigh joint, you'll get the most satisfactory results if the bird is roasted without the old-fashioned technique of trussing, or tying the legs and wings close to the body. Trussing actually slows cooking at the thigh joint.

Untrussed, the skin around the legs and over the breast browns more evenly and looks more appetizing. Moreover, untrussed birds are easier to prepare for roasting and simpler to serve because there are no strings to remove. Also the position of the legs, standing away from the body, makes it less awkward to get the knife into the hip joint as you carve.

To roast, place turkey, breast side up, on a V-shaped rack in a shallow roasting pan large enough to hold turkey comfortably. To give the bird better balance as it roasts and when carving, fold the wing tips underneath the back. Insert a meat thermometer through the thickest part of breast to the bone. (Use a meat thermometer even if turkey has a pop-up thermometer; our testing indicates that sometimes the bird is overcooked before thermometer pops up.) Rub body with 2 tablespoons softened butter or margarine. Roast on the lowest oven rack according to the chart on page 29.

Making giblet gravy. While the turkey is roasting, place neck and giblets (except liver) in a 2-quart (1.9-liter) pan and cover with 4 cups (950 ml) water. Bring to a boil over high heat. Cover, reduce heat, and simmer until tender (about 1½ hours). Strain and reserve broth. Strip meat from neck; chop giblets and neck meat, cover, and refrigerate.

When turkey is done, transfer to a platter or cutting board and let stand in a warm place for 15 to 30 minutes before carving. (This waiting period allows the juices to settle back into the meat, so that it will be as juicy as possible.)

Add 1 cup (240 ml) of reserved broth to drippings in roasting pan. Place over medium heat and scrape browned particles free from the pan; pour mixture into a large measuring cup. The fat will rise to the top. Spoon off the fat and reserve it.

Determine the amount of gravy you want: For each 1 cup gravy, you'll need 1 cup (240 ml) broth mixture, 2 tablespoons all-purpose flour, and 1 to 2 tablespoons (15 to 30 ml) of the reserved fat. Put flour and fat in a 2- to 3-quart (1.9- to 2.8-liter) pan. Cook, stirring, over medium heat until mixture is golden brown. Remove from heat and whisk in the broth mixture. Return to heat and stir until mixture boils and thickens. If gravy is thicker than you like, stir in more broth. Add chopped giblets and season gravy to taste with salt and pepper. Pour gravy into a bowl or gravy boat.

Carving the bird. Spoon out stuffing, transfer to a bowl, and keep warm. For a neat, professional carving job, make sure that your knife is good and sharp. Remove thighs and legs from turkey by pulling leg down and severing thigh from body at hip joint (insert knife directly into joint and cut through it). Locate joint between drumstick and thigh; pull down on leg and sever joint to separate drumstick. Thinly slice thigh and leg meat. Make a horizontal cut under ribs from neck to base of thigh, cutting through to bone. Then slice downward toward this cut to remove breast meat in thin slices. Cut off wings at shoulder joint, then cut wing sections apart.

HOW TO STUFF A TURKEY

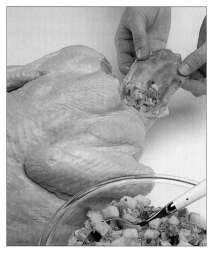

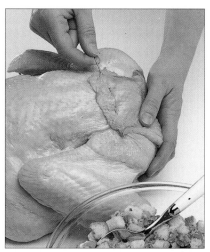

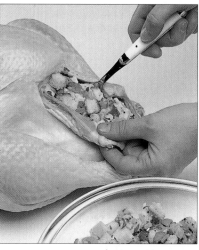

1 Place turkey on work surface, breast side down; lightly fill neck cavity with stuffing.

2 Bring neck skin up to cover opening. With a metal skewer, fasten neck skin to back, threading skewer in and out several times through neck and back skin.

3 Turn turkey over and loosely pack body cavity with stuffing. (Place any leftover stuffing in a baking dish; bake, covered, with turkey for last hour of roasting time.)

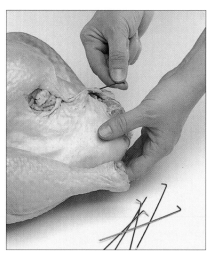

4 Skewer body cavity closed as you did the neck. If turkey has tail attached, push it into cavity before skewering. Leave legs free to help them cook at the joint.

5 Bend wing tips down and push under body; wing tips support neck and help keep turkey level on rack.

6 When turkey is done, remove from oven and let stand for at least 15 minutes; this allows juices to settle before carving. Transfer turkey to platter, remove skewers, and add a festive garnish, such as fresh herbs and lady apples.

Fish & Shellfish

Fish and shellfish suit today's taste for light, healthful meals that do not compromise on flavor. There is a variety of seafood to match every style of cooking, from elegant (poached sole or sautéed scampi) to casually festive (cracked crab or pan-fried trout). Fish and shellfish are generally lower in fat than red meat, and the fatty acid in fish oils is considered helpful in lowering the risk of heart disease.

Fresh fish—whether caught in wild waters or farm-raised—is widely available; but it's important to buy it from a reliable source with a rapid turnover. It's easy to judge freshness: All seafood should have a clean, pleasant odor and never smell "fishy"; whole fish should look plump and shiny, with clear and full (not sunken) eyes. Fillets and steaks should have a moist, freshly cut appearance and firm flesh with a close-grained texture. Keep fresh fish well wrapped and refrigerated; and be sure to cook it within one to two days of purchase.

Shellfish, too, are highly perishable. Buy shrimp, crabs, clams, mussels, oysters, and scallops no more than one day in advance; refrigerate them in covered containers until needed. In this chapter, you'll find shopping and preparation tips for each type of shellfish.

Frozen fish and shellfish may be fresher than chilled fish that has been in storage for days. Select a package that is solidly frozen but not icy on the outside. Thaw the fish in the refrigerator, cook it when thawed, and don't refreeze. Pat thawed fish or shellfish dry with paper towels before coating it with flour, crumbs, or batter.

How long to cook fish

Fish overcooks quickly, leaving it dry and flavorless. As a rough guide, allow 8 to 10 minutes of cooking time per 1 inch (2.5 cm) of thickness. Lay the fish flat on a counter, measure its thickest portion (by eye or with a ruler), and calculate the approximate cooking time.

To test for doneness, near the end of the estimated cooking time, cut a small slit in the center of the thickest portion of the fish and check its texture: The flesh inside should be slightly opaque and should have lost its wet look. Take the fish off the heat; it will finish cooking by the time it is placed on the table.

FISH

BAKING

For cooks short on time and energy, baked fish provides an excellent mealtime solution. If you keep a sharp eye on the clock and follow the tests for doneness, there's little chance of overcooking the fish. While the fish bakes, you'll have the opportunity to make a simple salad or side dish.

Vary the basic recipes that follow by using the different types of fish suggested, and be sure to select the freshest fish the market has to offer.

Baked Fish Provençal

- 3 teaspoons (15 ml) olive oil
- 4 ounces (115 g) mushrooms, thinly sliced
- 2 cloves garlic, minced or pressed
- 2 medium-size tomatoes (about 12 oz./340 g total), peeled and chopped
- ⅓ cup (15 g) chopped fresh basil
- ¼ cup (35 g) brine-cured olives, pitted and slivered
- 1 tablespoon drained capers
- ½ teaspoon salt
- 4 fish steaks, such as halibut, cod, salmon, or swordfish (about 6 oz./170 g each), 1 inch (2.5 cm) thick
  Basil leaves (optional)

Heat 2 teaspoons of the oil in a wide nonstick frying pan over medium heat. Add mushrooms and garlic; cook, stirring frequently until mushrooms are soft (about 4 minutes). Add tomatoes, basil, olives, capers, and ¼ teaspoon of the salt; cook until heated through (about 2 minutes).

Oil an 8- by 12-inch (20- by 30-cm) baking pan with the remaining 1 teaspoon oil. Arrange fish in a single layer in the pan; sprinkle the remaining ¼ teaspoon salt over fish, then spoon hot mushroom mixture over fish.

Bake fish, uncovered, in a 400°F (205°C) oven until just opaque but still moist in thickest part; cut to test (12 to 15 minutes). Transfer to a platter. Garnish with basil leaves, if desired. *Makes 4 servings*

PER SERVING: *220 calories, 28 g total fat, 1 g saturated fat, 44 mg cholesterol, 655 mg sodium, 6 g carbohydrates, 2 g fiber, 30 g protein, 91 mg calcium, 2 mg iron*

Baked Fish Florentine

- 4 teaspoons (20 ml) olive oil
- 4 mild-flavored white fish fillets, such as red snapper or sea bass (about 6 oz./170 g each), ¼ inch (6 mm) thick
- ¾ teaspoon salt
- ¼ teaspoon pepper
- ¼ cup (60 ml) mayonnaise
- 2 tablespoons (30 ml) reduced-fat sour cream
- 2 tablespoons grated Parmesan cheese
- 2 teaspoons all-purpose flour
- 2 bunches spinach (about 1½ lbs./680 g total), stemmed, well rinsed, and patted very dry
- ¼ teaspoon paprika

Coat the bottom of a 9- by 13-inch (23- by 33-cm) baking pan with 1 teaspoon of the oil. Arrange fish in a single layer in dish and sprinkle with ¼ teaspoon of the salt and the pepper.

In a small bowl, whisk together mayonnaise, sour cream, Parmesan cheese, and flour until smooth; spread over fish.

Bake fish, uncovered, in a 400°F (205°C) oven until just opaque but still moist in thickest part; cut to test (about 10 minutes).

Meanwhile, heat remaining oil in a wide nonstick frying pan over medium-high heat until hot but not smoking. Add spinach, cover, and cook, stirring occasionally, until wilted (about 2 minutes). Add remaining ½ teaspoon salt and stir to combine.

Arrange spinach in a single layer on a platter; place cooked fish on top. Spoon any extra sauce from baking dish over fish and sprinkle with paprika. *Makes 4 servings*

PER SERVING: *365 calories, 20 g total fat, 4 g saturated fat, 76 mg cholesterol, 746 mg sodium, 6 g carbohydrates, 3 g fiber, 40 g protein, 216 mg calcium, 4 mg iron*

PREPARING PARCHMENT-BAKED FISH FILLETS

1 Stir spice mixture into softened butter. The butter-spice mixture will create a rich, aromatic sauce when baked.

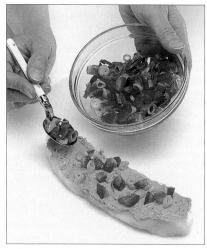

2 Cut cooking parchment, then place a piece of fish in the center of each. After spreading butter-spice mixture on fish, sprinkle tomato and green onion mixture on top.

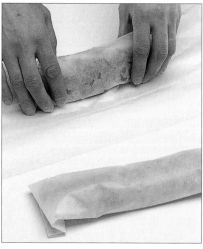

3 To enclose fish in parchment, first fold edge of parchment closest to you over fish, then fold forward with fish inside.

4 With cut edge of parchment down, make two folds at each open end, pressing to crease lightly and tucking ends under to hold in place.

5 To serve, cut packets down center of top with a sharp knife or scissors. The fish will be moist and bathed in a colorful sauce. Rice pilaf makes a fine accompaniment.

FISH *continued*

Parchment-Baked Fish Fillets

PICTURED ON FACING PAGE

2 tablespoons butter or margarine, softened

2 teaspoons minced fresh ginger or ½ teaspoon ground ginger

1 teaspoon ground coriander

1 teaspoon ground cumin

1 teaspoon ground turmeric

¼ teaspoon fennel seeds, crushed

⅛ teaspoon ground red pepper (cayenne)

4 lingcod, sea bass, or other white fish fillets (about 6 oz./ 170 g each), ¾ inch (2 cm) thick

2 medium-size tomatoes (about 12 oz./340 g total), seeded and finely chopped

2 green onions (including tops), thinly sliced

1 teaspoon salt

Place butter in a small bowl. In another small bowl, combine ginger, coriander, cumin, turmeric, fennel seeds, and ground red pepper. Stir spice mixture into butter; set aside.

Cut 4 sheets of cooking parchment, each about 4 times the width of the fish and 6 inches (15 cm) longer than the fish. About 1 inch (2.5 cm) in from edge of long sides, center a piece of fish on each piece of parchment.

In another small bowl, combine tomatoes and green onions. Spread each piece of fish with one fourth of the butter mixture, then top with one fourth of the tomato mixture. Sprinkle with salt.

For each packet, fold edge of parchment closest to you over fish, then fold forward with fish to enclose. With cut edge of parchment down, make 2 folds in parchment at each open end, pressing to crease lightly and tucking ends under to hold in place.

Place packets, smooth side up, on a large baking sheet. Bake in a 500°F (260°C) oven until fish is just opaque but still moist in thickest part; cut a tiny slit through parchment into fish to test (10 to 15 minutes).

Cut packets down center of top with scissors, then tear back parchment to expose fish.   *Makes 4 servings*

PER SERVING: *226 calories, 9 g total fat, 4 g saturated fat, 104 mg cholesterol, 719 mg sodium, 5 g carbohydrates, 1 g fiber, 31 g protein, 47 mg calcium, 2 mg iron*

Snappy Snapper

4 rockfish fillets (about 1 lb./455 g total)

1 lime

1 teaspoon olive oil

1 small red or green bell pepper (about 6 oz./170 g), sliced

1 small onion, sliced

1 clove garlic, minced or pressed

1 can (14½ oz./415 g) Italian-style stewed tomatoes

1 tablespoon drained capers

Chopped parsley

Rinse fish; arrange in a single layer in a shallow 2- to 2½-quart (1.9- to 2.4-liter) casserole. Squeeze lime juice over fish.

Bake, uncovered, in a 350°F (175°C) oven until just opaque but still moist in its thickest part; cut to test (15 to 20 minutes).

Meanwhile, heat oil over high heat in a wide nonstick frying pan until hot but not smoking. Add pepper, onion, and garlic; stir until onion is lightly browned (about 5 minutes). Add tomatoes and their liquid, and capers. Bring to a boil. Reduce heat to medium and simmer, uncovered, until liquid evaporates (about 10 minutes).

Spoon juice from baked fish into tomato mixture. Boil, uncovered, to reduce slightly (about 1½ minutes). Spoon sauce over fish. Sprinkle with chopped parsley.   *Makes 4 servings*

PER SERVING: *169 calories, 3 g total fat, 0.6 g saturated fat, 40 mg cholesterol, 426 mg sodium, 13 g carbohydrates, 3 g fiber, 23 g protein, 55 mg calcium, 1 mg iron*

What Is Rockfish?

Marketed as "Pacific snapper" on the West Coast, rockfish is actually a member of the ocean perch family and bears little resemblance to the true red snapper found only in Atlantic waters. Some types of rockfish are the widow, canary, China, and yelloweye. Rockfish is also sold as Pacific Ocean perch. If you live on the East Coast, use Atlantic Ocean perch (also called redfish and rosefish) or black sea bass in recipes calling for rockfish.

FISH *continued*

PAN-FRYING

Fish fillets, fish steaks, or small whole fish turn into glorious golden morsels when pan-fried, and a crisp crust encloses the tender, mild flesh. A nonstick frying pan allows you to cook the fish with little fat.

Because they cook so quickly, thin fillets brown better if they're first dusted with flour or coated with crumbs. Firmer, thicker pieces don't need coating to brown well, but you may enjoy the flavor boost.

Fish Fillets with Almond Butter

    1 large egg
    1 tablespoon (15 ml) water
    ¾ cup (about 2¼ oz./60 g) grated Parmesan cheese
    ⅓ cup (20 g) chopped parsley
    ½ teaspoon salt
    ¾ teaspoon pepper
       About ½ cup (60 g) all-purpose flour
    2 tablespoons (30 ml) olive oil
    4 flounder fillets (about 1½ lbs./680 g total)
    ¼ cup (55 g) butter
    ¼ cup (31 g) sliced almonds
    3 tablespoons (45 ml) lemon juice

In a pie pan, beat egg and water until well blended. In another pie pan, combine Parmesan cheese, parsley, salt, and pepper. Have flour ready in a third pie pan. Heat 1 tablespoon (15 ml) of the oil in a wide nonstick frying pan over medium heat until hot but not smoking.

While oil is heating, dredge a piece of fish in flour on all sides; shake off excess. Dip into egg mixture, then into cheese mixture. Place two fish fillets in hot pan. Cook until fish is golden brown and just opaque but still moist in thickest part; cut to test (about 2 minutes per side, depending on thickness). Transfer fish to a platter and keep warm. Repeat with remaining oil and fish.

Melt butter in a 1-quart (950-ml) pan over medium heat. When butter foams, stir in almonds; cook, stirring, just until almonds begin to brown. Turn off heat and stir in lemon juice. Spoon sauce over fish and serve immediately.   *Makes 4 servings*

PER SERVING: *500 calories, 29 g total fat, 12 g saturated fat, 178 mg cholesterol, 916 mg sodium, 15 g carbohydrates, 1 g fiber, 43 g protein, 279 mg calcium, 2 mg iron*

Hemingway's Trout

    4 whole cleaned trout (about 1 lb./455 g each)
    1 cup (240 ml) 2% milk
    6 green onions (including tops), chopped
    ¼ cup (60 ml) lemon juice
    2 tablespoons chopped parsley
    ½ teaspoon pepper
    1 teaspoon salt
    4 slices bacon (about 2¼ oz./63 g)
    ⅓ cup (40 g) all-purpose flour
    2 tablespoons yellow cornmeal
       Lemon wedges (optional)

Arrange fish in a single layer in a 9- by 13-inch (23- by 33-cm) baking pan; pour milk over fish and let stand for 10 minutes. In a small bowl, combine green onions, lemon juice, parsley, and pepper. Remove fish from milk; sprinkle cavities of fish with ½ teaspoon of the salt, then spread with onion mixture.

In a wide nonstick frying pan over medium heat, cook bacon until crisp. Remove bacon from pan, drain, and set aside. Leave 3 tablespoons (45 ml) drippings in pan; reserve remaining drippings.

Combine flour, cornmeal, and the remaining ½ teaspoon salt on a piece of wax paper; coat trout in mixture on all sides.

Heat the 3 tablespoons (45 ml) bacon drippings in pan over medium heat; arrange half the fish in pan. Cook, turning once, until just opaque but still moist in thickest part; cut to test (about 10 minutes total). Transfer fish to a platter; keep warm. Cook remaining fish, adding reserved drippings as needed. Slip a crisp bacon slice into cavity of each fish. Garnish with lemon wedges, if desired.   *Makes 4 servings*

PER SERVING: *424 calories, 23 g total fat, 6 g saturated fat, 106 mg cholesterol, 784 mg sodium, 106 g carbohydrates, 1 g fiber, 37 g protein, 114 mg calcium, 4 mg iron*

Fish Steaks with Rosemary Sauce

      4 halibut, salmon, or swordfish steaks (about 1½ lbs./680 g
         total)
      ½ teaspoon salt
      ¼ teaspoon pepper
      3 tablespoons all-purpose flour
      3 tablespoons (45 ml) olive oil
      3 green onions, thinly sliced
      2 cloves garlic, minced
      ⅓ cup (80 ml) white wine
      ¼ cup (60 ml) reduced-sodium chicken broth
    1½ teaspoons fresh rosemary or ¼ teaspoon dried rosemary
      3 tablespoons butter or margarine

Lightly sprinkle fish with salt and pepper. Dust with flour, shaking off excess.

Heat oil in a wide nonstick frying pan over medium-high heat until hot but not smoking. Add fish, without crowding, and cook, turning once, until just opaque but still moist in thickest part; cut to test (about 10 minutes). With a slotted spatula, transfer fish to a platter; keep warm.

Reduce heat to medium. Add green onions and garlic to pan and cook, stirring occasionally, until softened (about 1 minute). Add wine, broth, and rosemary to pan. Boil rapidly, scraping browned particles free from pan, until mixture is reduced by half. Swirl in butter. Spoon sauce over fish and serve immediately.   *Makes 4 servings*

PER SERVING: *348 calories, 22 g total fat, 7 g saturated fat, 68 mg cholesterol, 466 mg sodium, 6 g carbohydrates, 0.5 g fiber, 30 g protein, 85 mg calcium, 2 mg iron*

POACHING & STEEPING

Poaching is an excellent way to prepare seafood. The fish simmers in a seasoned broth that adds its own delicate flavor. Any variety of fish can be poached, and all forms of fish—fillets, steaks, whole fish, or even packages of frozen fish fillets—lend themselves to poaching.

Steeping, or cooking food with the residual heat of hot liquid, makes the tricky art of poaching lean, delicate-textured seafood more controllable. For information on the basic steeping technique for fish, see page 37.

Pan Poaching to Suit Any Fish

In the classic method of poaching, fish is immersed in a seasoned liquid. After the fish cooks, the liquid may be reduced, then combined with butter and flour to make a sauce. In this short-cut method, you poach with less liquid, then boil the pan juices alone for a few minutes to thicken and concentrate them.

Our directions include two poaching broths. The *Onion-Wine Broth* suits fish with a mild to moderate flavor, such as lingcod, halibut, or snapper. The *Tomato-Herb Broth* is best with moderate to more richly flavored fish, such as rockfish, salmon, or tuna.

Have ready four 8-ounce (230-g) *fish* fillets, steaks, or small whole cleaned fish. Prepare *poaching broth* in a wide nonstick frying pan and bring to a slow boil. Arrange fish in a single layer in pan. Cover and reduce heat so broth simmers.

Cook thin fillets ¼ to ⅓ inch (6 to 8 mm) thick without turning until done; cut to test (3 to 4 minutes). Simmer pieces ½ to 1 inch (1 to 2.5 cm) thick, or whole fish up to 1½ inches (3.5 cm) thick, until just opaque but still moist in thickest part; cut to test (4 to 10 minutes).

With a wide spatula, remove fish to a warm platter; cover and keep warm. Boil juices in pan over high heat until reduced to a medium-thick sauce. Season to taste with *salt, pepper,* and *lemon juice;* pour over fish.   *Makes 4 servings*

Onion-Wine Broth

Heat 4 teaspoons *butter* or margarine in a wide nonstick frying pan over medium heat. Add 4 *green onions,* thinly sliced, and 2 cloves *garlic,* minced. Cook, stirring, until soft (about 3 minutes). Stir in 1 cup (240 ml) each dry *white wine* and reduced-sodium *chicken broth* (or 2 cups/480 ml chicken broth only), 1 teaspoon *lemon juice,* ½ teaspoon *salt,* and ¼ teaspoon *pepper.*

Tomato-Herb Broth

Heat 2 teaspoons *olive oil* in a wide nonstick frying pan over medium heat. Add 1 medium-size *onion,* chopped, and 1 clove *garlic,* minced. Cook, stirring, until soft (about 3 minutes). Stir in 1 large *tomato,* diced; ½ cup (120 ml) reduced-sodium *chicken broth;* ½ teaspoon each dried *basil, oregano,* and *salt;* and a pinch of *pepper.* Bring to a boil; cover, reduce heat, and simmer for 5 minutes before adding fish.

FISH *continued*

Rolled Sole Fillets with Dill Sauce

2 teaspoons butter or margarine

1 medium carrot, cut into julienne strips

1 large stalk celery, cut into julienne strips

White part of 1 medium-size leek (about 2 oz./55 g) or 2 small green onions, cut into julienne strips

¼ cup (10 g) chopped fresh dill

4 sole fillets (about 1½ lbs./680 g total), ½ inch (1 cm) thick

¾ teaspoon salt

¼ teaspoon pepper

About ½ cup (120 ml) water

About ½ cup (120 ml) dry white wine

¼ cup (60 ml) half-and-half (light cream)

1½ teaspoons cornstarch mixed with 1 tablespoon (15 ml) water

Melt butter in a wide nonstick frying pan over medium heat. Add carrot, celery, and leek; cook, stirring frequently, for 2 minutes. Cover pan, reduce heat to low, and continue cooking, stirring occasionally, until vegetables are tender (about 5 minutes). Remove pan from heat and stir in 2 tablespoons of the dill. Let cool slightly. Measure 1 tablespoon of the cooked vegetables; mince and set aside.

Place a fish fillet, skinned side down, on work surface. Sprinkle with salt, pepper, and a little of the remaining dill. Place a small bundle of butter-steamed vegetable strips across one end of fillet; roll fillet into a cylinder. Repeat until all fillets are filled and rolled. Without crowding, arrange fish rolls, seam side down, in a wide nonstick frying pan at least 2 inches (5 cm) deep. (At this point, you may cover and refrigerate for up to 4 hours.)

Pour enough water and wine over fish so poaching liquid is ½ inch (1 cm) deep. Heat, uncovered, over high heat, just until small bubbles form. Immediately reduce heat, cover pan, and simmer fish until just opaque but still moist in thickest part; cut to test (about 8 minutes). With a slotted spatula, transfer rolls to a platter; cover loosely and keep warm.

Measure ½ cup (120 ml) of poaching liquid (discard remainder) and return to frying pan. Bring to a boil over medium-high heat and cook until reduced to about ⅓ cup (80 ml). Stir in half-and-half and cornstarch mixture; cook, stirring, until slightly thickened (about 1 minute). Stir in remaining dill and reserved minced vegetables. Spoon sauce over fish. *Makes 4 servings*

PER SERVING: *226 calories, 6 g total fat, 3 g saturated fat, 92 mg cholesterol, 598 mg sodium, 7 g carbohydrates, 1 g fiber, 33 g protein, 84 mg calcium, 2 mg iron*

Steeped Trout with Ginger

2 cleaned whole trout (about 1 lb./455 g each) Lemon slices

1 tablespoon (15 ml) reduced-sodium soy sauce

¼ cup (25 g) green onion slivers (about 1 in./2.5 cm)

1 pound (455 g) spinach, roots and tough stems trimmed

3 tablespoons (45 ml) vegetable oil

1 large clove garlic, minced

½ tablespoon fresh ginger slivers

Steep fish according to directions on page 37, adding a few lemon slices to steeping liquid; reserve steeping liquid. Place hot fish on serving platter. Drizzle with soy sauce and sprinkle with onion slivers. Plunge spinach into hot liquid in which the fish was steeped and stir until wilted (1 to 2 minutes). Drain, then arrange spinach around fish.

Heat oil in a small nonstick frying pan over medium-high heat just until oil is hot. Add garlic and ginger. Cook, stirring, just until garlic is light golden (about 1 minute); pour over fish. *Makes 2 servings*

PER SERVING: *465 calories, 32 g total fat, 5 g saturated fat, 92 mg cholesterol, 514 mg sodium, 8 g carbohydrates, 5 g fiber, 39 g protein, 245 mg calcium, 7 mg iron*

GRILLING & BROILING

The natural juices of fish are sealed in by grilling and broiling. To prevent fish from sticking to the grill or broiler-pan rack, make sure the rack is clean before you start cooking. To cook and turn the delicate fish pieces on a grill without destroying them, use a grill topper, a smooth sheet-steel screen perforated with holes (you can make your own by placing a double thickness of heavy-duty foil over a regular grill, then poking holes through it). Spray the topper or foil with nonstick cooking spray or coat with vegetable oil before arranging the fish on top. Or place the fish in an oiled, hinged wire basket—instead of turning the fish with a spatula, just turn the basket. For broiling, line the rack with foil and oil it before placing the fish on top.

Grilled Tuna Steaks

4 tuna (ahi) steaks (about 7 oz./200 g each), 1 inch (2.5 cm) thick

3 tablespoons (45 ml) lime juice

2 tablespoons (30 ml) reduced-sodium soy sauce

1 tablespoon minced garlic

1 tablespoon minced fresh ginger

Lime wedges

Oriental sesame oil (optional)

Rinse tuna and pat dry. Place in a 9- by 13-inch (23- by 33-cm) baking pan.

In a small bowl, combine lime juice, soy sauce, garlic, and ginger; pour over fish. Cover airtight and chill for at least 1 hour or up until next day; turn fish occasionally.

Place fish on a lightly oiled grill rack 4 to 6 inches (10 to 15 cm) above a bed of hot coals (you can hold your hand at grill level only 1 to 2 seconds). Cook, turning once, until fish is browned on outside but still pink in center; cut to test (6 to 7 minutes). Accompany with lime and sesame oil to add to taste. *Makes 4 servings*

PER SERVING: *260 calories, 9 g total fat, 2 g saturated fat, 67 mg cholesterol, 220 mg sodium, 1 g carbohydrates, 0 g fiber, 42 g protein, 4 mg calcium, 2 mg iron*

Barbecued Salmon

1 or 2 salmon fillets (3 to 4 lbs./1.35 to 1.8 kg total)

½ cup (120 ml) rosé or dry white wine

¼ cup (55 g) butter or margarine, melted, or ¼ cup (60 ml) vegetable oil

¼ cup (60 ml) lemon juice

¼ cup (60 ml) reduced-sodium soy sauce

Parsley sprigs

Lemon wedges

Rinse salmon and pat dry. Cut heavy-duty foil to the same size as salmon; place fish on foil, skin side down.

In a small bowl, combine wine, butter, lemon juice, and soy sauce. In a grill with a lid, place fish, foil side down, on a grill 4 to 6 inches (10 to 15 cm) above a solid bed of low coals (you can hold your hand at grill level only 6 to 7 seconds). Brush fish generously with butter mixture. Cover grill and open vents. Cook, basting with butter mixture about every 5 minutes, until fish is just opaque but still moist in thickest part; cut to test (15 to 20 minutes).

To serve, slide fish, still on foil, onto a board. Slice fish down to skin and lift each serving away from skin. Reheat butter mixture and offer to spoon over fish. Garnish with parsley sprigs and lemon wedges, if desired. *Makes 8 to 10 servings*

PER SERVING: *286 calories, 15 g total fat, 5 g saturated fat, 101 mg cholesterol, 391 mg sodium, 1 g carbohydrates, 0 g fiber, 32 g protein, 24 mg calcium, 2 mg iron*

Orange Barbecued Salmon

Follow recipe for *Barbecued Salmon*, but substitute *orange juice* for the wine in the basting sauce and increase the *lemon juice* to 5 tablespoons (75 ml).

Halibut with Avocado Salsa

½ cup (20 g) chopped fresh basil

1 tablespoon (15 ml) olive oil

½ teaspoon grated lime peel

⅓ cup (80 ml) lime juice

6 halibut steaks (about 6 oz./170 g each)

1 large avocado (about 12 oz./340 g), pitted, peeled, and diced

1 large tomato (about 8 oz./230 g), cored and chopped

2 tablespoons chopped green onion

Salt

Ground red pepper (cayenne)

In a small bowl, mix basil, oil, lime peel, and lime juice.

Rinse fish and pat dry. Place fish in a 9- by 13-inch (23- by 33-cm) baking pan. Pour ¼ cup (60 ml) of the lime mixture over fish and turn to coat. Chill for 30 minutes to 1 hour.

In a medium-size bowl, combine avocado, tomato, and green onion. Add remaining lime mixture, and salt and ground red pepper to taste; stir to combine.

Place fish on a broiler-pan rack. Broil about 4 inches (10 cm) from heat, turning once, until just barely opaque but still moist in thickest part; cut to test (8 to 12 minutes). Transfer fish to a platter and spoon avocado salsa over fish. *Makes 6 servings*

PER SERVING: *252 calories, 12 g total fat, 2 g saturated fat, 44 mg cholesterol, 85 mg sodium, 6 g carbohydrates, 2 g fiber, 30 g protein, 86 mg calcium, 2 mg iron*

HOW TO MAKE SCAMPI

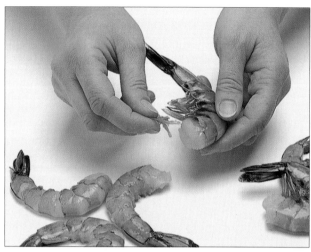

1 To clean shrimp, start by pulling off legs. Then slip your thumbs under shell, split it apart, and remove it. For a more attractive presentation, leave tail intact.

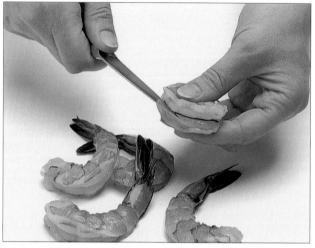

2 To devein, make a shallow cut down back of shrimp. Pick out the black vein with the tip of a knife, then rinse shrimp under cold water to wash away any remaining bits of vein.

3 After adding shrimp to pan, stir frequently and shake pan occasionally. Shrimp will begin to curl as they cook; when they've just turned pink outside and opaque inside, they're done. If overcooked, they will be dry and tough.

4 A big platter of sautéed shrimp, served with plenty of lemon, makes a most tempting main dish. Pasta (perhaps fettuccine mixed with basil and capers) would make an ideal accompaniment.

SHELLFISH

SHRIMP

Shrimp come in many sizes. The tiny ones (150 to 180 per lb./455 g) are always sold cooked and shelled, and are an excellent choice for salads and seafood cocktails. Larger sizes are sold raw (in the shell) or cooked (in the shell or shelled).

When you plan to use one of the larger sizes, raw shrimp in the shell are usually the best buy. See the photos on the facing page for how to clean shrimp.

Use any shrimp—fresh, or frozen and thawed—within a day after purchase; and, of course, store the shellfish in the refrigerator. For each serving, allow ⅓ to ¼ pound (150 to 115 g) raw shelled shrimp (about ⅓ to ½ lb./150 to 230 g unshelled). Select shrimp that are firm, moist, and fresh-smelling; there should be "bounce," or resilience, to the flesh.

Scampi

PICTURED ON FACING PAGE

About 1½ pounds (680 g) large shrimp, shelled and deveined, tails attached
3 tablespoons butter or margarine
¼ cup (25 g) minced green onions
3 cloves garlic, minced
2 tablespoons (30 ml) dry white wine or vermouth
¾ teaspoon grated lemon peel
1 tablespoon (15 ml) lemon juice
½ teaspoon salt
¼ cup (15 g) minced parsley

Pat shrimp dry with paper towels; set aside. Melt butter in a wide nonstick frying pan over medium heat. Stir in green onions and garlic; cook until soft, stirring frequently (about 7 minutes). Add wine, lemon peel, lemon juice, and salt; cook until bubbly.

Add shrimp to pan and increase heat to high. Cook, stirring frequently, until shrimp turn pink on outside and are opaque in center; cut to test (3 to 4 minutes). Stir in parsley. *Makes 4 servings*

PER SERVING: *236 calories, 11 g total fat, 6 g saturated fat, 234 mg cholesterol, 570 mg sodium, 3 g carbohydrates, 0.4 g fiber, 29 g protein, 91 mg calcium, 4 mg iron*

Coriander-Curry Shrimp

1 large onion, thinly sliced
1 clove garlic, minced
2 tablespoons (30 ml) water
1 teaspoon olive oil
1 tablespoon ground coriander
1 tablespoon curry powder
¼ teaspoon ground red pepper (cayenne)
⅔ cup (160 ml) pineapple-coconut juice (or ⅔ cup/160 ml pineapple juice and ¼ cup/20 g shredded, sweetened, dried coconut)
2 teaspoons cornstarch
1½ pounds (680 g) large shrimp, shelled and deveined
2 tablespoons minced parsley
6 cups (595 g) hot cooked pasta
Salt
Lime wedges

Place onion, garlic, water, and oil in a wide nonstick frying pan. Cook over high heat, stirring frequently, until water evaporates and onions are soft and start to brown slightly (about 5 minutes). Add coriander, curry powder, and ground red pepper; stir to blend.

In a small bowl, combine pineapple-coconut juice and cornstarch; stir until smooth. Add shrimp to pan and cook over high heat, stirring constantly, for about 2 minutes. Pour in pineapple-coconut juice mixture and stir until mixture boils and shrimp turn pink on outside and are opaque in center; cut to test (about 3 more minutes). Stir in parsley.

Mound hot pasta on a platter or plates and spoon the shrimp mixture on top. Season with salt and offer with lime wedges. *Makes 6 servings*

PER SERVING: *354 calories, 5 g total fat, 1 g saturated fat, 140 mg cholesterol, 149 mg sodium, 51 g carbohydrates, 3 g fiber, 26 g protein, 79 mg calcium, 5 mg iron*

PREPARING GREAT WESTERN CRAB CAKES

1 Spread crabmeat in a pan lined with paper towels and pat dry with more paper towels. Pick over crabmeat, removing any bits of shell or cartilage.

2 Spoon portions of crab cake mixture (roughly 2 tablespoons each) into frying pan. Using back of a spoon, gently spread mixture into flat cakes about 2½ inches (6 cm) in diameter.

3 When bottoms of cakes are lightly browned, turn with spatula and cook second side until browned. It's best to use a plastic or nylon spatula with nonstick pans.

4 Both the crab cakes and salad are served with the same lusciously lemony wine sauce. Bibb lettuce, mizuna (a Japanese salad green), and edible flowers make a suitably elegant salad.

SHELLFISH *continued*

CRAB

If buying live crabs, select the ones that are active, and once you get them home, loosely cover them and refrigerate for up to 12 hours. To cook, drop them into a large pan of boiling water that covers the crabs by 2 or 3 inches (5 to 8 cm). Put a lid on the pan and cook for 8 to 12 minutes. Drain and rinse.

Store-bought cooked, unshelled crabs should have a fresh, sweet smell. Rinse them before using.

Great Western Crab Cakes

PICTURED ON FACING PAGE

¾ cup (180 ml) reduced-sodium chicken broth
¾ cup (180 ml) dry white wine
¼ cup (60 ml) lemon juice
2 teaspoons cornstarch
1 teaspoon sugar
About 2 tablespoons butter or margarine
1 pound (455 g) shelled cooked crab
⅓ cup (80 ml) mayonnaise
2 large eggs
½ cup (50 g) thinly sliced green onions
¼ cup (38 g) minced red bell pepper
¼ cup (30 g) thinly sliced celery
2 tablespoons (30 ml) Dijon mustard
1 clove garlic, minced or pressed
⅛ teaspoon ground red pepper (cayenne)
8 cups (about 8 oz./230 g) mixed salad greens, rinsed and crisped

In a 2-quart (1.9-liter) pan, bring broth and wine to a boil over high heat; reduce mixture to ¾ cup/180 ml (about 6 minutes). In a small bowl, mix together lemon juice, cornstarch, and sugar; slowly stir into broth mixture. Continue to stir until sauce boils (about 10 seconds). Stir in 2 teaspoons of the butter; set sauce aside and keep warm.

Line a rimmed pan with paper towels. Place crabmeat in pan and pat dry with additional paper towels. Pick over crabmeat for any shells or cartilage.

To prepare crab cakes, in a large bowl, combine mayonnaise, eggs, green onions, bell pepper, celery, mustard, garlic, and ground red pepper; stir well. Fold crab into mayonnaise mixture. Do not overmix.

Melt 2 teaspoons of the butter in each of 2 large,

wide nonstick frying pans over medium-high heat (or use 1 pan and cook in 2 batches). Spoon 6 mounds of crab mixture (about 2 rounded tablespoons each) into each pan; gently spread with back of spoon into cakes 2½ inches (6 cm) in diameter. Cook until bottoms are lightly browned (about 4 minutes). With a wide spatula, carefully turn cakes over; cook to brown other sides (about 4 more minutes). Transfer 3 cakes to each of 4 plates.

In a large bowl, mix greens with ⅓ cup (80 ml) reserved lemon sauce; place some greens on each plate. Spoon remaining lemon sauce around cakes. *Makes 4 servings*

PER SERVING: *378 calories, 25 g total fat, 7 g saturated fat, 246 mg cholesterol, 790 mg sodium, 8 g carbohydrates, 1 g fiber, 28 g protein, 184 mg calcium, 3 mg iron*

Cracked Crab with Two Sauces

Cooked whole crab in shell (allow 1 lb./455 g of crab in shell per person; soft-shell crabs are not suitable)
Piquant Sauce (recipe follows)
Tartar Sauce (recipe follows)

Clean and crack cooked crab. Mound on a tray; cover and chill until serving time. Pass one or both sauces in separate bowls at the table. Provide nutcrackers and small forks for removing meat from shells. *Makes 4 servings*

Piquant Sauce. In a 1-quart (950-ml) pan, combine ½ cup (120 ml) tomato-based *chili sauce*, ¼ cup (60 ml) *lemon juice*, and 2 tablespoons each *butter* or margarine, *sugar*, and *Worcestershire*. Bring to a boil over medium heat, stirring. Serve hot. *Makes about 1 cup (240 ml)*

PER SERVING WITH CRAB: *237 calories, 8 g total fat, 4 g saturated fat, 129 mg cholesterol, 918 mg sodium, 17 g carbohydrates, 0 g fiber, 24 g protein, 128 mg calcium, 1 mg iron*

Light Tartar Sauce. In a small bowl, combine ¼ cup (60 ml) each reduced-calorie *mayonnaise*, reduced-fat *sour cream*, plain nonfat *yogurt*, and chopped *dill pickle*. Add 2 tablespoons chopped *green onion*, 1 tablespoon chopped *capers*, ½ teaspoon *Dijon mustard*, and ⅛ teaspoon each *salt* and *pepper*, and stir to combine. *Makes about ¾ cup (180 ml)*

PER SERVING WITH CRAB: *195 calories, 8 g total fat, 2 g saturated fat, 124 mg cholesterol, 799 mg sodium, 4 g carbohydrates, 0.1 g fiber, 25 g protein, 154 mg calcium, 1 mg iron*

SHELLFISH *continued*

CLAMS & MUSSELS

Although live hard-shell clams and mussels need a bit of attention, they're well worth the little effort it takes to clean and cook them. When using fresh clams or mussels, plan to serve them within 24 hours of purchase and keep them loosely covered in the refrigerator until you're ready to prepare them.

Just before cooking, scrub clam and mussel shells thoroughly under cold water with a stiff-bristled brush; also pull the wiry "beards" from the mussels. If shells gap, tap them. The ones that don't close are dead; discard them. If shells don't open after cooking, the clam or mussel needs to cook longer.

Steamed Clams or Mussels

- 2 *teaspoons olive oil or vegetable oil*
- 1 *medium-size onion, chopped*
- 3 *cloves garlic, minced or pressed*
- 1 *cup (240 ml) dry white wine or reduced-sodium chicken broth*
- ½ *cup (120 ml) water*
- 1 *large tomato (about 8 oz./230 g), diced*
- ¾ *teaspoon dried oregano*
- ½ *teaspoon dried basil*
- ¼ *teaspoon salt*
- ¼ *teaspoon pepper*
- 4 *dozen live hard-shell clams or mussels, well scrubbed (beards removed)*
- ¼ *cup (15 g) chopped parsley*

Heat oil in a 6-quart (6-liter) pan over medium heat. Add onion and garlic; cook, stirring, until onion is soft (3 to 4 minutes). Stir in wine, water, tomato, oregano, basil, salt, and pepper; bring to a boil. Cover, reduce heat, and simmer for 5 minutes.

Add clams or mussels; cover and simmer, shaking pan and stirring occasionally, until clams or mussels open (8 to 12 minutes). Stir in parsley. Ladle clams or mussels and broth into individual bowls.
Makes 4 servings

PER SERVING: *228 calories, 4 g total fat, 0.5 g saturated fat, 61 mg cholesterol, 247 mg sodium, 13 g carbohydrates, 2 g fiber, 24 g protein, 118 mg calcium, 26 mg iron*

Steamed Clams or Mussels Latin-Style

Prepare *Steamed Clams or Mussels*, but substitute ½ teaspoon ground *cumin* and ¼ teaspoon each *salt* and *liquid hot pepper seasoning* for the basil; reduce oregano to ½ teaspoon. Add 1 thinly sliced *chorizo sausage* (about 2½ oz./70 g) when adding wine and water.

OYSTERS

Before you buy shucked (shelled) oysters, be sure they're fresh. Check the lid for an expiration date and inspect the liquor (juices) surrounding the oysters—at least two thirds of it should look clear rather than milky. As a rule of thumb, allow about 4 ounces/115 g (¼ pint) shucked oysters per person.

When buying oysters in the shell, select ones that are tightly closed, feel heavy for their size, and smell fresh. Remove oysters from plastic bags to store; to stay alive, they need air. Cover them with damp paper towels and refrigerate.

Half-Shell Oysters with Vinegar-Soy Sauce

- ⅓ *cup (80 ml) balsamic vinegar*
- ⅓ *cup (80 ml) reduced-sodium soy sauce*
- 2 *tablespoons thinly sliced green onion*
- 2 *dozen chilled small to medium-size oysters, scrubbed and shucked*

To prepare sauce, in a small bowl, combine vinegar, soy sauce, and green onion.

Serve oysters on half shells cold or on ice with sauce to add to taste.
Makes ⅔ cup/160 ml sauce (8 servings)

PER SERVING WITH 1 TABLESPOON SAUCE: *36 calories, 1 g total fat, 0.3 g saturated fat, 23 mg cholesterol, 365 mg sodium, 3 g carbohydrates, 0 g fiber, 4 g protein, 22 mg calcium, 3 mg iron*

Half-Shell Oysters with Mignonette Sauce

Prepare *Half-Shell Oysters* as above. To prepare sauce, in a small bowl, combine ½ cup (120 ml) *white wine vinegar*, ¼ cup (60 ml) *water*, 1½ tablespoons minced *shallot*, and ¾ teaspoon *pepper*.
Makes about ¾ cup (180 ml) sauce

SCALLOPS

Most fish markets sell two varieties of scallops, distinguished mainly by size. The smaller type of scallop (½ in./1 cm diameter) is the bay scallop; the larger (1 to 1½ in./2.5 to 3.5 cm diameter) and more common variety is the sea scallop. Allow about ¼ to ⅓ pound (115 to 150 g) shucked scallops per person. Select sweet-smelling scallops packed in little or no liquid. The two varieties can be used interchangeably, but whole sea scallops need to cook a little longer than bay scallops. Thaw frozen scallops in the refrigerator. Rinse scallops well and pat dry with paper towels before cooking.

Lemon Scallops with Fusilli

8 ounces (230 g) fusilli, ruote, or other medium-size
    fancy-shaped dried pasta (see page 100)
¼ cup (60 ml) dry white wine
¼ teaspoon grated lemon peel
2 tablespoons (30 ml) lemon juice
2 green onions (including tops), thinly sliced
2 tablespoons drained capers
2 cloves garlic, minced or pressed
1 teaspoon dried rosemary
½ teaspoon dried basil
8 ounces (230 g) bay scallops, rinsed and patted dry
¼ cup (55 g) butter or margarine
    Chopped parsley

Bring 2 quarts (1.9 liters) water to a boil in a 4- to 5-quart (3.8- to 5-liter) pan over high heat. Stir in pasta and cook just until tender to bite (8 to 10 minutes); or cook according to package directions.

Meanwhile, in a wide nonstick frying pan, combine wine, lemon peel, lemon juice, green onions, capers, garlic, rosemary, and basil. Bring to a boil over high heat, stirring often, until liquid is reduced by half. Add scallops, stirring just until coated with lemon mixture and heated through (about 30 seconds). Remove from heat and add butter all at once, stirring constantly to incorporate.

Drain pasta and add to scallop mixture. Lift with 2 forks until coated. Sprinkle with parsley.
Makes 4 servings

PER SERVING: *373 calories, 13 g total fat, 8 g saturated fat, 50 mg cholesterol, 407 mg sodium, 47 g carbohydrates, 2 g fiber, 17 g protein, 45 mg calcium, 3 mg iron*

Broiled Sesame-Honey Scallops

2 tablespoons sesame seeds
1 pound (455 g) sea scallops, rinsed and patted dry
2 tablespoons (30 ml) lemon juice
2 tablespoons (30 ml) olive oil
1 tablespoon (15 ml) reduced-sodium soy sauce
2 teaspoons honey
1 clove garlic, minced
½ teaspoon ground ginger
¼ teaspoon salt
⅛ teaspoon crushed red pepper flakes (or to taste)

Toast sesame seeds in a small frying pan over medium heat, shaking pan often, until sesame seeds turn golden (5 to 6 minutes). Pour from pan and set aside.

Cut scallops into pieces, if needed, so all scallops are about the same size.

In a medium-size bowl, combine lemon juice, oil, soy sauce, honey, garlic, ginger, salt, and red pepper flakes. Add scallops and mix until well coated. Marinate for 15 minutes, stirring occasionally.

Lift scallops from marinade (reserve marinade) and thread on eight 8- to 10-inch (20- to 25-cm) skewers. Arrange skewers on broiler-pan rack and broil about 6 inches (15 cm) below heat, basting with reserved marinade, just until scallops are opaque but still moist in center; cut to test (about 5 minutes). Sprinkle broiled scallops with toasted sesame seeds.
Makes 4 servings

PER SERVING: *202 calories, 10 g total fat, 1 g saturated fat, 38 mg cholesterol, 470 mg sodium, 8 g carbohydrates, 0 g fiber, 20 g protein, 76 mg calcium, 1 mg iron*

Sizing Scallops

Sea scallops can vary in size. If some are much bigger than others, cut them into equal pieces so that they will cook more uniformly.

When substituting sea scallops for bay scallops, you have an alternative to cooking the dish a bit longer to allow for the difference in size: Cut the sea scallops crosswise into quarters. These pieces will be roughly the size of bay scallops.

MEATS

From a basic burger to a stately roast, meat holds center stage in many meals. It gets top billing in some of the world's greatest recipes and, like a prima donna, requires careful handling to bring out its best. But if you follow our guidelines for buying and cooking meat, each of the recipes in this chapter will yield tender, juicy results.

Buying meats

Although proper cooking will tenderize tougher cuts, the tenderness of a cut of meat is determined by its anatomical origin. The least-exercised parts of an animal (those in the middle of the back, called the loin) are the most tender; the parts adjacent to the loin (the round and flank) get more exercise and are less tender; and really hard-working muscles, such as the shoulder (or chuck) and neck, yield relatively tough meat. Price is related to tenderness.

Look at the primal cut and retail cut charts for each type of meat. They will familiarize you with where many of the cuts used in the recipes come from, and with marketing terms. How much meat to buy for a meal depends on appetites, but (uncooked) 4 to 6 ounces (115 to 170 g) per serving of boneless chops, steaks, and roasts; or 8 ounces (230 g) of bone-in chops, roasts, or steaks; or 1 pound (455 g) of spareribs, short ribs, or shanks is a good amount.

Cooking methods

Your goal, in cooking meat, is to preserve the natural tenderness or to tenderize naturally somewhat tough cuts. Tender cuts—pork tenderloin, for example—can be cooked by dry-heat methods such as roasting. Tougher cuts, such as beef chuck, require moist-heat methods, such as braising, to break down the connective tissue.

Today, livestock is bred and fed to be leaner than ever, and processors remove much of the fat from the outside of retail cuts (we encourage you to trim any remaining visible fat). But lean meats, even when they are tender cuts, cook and toughen more quickly than fattier meats. That's why it's essential to pay close attention to the cooking time.

The cooking times and temperatures in the chart on the following page should be used for simple roasting. Recipes in this chapter include additional steps and ingredients, and may vary from these basic guidelines.

Basic Meat Roasting Time & Temperature Chart

Cut	Oven temperature	Weight	Doneness		Roasting time
Beef (See Illustration, page 72)					
Standing rib	350°F (175°C)	4–6 lbs. (1.8–2.7 kg)	125°F/52°C*	(very rare)	1¼–1¾ hrs.
			135°F/57°C*	(medium-rare)	1¾–2¼ hrs.
			145°F/63°C*	(medium-well)	2–2½ hrs.
Standing rib	350°F (175°C)	8–10 lbs. (3.6–4.5 kg)	125°F/52°C*	(very rare)	2–2½ hrs.
			135°F/57°C*	(medium-rare)	2½–3 hrs.
			145°F/63°C*	(medium-well)	2¾–3¼ hrs.
Rib eye, tied	350°F (175°C)	4–6 lbs. (1.8–2.7 kg)	125°F/52°C*	(very rare)	1¼–1¾ hrs.
			135°F/57°C*	(medium-rare)	1¾–2 hrs.
			145°F/63°C*	(medium-well)	1¾–2¼ hrs.
Tenderloin	450°F (230°C)	4–5 lbs. (1.8–2.3 kg)	125°F/52°C*	(very rare)	20–35 mins.
			135°F/57°C*	(medium-rare)	35–45 mins.
			145°F/63°C*	(medium-well)	45–55 mins.
Boneless rump	325°F (165°C)	4–6 lbs. (1.8–2.7 kg)	130°F/55°C*	(very rare)	1¾–2¼ hrs.
			140°F/60°C*	(medium-rare)	2–2½ hrs.
Tri-tip	425°F (220°C)	1½–2 lbs. (680–905 g)	125°F/52°C*	(very rare)	20–35 mins.
			135°F/57°C*	(medium-rare)	30–45 mins.
			145°F/63°C*	(medium-well)	40–55 mins.
Veal					
Loin	325°F (165°C)	3–4 lbs. (1.35–1.8 kg)	155°F/68°C*	(medium-well)	1¾–2½ hrs.
Leg, boned & tied	325°F (165°C)	2–3 lbs. (905 g–1.35 kg)	155°F/68°C*	(medium-well)	1¼–1¾ hrs.
Shoulder, boned & tied	325°F (165°C)	2½–3 lbs. (1.15–1.35 kg)	155°F/68°C*	(medium–well)	1¼–1¾ hrs.
Fresh Pork (See Illustration, page 80)					
Loin, bone-in	350°F (175°C)	3–5 lbs. (1.35–2.3 kg)	155°F/68°C**		1–1½ hrs.
Loin, boned & tied	400°F (205°C)	2–4½ lbs. (905 g–2 kg)	150°F/66°C*		¾–1¼ hrs.
Crown, unstuffed	350°F (175°C)	6–10 lbs. (2.7–4.5 kg)	155°F/68°C**		1¼–1¾ hrs.
Shoulder (butt)	375°F (190°C)	3–7 lbs. (1.35–3.2 kg)	155°F/68°C*		1½–3¾ hrs.
Leg, boned & tied	350°F (175°C)	3½–4 lbs. (1.6–1.8 kg)	150°F/66°C*		1½–2 hrs.
Tenderloin***	450°F (230°C)	½–1 lb. (230–455 g)	150°F/66°C*		12–20 mins.
Smoked Pork fully cooked (See Illustration, page 80)					
Ham	325°F (165°C)	5–7 lbs. (2.3–3.2 kg)	140°F/60°C*		1–1¼ hrs.
Loin	325°F (165°C)	3–5 lbs. (1.35–2.3 kg)	140°F/60°C*		1–1¼ hrs.
Picnic shoulder	325°F (165°C)	5–8 lbs. (2.3–3.6 kg)	140°F/60°C*		1–1½ hrs.
Shoulder, boned & tied	325°F (165°C)	2–4 lbs. (905 g–1.8 kg)	140°F/60°C*		¾–1 hr.
Lamb (See Illustration, page 89)					
Leg, whole, bone-in	350°F (175°C)	5–7 lbs. (2.3–3.2 kg)	135°F/57°C**	(medium-rare)	1½–2 hrs.
			145°F/63°C**	(medium)	1¾–2¼ hrs.
			155°F/68°C**	(medium-well)	2–2½ hrs.
Leg, boned & tied	350°F (175°C)	3½–5 lbs. (1.6–2.3 kg)	135°F/57°C*	(medium-rare)	1¼–2 hrs.
			145°F/63°C*	(medium)	1½–2¼ hrs.
			155°F/68°C*	(medium-well)	1¾–2½ hrs.
Crown, unstuffed	450°F (230°C)	3–5 lbs. (1.35–2.3 kg)	135°F/57°C**	(medium-rare)	20–30 mins.
			145°F/63°C**	(medium)	25–35 mins.
			155°F/68°C**	(medium-well)	30–40 mins.
Shoulder, bone-in	350°F (175°C)	4–6 lbs. (1.8–2.7 kg)	135°F/57°C**	(medium-rare)	1½–1¾ hrs.
			145°F/63°C**	(medium)	1½–2 hrs.
			155°F/68°C**	(medium-well)	2–2½ hrs.
Shoulder, boned & tied	350°F (175°C)	3½–4 lbs. (1.6–1.8 kg)	135°F/57°C*	(medium-rare)	1–1¼ hrs.
			145°F/63°C*	(medium)	1–1½ hrs.
			155°F/68°C*	(medium-well)	1¼–1¾ hrs.
Rib rack***	475°F (245°C)	1½–2½ lbs. (680 g–1.15 kg)	135°F/57°C*	(medium-rare)	10–15 mins.
			145°F/63°C*	(medium)	15–20 mins.
			155°F/68°C*	(medium-well)	20–30 mins.

Insert meat thermometer into center of the thickest part of meat
**Insert meat thermometer through the thickest part of meat to the bone*

***Briefly pan-brown before roasting*

ROASTING & CARVING A STANDING RIB ROAST

1 Place roast, fat side up, on a rack in a shallow baking pan. Insert a meat thermometer in center of the thickest part of meat; roast, uncovered, until thermometer registers desired degree of doneness (see chart, page 67). Remove roast from oven and let stand in a warm place for 10 to 20 minutes. This allows juices to settle into meat so they are not lost in carving.

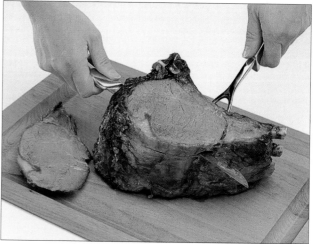

2 Transfer roast to a carving board; reserve cooking juices in pan for making sauce. Place roast on board, large end down, with ribs near your left hand. Insert large fork between ribs to brace roast as you carve. Cutting just up to the bone, cut meat toward the ribs and across the grain into slices ¼ to ½ inch (6 mm to 1 cm) thick.

3 Free the slice from rib by cutting down along edge of rib. Set slice aside on the board or transfer to a serving platter before continuing to carve the roast.

4 After slicing below first rib, cut bone off and set aside. Continue slicing meat and removing rib bones. Reserve bones, if you wish, for making broth or soup.

BEEF

DRY ROASTING

When it comes to beef roasts, the standing rib is king. The same cut, boned and tied, is sold as a rib-eye roast. Equally impressive, and even more tender, is the tenderloin—4 to 5 pounds (1.8 to 2.3 kg) of succulent meat, with no bones and trimmed of fat. All three of these roasts are naturally tender cuts that you cook with dry heat, using the same basic method of oven roasting (see the chart, page 67, for oven temperatures and approximate cooking times).

You can use dry heat to roast other less expensive (and less tender) cuts, too, such as sirloin tip and certain boneless cuts from the chuck (cross rib, eye roast). These are at their best when dry roasted rare to medium—still pink and juicy inside. They get very firm when cooked until well-done.

Standing Rib Roast

PICTURED ON FACING PAGE

- 1 standing rib beef roast (4 to 6 lbs./1.8 to 2.7 kg)
- ⅔ cup (160 ml) reduced-sodium beef broth, dry red wine, or water
- ¼ teaspoon salt
- ¼ teaspoon pepper

Place roast, fat side up, on a rack in a pan large enough to hold it comfortably. Insert a meat thermometer into thickest part of meat. Roast, uncovered, in a 350°F (175°C) oven until meat thermometer registers desired degree of doneness (see chart, page 67).

Remove roast from oven and transfer to a carving board or platter. Let roast stand in a warm place for 10 to 20 minutes before carving.

Meanwhile, skim and discard fat from pan drippings; pour broth into pan and place over medium-high heat. Cook, stirring and scraping browned particles free from pan, until sauce is reduced to ½ to ⅓ cup (120 to 80 ml). Stir in salt and pepper.

Slice meat and spoon a small amount of sauce over each slice. *Makes 8 to 10 servings*

PER SERVING: *579 calories, 47 g total fat, 19 g saturated fat, 136 mg cholesterol, 209 mg sodium, 0.1 g carbohydrates, 0 g fiber, 37 g protein, 18 mg calcium, 4 mg iron*

Beef Tenderloin with Cabernet-Cherry Sauce

- 4 cloves garlic, minced or pressed
- 1½ teaspoons grated orange peel
- 1½ teaspoons black peppercorns
- 1½ teaspoons dried thyme
- ½ teaspoon coriander seeds
- ½ teaspoon dried oregano
- ¼ teaspoon ground cinnamon
- ⅛ teaspoon ground allspice
- 1 center-cut beef tenderloin (about 5 lbs./2.3 kg), fat-trimmed and tied
- 3 cups (710 ml) reduced-sodium beef both
- 1½ cups (360 ml) cabernet sauvignon
- 1½ cups (215 g) dried tart cherries
- 2½ tablespoons red currant jelly
- 2 tablespoons cornstarch mixed with ¼ cup (60 ml) water
   Salt and pepper

In a small bowl, combine garlic, orange peel, peppercorns, thyme, coriander, oregano, cinnamon, and allspice. Rub mixture over beef. Place beef in a pan large enough to hold it comfortably. Insert a meat thermometer into thickest part of meat. Roast in a 450°F (230°C) oven until meat thermometer registers desired degree of doneness (see chart, page 67).

Meanwhile, in a 3- to 4-quart (2.8- to 3.8-liter) pan, combine 2 cups (470 ml) of the broth, the wine, cherries, and jelly; bring to a boil over high heat. Cover, reduce heat, and simmer until cherries soften (15 to 20 minutes).

When roast is done, transfer to a cutting board. Snip strings free; remove. Let roast stand in a warm place for about 15 minutes.

Meanwhile, add remaining 1 cup (240 ml) broth to pan; stir over medium heat to loosen browned particles from pan. Pour broth mixture into cherry mixture; bring to a boil. Add cornstarch mixture, and stir until sauce boils. Add salt and pepper to taste. Pour into a bowl.

Slice roast into thick or thin slices as desired; serve with sauce. *Makes 10 to 12 servings*

PER SERVING: *415 calories, 16 g total fat, 6 g saturated fat, 128 mg cholesterol, 287 mg sodium, 19 g carbohydrates, 0.1 g fiber, 44 g protein, 25 mg calcium, 6 mg iron*

PREPARING ASIAN SHORT RIBS

1 Toast sesame seeds in a small, dry frying pan over medium heat, stirring often so that seeds do not scorch. As soon as seeds are golden and fragrant, transfer them to a blender container (don't leave seeds in hot pan or they will scorch).

2 Scoring the meat allows it to cook faster and the marinade to penetrate more deeply. With ribs bone side down, use a sharp paring knife to make a series of parallel diagonal cuts, about ¾ inch (2 cm) apart, in the meat, cutting halfway to the bone. Then make a second set of cuts perpendicular to the first set in the same manner.

3 For easy cleanup, marinate ribs in a heavy-duty zip-seal food-storage bag. Turn over top edge of bag like a cuff so it will stand steady. Place ribs in bag, then pour in marinade. Seal bag and turn to coat ribs with marinade. Place bag in a shallow pan and refrigerate for at least 4 hours, or overnight, turning occasionally.

4 Though Asian in inspiration, the short ribs are right at home with all-American corn on the cob; cut the ears of corn into short lengths for easy eating. Round out the meal with salad greens and cherry tomatoes.

BEEF *continued*

BROILING & GRILLING

Broiled or grilled, tender beef cuts such as porterhouse steaks or a whole tenderloin need little but careful timing to cook them to perfection—rare or medium-rare doneness is recommended for optimal flavor and juiciness. To tenderize tougher cuts (short ribs and flank steak, for example), marinate before broiling and grilling.

Broil beef on a rack in a large, shallow pan and use tongs to turn the meat over when browned—don't use a fork, which will pierce the meat and allow the juices to run out. Test doneness by cutting into center of the thickest portion.

To grill beef, test the heat level (see page 94), position the rack over the heat source as recommended in the recipe, then add the meat. If desired, smoke the meat using hardwood chips (see page 42) to add a complementary flavor.

Red Wine Steak

⅓ cup (80 ml) dry red wine
1 tablespoon (15 ml) olive oil
2 cloves garlic, peeled and crushed
2 boneless shell steaks, about 1 pound (455 g) each, 1½ inches (3.5 cm) thick, or 2 pounds (905 g) top sirloin, 1½ inches (3.5 cm) thick
½ teaspoon salt
¼ teaspoon pepper

In a small bowl, combine wine, oil, and garlic. Place steaks, side by side, in a 9- by 12-inch (23- by 30-cm) baking pan. Pour wine mixture over steaks. Let stand at room temperature for about 1 hour, or refrigerate for up to 8 hours.

Reserving marinade, transfer steaks to a broiler-pan rack. Broil about 6 inches below heat, brushing with the marinade and turning once, until done to your liking; cut to test (about 7 minutes per side for rare).

Transfer steaks to a carving board and cut into slices. Sprinkle with salt and pepper. *Makes 4 servings*

PER SERVING: *430 calories, 26 g total fat, 10 g saturated fat, 138 mg cholesterol, 371 mg sodium, 0.7 g carbohydrates, 0.1 g fiber, 43 g protein, 22 mg calcium, 5 mg iron*

Asian Short Ribs

PICTURED ON FACING PAGE

2 tablespoons sesame seeds
⅓ cup (70 g) sugar
⅓ cup (80 ml) reduced-sodium chicken broth
⅓ cup (80 ml) reduced-sodium soy sauce
3 tablespoons (45 ml) bourbon or applejack
2 tablespoons (30 ml) Oriental sesame oil or vegetable oil
1 small onion, cut into 8 wedges
1 teaspoon chopped fresh ginger
1 clove garlic, quartered
1 green onion (including top), finely chopped
4 pounds (1.8 kg) lean, well-trimmed beef short ribs, cut into 3- to 4-inch (8- to 10-cm) lengths

Stir sesame seeds in a small, dry frying pan over medium heat until golden (about 3 minutes). Pour seeds into a blender and add sugar, broth, soy sauce, bourbon, oil, onion, ginger, and garlic. Whirl until smoothly puréed, then stir in green onion and set aside.

Place each rib bone side down and score meat with a sharp knife in a crisscross pattern. Make one set of parallel cuts ¾ inch (2 cm) apart, cutting through meat halfway to bone. Then make a second series of cuts perpendicular to the first set, in same manner. Place ribs in a large zip-seal plastic bag. Pour marinade over ribs; seal bag securely and turn to coat with marinade. Place bag in a shallow baking pan. Refrigerate for about 4 hours, or overnight, turning bag occasionally.

Lift ribs from marinade and drain briefly (reserve marinade). Place ribs on a lightly greased grill 4 to 6 inches (10 to 15 cm) above a solid bed of medium coals (you can hold your hand at grill level only 4 to 5 seconds). Cook, turning and basting often with marinade, until ribs are well browned on all sides and meat near bone is done to your liking; cut to test (about 30 minutes for medium-rare).
Makes 4 servings

PER SERVING: *496 calories, 29 g total fat, 11 g saturated fat, 114 mg cholesterol, 700 mg sodium, 17 g carbohydrates, 0.8 g fiber, 40 g protein, 57 mg calcium, 5 mg iron*

Beef Primal Cuts

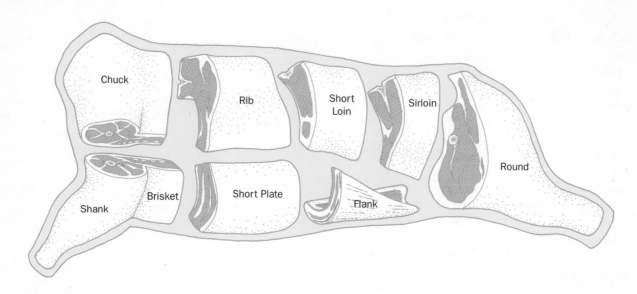

Retail Cuts and How to Cook Them

7-Bone Pot Roast
(From the Chuck)
Braise

Blade Roast
(From the Chuck)
Braise

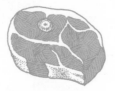

Arm Pot Roast
(From the Chuck)
Braise

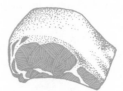

Rib Roast
(From the Rib)
Roast

**Boneless Rolled
Rump Roast**
(From the Round)
Braise • Roast

Bottom Round Roast
(From the Round)
Braise • Roast

Porterhouse Steak
(From the Short Loin)
Broil • Pan-broil
Pan-fry • Grill

T-Bone Steak
(From the Short Loin)
Broil • Pan-broil
Pan-fry

Top Loin Steak
(From the Short Loin)
Broil • Pan-broil
Stir-fry • Grill

Round Steak
(From the Round)
Braise • Pan-fry

Shank Cross Cuts
(From the Shank)
Braise

Short Ribs
(From the Chuck)
Braise • Grill

Corned Brisket
(From the Brisket)
Braise

Flank Steak
(From the Flank)
Pan-fry • Grill • Stir-fry

Tip Roast
(From the Round)
Braise • Roast

BEEF *continued*

PAN-FRYING

The pan-fried beef entrées on this page provide hearty dinners in a hurry. Both calf's liver and flank steak are ideal for pan-frying because they cook quickly, and are moist, tender, and flavorful if not cooked beyond medium-rare.

These recipes require only a single frying pan for both the meat and its accompaniment. For the liver, bacon drippings are used to fry onions, its classic companion. And the pan juices and tasty browned bits from frying the flank steak become part of the sauce for the meat.

A nonstick frying pan allows you to keep the fat to a minimum.

Pan-Fried Liver & Onions

    4 slices bacon (about 2¼ oz./63 g total)
    4 medium-size onions, cut into slices ¼ inch (6 mm) thick
    ½ teaspoon salt
    ¼ teaspoon pepper
 1½ pounds (680 g) calf's liver, in one piece
    ¼ cup (30 g) all-purpose flour

In a wide nonstick frying pan over medium heat, cook bacon until crisp (about 6 minutes). Remove bacon from pan, drain on paper towels.

Pour off and reserve all but 1 tablespoon (15 ml) bacon drippings. Add onions to pan and cook over medium-high heat, stirring often and adding more drippings as needed, until onions are golden (about 20 minutes). Sprinkle with salt and pepper. With a slotted spoon, remove onions from pan; keep warm.

Trim membrane from liver. Rinse liver, pat dry, and cut into 8 slices, ½ inch (1 cm) thick. Coat each slice in flour; shake off excess. Cook over medium-high heat, turning once and adding more drippings if needed, until liver is browned on both sides but still pink in center; cut to test (about 2 minutes per side). Spoon onions onto plates; top with liver and bacon.   *Makes 4 servings*

PER SERVING: *363 calories, 13 g total fat, 4 g saturated fat, 532 mg cholesterol, 472 mg sodium, 27 g carbohydrates, 3 g fiber, 34 g protein, 53 mg calcium, 9 mg iron*

Flank Steak with Mustard-Caper Sauce

    2 tablespoons (30 ml) olive oil
    1 flank steak (about 1½ lbs./680 g)
    ¼ cup (60 ml) reduced-sodium beef broth
    ¼ cup (60 ml) dry red wine
 1½ tablespoons drained capers
    1 tablespoon (15 ml) Dijon mustard
    1 teaspoon Worcestershire
    1 tablespoon butter or margarine

Heat oil in a wide nonstick frying pan over medium-high heat. Place meat in pan and cook, uncovered, turning once, until meat is browned on both sides and cooked to desired degree of doneness (about 3 to 4 minutes per side for rare).

Transfer meat to a cutting board; keep warm. Add broth and wine to pan, scraping browned particles free from pan. Add capers, mustard, and Worcestershire; stir briskly to blend. Remove from heat and swirl in butter until blended.

Cut meat across the grain into thin diagonal slices; transfer to a platter. Spoon mustard-caper sauce over meat.   *Makes 4 servings*

PER SERVING: *410 calories, 28 g total fat, 10 g saturated fat, 96 mg cholesterol, 436 mg sodium, 0.9 g carbohydrates, 0 g fiber, 34 g protein, 11 mg calcium, 3 mg iron*

Perfect Pan-Frying

In pan-frying, meat is cooked quickly in a small amount of fat over medium-high heat, so it should be of a cut and thickness that will cook in a short time. Steaks from the rib and loin pan-fry beautifully, but minute steaks, boneless blade steaks, tip steaks, and top round steaks will be tough if they are done beyond medium.

Start by heating the fat in the pan; when it's hot but not smoking, add the meat and cook it on one side until nicely browned. Turn the meat with tongs and brown it well. If necessary, fry the meat in batches to avoid crowding, removing the cooked pieces to a platter; keep warm.

BEEF *continued*

STIR-FRYING

Beef goes a long way in a stir-fry when coupled with lots of vegetables and served with rice, or with tortillas, as in the recipe below. Certainly, tender boneless rib or loin steaks, fat-trimmed and cut across the grain, are an ideal choice. But less-tender cuts (like flank and top round), fat-trimmed and sliced in the same way, can be used, too. Stir-fry these tougher cuts until medium-rare or rare to keep them moist.

Beef Fajitas

- 1   *flank steak (about 1 lb./455 g), fat trimmed*
- 3   *tablespoons (45 ml) orange juice*
- 3   *tablespoons (45 ml) red wine vinegar*
- 1   *teaspoon cumin seeds*
- 1   *teaspoon dried oregano*
- 1   *teaspoon salt*
- 2   *cloves garlic, minced*
- ¼   *teaspoon hot pepper seasoning*
- 1   *large onion, thickly sliced*
- 1   *large green or red bell pepper (about 8 oz./230 g), stemmed, halved, and seeded*
  About 2 teaspoons olive oil or vegetable oil
- 6   *warm burrito-size flour tortillas*
  About 3 cups (86 g) shredded iceberg lettuce
  Purchased salsa

Cut steak diagonally across the grain into slices ⅛ inch (3 mm) thick. In a large bowl, combine orange juice, vinegar, cumin, oregano, salt, garlic, and hot pepper seasoning. Add meat; stir to coat evenly. Marinate for 10 minutes or for up to 1 hour at room temperature.

   Meanwhile, place onion and bell pepper in a broiler pan; broil 4 to 6 inches (10 to 15 cm) below heat for about 10 minutes, turning as needed to brown all sides evenly. Remove pan from broiler and cover tightly with foil (see page 124); set aside for at least 5 minutes to cool slightly. Pull off and discard pepper skin. Cut pepper into thin slices; separate onion into rings. Transfer to a platter.

   Heat 2 teaspoons of the oil in a wok or wide nonstick frying pan over high heat. Add half the beef slices and stir-fry until barely pink (3 to 5 minutes).

Transfer to platter. Repeat to cook remaining beef, adding more oil, if needed. Spoon into warm tortillas with onion, pepper, lettuce, and salsa.
Makes 4 servings

PER SERVING: *546 calories, 21 g total fat, 6 g saturated fat, 59 mg cholesterol, 803 mg sodium, 58 g carbohydrates, 5 g fiber, 31 g protein, 167 mg calcium, 6 mg iron*

Citrus Beef Stir-Fry

- 2   *large oranges (about 1 lb./455 g total)*
- 3   *tablespoons (45 ml) dry sherry*
- 3   *tablespoons (45 ml) reduced-sodium soy sauce*
- 2   *tablespoons (30 ml) minced fresh ginger*
- 1   *pound (455 g) boneless lean beef, such as top sirloin, fat trimmed*
- 2   *teaspoons cornstarch*
- 2   *tablespoons (30 ml) vegetable oil*
- 3   *large stalks celery, thinly sliced*
- 1   *cup (about 1¼ oz./38 g) bean sprouts*
- 1   *cup (about 2½ oz./70 g) Chinese pea pods (snow peas), ends and strings removed*

Grate peel from one of the oranges. Squeeze juice from both oranges into a large bowl; mix in peel, sherry, soy sauce, and ginger.

   Cut meat diagonally across grain into slices ⅛ inch (3 mm) thick. Add to bowl and stir to combine. Let stand for at least 5 minutes; stir several times. Drain marinade into a small bowl and mix with cornstarch.

   Heat 2 teaspoons of the oil in a wok or wide non-stick frying pan over high heat. Add half the beef and stir-fry until barely pink (3 to 5 minutes); transfer to a clean bowl. Repeat with remaining beef, adding more oil, if needed; transfer to bowl.

   Heat remaining oil; add celery, sprouts, and pea pods to pan. Stir until pea pods turn bright green (about 1 minute). Add marinade; stir until mixture boils. Return meat to pan and stir-fry just to heat through.   *Makes 4 servings*

PER SERVING: *280 calories, 12 g total fat, 3 g saturated fat, 69 mg cholesterol, 552 mg sodium, 13 g carbohydrates, 1 g fiber, 26 g protein, 46 mg calcium, 4 mg iron*

BRAISING

Less-tender cuts of beef, such as brisket and rump (see "Retail Cuts," page 72), need to cook slowly with moist heat to become tender. The technique, called "braising," requires gentle simmering in liquid in a tightly covered pan. Short ribs lend themselves to a variety of cooking techniques (we grill them on page 71), but braising gives them particular succulence.

Browning the meat to develop a richer color and flavor may be done before the braising, as in the Beef Pot Roast recipe on page 77, or afterward.

Spiced Short Ribs

    8 lean beef short ribs (about 4 lbs./1.8 kg total)
    ¼ teaspoon pepper
    ¼ cup (30 g) all-purpose flour
    4 medium-size onions, thinly sliced
    2 cloves garlic, minced or pressed
    1 bay leaf
    ½ teaspoon ground ginger
    ½ teaspoon dried rosemary
    3 whole cloves
    2 cups (470 ml) reduced-sodium beef broth
    1½ tablespoons (23 ml) red wine vinegar
    1½ teaspoons Dijon mustard
    ¼ teaspoon salt
    ¼ cup (15 g) chopped parsley

Sprinkle ribs with pepper. Roll in flour, then shake off excess. Place about half the onions in a 4- to 5-quart (3.8- to 5-liter) ovenproof pan; arrange ribs on top of onions, then cover with remaining onions. Add garlic, bay leaf, ginger, rosemary, and cloves. Pour broth over all.

Cover tightly and bake in a 350°F (175°C) oven until meat is very tender when pierced (3 to 3½ hours; check periodically after 2½ hours). Remove meat to a rimmed platter; keep warm. Skim fat from cooking liquid, then stir in vinegar and mustard. Bring to a boil over high heat and continue to boil, stirring, until sauce is slightly reduced (about 3 minutes). Stir in salt. Pour sauce over ribs; sprinkle with parsley.   *Makes 4 servings*

PER SERVING: *425 calories, 19 g total fat, 8 g saturated fat, 110 mg cholesterol, 623 mg sodium, 21 g carbohydrates, 3 g fiber, 40 g protein, 63 mg calcium, 5 mg iron*

Alsatian Beef Brisket with Broth

    1 beef brisket (4 to 4½ lbs./1.8 to 2 kg)
       About 3 quarts (2.8 liters) reduced-sodium beef broth
    1 large onion, thinly sliced
    2 bay leaves
    2 cloves garlic
    1 teaspoon black peppercorns
    ½ teaspoon whole cloves
    ½ teaspoon dried thyme
    1 small dried hot red chile
    6 parsley sprigs
       Coarse salt
       Prepared horseradish
       Dijon mustard

Trim surface fat from beef. In a 12- by 14-inch (30- by 35.5-cm) baking pan (at least 2½ in./6 cm deep), combine beef, 3 cups (710 ml) of the broth, the onion, bay leaves, garlic, peppercorns, cloves, thyme, chile, and parsley. Cover tightly with foil. Bake in a 325°F (165°C) oven until beef is very tender when pierced (3½ to 4 hours). At this point, you may cool, cover, and chill up until next day. Lift off and discard fat. Reheat meat, tightly covered, in a 325°F (165°C) oven until hot (about 45 minutes).

Lift out meat and place on a platter; keep warm. Pour pan juices, a little at a time, through a fine strainer into a 1- to 2-quart (950-ml to 1.9-liter) glass measure or gravy separator. Skim off and discard fat. Measure juices and pour into a 4- to 5-quart (3.8- to 5-liter) pan; add enough broth to make 10 to 12 cups (2.4 to 2.9 liters) total. Bring broth to a boil. Immediately, ladle into soup bowls and serve as a first course.

Cut beef diagonally across the grain into thin slices. Accompany with salt, horseradish, and mustard to add to taste.   *Makes 8 to 10 servings*

PER SERVING: *256 calories, 11 g total fat, 4 g saturated fat, 89 mg cholesterol, 953 mg sodium, 4 g carbohydrates, 0.4 g fiber, 34 g protein, 17 mg calcium, 3 mg iron*

HOW TO MAKE BEEF POT ROAST

1 When oil is hot but not smoking, place meat in pan and cook, turning until browned on all sides. Browning adds flavor to meat and to the pan juices that will be used for the gravy. Use two spoons to support the meat when turning.

2 When pot roast is done, transfer meat and vegetables to a rimmed platter and keep warm. Skim fat from pan drippings with a spoon. Measure drippings and add enough water to make 2 cups (470 ml).

3 To make a smooth sauce, whisk flour into butter, then remove from heat and gradually whisk in reserved drippings. Season with salt and pepper, return pan to heat, and cook, stirring, until sauce is thick.

4 The pot roast comes to the table on a handsome platter, surrounded with deliciously tender carrots, turnips, and onions; a sprinkling of chopped fresh parsley brightens the dish. Slice the roast at the table and pass the sauce in a gravy boat.

BEEF *continued*

Beef Pot Roast

PICTURED ON FACING PAGE

- ¼ cup (30 g) plus 1 tablespoon all-purpose flour
- 1 boneless beef rump roast or chuck roast (4 to 5 lbs./1.8 to 2.3 kg)
- 1 tablespoon (15 ml) olive oil
- 2 cups (470 ml) reduced-sodium beef broth
- 2 cups (470 ml) water
- 1½ teaspoons dried thyme
- 1⅛ teaspoons pepper
- 1 bay leaf
- 3 medium-size turnips (about 1¾ lbs./795 g total), peeled and quartered
- 8 medium-size carrots, cut into 3-inch (8-cm) lengths
- 12 small white boiling onions (about 8 oz./230 g total), peeled
- 1 tablespoon butter or margarine
- ¼ teaspoon salt
- 2 tablespoons chopped parsley (optional)

Coat meat with the ¼ cup (30 g) flour, then shake off excess. Heat oil in a 5- to 6-quart (5- to 6-liter) oven-proof pan over medium-high heat until hot but not smoking. Add meat and brown well on all sides. Add broth, water, thyme, 1 teaspoon of the pepper, and the bay leaf; bring to a boil. Cover tightly and cook in a 350°F (175°C) oven for 1½ hours.

Lay turnips, carrots, and onions on and around meat. Cover tightly and continue to bake until meat and vegetables are tender when pierced (about 45 minutes).

Transfer meat and vegetables to a platter and keep warm. Skim and discard fat from drippings. Pour drippings into a 2-cup (470-ml) measure and add water, if necessary, to make 2 cups (470 ml) total.

Melt butter in a small pan over medium heat. Add remaining 1 tablespoon flour and cook, stirring, until bubbly; remove from heat. With a whisk, gradually stir in reserved drippings. Stir in salt and remaining ⅛ teaspoon pepper. Return pan to medium heat and cook, stirring, until sauce boils and thickens (about 4 minutes). Pour sauce into a small bowl. Garnish meat and vegetables with parsley, if desired, and ac-company with sauce. Slice meat at the table.
Makes 8 servings

PER SERVING: *426 calories, 15 g total fat, 5 g saturated fat, 136 mg cholesterol, 453 mg sodium, 19 g carbohydrates, 5 g fiber, 53 g protein, 70 mg calcium, 6 mg iron*

GROUND BEEF

Ground lean beef can come from many different cuts, such as round and chuck, and usually contains some fat to make it juicy. Look at the label to check the percentage of fat (or, expressed another way, the percentage of lean meat). Grinding your own lean cubes of beef is easy to do in a food processor, or you can ask the butcher to trim and grind the cut of beef you have selected.

Basic Hamburgers

- 1 pound (455 g) ground lean beef
- 1 small onion, chopped
- 2 teaspoons Dijon mustard
- 1 teaspoon Worcestershire
- ½ teaspoon salt
- ¼ teaspoon pepper
- 4 hamburger buns, split and toasted

Crumble ground beef into a large bowl. Add onion, mustard, Worcestershire, salt, and pepper, and mix well. Divide mixture into 4 equal portions; lightly shape each portion into a patty ½ inch (1 cm) thick.

Place burgers on broiler-pan rack. Broil about 6 inches (15 cm) below the heat, turning once, until burgers are browned on both sides and done to your liking; cut to test (2 to 3 minutes per side for medium-rare). Serve patties on toasted buns.
Makes 4 servings

PER SERVING: *357 calories, 17 g total fat, 6 g saturated fat, 70 mg cholesterol, 651 mg sodium, 24 g carbohydrates, 1 g fiber, 24 g protein, 77 mg calcium, 3 mg iron*

Cheese-Stuffed Hamburgers

Prepare mixture for *Basic Hamburgers*. Divide mixture into 8 equal portions; shape each portion into a patty about ¼ inch (6 mm) thick.

In a small bowl, stir together 1 cup (about 4 oz./115 g) shredded sharp *Cheddar cheese*, 2 tea-spoons *catsup*, and 1 tablespoon finely chopped *green onion* (including top). Spread equal amounts of filling over 4 of the patties to within ¼ inch (6 mm) of edges. Dampen edge of each patty with water. Top with remaining patties and pinch edges of meat to-gether to completely enclose cheese filling. Cook as for *Basic Hamburgers*. Serve patties on toasted buns.
Makes 4 servings

MAKING STUFFED MEATLOAF

1 Soften dried tomatoes by soaking in a small bowl with boiling water to cover for about 10 minutes. Then drain well and squeeze out excess liquid. To dice tomatoes, cut lengthwise into strips, then crosswise into small bits.

2 In a large bowl, combine sautéed onion, bread crumbs, beef, Italian sausage, pimentos, whole egg and egg whites, garlic, herbs, and pepper. Mix with a spoon or your hands until completely blended. Wash your hands with soap and warm water after this step (as you should always do after handling raw meat).

3 Spoon one third of meat mixture into loaf pan, then spoon half of the tomato-cheese mixture over it. Top with another one third meat mixture and then the remaining tomato-cheese mixture. Cover with a final layer of meat.

4 Bands of flavorful stuffing make this meatloaf more than everyday fare. Serve it with tiny green peas and pearl onions and velvety mashed potatoes laced with butter and touched with paprika. Garnish each plate with a sprig of parsley.

BEEF *continued*

Stuffed Meatloaf

PICTURED ON FACING PAGE

1   cup (about 2 oz./55 g) dried tomatoes (not packed in oil)

2   tablespoons (30 ml) marsala

1   teaspoon olive oil

1   large red onion (about 12 oz./340 g), chopped

5   slices sourdough sandwich bread (about 5 oz./140 g total), torn into pieces

1½ pounds (680 g) ground lean beef

4   ounces (115 g) reduced-fat or regular mild Italian sausage, casings removed and meat crumbled

1   jar (about 4 oz./115 g) diced pimentos, drained

1   large egg

2   large egg whites

2   cloves garlic, minced or pressed

½   teaspoon dried thyme

¼   teaspoon ground sage

⅓   cup (20 g) chopped Italian or regular parsley

¼   cup (about ¾ oz./20 g) grated Parmesan cheese

¼   teaspoon pepper

2   tablespoons chopped capers

1¼ cups (50 g) lightly packed fresh basil, chopped

2   ounces (55 g) thinly sliced prosciutto or ham, chopped

¼   cup (about 1 oz./29 g) shredded fontina cheese
    Italian or regular parsley sprigs

Place tomatoes in a medium-size bowl and add boiling water to cover. Let stand until soft (about 10 minutes), stirring occasionally. Drain well; gently squeeze out excess liquid. Finely chop tomatoes and return to bowl. Drizzle with marsala and set aside.

Heat oil in a wide nonstick frying pan over medium-high heat. Add onion and cook, stirring, until it begins to brown (about 10 minutes); add some water, ¼ cup (60 ml) at a time, if pan appears dry. Transfer onion to a large bowl and let cool slightly.

In a food processor or blender, whirl bread to form fine crumbs. Add crumbs to onion. Add beef, sausage, pimentos, egg, egg whites, garlic, thyme, sage, chopped parsley, Parmesan cheese, and pepper; mix until very well blended. To chopped tomatoes, add capers, basil, prosciutto, and fontina cheese.

Divide meat mixture into thirds. Spread one third of the meat mixture evenly in a 5- by 9-inch (12.5- by 23-cm) loaf pan. Cover with half the tomato-cheese mixture. Top evenly with another one third of the meat mixture and cover with remaining tomato-cheese mixture. Cover evenly with remaining meat mixture.

Bake in a 350°F (175°C) oven until meatloaf is well browned on top (1 to 1¼ hours). Invert meatloaf onto a platter or cutting board; let sit for at least 5 minutes or until cool before slicing. Garnish with parsley sprigs.   *Makes 8 to 10 servings*

PER SERVING: *363 calories, 21 g total fat, 8 g saturated fat, 98 mg cholesterol, 531 mg sodium, 18 g carbohydrates, 3 g fiber, 24 g protein, 111 mg calcium, 3 mg iron*

Beef Tacos

1   pound (455 g) ground lean beef chuck

3   green onions, thinly sliced

2   teaspoons mild or medium chili powder

1   teaspoon ground cumin

½   teaspoon dried oregano

¼   teaspoon pepper

⅓   cup (80 ml) chili sauce

1   teaspoon Worcestershire

8   corn tortillas (about 6-in./15-cm diameter)

1   tablespoon olive oil or vegetable oil
    Fillings: Shredded iceberg lettuce, tomato wedges, chopped green onions, shredded sharp Cheddar cheese

Crumble beef into a wide nonstick frying pan and cook, stirring frequently, over medium-high heat until browned. Add green onions and cook, stirring, until soft (about 5 minutes). Stir in chili powder, cumin, oregano, and pepper until well combined. Reduce heat to medium, add chili sauce and Worcestershire, and cook, stirring, until heated through (about 1 minute). Pour into a bowl and keep warm.

Rinse frying pan and wipe dry. Placed over medium-high heat until hot. One at a time, lightly brush both sides of tortilla with a little of the oil. Place tortilla in frying pan and cook on one side until slightly crisp (about 30 seconds); turn over and fold in half (cooked side in). Cook on second side until slightly crisp (about 30 more seconds). Transfer to paper towels to drain. Repeat to cook remaining tortillas. Keep tortillas warm until all are cooked. Fill each taco shell with 2 to 3 tablespoons beef mixture and add fillings to taste.   *Makes 4 servings*

PER SERVING: *475 calories, 29 g total fat, 10 g saturated fat, 85 mg cholesterol, 489 mg sodium, 31 g carbohydrates, 3 g fiber, 24 g protein, 121 mg calcium, 4 mg iron*

PORK

Today's modern methods of breeding and feeding now produce fresh pork that comes to market much younger and leaner than it did a few decades ago—a boon to those who relish this rich-tasting, nutritious meat but are concerned about calories and fat.

To be tender, moist, and flavorful, cuts of lean pork must not overcook. For best results, when roasting pork, insert a meat thermometer into the thickest part of the meat and cook to 150° to 155°F (66° to 68°C). This is well beyond the temperature required to destroy trichinae—a parasite that is rare in U.S. hogs that have been raised in sanitary condi-

tions. At this internal temperature, pork will be white in color. When broiled, grilled, or stir-fried, pork may show a blush of color when first cut; this is fine. (See the chart on page 67 for oven temperatures and approximate cooking times.)

Check your supermarket or butcher not only for pork roasts, chops, and ribs, but also for tenderloins, strips (ideal for stir-frying), and lean cubes (great for grilling). Complement pork with the mellow sweetness of fruit (apples are a traditional accompaniment) or with such robust vegetables as cauliflower, broccoli, or cabbage—and certainly with sauerkraut.

Pork Primal Cuts

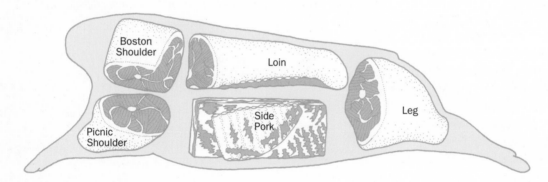

Retail Cuts and How to Cook Them

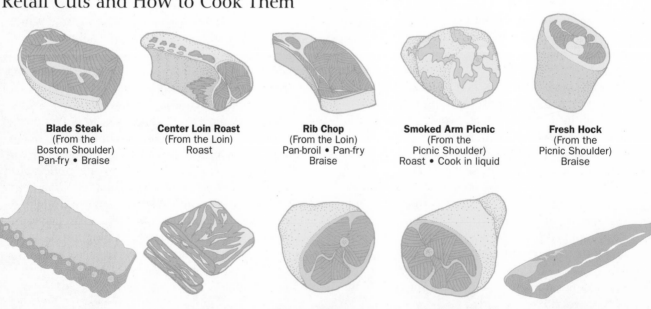

Blade Steak
(From the
Boston Shoulder)
Pan-fry • Braise

Center Loin Roast
(From the Loin)
Roast

Rib Chop
(From the Loin)
Pan-broil • Pan-fry
Braise

Smoked Arm Picnic
(From the
Picnic Shoulder)
Roast • Cook in liquid

Fresh Hock
(From the
Picnic Shoulder)
Braise

Back Ribs
(From the Loin)
Roast • Grill • Broil

Slab Bacon
(From the Side Pork)
Broil • Pan-fry

Rump Butt Portion
(From the Leg)
Roast • Cook in liquid

Shank Portion
(From the Leg)
Roast • Cook in liquid

Tenderloin
(From the Loin)
Roast • Pan-fry

DRY ROASTING

The aroma of pork roasting in the oven promises a feast close at hand. Because fresh pork cuts vary little in tenderness, you can dry roast most of them (see the chart on page 67); pork shoulder, with ample marbling, tolerates this type of cooking best. Marinate the pork, baste with a sauce, or simply roast the meat unadorned.

Though pork ribs have a high ratio of bone to meat, this has never detracted from their popularity. Part of their appeal, in fact, is the satisfaction of chewing on the bones to get every last morsel of meat. Today, many people favor pork back ribs over spareribs because they are leaner and easier to cut apart. You can cook both types of ribs in a variety of ways, but pork back ribs are especially good dry roasted, as suggested here.

Pork Tenderloins with Onion-Apple Cream

    2   pork tenderloins (12 oz. to 1 lb./340 g to 455 g each), well
        trimmed

        About 1 teaspoon salt

        About ½ teaspoon pepper

    3   tablespoons (45 ml) Dijon mustard

    4   teaspoons (20 ml) olive oil

    1   large onion, diced

    1   large Golden Delicious apple (about 8 oz./230 g),
        thinly sliced

    ¼   cup (60 ml) dry sherry

    1½ cups (360 ml) reduced-sodium chicken broth

    ¼   cup (60 ml) reduced-fat sour cream

    2   tablespoons butter or margarine

Place both pork tenderloins slightly apart on a rack in a 10- by 15-inch (25- by 38-cm) baking pan. Sprinkle with 1 teaspoon of the salt and ½ teaspoon of the pepper. Brush with half the mustard. Roast, uncovered, in a 425°F (220°C) oven, basting with any pan juices, until a meat thermometer inserted in thickest part of meat registers 150°F (63°C) and meat in center is no longer pink; cut to test (20 to 25 minutes).

Just before pork is done, heat oil in a wide nonstick frying pan over medium heat. Add onion and cook, stirring often, until soft (about 5 minutes). Transfer pork to a cutting board; keep warm.

Add apple to onion mixture and cook, stirring frequently, until softened (about 5 minutes). Stir in sherry. Add broth and cook until slightly reduced (about 5 minutes). Stir in the remaining mustard, sour cream, and any pork juices from the platter; season with a pinch of salt and pepper. Reduce heat to low and swirl in butter.

Carve the pork into slices about ¼ inch (6 mm) thick; transfer to a platter. Serve topped with the sauce.   *Makes 4 to 6 servings*

PER SERVING: *345 calories, 16 g total fat, 6g saturated fat, 97 mg cholesterol, 936 mg sodium, 13 g carbohydrates, 2 g fiber, 30 g protein, 24 mg calcium, 2 mg iron*

Pork Tenderloins with Dried Apricot Chutney

Bake pork tenderloins as directed in *Pork Tenderloins with Onion-Apple Cream*, but omit the onion-apple cream and serve with *Dried Apricot Chutney* (see page 145) instead.

Roasted Pork Back Ribs

    2   tablespoons black peppercorns

    1   tablespoon fennel seeds

    1   tablespoon ground sage

    3   pounds (1.35 kg) pork back ribs (2 slabs, about 1½ lbs./
        680 g each)

        Salt

In a blender, whirl together peppercorns, fennel seeds, and sage (or crush with mortar and pestle to a coarse powder).

Rinse ribs. Rub ribs to coat all over with ground herb mixture. Set ribs, cupped side down, on a rack in a baking pan just long enough to hold meat. Bake in a 450°F (230°C) oven for 30 minutes; turn curved side up and bake for 10 more minutes. (When drippings in pan start to smoke, add water to cover pan bottom.) Turn ribs over again and bake until sizzling and well browned under herb rub (10 to 15 more minutes). Cut ribs apart and sprinkle with salt to taste. Serve hot or cold.   *Makes 4 servings*

PER SERVING: *624 calories, 49 g total fat, 18 g saturated fat, 194 mg cholesterol, 169 mg sodium, 3 g carbohydrates, 0.8 g fiber, 41 g protein, 114 mg calcium, 4 mg iron*

PORK *continued*

BRAISING

You can braise various cuts of pork the same way you do beef—just cook in liquid in a tightly covered container, either on top of the stove or in the oven. But because the texture of pork is finer than that of beef, it requires somewhat less cooking time. Small cubes will braise more quickly than large ones.

Fruit-Stuffed Pork Chops

PICTURED ON FACING PAGE

1 package (12 oz./340 g) diced mixed dried fruits, chopped
1 cup (240 ml) water
¼ cup (30 g) chopped celery
¼ cup (43 g) chopped onion
½ teaspoon dried rosemary
¾ teaspoon salt
½ teaspoon pepper
4 large rib or loin pork chops (about 8 oz./230 g each), 1 inch (2.5 cm) thick
¼ teaspoon dried thyme
1 tablespoon (15 ml) olive oil
1 cup (240 ml) apple juice
¼ cup (60 ml) reduced-sodium chicken broth
1½ teaspoons cornstarch mixed with 1 tablespoon (15 ml) water

In a 1- to 2-quart (950-ml to 1.9-liter) pan over medium heat, combine fruits, water, celery, onion, rosemary, and ¼ teaspoon each of the salt and pepper. Bring to a boil. Cover, reduce heat, and simmer, stirring occasionally, until dried fruits are tender and liquid absorbed (about 15 minutes); set aside.

Meanwhile, with a small sharp knife, cut a 3-inch (8-cm) horizontal slit through meat side of chop almost to bone to form a pocket. Stuff each pocket with about 3 tablespoons of the fruit mixture. Set aside remaining filling. Press meat together to close pocket.

In a small bowl, mix the remaining ½ teaspoon salt and ¼ teaspoon pepper with thyme; rub this mixture into one side of each chop.

Heat oil in a wide nonstick frying pan over medium heat until hot but not smoking. Add chops (in batches if necessary to prevent crowding) and cook until well browned on both sides (about 2 minutes per side). Pour in apple juice and broth, and bring to a boil over medium heat. Cover, reduce heat, and simmer until meat is no longer pink at bone; cut to test (35 to 40 minutes). Turn chops over after 20 minutes.

Lift out chops; arrange on a platter and keep warm. Pour drippings into a 2-cup (470-ml) measure; skim and discard fat. Return liquid to pan and bring to a boil over medium heat. Stir cornstarch mixture to recombine and add to pan along with reserved fruit filling. Cook, stirring, over medium heat until sauce boils and thickens slightly (about 1 minute). Pour sauce over chops.   *Makes 4 servings*

PER SERVING: *656 calories, 32 g total fat, 11 g saturated fat, 96 mg cholesterol, 523 mg sodium, 64 g carbohydrates, 5 g fiber, 32 g protein, 61 mg calcium, 4 mg iron*

Southwest Stew

12 ounces (340 g) boneless pork center loin, top loin, or shoulder (fat trimmed), cut into ¾-inch (2-cm) chunks
5 cups (1.2 liters) reduced-sodium chicken broth
2 cups (340 g) chopped yellow onions
4 cloves garlic, minced
1½ tablespoons New Mexico, California, or regular chili powder
1 teaspoon dried oregano
3 cans (14½ oz./415 g each) hominy, rinsed and drained
1 can (7 oz./200 g) diced green chiles
Sliced green onions
Lime wedges

In a 5- to 6-quart (5- to 6-liter) pan, combine pork, ⅓ cup (80 ml) of the broth, the yellow onions, and garlic. Cover tightly and bring to a boil over high heat. Reduce heat, cover, and simmer for 10 minutes.

Uncover, increase heat to medium-high, and stir until juices evaporate and drippings stick to pan and turn deep brown (about 4 minutes). Add 2 tablespoons (30 ml) of the remaining broth and stir to scrape browned particles free. Add chili powder and oregano; stir for 15 seconds.

Stir in remaining broth, hominy, and chiles. Bring to a boil, reduce heat, and simmer, covered, until flavors are blended (about 10 minutes). Season to taste with green onions and lime.   *Makes 4 servings*

PER SERVING: *423 calories, 8 g total fat, 2 g saturated fat, 54 mg cholesterol, 1,738 mg sodium, 57 g carbohydrates, 11 g fiber, 28 g protein, 87 mg calcium, 4 mg iron*

PREPARING FRUIT-STUFFED PORK CHOPS

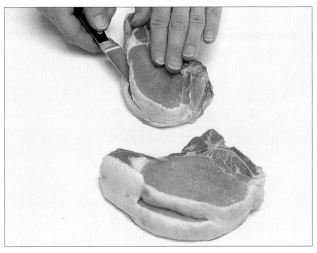

1 To make a pocket for stuffing, use a small, sharp knife to cut a 3-inch (8-cm) horizontal slit through meat side of chop almost to bone.

2 Holding chop in your hand, spoon about 3 tablespoons fruit filling into pocket. Press edges of meat together to close pocket (you will not need to skewer). Set the leftover filling aside to add to the sauce.

3 Brown the stuffed, herb-rubbed chops in hot oil, working in batches, if necessary, to avoid crowding. The moist, slightly spicy stuffing should stay neatly inside chops, even when you turn them.

4 The glossy, deeply savory sauce for the chops is chunky with bits of fruit. Broccoli is a good choice for an accompanying vegetable; serve plain rice, or try a mixture of white and wild rice.

PORK *continued*

STIR-FRYING

Fat-trimmed and thinly sliced pork is ideal for stir-frying. The slender pieces of meat cook in a flash.

Stir-Fried Spiced Pork on Couscous

   1   *pound (455 g) boneless pork loin or shoulder, fat trimmed*
   4   *cups (about 10 oz./285 g) shredded red cabbage*
   ¼   *cup (60 ml) seasoned rice vinegar (or ¼ cup/60 ml distilled white vinegar plus 1 tablespoon sugar)*
 2¾   *cups (650 ml) reduced-sodium chicken broth*
   ½   *cup (120 ml) orange juice*
   4   *teaspoons cornstarch*
   2   *tablespoons (30 ml) reduced-sodium soy sauce*
   1   *teaspoon ground coriander*
   ½   *teaspoon ground cumin*
   ¼   *teaspoon ground red pepper (cayenne)*
   1   *cup (6 oz./170 g) couscous*
   6   *teaspoons (30 ml) vegetable oil*
   1   *large onion, thinly sliced*
   1   *tablespoon minced fresh ginger*
   2   *cloves garlic, minced or pressed*
   ¼   *cup (10 g) chopped fresh mint or cilantro*

Cut pork into slices ¼ inch (6 mm) thick, then stack slices and cut into strips ¼ inch (6 mm) wide; set aside.

In a large bowl, combine cabbage and vinegar mixture; set aside.

To prepare sauce, in a small bowl, combine ¾ cup (180 ml) of the broth, the orange juice, cornstarch, soy sauce, coriander, cumin, and ground red pepper; set aside.

In a 1½- to 2-quart (1.4- to 1.9-liter) pan, bring remaining 2 cups (470 ml) broth to a boil. Stir in couscous, cover pan tightly, remove from heat, and let stand until liquid is absorbed (about 5 minutes).

Meanwhile, place a nonstick wok or wide nonstick frying pan over high heat. When pan is hot, add 2 teaspoons of the oil and half the pork; stir-fry until pork is lightly browned (about 3 minutes). Remove pork from pan; add 2 more teaspoons oil and remaining pork, and repeat. Add to cooked meat.

Add 2 more teaspoons of the oil, the onion, ginger, and garlic to pan; stir-fry over high heat until

soft (about 2 minutes). Stir reserved sauce to recombine and add to pan. Stir until sauce boils (about 2 minutes), then return pork to pan.

Place cabbage on a large platter. Mound hot couscous on cabbage. Spoon pork and sauce over couscous. Sprinkle with mint.   *Makes 4 servings*

PER SERVING: *496 calories, 14 g total fat, 3 g saturated fat, 67 mg cholesterol, 1,057 mg sodium, 55 g carbohydrates, 4 g fiber, 34 g protein, 90 mg calcium, 2 mg iron*

Stir-Fried Pork with Asparagus & Peppers

PICTURED ON FACING PAGE

   1   *pound (455 g) boneless pork loin or shoulder, fat trimmed*
   3   *tablespoons (45 ml) reduced-sodium soy sauce*
   1   *tablespoon (15 ml) sake (rice wine)*
   2   *teaspoons minced fresh ginger*
   1   *clove garlic, minced*
 1½   *pounds (680 g) slender asparagus, cut into 4-inch (10-cm) lengths*
   1   *large red bell pepper (about 6 oz./170 g), stemmed, seeded, and cut into strips ¼ inch (6 mm) wide*
   ½   *cup (120 ml) plus 3 tablespoons (45 ml) chicken broth*
   1   *teaspoon cornstarch*
   2   *teaspoons vegetable oil*
   1   *tablespoon sliced green onion*

Cut pork into slices ¼ inch (6 mm) thick, then stack slices and cut into strips ¼ inch (6 mm) wide. In a bowl, mix pork, soy sauce, sake, ginger, and garlic; let stand for about 30 minutes.

Place asparagus, bell pepper, and ½ cup (120 ml) of the broth in a wok or wide nonstick frying pan over high heat; cover. Stir occasionally until vegetables are tender-crisp to bite (about 4 minutes). Drain, transfer to a platter, and keep warm.

Holding back meat, drain marinade into a 1-cup (240-ml) measure. Stir remaining 3 tablespoons broth and the cornstarch into marinade. Add oil to pan over high heat. Add pork and stir-fry until meat is no longer pink in center; cut to test (2 to 3 minutes). Add marinade and stir until it boils. Return vegetables to pan and stir until heated through (about 1 minute). Sprinkle with onion.   *Makes 4 servings*

PER SERVING: *234 calories, 9 g total fat, 2 g saturated fat, 60 mg cholesterol, 581 mg sodium, 11 g carbohydrates, 2 g fiber, 28 g protein, 63 mg calcium, 3 mg iron*

STIR-FRYING PORK WITH ASPARAGUS & PEPPERS

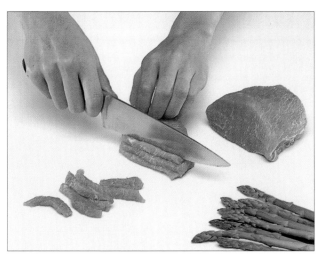

1 Be sure pork is well trimmed of fat before you cut it. For easier slicing, place meat in freezer for 15 minutes to firm it. First cut pork into slices ¼ inch (6 mm) thick, then stack slices and cut into strips ¼ inch (6 mm) wide. Pork will marinate for about 30 minutes.

2 Asparagus and bell peppers are cut into pieces of similar size for uniform cooking. Place vegetables in a wok or frying pan with ½ cup (120 ml) broth, cover, and cook over high heat, stirring occasionally. This "stir-steaming" produces tender-crisp vegetables. Transfer vegetables to a platter when cooked.

3 Heat oil in wok or frying pan over high heat; add marinated pork strips and cook, stirring constantly, until meat is no longer pink in center. Because strips of pork are thin, they will cook in just 2 to 3 minutes. The marinade is then added and cooked with the pork just until thickened.

4 The vegetables are returned to the pan at the end to reheat. The two-stage cooking of the vegetables and meat yields a dish in which the pork is tender and juicy, and the vegetables are tender-crisp and bright. The cornstarch-thickened sauce glazes the pork, asparagus, and peppers. The classic partner for a stir-fry is hot steamed rice.

PORK *continued*

BROILING & GRILLING

Broiling and grilling are both savory ways to cook fresh pork. Shoulder, rib, and loin chops—as well as the tenderloin—require just minutes under (or over) intense heat. To give chops enough time to cook without overbrowning, broil about 6 inches (15 cm) from the heat. Test the meat for doneness at the minimum recommended cooking time.

To grill pork, let charcoal briquets burn down to the desired heat and spread in a solid layer under meat. Or adjust gas grill to desired heat and close lid to cover. You can rub the meat with a spice mixture before cooking, and baste often to add moisture. The inimitable glaze on the Killer Ribs (at right) is achieved by brushing on a peachy barbecue sauce.

Broiled Pork Chops with Tomato-Cilantro Salsa

    1   teaspoon ground cumin
    ¾   teaspoon ground coriander
    ¾   teaspoon dried oregano
    1   teaspoon salt
    ¼   teaspoon sugar
    4   shoulder pork chops (about 8 oz./230 g each), ½ inch (1 cm) thick
    1   large tomato (about 8 oz./230 g), chopped
    ¼   cup (10 g) chopped cilantro
    3   green onions, thinly sliced
    1   tablespoon (15 ml) balsamic vinegar

In a small bowl, combine ¾ teaspoon of the cumin, the coriander, ½ teaspoon each of the oregano and salt, and the sugar. Rub into chops. Place chops on broiler-pan rack and broil about 6 inches (15 cm) below heat, turning once, until meat is no longer pink at bone; cut to test (5 to 6 minutes per side).

Meanwhile, to make salsa, in a medium bowl, combine tomato, cilantro, green onions, vinegar, remaining ¼ teaspoon each cumin and oregano, and remaining ½ teaspoon salt. Spoon salsa over chops before serving.   *Makes 4 servings*

PER SERVING: *512 calories, 40 g total fat, 14 g saturated fat, 145 mg cholesterol, 664 mg sodium, 4 g carbohydrates, 1 g fiber, 32 g protein, 32 mg calcium, 3 mg iron*

Killer Ribs

        About 5 pounds (2.3 kg) pork back ribs
    1   large onion, coarsely chopped
    1   tablespoon dried basil
    2   teaspoons ground cinnamon
    1½ teaspoons ground allspice
    1½ teaspoons ground ginger
    1   or 2 teaspoons crushed red pepper flakes
    3   bay leaves
    3   cloves garlic, minced or pressed
    1   can (about 1 lb./455 g) sliced peaches, drained
    1   bottle (18 oz./510 ml) prepared barbecue sauce

Trim and discard excess fat from ribs. Place ribs in an 8- to 10-quart (8- to 10-liter) pan; add onion, basil, cinnamon, allspice, ginger, 1 teaspoon of the red pepper flakes, the bay leaves, and garlic.

Fill pan with just enough water to cover ribs. Cover pan and bring water to a boil over high heat. Reduce heat and simmer until meat is tender when pierced (about 50 minutes).

Meanwhile, in a blender or food processor, whirl peaches until smoothly puréed. Transfer peaches to a medium-size bowl. Stir in barbecue sauce and remaining 1 teaspoon red pepper flakes, if using. Pour about half the sauce into a bowl to serve with the cooked ribs; use remainder for basting.

Drain ribs; place on a grill 4 to 6 inches (10 to 15 cm) above a solid bed of medium coals (you can hold your hand at grill level only 4 to 5 seconds). Baste frequently with peach sauce and turn ribs as needed to develop a rich brown glaze (about 20 minutes). Cut ribs between bones and accompany with more sauce added to taste.   *Makes 6 to 8 servings*

PER SERVING: *686 calories, 48 g total fat, 17 g saturated fat, 184 mg cholesterol, 757 mg sodium, 23 g carbohydrates, 1 g fiber, 40 g protein, 115 mg calcium, 4 mg iron*

PAN-FRYING

Bone-in or boneless, pan-fried pork is a speedy solution for the busy cook. Choose chops or steaks cut from the shoulder, leg, or loin. Tenderloin medallions are also perfect for pan-frying. Pounded thin, they cook in less than 2 minutes.

Pork Chops with Olives

 2 teaspoons olive oil
 4 center-cut loin pork chops (about 8 oz./230 g each),
    ¾ inch (2 cm) thick
 ¾ cup (180 ml) dry white wine
 ½ cup (120 ml) reduced-sodium chicken broth
 3 tablespoons sliced pimento-stuffed olives
 1 teaspoon grated lime peel
 ½ teaspoon salt
 ¼ teaspoon pepper
 ¾ teaspoon cornstarch mixed with 1 tablespoon (15 ml) water
 1 tablespoon butter or margarine
 2 tablespoons chopped parsley

Heat oil in a wide nonstick frying pan over medium-high heat. Cook chops, turning once, until they are browned on both sides and meat at bone is no longer pink; cut to test (6 to 8 minutes per side).

Lift out chops; arrange on a rimmed platter and keep warm. Add wine, broth, olives, and lime peel to pan. Boil over high heat until liquid is reduced to about 1 cup/240 ml (about 2 minutes). Add any juices that have accumulated on platter, salt, and pepper. Stir cornstarch mixture to recombine; add to pan. Cook, stirring constantly, until sauce boils and is slightly thickened (about 1 minute). Remove from the heat and swirl in butter and parsley. Pour sauce over chops.   *Makes 4 servings*

PER SERVING: *396 calories, 27 g total fat, 10 g saturated fat, 120 mg cholesterol, 629 mg sodium, 1 g carbohydrates, 0.3 g fiber, 34 g protein, 54 mg calcium, 2 mg iron*

Pork Chops with Green Peppercorns

Follow directions for *Pork Chops with Olives*, but substitute 1½ tablespoons *green peppercorns*, rinsed and drained well, for olives.

Pork Tenderloin Cutlets with Mustard Cream

 2 pork tenderloins (12 oz. to 1 lb./340 g to 455 g each),
    fat trimmed
    About ½ teaspoon vegetable oil
 1 pound (455 g) mushrooms, thinly sliced
 2 tablespoons minced shallots or green onion
 3 cloves garlic, minced
 2 tablespoons (30 ml) balsamic vinegar
 ½ cup (120 ml) whipping cream
 3 tablespoons (45 ml) Dijon mustard
 1 teaspoon Worcestershire
 1 tablespoon (15 ml) lemon juice
 ½ teaspoon ground sage
 ¼ teaspoon sugar
    About ¼ cup (30 g) minced chives or green onion tops
    Salt and pepper

Cut tenderloins across the grain into slices 1 inch (2.5 cm) thick. Place pieces of meat well apart between sheets of plastic wrap. Pound firmly and gently with a mallet or small frying pan until meat is about ¼ inch (6 mm) thick.

Coat bottom of a wide nonstick frying pan lightly with oil. Place pan over medium-high heat. Add mushrooms, shallots, garlic, and vinegar; stir often until mushroom liquid evaporates and slices begin to brown lightly (10 to 12 minutes). Pour from pan into a medium-size bowl and keep warm.

Coat pan bottom lightly with more oil and place pan over high heat. When oil is hot, add some of the pork (do not crowd). Turn pieces just as edges turn white. Cook until meat is no longer pink in thickest part; cut to test (about 1½ to 2 minutes total). Transfer pork to bowl with mushrooms. Repeat until all pork is cooked.

Add cream, mustard, Worcestershire, lemon juice, sage, and sugar to pan. Stir over high heat until mixture boils vigorously; drain any liquid from pork and mushrooms into pan and return to a boil. Remove sauce from heat. Quickly arrange equal portions of the meat and mushrooms on dinner plates. Pour sauce over foods and sprinkle with chives. Season to taste with salt and pepper.
Makes 6 to 8 servings

PER SERVING: *216 calories, 10 g total fat, 5 g saturated fat, 91 mg cholesterol, 225 mg sodium, 5 g carbohydrates, 0.9 g fiber, 24 g protein, 25 mg calcium, 2 mg iron*

PORK *continued*

SMOKED PORK

Curing and smoking certain cuts of fresh pork gives additional moistness and flavor to the meat—ham from leg of pork, Canadian bacon from pork tenderloin, smoked loin from center-cut pork loin, picnic ham from the shoulder (or butt), for example. At one time, these smoked cuts, like their fresh counterparts, needed to be cooked; but today, most carry the label "fully cooked" or "ready to eat." This means, in theory, that you can serve them just as they are. However, if you want the meat hot, you have to heat it—and this can take almost as much time as cooking would.

Smoked Pork Loin Roast with Apples & Currants

1   fully cooked smoked pork loin roast (about 2½ to 3 lbs./1.15 to 1.35 kg), 4 to 6 bones, sawed through

2   tablespoons dried currants

3   tablespoons butter or margarine

4   large Golden Delicious apples (about 2 lbs./905 g), peeled

3   teaspoons sugar

Place roast, bone side down, in a pan large enough to hold it comfortably. Bake in a 350°F (175°C) oven until hot (120°F/49°C) in center (50 to 60 minutes).

Meanwhile, prepare the currants and apples. Place currants in a wide nonstick frying pan with about 1 teaspoon of the butter. Stir over high heat until currants puff (about 2 minutes). Pour currants from pan into a small bowl.

Cut apples in half, cut each half into 4 equal wedges; core. Add remaining butter to frying pan and melt over medium-high heat. Lay apple wedges in pan and cook until wedges are lightly browned and feel soft when pressed (15 to 20 minutes); turn wedges occasionally with a wide spatula.

Sprinkle apples with sugar, then return currants to pan; shake pan to mix. Brown apples a bit more (1 or 2 minutes). Transfer roast to a platter and add fruit. Slice roast into chops.   *Makes 4 to 6 servings*

PER SERVING: *455 calories, 25 g total fat, 9 g saturated fat, 118 mg cholesterol, 2,908 mg sodium, 33 g carbohydrates, 3 g fiber, 31 g protein, 11 mg calcium, 2 mg iron*

Baked Ham with Madeira Sauce

1   fully cooked half ham (6 lbs./2.7 kg), bone in, trimmed

½   cup (120 ml) Madeira

½   cup (110 g) firmly packed dark brown sugar

3   tablespoons (45 ml) Dijon mustard

Place ham, fat side up, in a pan large enough to hold it comfortably; insert meat thermometer into thickest part of meat to the bone. Roast, uncovered, in a 325°F (165°C) oven for 1 hour.

In a small bowl, combine Madeira, sugar, and mustard; brush half the sauce over ham. Return to oven and roast, uncovered, until thermometer registers 140°F (60°C) and glaze is browned (about 1 more hour); baste often with sauce.   *Makes 8 servings*

PER SERVING: *266 calories, 10 g total fat, 4 g saturated fat, 67 mg cholesterol, 1,843 mg sodium, 15 g carbohydrates, 0 g fiber, 26 g protein, 22 mg calcium, 2 mg iron*

Smoked Pork Chops with Sweet Potatoes

4   medium-size sweet potatoes (about 1½ lbs./680 g total)

2   tablespoons butter or margarine, melted

3   tablespoons firmly packed brown sugar

4   smoked pork chops (about 8 oz./230 g each), ¾ inch (2 cm) thick

¼   cup (60 ml) reduced-sodium chicken broth

2   tablespoons chopped mango chutney

Peel potatoes; halve lengthwise. Cut crosswise into slices ½ inch (1 cm) thick. Place in a 6-quart (6-liter) pan with water to cover. Cover pan, bring to a boil, and cook potatoes until just tender (about 7 minutes).

Pour 1 tablespoon butter into an 7- by 11-inch (18- by 28-cm) baking pan and stir in half the sugar. Arrange potatoes evenly in dish and sprinkle with remaining butter and sugar. Arrange chops over potatoes. In a small bowl, combine broth and chutney; spoon over chops.

Cover pan with foil and bake in a 350°F (175°C) oven for 10 minutes. Uncover, baste with juices, and continue to bake, basting often, until lightly browned (about 30 more minutes).   *Makes 4 servings*

PER SERVING: *510 calories, 22 g total fat, 8 g saturated fat, 106 mg cholesterol, 2,778 mg sodium, 51 g carbohydrates, 4 g fiber, 30 g protein, 37 mg calcium, 2 mg iron*

L A M B

Lambs are young animals, so almost any cut will be relatively tender. That's why nearly all cuts of lamb can be cooked with dry heat—roasting, broiling, pan-broiling, or pan-frying. The tougher cuts—those near the shoulder or shank—can be coaxed to juicy tenderness through braising.

The delicate and distinctive flavor of lamb marries well with all sorts of seasonings, from garlic, mustard, and rosemary to sweet spices and fruit. Long associated with springtime, lamb is often paired with tender spring vegetables and fresh mint.

Lamb has a fine-grained texture and is essentially a lean meat. Almost all cuts have under 200 calories per 3-ounce (85-g) cooked serving. Although the rib chops are deluxe cuts, lamb can be very economical. Bone-in or boneless leg or shoulder roasts can feed a small crowd. Made ahead, these roasts are delicious sliced and served cold in sandwiches or salads.

Most lamb lovers agree that the meat tastes its best when cooked medium-rare to medium—still red and juicy inside (see the chart on page 67 for meat roasting times and temperatures).

Lamb Primal Cuts

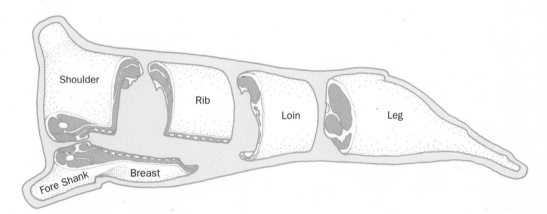

Retail Cuts and How to Cook Them

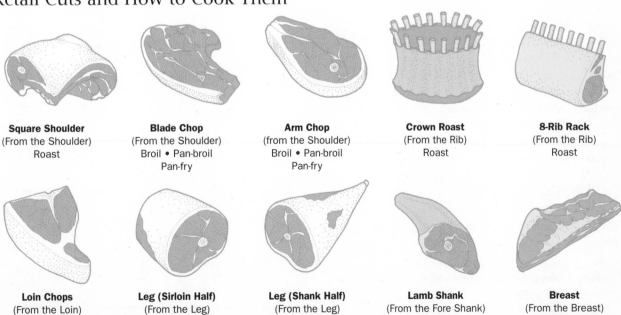

Square Shoulder
(From the Shoulder)
Roast

Blade Chop
(From the Shoulder)
Broil • Pan-broil
Pan-fry

Arm Chop
(from the Shoulder)
Broil • Pan-broil
Pan-fry

Crown Roast
(From the Rib)
Roast

8-Rib Rack
(From the Rib)
Roast

Loin Chops
(From the Loin)
Broil • Pan-fry

Leg (Sirloin Half)
(From the Leg)
Roast

Leg (Shank Half)
(From the Leg)
Roast

Lamb Shank
(From the Fore Shank)
Braise

Breast
(From the Breast)
Roast • Braise

DRY ROASTING

When a juicy lamb roast has star billing on your dinner menu, you can choose the supporting cast from a variety of side dishes. One established favorite from the Middle East is a pilaf of rice or cracked wheat. Also complementary are lightly cooked green vegetables, such as baby artichokes, asparagus, broccoli, or green beans.

Carving a leg of lamb is easy (see page 91), and the roast rack of lamb (in the recipe at right) separates neatly into chops. To dress up the platter for serving, surround the roast lamb with marmalade-glazed baby carrots, braised whole shallots, lemon wedges, or sprigs of fresh watercress.

Mustard-Coated Roast Leg of Lamb

PICTURED ON FACING PAGE

¼ cup (60 ml) Dijon mustard

1 tablespoon (15 ml) reduced-sodium soy sauce

1½ teaspoons dried rosemary, crumbled

½ teaspoon ground ginger

½ teaspoon sugar

½ teaspoon pepper

1 bone-in leg of lamb (5- to 6 lbs./2.3-to 2.7 kg), fat trimmed

2 cloves garlic, slivered

In a small bowl, combine mustard, soy sauce, rosemary, ginger, sugar, and pepper.

Place lamb on a rack in a pan large enough to hold it comfortably. With a small, sharp knife, cut small slits in surface of lamb and insert garlic slivers. With a brush, completely coat roast with mustard mixture. Insert a meat thermometer through thickest part of meat to the bone.

Roast, uncovered, in a 350°F (175°C) oven to degree of doneness preferred (see chart, page 67). Remove lamb to a platter; keep warm and let stand for 10 to 15 minutes before carving.

To carve, grasp narrow end of leg (protect hand with a potholder or cloth) and slice meat, cutting parallel to leg bone. *Makes 6 servings*

PER SERVING: *398 calories, 16 g total fat, 6 g saturated fat, 178 mg cholesterol, 476 mg sodium, 1 g carbohydrates, 0.1 g fiber, 57 g protein, 23 mg calcium, 4 mg iron*

Roast Rack of Lamb with New Potatoes

¼ cup (2 oz./55 g) butter or margarine, at room temperature

3 tablespoons minced parsley

1 small clove garlic, minced or pressed

1 rack of lamb (2 to 2½ lbs./905 g to 1.15 kg)

6 red thin-skinned potatoes (about 2½-in./6-cm diameter), scrubbed

Salt and pepper

To make parsley butter, in a small bowl, mash butter, parsley, and garlic. Rub about 1½ tablespoons of parsley butter over all sides of lamb. To check pan size, place lamb rack, fat side up, in a pan large enough to hold it comfortably; insert a meat thermometer through thickest part of meat. Remove roast from pan and set aside.

Place potatoes in same pan and cook in a 425°F (220°C) oven for 15 minutes. Add meat and cook until done to your liking (see chart, page 67) and potatoes are soft when squeezed. If lamb is done before potatoes, remove it from pan and keep warm.

To serve, cut lamb between ribs into individual chops; offer remaining parsley butter with lamb and potatoes. *Makes 4 servings*

PER SERVING: *682 calories, 54 g total fat, 26 g saturated fat, 169 mg cholesterol, 229 mg sodium, 16 g carbohydrates, 2 g fiber, 32 g protein, 39 mg calcium, 3 mg iron*

Roast Rack of Lamb with Root Vegetables

Follow recipe for *Roast Rack of Lamb with New Potatoes*, but substitute 2 medium-size *carrots* or 2 medium-size *parsnips*, cut into 2-inch (5-cm) lengths, for the potatoes. Cook as directed above, then add lamb.

Or use *celery root* (celeriac). Peel 1 celery root, cut into 2-inch (5-cm) wedges, and use instead of potatoes. Or, if you have room in the pan, cook all the vegetables along with the potatoes.

PREPARING MUSTARD-COATED ROAST LEG OF LAMB

1 Place leg of lamb on a rack in a pan large enough to hold meat comfortably. Using tip of a small, sharp knife, cut small slits all over surface of lamb. Insert a sliver of garlic into each slit.

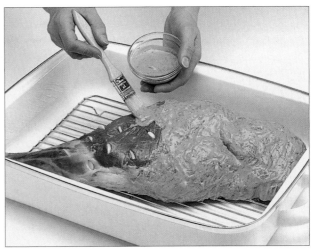

2 With a basting brush, completely coat leg of lamb with mustard mixture. If you don't have a basting brush, a small spatula is fine for this job.

3 There are two ways to check internal temperature of meat for doneness. You can insert a regular meat thermometer in roast before placing meat in oven, and check it when appropriate time has elapsed (see chart, page 67). Or, at appropriate time, pull out oven rack and quickly insert instant-read thermometer through thickest part of meat to bone.

4 When roast is done, transfer to a carving board, cover loosely, and let stand for 10 to 15 minutes (this allows juices to settle into meat so that they are not lost in carving). To carve, grasp bone at narrow end of roast (protect hand with a potholder or kitchen towel) and cut downward, parallel to bone.

LAMB *continued*

BRAISING

Shoulder, shank, and neck of lamb benefit from braising since their higher amount of tough connective tissue needs gentle, moist-heat cooking to tenderize it. When these cuts are braised, the juices make delicious sauces.

Braised Lamb with Vegetables

PICTURED ON FACING PAGE

　　3　*pounds (1.35 kg) boneless lamb shoulder or neck, cut into 1- to 2-inch (2.5- to 5-cm) chunks, fat trimmed*

　　1　*cup (240 ml) dry red wine*

　½　*cup (120 ml) Madeira or port*

　　2　*tablespoons (30 ml) reduced-sodium soy sauce*

1½　*cups (360 ml) reduced-sodium chicken broth*

　　2　*teaspoons mustard seeds*

　¾　*teaspoon dried thyme*

　¼　*teaspoon freshly ground black pepper*

　　1　*bay leaf*

1½　*to 2 pounds (680 to 905 g) small red or white thin-skinned potatoes, quartered*

　　8　*slender carrots, peeled and cut into 3-inch (8-cm) lengths*

　　6　*medium white turnips (about 1½ lbs./680 g total), peeled and quartered*

　12　*small white onions (about 6 oz./170 g total), peeled, or 2 cups (425 g) frozen pearl onions*

　12　*ounces (340 g) thin green beans, trimmed and halved diagonally*

　　3　*tablespoons (45 ml) whipping cream*

　　1　*tablespoon (15 ml) Dijon mustard*

　¼　*teaspoon salt*

Place meat in a 5- to 6-quart (5- to 6-liter) pan. Add red wine, Madeira, and soy sauce. Cover and bring to a boil over medium heat; reduce heat and simmer meat in its accumulated juices for 30 minutes. Uncover, increase heat to high, and boil until liquid evaporates and meat starts to sizzle in its own fat (about 10 minutes); stir frequently until meat is richly browned. Remove meat with a slotted spoon and set aside; pour off any fat from pan. Return meat to pan, add broth, mustard seeds, thyme, pepper, and bay leaf; stir to combine.

Lay potatoes, carrots, turnips, and onions on meat. Bring liquid to a boil; cover, reduce heat, and simmer until meat is very tender when pierced (about 30 minutes). Add beans and cook 5 more minutes.

With a slotted spoon, lift vegetables and meat from liquid and mound on an ovenproof platter. Cover loosely with foil and keep warm in a 150°F (66°C) oven.

Meanwhile, discard bay leaf from pan juices; add cream, mustard, and salt. Boil over high heat, stirring often, until sauce thickens slightly and is reduced to about 1¾ cups/420 ml (8 to 10 minutes). Spoon a little of the sauce over vegetables to give them a shiny glaze. Pour remaining sauce into a bowl and serve with the meat and vegetables.　*Makes 8 servings*

PER SERVING: *437 calories, 14 g total fat, 5 g saturated fat, 120 mg cholesterol, 575 mg sodium, 37 g carbohydrates, 6 g fiber, 39 g protein, 102 mg calcium, 5 mg iron*

Herbed Lamb Shanks

　　1　*tablespoon (15 ml) olive oil*

　　4　*lamb shanks (about 1 lb./455 g each), cracked*

　　2　*tablespoons all-purpose flour*

　　2　*large onions, sliced*

　　1　*large green bell pepper (about 6 oz./170 g), thinly sliced*

　　2　*cloves garlic, minced or pressed*

　　1　*cup (155 g) crushed canned tomatoes*

　½　*cup (120 ml) dry red wine or water*

　¾　*teaspoon dried savory*

　¾　*teaspoon dried thyme*

　¾　*teaspoon salt*

　¼　*teaspoon pepper*

Heat oil in a 5- to 6-quart (5- to 6-liter) pan over medium-high heat. Coat lamb shanks with flour, shaking off excess. Add shanks to pan two at a time, and cook over medium-high heat until browned on all sides. Transfer to a plate.

Add onions, bell pepper, and garlic to pan; cook, stirring often, until vegetables are lightly browned (about 5 minutes). Add tomatoes, wine, savory, thyme, salt, and pepper; bring to a boil. Add lamb shanks, reduce heat, and simmer, covered, until meat is very tender when pierced (about 2½ hours).

Transfer meat to a rimmed platter and keep warm. Skim and discard fat from pan juices. Serve meat with juices.　*Makes 4 servings*

PER SERVING: *718 calories, 37 g total fat, 14 g saturated fat, 241 mg cholesterol, 690 mg sodium, 19 g carbohydrates, 3 g fiber, 74 g protein, 88 mg calcium, 7 mg iron*

BRAISED LAMB WITH VEGETABLES

1 This recipe begins with "sweating" the meat in a heady mixture of red wine, Madeira, and soy sauce. As the lamb simmers, it releases its juices into the sauce. After 30 minutes, uncover pan so wine sauce can cook down; at this point, the lamb will begin to sizzle and brown in its own fat.

2 The vegetables are placed on top of the meat to steam rather than cook in the liquid. Keep the carrots, onions, potatoes, and turnips separate—they will be offered individually on the serving platter.

3 When the lamb and vegetables are done, use a slotted spoon to transfer them to a platter. Leave broth in pan; remove and discard bay leaf. Whisk in whipping cream, mustard, and salt, and boil over high heat until sauce is creamy and thick.

4 Arrange the lamb and vegetables individually on a large serving platter. Glaze the vegetables with a little of the sauce and some chopped parsley, if desired. Pour the remaining sauce into a gravy boat. Balance this rich fare by keeping the rest of the meal on the light side. Serve a crisp salad to start, and finish with fresh fruit or citrus sorbet.

LAMB *continued*

BROILING & GRILLING

Just about any cut of lamb—the butterflied leg, steaks, chops (from the shoulder, rib, and loin), boneless chunks, or ground meat patties—will grill or broil to perfection.

Before you cook the meat, trim the fat closely; melted fat dripping onto the hot coals can cause flare-ups and excessive smoke. Soy sauce–based marinades, dry rubs made from a mixture of herbs or spices, fillings (such as the mint pesto in the recipe at right), garlic-and-olive-oil basting sauces, and honey glazes are among the many choices for seasoning lamb that is to be grilled.

Lamb Chops with Honey-Lime Glaze

 3 tablespoons (45 ml) honey
 ½ teaspoon grated lime peel
 1 tablespoon (15 ml) lime juice
 1 teaspoon reduced-sodium soy sauce
 1 clove garlic, minced or pressed
 ½ teaspoon salt
 ¼ teaspoon ground ginger
 ¼ teaspoon pepper
 ⅛ teaspoon ground allspice
 4 large shoulder lamb chops (about 8 oz./230 g each), ¾ inch (2 cm) thick

In a small bowl, combine honey, lime peel, lime juice, soy sauce, garlic, salt, ginger, pepper, and allspice. Place chops in a 9- by 13-inch (23- by 33-cm) glass baking pan and spoon all but 2 tablespoons (30 ml) of the honey mixture over chops; turn to coat. Cover the pan and marinate for 30 minutes at room temperature or for up to 1 hour in the refrigerator.

Place chops on a broiler-pan rack and spread with half the reserved honey mixture. Broil about 6 inches (15 cm) below heat, turning once and spreading with remaining honey mixture, until done to taste; cut to test (about 10 minutes total for medium-rare).
Makes 4 servings

PER SERVING: *409 calories, 26 g total fat, 11 g saturated fat, 127 mg cholesterol, 348 mg sodium, 11 g carbohydrates, 0 g fiber, 32 g protein, 28 mg calcium, 3 mg iron*

Grilled Lamb Chops with Mint Pesto

 1 cup (40 g) fresh mint
 ½ cup (65 g) pine nuts
 ¼ cup (about ¾ oz./20 g) grated Parmesan cheese
 3 cloves garlic
 3 tablespoons (45 ml) olive oil
 12 lamb rib chops (about 2½ lbs./1.15 kg total), cut 1 inch (2.5 cm) thick
 Salt

To prepare mint pesto, in a blender or food processor, whirl mint, pine nuts, Parmesan cheese, garlic, and olive oil until smoothly puréed.

With a small, sharp knife, trim fat from chops. Cut a 3-inch (8-cm) slit through trimmed edge of each chop almost to bone to form a pocket (see page 83 for how to make a pocket). Fill pockets equally with pesto.

Place lamb on a grill above a solid bed of hot coals (you can hold your hand at grill level for only 2 to 3 seconds). Cook, turning to brown evenly, until done to taste; cut to test (7 to 10 minutes total for medium rare). Add salt to taste.
Makes 12 servings (¾ cup/180 ml pesto)

PER SERVING: *182 calories, 13 g total fat, 3 g saturated fat, 44 mg cholesterol, 72 mg sodium, 1 g carbohydrates, 0.7 g fiber, 15 g protein, 36 mg calcium, 2 mg iron*

Firing Up the Grill

When it comes to grills, the gas and electric types are easiest to start and clean, but many people still prefer to cook over a fire made with charcoal briquets. Allow 20 to 30 minutes to ignite the briquets. The coals are ready to use when spotted or coated with white ash. Spread the coals out in a solid, even layer over the bottom of the grill. At this point, you should determine the temperature and prepare for cooking: If you can hold the palm of your hand level over the coals at grill level for just 2 or 3 seconds, the fire is hot; for 4 to 5 seconds, the fire is medium; and for 6 to 7 seconds, the fire is low. The recipes in this book will specify the proper heat level.

VEAL

Because it comes from very young, milk-fed calves, veal is tender and lean, with very little internal fat marbling and external fat. Its delicacy demands special care in cooking.

For roasting, choose a shoulder or leg of veal; you can also use the loin, but it's usually more expensive. Chops and boneless veal (called "cutlets" or "scallops") are best when quickly cooked to be juicy and tender. Otherwise, slow, moist heat makes the most of this exquisitely flavored meat.

Wiener Schnitzel

- 8 veal cutlets (about 1½ lbs./680 g total), ⅓ inch (8 mm) thick
- ½ teaspoon salt
- ¼ teaspoon pepper
- ¼ cup (30 g) all-purpose flour
- 2 large eggs lightly beaten with 1 tablespoon (15 ml) water
- 1 cup (100 g) plain fine dry bread crumbs
- 4 tablespoons (60 ml) olive oil
- 1 lemon, cut into 8 wedges (optional)
  Parsley (optional)

Place cutlets between sheets of plastic wrap and gently pound with flat side of a mallet to ¼ inch (6 mm) thick. Sprinkle veal with salt and pepper; set aside.

Place flour, egg mixture, and bread crumbs in three separate pie pans. Coat cutlets with flour (shaking off excess); dip in egg mixture, then in bread crumbs, shaking off excess. Place cutlets on a flat surface and, with your hands, press in crumbs.

Heat 1 tablespoon (15 ml) of the oil for each 2 cutlets in a wide nonstick frying pan over medium-high heat until hot but not smoking. Add 2 cutlets at a time and cook until golden brown on both sides (about 1 minute per side). Drain briefly on paper towels; arrange on a platter and keep warm. Repeat with remaining oil and cutlets until all cutlets are cooked. Garnish with lemon and parsley, if desired. Serve immediately.   *Makes 4 servings*

PER SERVING: *474 calories, 21 g total fat, 4 g saturated fat, 239 mg cholesterol, 647 mg sodium, 26 g carbohydrates, 1 g fiber, 44 g protein, 86 mg calcium, 4 mg iron*

Veal Piccata

- ¼ cup (30 g) all-purpose flour
- ¾ teaspoon salt
- ¼ teaspoon pepper
- 8 veal cutlets (about 1½ lbs./680 g total), ⅓ inch (8 mm) thick
- 4 tablespoons (60 ml) olive oil
- ⅔ cup (160 ml) dry white wine
- 2 tablespoons (30 ml) lemon juice
- 2 tablespoons chopped parsley
- 1 teaspoon grated lemon peel
- 2 tablespoons butter or margarine
  Lemon slices

Place cutlets between sheets of plastic wrap and gently pound with a mallet to ¼ inch (6 mm) thick.

In a pie pan, mix flour, salt, and pepper. Coat meat with flour mixture.

Heat 1 tablespoon (15 ml) of the oil for each 2 cutlets in a wide nonstick frying pan over medium-high heat until hot but not smoking. Add 2 cutlets at a time and cook until browned on both sides (about 1 minute per side). Drain briefly on paper towels; arrange on a platter and keep warm. Repeat with remaining oil and cutlets until all cutlets are cooked.

Add wine and lemon juice to pan; bring to a boil. Remove pan from heat and stir in parsley and lemon peel. Swirl in butter until melted. Spoon sauce over veal and garnish with lemon slices.
Makes 4 servings

PER SERVING: *411 calories, 22 g total fat, 6 g saturated fat, 148 mg cholesterol, 584 mg sodium, 7 g carbohydrates, 0.3 g fiber, 37 g protein, 22 mg calcium, 2 mg iron*

Veal Piccata with Mushrooms

Cook veal as in *Veal Piccata* recipe. When all veal is cooked, add about 8 ounces (230 g) sliced *mushrooms* (see page 132 for mushroom ideas) to pan. Cook, stirring frequently, until mushrooms are soft (about 4 minutes), then continue with recipe.

Using a Steel

With a bit of care, a good knife can last a lifetime—and is useful as long as you keep it properly sharpened. And sharp knives are safer; dull ones are more likely to slip and cut you.

A steel doesn't actually sharpen a knife; what it does is reset the blade edge, remove and smooth out minuscule burrs, and realign the almost invisible teeth that form the cutting edge. (Serrated knives, with their big teeth, never need resetting.)

For safety, choose a steel that has a handle guard to protect your fingers. To use the steel, hold it in front of you; then position the heel of the knife at the top of the steel, with the cutting edge at about a 20-degree angle to the steel. With your wrist relaxed, draw the blade from heel to tip toward you across the steel (see Illustration 1). Use light pressure and keep the 20-degree angle constant; if you press too hard or let the knife veer to a wider angle, you may nick its edge.

Reset the other side of the knife blade on the underside of the steel. Using the same angle, gently glide the knife, from tip to heel, away from you (see Illustration 2). You'll probably need to make a total of only 10 to 12 strokes, alternating from side to side. Then carefully wipe the steel and blade clean.

Use the steel often, especially before any significant amount of cutting or carving.

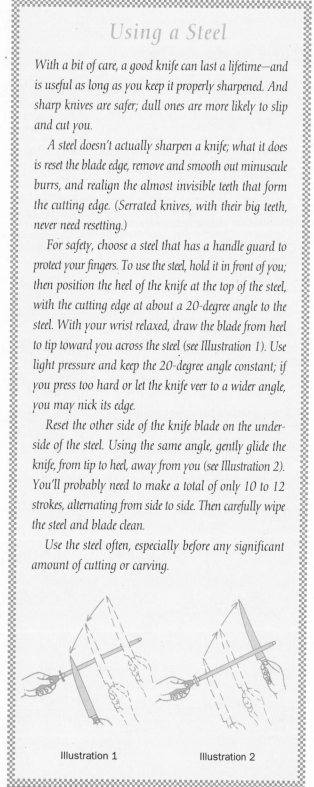

Illustration 1   Illustration 2

Veal Chops with Rich Cream Sauce

4   rib or loin veal chops (about 8 oz./230 g each), ½ to ¾ inch (1 to 2 cm) thick
¾   teaspoon ground sage
¼   teaspoon salt
¼   teaspoon pepper
4   tablespoons (2 oz./55 g) butter or margarine
1   tablespoon (15 ml) olive oil
¼   cup (60 ml) reduced-sodium chicken broth
¼   cup (60 ml) dry vermouth
1   tablespoon (15 ml) whipping cream
1   tablespoon chopped parsley (optional)

Sprinkle chops with ¼ teaspoon of the sage and the salt and pepper. Melt 1 tablespoon of the butter with the oil in a wide nonstick frying pan over high heat until hot and bubbly. Add chops and cook until browned on outside and still slightly pink on the inside; cut to test (2 to 3 minutes per side). Arrange chops on a platter and keep warm. Discard fat from pan.

Add broth, vermouth, and remaining ½ teaspoon sage to pan and boil over high heat, scraping browned particles free from pan, until reduced to 2 to 3 tablespoons (30 to 45 ml) and slightly thickened. Reduce heat to medium-low. Whisk in cream, any veal juices that have collected on platter, and parsley. Whisk in remaining 3 tablespoons butter. Spoon sauce over chops.   *Makes 4 servings*

PER SERVING: *411 calories, 30 g total fat, 14 g saturated fat, 164 mg cholesterol, 386 mg sodium, 0.9 g carbohydrates, 0 g fiber, 29 g protein, 23 mg calcium, 1 mg iron*

Baked Veal Shanks with Risotto

- 2 tablespoons butter or margarine
- 6 meaty veal shanks (about 4 lbs./1.8 kg total), 2 inches (5 cm) thick
- 1 cup (240 ml) dry white wine
- 4 cups (950 ml) reduced-sodium chicken broth
- 2 tablespoons grated lemon peel
- 1 teaspoon dried oregano
- 1 teaspoon dried thyme
- 2 cups (400 g) arborio rice or short-grain white rice
  About 2 cups (470 ml) boiling water
- ¼ cup (15 g) minced parsley
- 2 cloves garlic, minced or pressed
- ¼ cup (about ¾ oz./20 g) grated Parmesan cheese

Heat butter in an 11- by 17-inch (28- to 43-cm) baking pan in a 475°F (245°C) oven until melted and sizzling (about 2 minutes). Place veal shanks in a single layer in pan. Bake, uncovered, for 30 minutes; turn shanks over and continue to bake until meat is well browned (about 10 more minutes).

Remove pan from oven and reduce temperature to 375°F (190°C). Add wine to pan and stir to scrape browned particles free from pan. Add broth, 1 tablespoon of the lemon peel, the oregano, and thyme; stir again. Cover pan tightly with foil and bake until meat is tender enough to pull apart easily (about 1½ hours).

Uncover pan; stir rice and water into pan juices. Bake, uncovered, stirring rice and veal shanks occasionally, until liquid is absorbed and rice is tender to bite (about 25 minutes). If rice begins to dry out before it is done, add more water, about ¼ cup (120 ml) at a time.

In a small bowl, combine parsley, garlic, and remaining 1 tablespoon lemon peel; set aside. Remove veal from pan; keep warm. Stir Parmesan cheese into rice, then spoon rice onto 6 plates. Top each serving with a veal shank. Sprinkle veal with parsley mixture. *Makes 6 servings*

Per serving: 432 calories, 9 g total fat, 4 g saturated fat, 96 mg cholesterol, 545 mg sodium, 54 g carbohydrates, 0.8 g fiber, 30 g protein, 74 mg calcium, 4 mg iron

Veal Stew with Artichokes

- 2 pounds (905 g) boneless veal shoulder, cut into 1-inch (2.5-cm) cubes
- ¼ cup (30 g) all-purpose flour
- 2 tablespoons (30 ml) olive oil or vegetable oil
- 1 large onion, chopped
- 2 cloves garlic, minced or pressed
- 2 cups (270 ml) reduced-sodium chicken broth
- ½ cup (120 ml) dry white wine
- 1 teaspoon salt
- ¾ teaspoon dried rosemary or 1 tablespoon chopped fresh rosemary
- 1 package (9 oz./255 g) frozen artichoke hearts, thawed
- ¼ cup (60 ml) whipping cream
  About 3 cups (11 oz./310 g) hot cooked buttered noodles
  Grated Parmesan cheese

Trim and discard any fat or tough membrane from meat. Coat veal with flour, shaking off excess. Heat 2 teaspoons of the oil in a 5- to 6-quart (5- to 6-liter) nonstick pan over medium-high heat until hot but not smoking. Add one third of the veal to pan, and cook until well browned on all sides; lift out with a slotted spoon and set aside. Repeat, in batches, with remaining oil and veal.

Add onion and garlic to pan and cook, stirring, over medium-low heat until onion is soft (about 5 minutes). Stir in broth, wine, salt, and rosemary; bring to a boil. Reduce heat, return veal to pan, and simmer, covered, until veal is tender when pierced (about 45 minutes).

Add artichokes and cook, covered, until artichokes are tender when pierced (about 5 minutes). Stir in cream. Increase heat to high and cook, uncovered, stirring, until sauce is slightly thickened (about 4 minutes).

To serve, spoon stew over noodles and offer Parmesan cheese at the table. *Makes 6 servings*

Per serving: 453 calories, 20 g total fat, 8 g saturated fat, 177 mg cholesterol, 742 mg sodium, 31 g carbohydrates, 5 g fiber, 36 g protein, 74 mg calcium, 3 mg iron

PASTA

Pasta has so much to recommend it: This inexpensive, lowfat source of complex carbohydrates cooks quickly; its neutral flavor lets you combine it with all sorts of foods and flavorings; and, of course, almost everybody loves it. Our recipes showcase various pastas, along with an appealing selection of classic and innovative sauces, toppings, and stuffings.

One of the best things about pasta is that it comes in hundreds of different shapes and sizes (and several colors, too). Don't feel bound by old-fashioned rules about matching pastas and sauces: Just take a look at the pasta photo on page 100 and you'll realize that you can put a new twist on just about any pasta dish by simply switching to another pasta shape. Still, there are reasons for traditional sauce partnerships: Angel hair pasta calls for a light, brothy sauce, while thicker strands, such as spaghetti, require smooth, clingy sauces; tubes, twists, and cuplike shapes are ideal for catching and holding the bits in chunky sauces and casserole fillings. And the flat surfaces of ribbon-shaped pastas, such as fettuccine, provide the perfect backdrop for thick, creamy sauces.

How to cook pasta

The cooking times for pasta depend on whether it's dried or fresh, and on its size and shape, but the doneness test is the same for all: It should be al dente, an Italian term meaning "to the tooth," or tender yet firm to the bite, with no hard, white core at the center. That's how pasta tastes best.

No matter how much pasta you plan to cook, use a large pot and a generous amount of water to keep the pasta from sticking together. You don't need to salt the water.

Bring the water to a rolling boil. Add short pasta all at once and long pasta in two or three batches, pushing the first strands down to submerge them before adding the next; stir the pasta to prevent clumping. Begin timing and return the water to a boil. Cook the pasta, uncovered, according to the recipe or package directions. As soon as the pasta is done, drain it in a colander and serve. It's not necessary to rinse pasta after cooking unless you're using it in a salad or need to cool lasagne noodles so you can handle them.

To estimate pasta quantities, use this basic guideline: 2 ounces (55 g) dried pasta will make about 1 cup (85 g) cooked pasta.

One-Hour Lasagne

8 ounces (230 g) lasagne

12 ounces (340 g) mild or hot Italian sausages, casings removed

1 tablespoon (15 ml) balsamic vinegar

½ teaspoon fennel seeds

1 jar (28 to 32 oz./830 to 950 ml) prepared pasta sauce, such as marinara

1 package (10 oz./285 g) frozen chopped spinach, thawed and squeezed dry

1 carton (15 oz./428 g) lowfat ricotta cheese

⅛ teaspoon ground nutmeg

2 cups (about 8 oz./230 g) shredded mozzarella cheese

½ cup (about 1½ oz./40 g) grated Parmesan cheese

In a 5- to 6-quart (5- to 6-liter) pan, bring about 4 quarts (3.8 liters) water to a boil over high heat; stir in lasagne and cook until just tender to bite (8 to 10 minutes); or cook according to package directions. Drain, immerse in cold water, and drain again.

Chop or crumble sausages. Cook in a wide non-stick frying pan over medium-high heat, stirring often, until tinged with brown (about 10 minutes). Drain and discard all but 1 tablespoon (15 ml) of the drippings. Add vinegar and fennel seeds to pan. Stir over high heat just until mixture is hot (about 30 seconds). Remove pan from heat and stir in pasta sauce.

In a medium-size bowl, mix spinach with ricotta cheese and nutmeg; set aside.

In a 9- by 13-inch (23- by 33-cm) baking pan at least 1¾ inches (4.5 cm) deep, layer one third of the sauce, half the pasta, half the ricotta mixture, half the mozzarella, and one third of the Parmesan cheese. Repeat layers, ending with sauce and Parmesan cheese.

Bake, uncovered, in a 375°F (190°C) oven until pasta is hot in the center (30 to 35 minutes).

Let cool for 10 minutes. Cut portions and lift out with a spatula.   *Makes 8 servings*

PER SERVING: *453 calories, 23 g total fat, 10 g saturated fat, 64 mg cholesterol, 1,238 mg sodium, 37 g carbohydrates, 1 g fiber, 24 g protein, 374 mg calcium, 3 mg iron*

Vegetable Lasagne

8 ounces (230 g) lasagne

4 large carrots, cut into slices ¼ inch (6 mm) thick

3 large zucchini (about 1 lb./455 g total), cut into slices ¼ inch (6 mm) thick

2 tablespoons (30 ml) olive oil or vegetable oil

1 medium-size onion, finely chopped

8 ounces (230 g) mushrooms, thinly sliced

1 teaspoon dried basil

1 teaspoon dried oregano

1 teaspoon dried thyme

1 jar (32 oz./950 ml) marinara sauce

2 packages (10 oz./285 g each) frozen chopped spinach, thawed and squeezed dry

8 ounces (230 g) lowfat ricotta cheese

3 cups (about 12 oz./340 g) shredded mozzarella cheese

¼ cup (about ¾ oz./20 g) grated Parmesan cheese

In a 5- to 6-quart (5- to 6-liter) pan, bring about 4 quarts (3.8 liters) water to a boil over high heat. Stir in lasagne and carrots; cook for 6 minutes. Stir in zucchini; continue to cook just until lasagne is tender to bite (4 to 5 more minutes). Drain well; set lasagne and vegetables aside separately.

In same pan, heat oil over high heat; add onion, mushrooms, basil, oregano, and thyme. Cook, stirring often, until onion is soft and all liquid has evaporated (5 to 8 minutes). Remove pan from heat, stir in marinara sauce, and set aside.

In a medium-size bowl, combine spinach and ricotta cheese; set aside.

Spread one third of the sauce in a shallow 2½- to 3-quart (2.4- to 2.8-liter) baking pan. Arrange half the lasagne over sauce. Add half each of the blanched carrots and zucchini, the spinach mixture, and mozzarella cheese. Repeat layers, ending with sauce and Parmesan cheese.

Bake, uncovered, in a 400°F (205°C) oven until hot in center (about 25 minutes). Let stand for about 10 minutes before serving.   *Makes 6 servings*

PER SERVING: *578 calories, 26 g total fat, 11 g saturated fat, 56 mg cholesterol, 1,359 mg sodium, 64 g carbohydrates, 6 g fiber, 28 g protein, 590 mg calcium, 6 mg iron*

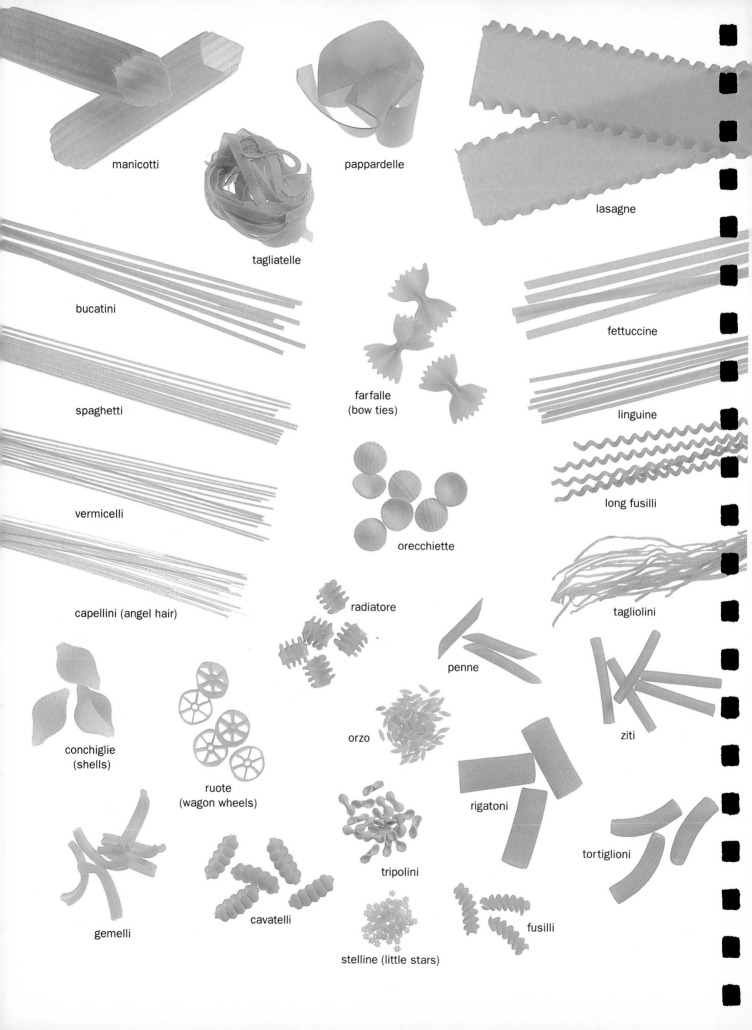

manicotti

pappardelle

lasagne

tagliatelle

bucatini

fettuccine

spaghetti

farfalle
(bow ties)

linguine

vermicelli

long fusilli

orecchiette

capellini (angel hair)

radiatore

tagliolini

penne

conchiglie
(shells)

orzo

ziti

ruote
(wagon wheels)

rigatoni

gemelli

tripolini

tortiglioni

cavatelli

fusilli

stelline (little stars)

Orzo with Shrimp, Feta & Artichoke Hearts

¾ cup (180 ml) reduced-sodium chicken broth

¼ cup (60 ml) dry white wine

1 tablespoon finely shredded lemon peel

8 ounces (230 g) orzo pasta

1 cup (150 g) frozen tiny peas

1 jar (6 oz./170 g) quartered marinated artichoke hearts, drained and thinly sliced

8 ounces (230 g) shelled cooked medium-size shrimp

½ cup (about 2¼ oz./63 g) feta cheese, crumbled

In a 5- to 6-quart (5- to 6-liter) pan, bring about 4 quarts (3.8 liters) water to a boil over high heat. Meanwhile, in a 2- to 3-quart (1.9- to 2.8-liter) pan, combine broth, wine, and lemon peel. Cover; bring to a boil over high heat. Remove from heat; keep warm.

Stir pasta into boiling water and cook until just tender to bite (about 5 minutes); or cook according to package directions. About 1 minute before pasta is done, add peas; drain pasta and peas well.

Mix pasta and peas with broth mixture, artichokes, shrimp, and all but 2 tablespoons of the feta. Transfer to a serving bowl or 4 individual plates. Sprinkle with remaining feta. *Makes 4 servings*

PER SERVING: *399 calories, 9 g total fat, 3 g saturated fat, 126 mg cholesterol, 707 mg sodium, 52 g carbohydrates, 6 g fiber, 25 g protein, 137 mg calcium, 5 mg iron*

Pesto for Pasta

2 cups (80 g) lightly packed fresh basil

1 cup (about 3 oz./80 g) grated Parmesan cheese

½ to ⅔ cup (120 to 160 ml) olive oil

1 or 2 cloves garlic (optional)

Hot cooked pasta (see box at right)

Butter or margarine (optional, see box at right)

In a blender or food processor, whirl basil, cheese, ½ cup (120 ml) of the oil, and garlic, if using, until smoothly puréed; add more oil, if needed. *Makes about 1½ cups (360 ml)*

PER TABLESPOON: *75 calories, 7 g total fat, 2 g saturated fat, 5 mg cholesterol, 110 mg sodium, 0.4 g carbohydrates, 0.1 g fiber, 3 g protein, 86 mg calcium, 0.2 mg iron*

Cilantro Pesto

Follow directions for *Pesto for Pasta*, but omit basil; instead, use 2 cups (80 g) firmly packed *cilantro*. Decrease cheese to ½ cup (40 g), decrease oil to ¼ cup (60 ml), and use only 1 clove garlic. Add ¼ cup (30 g) *pine nuts* (toasted, if desired) and 1 teaspoon grated *lime peel*.   *Makes about ¾ cup (180 ml)*

Spinach-Herb Pesto

Follow directions for *Pesto for Pasta*, but omit basil; instead use 1½ cups (43 g) lightly packed *spinach leaves* and ¼ cup (10 g) lightly packed *fresh tarragon*, thyme, marjoram, or oregano. Decrease cheese to ½ cup (40 g).   *Makes about 1 cup (240 ml)*

Dried Tomato Pesto

Follow directions for *Pesto for Pasta*, but add ¼ cup (41 g) chopped, drained *dried tomatoes* packed in oil. Decrease *cheese* to ½ cup (40 g). Use 2 cloves *garlic*. *Makes about 1¼ cups (300 ml)*

Pasta for Pesto & Other Pesto Tips

• *To serve any of these pesto sauces with pasta, add about ½ cup (120 ml) of the pesto and ¼ cup (55 g) olive oil, butter, or margarine (at room temperature), if desired, to 4 cups (397 g) hot cooked fettuccine, spaghetti, linguine, or similar pasta. Mix well with 2 forks; serve with grated Parmesan cheese and additional pesto to add to taste.*

• *To toast whole pine nuts, cook, stirring frequently, in a small, dry frying pan over medium-low heat until lightly browned (3 to 6 minutes). Immediately tip toasted nuts out of hot pan so that they do not burn.*

• *To store pesto, refrigerate or freeze it. It will darken slightly as it stands; covering the pesto with a thin layer of oil will help preserve the color.*

◄ *A Variety of Pastas*

LOWFAT SPAGHETTI & MEATBALLS

1 For the freshest, leanest ground beef, chop well-trimmed top round in a food processor. Process for only about 30 seconds—just until coarsely ground.

2 Add drained bulgur to seasoned ground beef and mix well. Bulgur bulks up meatballs without adding fat, and helps keep them moist.

3 Use about ¼ cup (55 g) beef mixture for each meatball. Shape meatballs with a gentle touch; squeezing or compressing mixture will make meatballs hard.

4 Combine mushrooms, garlic, basil, red pepper flakes, and water, and cook over high heat, stirring often. When liquid has evaporated, mushrooms will begin to brown.

5 After 10 minutes of simmering, the tomato sauce will be flavorful and fragrant. Add meatballs, one at a time, being careful not to splatter hot sauce; simmer for 5 minutes longer.

6 Serve generous portions of spaghetti, meatballs, and sauce with a clear conscience: Even with three good-sized meatballs, each irresistible serving has just 5 grams of fat.

Lowfat Spaghetti & Meatballs

PICTURED ON FACING PAGE

¾ cup (131 g) bulgur (cracked wheat)

1½ cups (360 ml) boiling water

12 ounces (340 g) beef top round, fat trimmed, or 12 ounces (340 g) ground beef with 15% or less fat

1 large onion, chopped

4 cloves garlic, minced or pressed

1 teaspoon dried oregano

½ teaspoon salt

¼ teaspoon pepper

8 ounces (230 g) mushrooms, sliced

1 tablespoon dried basil

¾ teaspoon crushed red pepper flakes

¼ cup (60 ml) water

About 1¼ cups (300 ml) reduced-sodium beef broth

1 can (28 oz./795 g) crushed tomatoes

1½ pounds (680 g) spaghetti

Chopped parsley

Grated Parmesan cheese

In a large bowl, mix bulgur with boiling water. Let stand until grains are tender to bite (10 to 15 minutes).

Meanwhile, cut beef into ½-inch (1-cm) cubes. Place cubes in a food processor and whirl until coarsely ground. Transfer ground beef to a large bowl. Add onion, half the minced garlic, the oregano, salt, and pepper.

Drain bulgur. Add bulgur to meat mixture; mix well and shape into 15 meatballs, using about ¼ cup (55 g) mixture for each. Space meatballs apart in a lightly oiled 10- by 15-inch (25- by 38-cm) rimmed baking pan. Bake in a 425°F (220°C) oven until meatballs are well browned (25 to 30 minutes).

Meanwhile, in a 3- to 4-quart (2.8- to 3.8-liter) pan, combine mushrooms, remaining garlic, the basil, red pepper flakes, and the ¼ cup (60 ml) water. Cook over high heat, stirring often, until juices evaporate and vegetables begin to brown (about 10 minutes).

Add ¼ cup (60 ml) of the broth to pan, stirring to scrape browned particles from pan. Stir often until liquid evaporates and mushrooms begin to brown again. Repeat this once or twice more, using ¼ cup (60 ml) broth each time, until mushrooms are well browned. Add tomatoes and reduce heat; cover, and simmer for 10 minutes. Add meatballs; cover and simmer for about 5 minutes. (If sauce sticks, stir in a little more broth.)

While mushrooms are browning, in a 5- to 6-quart (5- to 6-liter) pan, bring about 4 quarts (3.8 liters) water to a boil over high heat. Stir in spaghetti and cook until just tender to bite (7 to 10 minutes); or cook according to package directions. Drain.

In same pan, bring ⅓ cup (80 ml) of the broth to a boil; add pasta and mix to coat. Pour pasta into individual bowls; top with meatballs, sauce, and parsley. Add Parmesan cheese to taste.   *Makes 5 servings*

PER SERVING: *736 calories, 5 g total fat, 1 g saturated fat, 39 mg cholesterol, 687 mg sodium, 133 g carbohydrates, 10 g fiber, 40 g protein, 117 mg calcium, 9 mg iron*

Marinara Spaghetti

2 tablespoons (30 ml) olive oil or vegetable oil

1 large onion, finely chopped

1 large carrot, finely chopped

2 cloves garlic, minced or pressed

1 can (28 oz./795 g) tomatoes, coarsely chopped, liquid reserved

1 can (1 lb./455 g) tomato purée

¼ cup (60 ml) dry red wine

1¼ teaspoons salt

1 teaspoon pepper

1 teaspoon dried basil

1 teaspoon dried oregano

1 teaspoon sugar

1 bay leaf

1½ pounds (680 g) spaghetti

½ cup (about 1½ oz./40 g) grated Parmesan cheese

Heat oil in a 6- to 8-quart (6- to 8-liter) nonstick pan over medium heat. Add onion, carrot, and garlic; cook until vegetables are tender (8 to 9 minutes). Add tomatoes and their liquid, tomato purée, wine, salt, pepper, basil, oregano, sugar, and bay leaf. Reduce heat; cover and simmer until richly flavored (about 45 minutes). Remove bay leaf.

In a 5- to 6-quart (5- to 6-liter) pan, bring about 4 quarts (3.8 liters) water to a boil over high heat. Stir in pasta and cook until just tender to bite (about 12 minutes); or cook according to package directions. Drain. Transfer pasta to individual serving bowls; ladle some sauce over each serving and sprinkle with Parmesan cheese.   *Makes 8 servings*

PER SERVING: *434 calories, 7 g total fat, 2 g saturated fat, 4 mg cholesterol, 836 mg sodium, 79 g carbohydrates, 5 g fiber, 15 g protein, 141 mg calcium, 5 mg iron*

Ham-Stuffed Manicotti

8 ounces (230 g) manicotti shells

2 cups (about 6 oz./160 g) shredded Parmesan cheese

1 carton (15 oz./428 g) lowfat ricotta cheese

8 ounces (230 g) cooked ham, cut into ½-inch (1-cm) cubes

½ cup (3 oz./85 g) diced red bell pepper

1 large egg

¼ cup (25 g) fine dry seasoned bread crumbs

2 cups (16 oz./470 ml) prepared pasta sauce

1 cup (about 4 oz./113 g) shredded mozzarella

In a 5- to 6-quart (5- to 6-liter) pan, bring about 4 quarts (3.8 liters) of water to a boil over high heat. Stir in manicotti shells and cook until just tender to bite (about 12 minutes); or cook according to package directions. Drain and rinse with cold water.

Meanwhile, in a large bowl, combine half the Parmesan cheese with the ricotta, ham, bell pepper, egg, and bread crumbs.

Fill each of 12 cooled manicotti shells (you will have more, but a couple may break) equally with the cheese-ham mixture. Lay filled manicotti in a lightly oiled 9- by 13-inch (23- by 33-cm) baking pan. Cover stuffed manicotti with sauce, mozzarella, and remaining Parmesan.

Bake in a 350°F (175°C) oven until sauce is hot and bubbling (about 45 minutes); cool 10 minutes before serving. *Makes 6 servings*

PER SERVING: *576 calories, 24 g total fat, 12 g saturated fat, 110 mg cholesterol, 1,685 mg sodium, 52 g carbohydrates, 1 g fiber, 35 g protein, 621 mg calcium, 3 mg iron*

Penne with Sausage, Roasted Peppers & Greens

8 ounces (230 g) turkey Italian sausage, casings removed

1 medium-size onion, chopped

3 cloves garlic, minced

12 ounces (340 g) penne

1 can (15 oz./425 g) no-salt-added tomato sauce

½ cup (120 ml) dry red wine

1 jar (7¼ oz./208 g) peeled roasted red peppers, drained and cut into thin strips

3 cups (about 3 oz./85 g total) thinly sliced mustard greens

¼ cup (about ¾ oz./20 g) shredded Parmesan cheese

In a 5- to 6-quart (5- to 6-liter) pan, bring 4 quarts (3.8 liters) water to a boil over high heat.

Meanwhile, chop or crumble sausage and place in a 3- to 4-quart (2.8- to 3.8-liter) pan. Add onion and garlic; cook over medium-high heat, stirring often, until sausage is browned (about 10 minutes).

Stir pasta into boiling water and cook until just tender to bite (about 8 minutes); or cook according to package directions.

While pasta cooks, add tomato sauce, wine, and peppers to sausage mixture; cook over high heat, stirring often. Stir in mustard greens and all but 1 tablespoon of the Parmesan cheese.

Drain pasta, then mix with tomato sauce mixture. Transfer to a serving bowl or to 4 individual plates. Sprinkle with remaining cheese. *Makes 4 servings*

PER SERVING: *540 calories, 10 g total fat, 3 g saturated fat, 34 mg cholesterol, 616 mg sodium, 84 g carbohydrates, 5 g fiber, 26 g protein, 156 mg calcium, 7 mg iron*

Parmesan Cheese

If you love Italian food, Italian Parmesan—the real thing—makes the ideal finishing touch for your pasta dishes. Parmesan imported from the area where this cheese originated has the words "Parmigiano-Reggiano" stamped on the rind—it's considered the best you can buy. Unlike domestic Parmesan, which is aged for 14 months or less, Parmigiano-Reggiano is usually aged for two years, producing a complex, sharp-sweet flavor and a granular texture perfect for grating.

It takes only a moment to grate or shred a chunk of Parmesan in a food processor. When the cheese is freshly grated or shredded, its flavor is at its peak. And cheese that's just been grated or shredded melts more easily as well.

You may have to visit your supermarket deli counter (or a gourmet shop) to get Parmigiano-Reggiano. It's relatively expensive, but a little goes a long way. And you'll taste a world of difference with every bite.

Angel Hair Pasta & Vegetables

2 cups (470 ml) reduced-sodium vegetable broth or chicken broth

½ cup (1¼ oz./38 g) dried tomatoes (not packed in oil), minced

¼ teaspoon crushed red pepper flakes (optional)

1 pound (455 g) carrots, thinly sliced

1 cup (150 g) frozen pearl onions

12 ounces (340 g) angel hair (capellini) pasta

12 ounces (340 g) broccoli flowerets

3 tablespoons drained capers

¼ cup (about ¾ oz./20 g) shredded Parmesan cheese

In a 5- to 6-quart (5- to 6-liter) pan, bring about 4 quarts (3.8 liters) water to a boil over high heat.

Meanwhile, in a 1- to 2-quart (950-ml to 1.9-liter) pan, bring broth, tomatoes, and red pepper flakes to a boil over high heat; reduce heat to low and keep warm.

Add carrots and onions to boiling water in large pan. Cook until onions are thawed and carrots are just tender when pierced (about 6 minutes).

Without removing carrots or onions, stir pasta into boiling water. Cook until pasta is just tender to bite (1 to 3 minutes); or according to package directions. After pasta has cooked for 1 minute, add broccoli. Drain pasta and vegetables in a colander, then mix with broth-tomato mixture. Add capers and Parmesan cheese.   *Makes 4 servings*

PER SERVING: *472 calories, 4 g total fat, 1 g saturated fat, 4 mg cholesterol, 596 mg sodium, 91 g carbohydrates, 10 g fiber, 20 g protein, 169 mg calcium, 5 mg iron*

Macaroni & Cheese

3 tablespoons plus 1 teaspoon butter or margarine

1 small onion, finely chopped

3 tablespoons all-purpose flour

2 cups (470 ml) 2% milk

2½ cups (about 10 oz./285 g) shredded extra-sharp Cheddar cheese

1 teaspoon Dijon mustard

½ teaspoon salt

¼ teaspoon white pepper

¼ teaspoon Worcestershire

8 ounces (230 g) elbow macaroni, rotelle, shells, rigatoni, or bow ties

In a 3- to 4-quart (2.8- to 3.8-liter) pan, melt 3 tablespoons of the butter over medium heat. Add onion and cook, stirring, until soft (about 3 minutes). Stir in flour and cook until bubbly. Remove pan from heat and stir in milk. Return pan to medium heat and cook, stirring, until sauce is smooth and thickened (about 8 minutes). Remove pan from heat and stir in 2 cups (about 8 oz./230 g) of the Cheddar cheese, the mustard, salt, pepper, and Worcestershire. Cook, stirring, until cheese melts (about 1 minute). Remove from heat.

Meanwhile, in a 5- to 6-quart (5- to 6-liter) pan, bring about 4 quarts (3.8 liters) water to a boil over high heat. Stir in pasta and cook until just tender to bite (about 5 minutes); or cook according to package directions. Drain and add to cheese sauce.

Coat a shallow 2½ to 3-quart (2.4- to 2.8-liter) baking dish with the remaining 1 teaspoon butter. Spoon macaroni mixture into pan and sprinkle with remaining ½ cup (about 2 oz./55 g) Cheddar cheese.

Bake, uncovered, in a 350°F (175°C) oven until cheese is bubbly and center of casserole is hot (about 30 minutes).   *Makes 6 servings*

PER SERVING: *450 calories, 24 g total fat, 15 g saturated fat, 73 mg cholesterol, 607 mg sodium, 37 g carbohydrates, 1 g fiber, 20 g protein, 454 mg calcium, 2 mg iron*

EGGS

Keep a supply of eggs on hand, and a tasty lunch or dinner is just moments away. Eggs are the key to an astonishing variety of satisfying, quick-to-prepare dishes, from rustic frittatas to elegant soufflés.

As you shop for this useful ingredient, choose only the freshest refrigerated eggs (check the date on the carton) and open the carton to check that the shells are clean and uncracked. The quality and soundness of the eggs are indicated by their grade. The most widely available eggs are Grade AA and A. Eggs are also sold by size—jumbo, extra-large, large, medium, and small. *All recipes in this book use large eggs.*

Generally speaking, eggs maintain good quality for as long as a month if stored in the refrigerator, but are in their prime for about the first week. The yolk of a very fresh egg is plump and sits up higher than the surrounding white, which is thick and dense. Freshness matters most when you're frying or poaching—or separating the eggs (the yolks of fresh eggs are less likely to break). Save slightly less fresh eggs for hard-cooking or scrambling, or use them for baking.

Safe storing & savvy cooking

Eggs can pick up off flavors right through their shells, so they should be stored in the carton (not in the refrigerator door) and kept away from strong-flavored foods such as fish. Turn the eggs broad end up; they'll keep better, and the yolks will remain more centered.

Eggs are delicate; even slight shifts of temperature can affect them appreciably in cooking. While eggs separate more easily when cold, those at room temperature will cook more evenly and the egg whites will beat up to a greater volume. If necessary, you can bring refrigerated eggs to room temperature quickly by covering them for a minute or two with hot tap water.

When you cook eggs, always use medium heat. The proteins begin to set at temperatures as low as 144°F (62°C); high heat and overcooking will toughen or curdle eggs.

Raw eggs may, on occasion, contain salmonella bacteria, which can cause a potentially life-threatening illness. For safety's sake, do not leave eggs or uncooked egg mixtures at room temperature for more than 2 hours, and avoid tasting uncooked mixtures containing eggs. Cooking eggs at 140°F (60°C) for 3½ minutes will kill salmonella.

SOFT-COOKED & HARD-COOKED EGGS

Though the expression "hard-boiled eggs" is familiar to us all, in fact you should never boil eggs, unless you are heat-treating them for a few seconds before poaching (see page 109). If you do boil them for any length of time, you court such mishaps as cracked shells and rubbery whites. Keep in mind that eggs are delicate and will cook at a gentle simmer.

To cook eggs in their shells: Place the eggs in a single layer in a pan without crowding and add cold water to cover the eggs by 1 inch (2.5 cm). Place the pan, uncovered, over high heat and bring the water to 200°F (95°C), or just under a full, rolling boil.

For soft-cooked eggs: If the simmering temperature noted above is reached in 8 to 11 minutes, the egg will have a soft, hot yolk, a surrounding clear, thin layer of white, and firm white against the shell; it should be served at once. As you increase the cooking time, the egg will firm a little more with each additional minute. Experiment with the timing until you achieve just the right consistency.

For hard-cooked eggs: When the water shows the first signs of a rolling boil, reduce the heat so that only an occasional bubble on the pan bottom glides upward. Cook the eggs, keeping the water barely bubbling like this, for 12 minutes, then plunge the eggs into cold water to stop the cooking. If you don't plan to use the cooled hard-cooked eggs right away, store them in the refrigerator.

To shell a hard-cooked egg: Tap the egg gently all over on a flat surface or with the back of a spoon. Under cold running water, roll the egg between the palms of your hands to loosen and peel off the shell.

SCRAMBLED EGGS

For tender, velvety-textured scrambled eggs, mix a little liquid into the eggs before cooking.

Break *eggs* into a bowl. Add 1 teaspoon to 1 tablespoon (15 ml) *milk, cream,* or *water* for each egg, plus a dash of *salt*. Beat with a fork until thoroughly blended but not frothy. Heat *fat* (1 teaspoon butter, margarine, vegetable oil, or bacon fat per egg) in a medium-size or wide nonstick frying pan over medium-low heat. Use an 8-inch (20-cm) pan for 2 to 4 eggs, a 10- or 12-inch (25- or 30-cm) pan for a larger quantity (but no more than 1 dozen).

When the pan is hot, pour in egg mixture. Cook eggs slowly and gently. Lift cooked portion to allow uncooked egg to flow underneath. Never rush eggs—they should cook slowly and gently. Cook the eggs to the texture you like, whether creamy or firm, and remove from the heat at once.

FRIED EGGS

You can fry eggs with virtually no fat by using a nonstick pan as the manufacturer directs. But most people prefer the added flavor of a little fat—butter, margarine, bacon fat, or vegetable oil.

For tender, evenly cooked eggs, the eggs should not be crowded in the pan or they will be hard to turn. Melt *fat* (1 teaspoon per egg) in a wide frying pan over medium heat. When the pan is hot, break *eggs* directly into pan. Eggs should begin to set almost immediately. For over-easy style, fry just until whites are set on one side, then with a spatula turn over and fry briefly on the other side. For opaquely covered yolks, don't turn the eggs; just cover the pan and cook for about 2 minutes.

BAKED EGGS

To cook eggs by this simple method, you'll need individual custard cups or ramekins. Because each egg bakes in its own dish, you can time each one according to individual preferences.

For each serving, rub a 1-cup (240-ml) custard cup or ramekin with ½ teaspoon *butter*; sprinkle with a pinch of *dried thyme* or fines herbes. Carefully break 1 *egg* into cup; top with 1 teaspoon *half-and-half (light cream)* and sprinkle with *salt, pepper,* and *paprika*. Bake in a 400°F (205°C) oven until egg is just set to your liking (about 10 minutes for firm); it will continue to cook slightly after removal from the oven.
Makes 1 serving

A Lower-Fat Solution

To reduce the fat and cholesterol in scrambled eggs and omelets, use 2 whole eggs plus 4 egg whites for 2 servings. Use a nonstick frying pan lightly rubbed with oil. Beat a little water into the egg mixture for creaminess. Serve the scrambled eggs with salsa or fill the omelet with fresh herbs or steamed vegetables.

POACHING EGGS FOR HUEVOS RANCHEROS

1 Heat-treating eggs before poaching keeps the poached eggs shapely. One by one, place up to 6 eggs in boiling water. Timing from when first egg is added, cook for exactly 8 seconds, then remove eggs in the order that you put them in.

2 To poach eggs, bring water just to a simmer in wide frying pan. Break heat-treated eggs close to surface of water. Adding vinegar to water helps the eggs hold their shape.

3 Test eggs for doneness by pressing yolk lightly with your finger. If you like soft yolks and firm whites, 3 to 5 minutes will do it. For firm yolks and whites, cook eggs for 7 to 10 minutes.

4 If poaching eggs in advance (a great idea to streamline preparation for a company meal), transfer immediately to a bowl of ice water when done. This quick-chills eggs and stops the cooking.

5 Piping-hot Huevos Rancheros makes a hearty brunch for Sunday-morning guests. Serve the plates of egg-topped tortillas with assorted garnishes—diced avocados, sliced radishes, and shredded cheese. Offer hot sauce, too, if you like.

POACHED EGGS

A beautifully poached egg has a well-centered yolk snugly surrounded by the white, and cooked just to the firmness you like. Once, perfect poached eggs required the freshest eggs possible, skillfully cooked to order one at a time and served immediately. But thanks to the precook treatment described below, you can now get the same excellent results from supermarket eggs in your own kitchen, with no special equipment or expertise. The secret to such perfection is to heat-treat the eggs before actually poaching them; this sets the thin layer of white just inside the shell; the thicker white surrounding the yolk increases in density, and the yolk is more securely centered.

To heat-treat eggs: In a 4- to 5-quart (3.8- to 5-liter) pan, bring enough water to a boil to cover an egg in the shell by 1 inch (2.5 cm). With the heat on high, gently lower eggs, one at a time, into the boiling water. Begin timing when you add the first egg (treat no more than 6 at a time). Cook for 8 seconds, then remove eggs in the same order that they were placed in the water. Don't worry if eggs crack. Use at once, or refrigerate for up to two days.

To poach heat-treated eggs: Fill a wide, deep frying pan with enough water to cover an egg out of the shell by about 1 inch (2.5 cm). Add 1 tablespoon (15 ml) white vinegar for each 1 quart (950 ml) of water (this helps firm the egg). Heat the water until 1 or 2 bubbles break the surface. Reduce the heat until bubbles form on the pan bottom and occasionally pop to the surface. Holding an egg as close to the surface as is comfortable, break each egg directly into the water (do not let eggs touch). Cook, uncovered, with the water barely simmering (it should not jiggle eggs), until eggs are done to your liking. Press egg yolk gently to check firmness. Soft yolks with firm whites take 3 to 5 minutes. Firm yolks and firm whites take 7 to 10 minutes. As soon as eggs are cooked, lift each one from pan with a slotted spoon and serve, or refrigerate for up to two days.

To make poaching easier for entertaining: We suggest prepoaching your eggs a day or two ahead and then reheating them at serving time. To do this, immerse poached eggs in a generous amount of ice water as soon as you lift them from the hot water. Cover and refrigerate for up to two days. To reheat, transfer cooked eggs to a bowl of very hot tap water until eggs are hot to the touch (5 to 10 minutes). Add more hot water, if needed. Lift eggs out with a slotted spoon.

Huevos Rancheros

PICTURED ON FACING PAGE

1 tablespoon (15 ml) olive oil

2 medium-size onions, chopped

1 large green bell pepper (about 8 oz./230 g), stemmed, seeded and chopped

2 cups (470 ml) reduced-sodium chicken broth or beef broth

1 can (1 lb./455 g) crushed tomatoes

¼ cup (43 g) canned diced green chiles

½ teaspoon ground cumin

½ teaspoon dried oregano

6 corn or flour tortillas (about 6-in./15-cm diameter)

6 hot poached (or fried) large eggs (see information at left or on page 107)

Garnishes: diced avocado, sliced radishes, shredded jack cheese or mild Cheddar cheese

To prepare hot sauce, heat oil in a wide nonstick frying pan over medium-high heat until hot but not smoking. Add onions and green pepper; cook until vegetables are soft (about 4 minutes). Add broth, tomatoes (break up with a spoon) and their liquid, chiles, cumin, and oregano; boil rapidly, stirring to prevent sticking, until sauce is reduced to about 2½ cups/590 ml (about 12 minutes). Pour into a bowl and keep sauce warm.

Rinse frying pan and wipe dry. Place pan over medium-high heat. Place tortillas, one at a time, in pan. Heat until soft and hot (about 30 seconds per side). Place immediately in a covered ovenproof container or foil packet and keep warm in a 200°F (95°C) oven until all tortillas are heated.

For each serving, place 1 tortilla on a plate; top with a well-drained poached (or a fried) egg and about ½ cup (120 ml) of the sauce. Top with the garnishes of your choice. *Makes 6 servings*

PER SERVING: *206 calories, 9 g total fat, 2 g saturated fat, 212 mg cholesterol, 480 mg sodium, 23 g carbohydrates, 3 g fiber, 10 g protein, 111 mg calcium, 3 mg iron*

HOW TO MAKE A FILLED OMELET

1 Use a fork to beat eggs, water, salt, and pepper in a small bowl. Prepare eggs for each omelet individually, and beat only until yolks and whites are mixed.

2 When foam on melted butter begins to subside, pour in egg mixture all at once.

3 As edges begin to set (almost as soon as egg mixture hits pan), carefully lift omelet with spatula and tilt pan so uncooked egg flows under cooked portion.

4 Vary omelets with seasonings and fillings. Here, omelet is sprinkled with herbs, then cheese is added (use about 2 teaspoons filling per egg). Sprinkle filling down center of omelet in line with pan handle for easier folding.

5 Run spatula around edge of omelet to loosen from pan. Begin fold, holding pan handle in your left hand. With your right hand, slide spatula under right edge of omelet, lift edge and fold about one third of omelet over center.

6 Switch pan to right hand. Holding pan over plate, gently shake pan to slide unfolded edge of omelet just onto plate. With a quick downward flick of the wrist, let folded section of omelet neatly fall over omelet edge on plate.

OMELETS & FRITTATAS

An omelet is one of the easiest, speediest, yet most elegant creations in cooking. Even with a filling added, the transition from eggshell to table happens almost like magic—in less than 5 minutes.

A frittata is prepared in the same manner as an omelet, but is left unfolded and is traditionally placed under the broiler to brown the topping.

An omelet pan generally has sides that curve outward from the bottom, making it easier to slide or roll out an omelet neatly. And a nonstick pan makes even the novice omelet-maker an expert.

For frittatas, which are often intended to serve more than one person, you need a wide frying pan with a flameproof handle.

Individual Omelet

> 2 large eggs
> 1 tablespoon (15 ml) water
> ¼ teaspoon salt
>   Dash of pepper
> 2 teaspoons butter or margarine

For each omelet, break eggs into a small bowl and add water, salt, and pepper. Beat with a fork just until yolks and whites are mixed.

In a 7- to 8-inch (18- to 20-cm) omelet pan over medium-high heat, melt butter and heat until foam begins to subside. Pour in egg mixture all at once. As edges begin to set (almost at once), lift with a spatula and tilt pan to let uncooked eggs flow underneath. When eggs no longer flow freely, run a spatula around edge to loosen from the pan.

To fold an omelet into thirds, hold the pan handle in your left hand. With your right hand slide the spatula under the right edge of omelet, lift edge, and fold about one third of omelet over the center. (If you're left-handed simply reverse this process.)

Switch pan to your right hand. Holding pan over a warm serving plate, gently shake pan to slide unfolded edge of omelet just onto plate. Flick your right wrist downward so that previously folded edge of omelet falls neatly over omelet edge on plate.
Makes 1 serving

PER SERVING: *217 calories, 18 g total fat, 8 g saturated fat, 446 mg cholesterol, 745 mg sodium, 1 g carbohydrates, 0 g fiber, 13 g protein, 55 mg calcium, 2 mg iron*

Filled Omelet

PICTURED ON FACING PAGE

Follow directions for *Individual Omelet*, but when egg no longer flows freely, sprinkle one or a combination of the following down center of omelet in line with pan handle. Use 2 teaspoons filling per egg and don't add too much, or it will complicate folding the omelet out of the pan. Try shredded *cheese* (jack, Cheddar, or Parmesan), chopped *fresh herbs*, diced *avocado*, sliced *mushrooms*, thinly sliced *ham* or prosciutto; small cooked *shrimp*, or diced *tomatoes*.

Country Omelet

> 2 slices bacon (about 1½ oz./45 g)
> ¼ cup (43 g) diced onion
> 1 small thin-skinned potato (about 3 oz./85 g), finely diced
> 2 teaspoons butter or margarine
> 4 large eggs
> ½ teaspoon salt
> ¼ teaspoon pepper
> ⅓ cup (about 1½ oz./40 g) shredded Swiss cheese
> 1 tablespoon minced parsley
> 2 tablespoons (30 ml) reduced-fat sour cream

In a wide nonstick frying pan, cook bacon over medium heat until crisp (about 5 minutes). Remove bacon, crumble, and set aside. Discard all but 2 teaspoons drippings. Reduce heat to medium-low and add onion and potato. Cook, stirring, until potato is fork-tender and slightly browned (about 10 minutes). Remove from pan and keep warm.

Melt butter in an 8-inch (20-cm) omelet pan over medium-high heat until foam begins to subside. Break eggs into a small bowl, add salt and pepper, and beat with a fork just until yolks and whites are mixed. Pour egg mixture into pan all at once. As edges begin to set, lift with a spatula or tilt pan to let uncooked eggs flow underneath. When eggs no longer flow freely and top of omelet is still moist (3 to 4 minutes), sprinkle eggs with bacon, potato-onion mixture, cheese, and parsley. Remove from heat. Spoon sour cream into center of omelet. Cut into wedges and serve.   *Makes 2 servings*

PER SERVING: *389 calories, 28 g total fat, 12 g saturated fat, 446 mg cholesterol, 896 mg sodium, 13 g carbohydrates, 1 g fiber, 22 g protein, 242 mg calcium, 2 mg iron*

Zucchini-Parmesan Frittata

6 large eggs

1 tablespoon (15 ml) water

⅛ teaspoon pepper

⅛ teaspoon ground nutmeg

3 tablespoons (45 ml) olive oil

1 small zucchini (about 4 oz./115 g), thinly sliced

1 small red bell pepper (about 4 oz./115 g), seeded and cut into ½-inch (1-cm) squares

⅓ cup (about 1 oz./27 g) grated Parmesan cheese

Break eggs into a small bowl. Add water, pepper, and nutmeg, and beat with a fork just until yolks and whites are mixed. Set aside.

Heat oil in a wide flameproof frying pan over medium heat. Add zucchini and bell pepper; cook, stirring, until soft (about 7 minutes). Spread vegetables evenly in pan. Pour egg mixture on top of vegetables. As edges begin to set, lift with a spatula and tilt pan to let uncooked eggs flow underneath. Cook until eggs begin to set on top but are still moist (about 5 minutes).

Remove frittata from heat and sprinkle with cheese. Broil about 6 inches (15 cm) below heat until puffy and lightly browned (about 2 minutes). Slide onto a plate and cut into wedges to serve.
Makes 4 to 6 servings

PER SERVING: *194 calories, 16 g total fat, 4 g saturated fat, 259 mg cholesterol, 175 mg sodium, 3 g carbohydrates, 0.4 g fiber, 10 g protein, 108 mg calcium, 1 mg iron*

Red Onion Frittata

Follow directions for *Zucchini-Parmesan Frittata*, but decrease oil to 2 tablespoons (30 ml). In place of zucchini and bell pepper, use 2 medium-size *red onions* (6 oz./170 g total), cut into slices ¼ inch (6 mm) thick and separated into rings, and 1 tablespoon (15 ml) *balsamic* or *red wine vinegar*. Cook over medium-high heat, stirring often, until onions are lightly browned (about 10 minutes). Reduce heat to medium and spread onions evenly in pan. Pour in egg mixture and proceed as directed above; omit Parmesan cheese.   *Makes 4 to 6 servings*

SOUFFLÉS

An aura of mystery has always surrounded soufflés, yet they're surprisingly simple to prepare once you've mastered a few techniques. For a main-dish soufflé, the base is simply a thick white sauce with eggs and your choice of vegetables, fish, poultry, meat, or cheese added. Make the sauce first, then beat the egg whites.

To achieve the greatest volume, separate the eggs carefully (see page 30). If a bit of yolk falls into the whites, remove it completely. If you can't remove all traces of yolk, save the eggs for another purpose—the smallest amount of yolk (or, for that matter, an oily bowl or beaters) will prevent the whites from beating up to their maximum volume.

You'll get the best results if the egg whites are at room temperature. For soufflés, the beaten whites should hold soft, moist peaks. Overbeaten whites become too dry and stiff, and they'll be difficult to fold into the sauce-yolk mixture. Worse still, they'll lose their ability to puff up further in the oven.

You lighten the heavy sauce by first stirring about one third of the beaten egg whites into it, then gently folding in the remainder of the egg whites.

A traditional soufflé dish is ideal but not essential. Any straight-sided, deep ovenproof baking dish will do, as long as its volume is equal to the dish size the recipe specifies. Be sure to oil or butter the dish well.

Once your soufflé is assembled and in the baking dish, put it directly into a preheated oven—it must be preheated because a soufflé needs to start baking at once; otherwise, the egg whites begin to deflate and the soufflé will not rise to its full volume.

The soufflé is done when the top is golden or feels firm to the touch, and jiggles only slightly when gently shaken. The French enjoy their soufflés, like their eggs, moist and creamy. Americans, on the other hand, often prefer theirs firmer.

After baking, your soufflé should be served immediately, but it can remain in the turned-off oven for about 10 minutes before it begins to collapse. It will continue to cook slightly, though, and become firmer.

Once you've mastered the Cheese Soufflé on the following page and wish to experiment, you can add 3 ounces (85 g) chopped cooked meat, fish, poultry, or vegetables; include the cheese or omit it, as you prefer. Stir the additions into the white sauce. Season the sauce mixture with ½ teaspoon herb or spice.

Cheese Soufflé

> About 3 tablespoons butter or margarine
>
> 3 tablespoons all-purpose flour
>
> ¼ teaspoon salt
>
> ⅛ teaspoon ground nutmeg
>
> Pinch of pepper
>
> 1 cup (240 ml) 2% milk
>
> 4 large eggs, separated
>
> ¾ cup (about 3 oz./85 g) shredded sharp Cheddar, Swiss, or Gruyère cheese

Preheat oven to 375°F (190°C). Melt 3 tablespoons of the butter in a 1-quart (950-ml) pan over medium heat. To make a roux (a cooked butter-flour base for sauces), stir in flour, ¼ teaspoon of the salt, nutmeg, and pepper; cook until mixture bubbles continuously for 1 minute. Remove pan from heat. Stirring constantly with a whisk, gradually add milk. Return to medium-high heat and cook, continuing to stir constantly, until sauce boils and thickens (about 5 minutes). Remove from heat.

With a whisk, lightly beat egg yolks to blend. Whisk in about 2 tablespoons (30 ml) of the sauce, then stir egg yolk mixture back into sauce. Stir in cheese until it melts; set aside.

With an electric mixer, beat egg whites on high speed until soft, moist, stiff peaks form. Stir about one third of the beaten whites into the sauce mixture. Then gently fold sauce into egg white mixture until blended; don't worry if some flecks of egg white remain visible.

Pour into a well-buttered 1½-quart (1.4-liter) soufflé dish. For a flat-top soufflé, gently smooth top with a spatula. For a "top-hat," draw a circle with the tip of a knife or a spoon on the surface of soufflé, 1 inch (2.5 cm) or so in from the rim. Bake for 20 minutes or until top is golden and center jiggles only slightly when gently shaken. When you do this test for doneness, make it quick and close the oven door promptly—if the temperature drops excessively, the soufflé may sink. Spoon onto plates.
Makes 4 servings

PER SERVING: *289 calories, 22 g total fat, 12 g saturated fat, 263 mg cholesterol, 482 mg sodium, 8 g carbohydrates, 0.2 g fiber, 14 g protein, 257 mg calcium, 1 mg iron*

QUICHE

Its versatility—along with its elegance—has made quiche very popular. You can serve it warm or at room temperature. The basic filling—eggs, milk, and cheese—is a snap to assemble. The pastry shell takes more time. We like Butter Pastry (page 167) for its tenderness and ease of handling. If you have trouble rolling it out, you can press it by hand into your pie pan or quiche dish. We recommend prebaking the crust so the filling doesn't make it soggy.

Quiche Lorraine

> Butter Pastry (see page 167)
>
> 8 slices bacon (about 4½ oz./126 g), crisply cooked, drained, and crumbled
>
> 1 cup (about 4 oz./113 g) shredded Swiss or Gruyère cheese
>
> 3 large eggs
>
> 1½ cups (360 ml) half-and-half (light cream)
>
> ½ teaspoon salt
>
> ⅛ teaspoon ground nutmeg

On a lightly floured board, roll out pastry to about ⅛ inch (3 mm) thick. Fit into a 9-inch (23-cm) pie pan, 1½ inches (3.5 cm) deep; flute edges. Or press into a quiche dish. Place a piece of foil inside pastry shell and partially fill with uncooked beans or rice. Bake in a 450°F (230°C) oven for 10 minutes. Lift off foil and beans; return pastry to oven until lightly browned (about 5 more minutes). Let cool. Reduce oven temperature to 350°F (175°C).

Scatter bacon in pastry shell; sprinkle evenly with cheese. In a medium-size bowl, beat eggs with half-and-half, salt, and nutmeg; pour over cheese. Bake until center is set when pan is shaken gently (35 to 40 minutes). Let stand for 10 minutes before cutting.
Makes 6 servings

PER SERVING: *417 calories, 30 g total fat, 17 g saturated fat, 184 mg cholesterol, 630 mg sodium, 21 g carbohydrates, 0.6 g fiber, 15 g protein, 267 mg calcium, 2 mg iron*

Cheese & Chile Quiche

Follow directions for *Quiche Lorraine*, but omit bacon, and substitute 1½ cups (about 6 oz./170 g) shredded *Cheddar cheese* for Swiss cheese. Sprinkle 1 can (4½ oz./130 g) diced *green chiles* over cheese before pouring in egg mixture. Sprinkle with ⅛ teaspoon ground *cumin* instead of nutmeg.

GRAINS & BEANS

Some of the world's great ethnic cuisines are based on grains and beans. These low-cost, lowfat staples are satisfying sources of protein. With their fairly muted flavors, rice, corn, and beans are amenable to just about any sort of seasoning.

Both grains and beans make excellent first courses, side dishes, or even entrées. A savory risotto is a fine prelude to an Italian meal, while curried lentils add spice to simple baked chicken. Hearty meatless chili is a wonderful main course, and is even more filling (and nutritious) if you ladle it over rice.

The recipes in this chapter highlight not only the great nutrition in grains and beans, but also their near-universal availability and versatility. Rice and cornmeal stand shelf-ready for meals in a flash. To shorten cooking time, our recipes call for canned beans, which should always be rinsed and drained to freshen their flavor and wash away excess sodium. We also provide directions for preparing dried beans from scratch. If you prefer these to canned, you might want to cook up a big batch and freeze them in recipe-size portions.

Explore the differences within the grain and bean families. You'll learn to love the subtleties of rice, and the changes that result when you vary the type called for in a recipe. And after you take our suggestions for beans, try your own substitutions, choosing from the many types available for different textures and flavors.

Shopping, storage & cooking

As a rule, count on beans to double in volume after cooking; grains expand to roughly three times their uncooked volume.

Although grains and dried beans have a long shelf life if stored airtight in a cool, dry place, two years is really their maximum storage time. Grains and beans both dry out with age. If you're using an old supply, you may need to add some more liquid toward the end of cooking, and simmer them longer.

When cooking grains and dried beans, keep the liquid at a moderate simmer, as cooking at a furious boil will turn beans and grains mushy. Stir gently, being careful not to mash as you mix.

GRAINS

Traditional Rice Pilaf

3 cups (710 ml) reduced-sodium beef broth
1 tablespoon butter or margarine
1 small onion, finely chopped
1½ cups (278 g) long-grain white rice, such as basmati
½ teaspoon salt
¼ teaspoon pepper
2 tablespoons chopped parsley (optional)

Bring broth to a boil in a 1- to 1½-quart (950-ml to 1.4-liter) pan.

Meanwhile, melt butter in a 2-quart (1.9-liter) non-stick pan over medium heat. Add onion and cook until soft (about 3 minutes). Add rice and cook, stirring occasionally, until rice is golden (about 3 minutes).

Add boiling broth, salt, and pepper to rice and return to a boil. Cover, reduce heat, and simmer until rice is just tender to bite and all liquid is absorbed (about 25 minutes). Fluff rice with a fork and mix gently with parsley. *Makes 4 servings*

PER SERVING: *282 calories, 4 g total fat, 2 g saturated fat, 8 mg cholesterol, 806 mg sodium, 57 g carbohydrates, 1 g fiber, 10 g protein, 9 mg calcium, 0.1 mg iron*

Mushroom Pilaf

Prepare *Traditional Rice Pilaf*, but substitute 8 ounces (230 g) fresh *mushrooms* (sliced) for onion, cooking them in the butter until soft. See page 132 for some mushroom suggestions.

Fruited Rice Pilaf

2¼ cups (530 ml) reduced-sodium chicken broth
1 cup (185 g) long-grain brown rice
½ teaspoon ground sage
¼ teaspoon salt
¼ teaspoon pepper
1 tablespoon butter or margarine
¼ cup (30 g) cashews, roughly chopped
¼ cup (35 g) raisins
¼ cup (35 g) coarsely chopped dried apricots
¼ cup (45 g) coarsely chopped pitted dates

In a 2-quart (1.9-liter) nonstick pan, combine broth, rice, sage, salt, and pepper. Cover and bring to a boil over high heat; reduce heat and simmer, covered, until rice is just tender to bite and all liquid is absorbed (about 45 minutes).

Just before rice is done, melt butter in a small nonstick frying pan over medium heat. Add cashews and cook, mixing, until golden (3 to 4 minutes). Add raisins, apricots, and dates; cook until heated through (about 1 minute). When rice is cooked, stir in cashews and dried fruits. *Makes 4 servings*

PER SERVING: *335 calories, 9 g total fat, 3 g saturated fat, 8 mg cholesterol, 413 mg sodium, 59 g carbohydrates, 4 g fiber, 6 g protein, 29 mg calcium, 2 mg iron*

Mexican Rice

2 teaspoons olive oil
1 small onion, finely chopped
2 cloves garlic, minced or pressed
1½ cups (278 g) long-grain white rice
3 cups (710 ml) reduced-sodium chicken broth
2 medium-size tomatoes (about 12 oz./340 g total), chopped
1 can (4½ oz./130 g) chopped mild green chiles
1 teaspoon chili powder
½ teaspoon salt
¼ teaspoon pepper
½ cup (20 g) chopped cilantro (optional)
½ cup (70 g) pimento-stuffed green olives, sliced

Heat oil in a 4-quart (3.8-liter) nonstick pan over medium-high heat until hot but not smoking. Add onion and garlic; cook until soft (2 to 3 minutes). Add rice and stir well; cook, stirring occasionally, until rice is golden (about 3 minutes). Add broth, tomatoes, chiles, chili powder, salt, and pepper. Cover and bring to a boil; reduce heat and simmer, covered, until rice is just tender to bite (about 25 minutes). Some liquid may still be left.

Turn off heat and stir in cilantro, if using, and olives. Let stand, covered, for 10 minutes. *Makes 4 servings*

PER SERVING: *352 calories, 6 g total fat, 1 g saturated fat, 0 mg cholesterol, 1,195 mg sodium, 65 g carbohydrates, 3 g fiber, 7 g protein, 49 mg calcium, 4 mg iron*

HOW TO MAKE CORN RISOTTO WITH SAGE

1 To slice kernels off corncob, use a sharp knife held flat against cob. Cut deeply enough to include bases of kernels, but don't slice fibrous surface from cob.

2 When onion is soft, add rice and cook, stirring, until rice loses its pearly appearance and becomes opaque (about 3 minutes).

3 Stir broth into rice and corn, and bring to a boil, stirring frequently. Reduce heat and simmer, uncovered, until rice is tender to the bite. For this easy risotto, the rice is stirred occasionally, not constantly, as in traditional recipes.

4 To preserve every bit of corn flavor, scrape milk from cobs into rice. Use dull side of knife and press, rather than cut.

5 Corn Risotto with Sage makes a tasty appetizer or side dish when served before or with simple foods such as chicken breasts or veal scallops. Paired with a salad, it can even be a light supper.

Risotto

2   tablespoons butter or margarine
1   medium-size onion, finely chopped
1   cup (200 g) short-grain white rice, such as arborio or pearl
⅛   teaspoon saffron (optional)
1   quart (950 ml) reduced-sodium chicken broth
½   cup (about 1½ oz./40 g) grated Parmesan cheese

Melt 1 tablespoon of the butter in a 3- to 4-quart (2.8- to 3.8-liter) nonstick pan over medium heat. Add onion and cook, stirring, until soft (about 5 minutes). Add rice and stir until rice looks opaque (about 3 minutes). Stir in saffron, if using, then mix in broth. Cook, uncovered, stirring occasionally, until mixture comes to a boil.

Adjust heat so rice boils gently; then cook, uncovered, until rice is just tender to bite and most of the liquid is absorbed (20 to 25 minutes). Toward end of cooking time, stir rice occasionally to prevent sticking. Turn off heat and stir in Parmesan cheese and remaining 1 tablespoon butter.   *Makes 4 servings*

PER SERVING: *317 calories, 11 g total fat, 6 g saturated fat, 23 mg cholesterol, 676 mg sodium, 45 g carbohydrates, 1 g fiber, 9 g protein, 149 mg calcium, 2 mg iron*

Corn Risotto with Sage

PICTURED ON FACING PAGE

3   medium-size ears yellow or white corn (about 1½ lbs./680 g total), husks and silk removed, or 1 package (10 oz./285 g) frozen corn kernels
1   tablespoon butter or margarine
1   large onion, finely chopped
1   cup (200 g) short-grain white rice, such as arborio or pearl
3½   cups (830 ml) reduced-sodium chicken broth
¼   cup (about ¾ oz./20 g) grated Parmesan cheese
¼   cup (about 1 oz./30 g) shredded fontina cheese
3   tablespoons chopped fresh sage or 2 teaspoons ground sage
    Fresh sage

If using fresh corn, with a sharp knife, cut kernels from cobs; set aside kernels and cobs, covered, so they don't dry out.

In a wide nonstick frying pan, melt butter over medium heat. Add onion and cook, stirring often, until soft (about 5 minutes). Add rice and stir until opaque (about 3 minutes). Stir in corn kernels. Mix in broth. Bring to a boil, stirring often. Reduce heat

and simmer, uncovered, stirring occasionally until rice is tender and most of the liquid is absorbed (20 to 25 minutes). Reduce heat to low and stir more often as mixture thickens.

Remove rice from heat. Holding cobs over rice, with dull side of a knife scrape them lengthwise so corn milk falls into rice mixture. Gently stir in Parmesan, fontina, and chopped sage; let stand until cheese melts (about 2 minutes).

Transfer to 5 shallow serving bowls. Garnish with fresh sage.   *Makes 4 to 6 servings*

PER SERVING: *283 calories, 7 g total fat, 4 g saturated fat, 16 mg cholesterol, 456 mg sodium, 46 g carbohydrates, 3 g fiber, 9 g protein, 104 mg calcium, 2 mg iron*

Soft Polenta with Two Cheeses

3   cups (710 ml) reduced-sodium chicken broth
3   cups (710 ml) water
2   cups (276 g) polenta or yellow cornmeal
12   ounces (340 g) teleme or jack cheese, thinly sliced
    About 1 cup (about 3 oz./80 g) shredded Parmesan cheese
    Coarsely ground pepper
    Extra-virgin olive oil or olive oil flavored with basil, chile, or another flavor (optional)
    Salt

In a 5- to 6-quart (5- to 6-liter) nonstick pan, combine broth, water, and polenta; stir to mix well. Bring to a boil over high heat, stirring often with a whisk or a spoon to prevent lumps. Reduce heat; simmer, uncovered, stirring often, until polenta feels creamy and smooth when tasted (at least 15 minutes).

Ladle half the polenta into a large, shallow serving bowl (or 6 to 8 individual bowls) and cover with half the teleme cheese and 1 cup (3 oz./80 g) of the Parmesan cheese. Cover with remaining polenta and top with the rest of the teleme cheese. Sprinkle with pepper. Accompany with more Parmesan cheese, olive oil, and salt to add to taste.   *Makes 6 to 8 servings*

PER SERVING: *388 calories, 19 g total fat, 11 g saturated fat, 60 mg cholesterol, 659 mg sodium, 32 g carbohydrates, 2 g fiber, 20 g protein, 522 mg calcium, 2 mg iron*

PREPARING BEAN ROLL-UPS

1 The filling for Bean Roll-Ups is a rich-tasting mixture of spinach, Neufchâtel cheese, Parmesan cheese, mayonnaise, horseradish, and allspice. Mix these ingredients in a medium-size bowl.

2 Divide spinach mixture among 6 tortillas. With a small spatula, spread spinach mixture almost to edges of tortillas. In same manner, cover spinach mixture with bean mixture. Top with sliced green onions and chopped parsley.

3 Roll up tortillas as tightly as possible without squeezing out filling. If not serving right away, refrigerate for up to 3 hours. Wrap or cover tortillas so they don't dry out in the refrigerator.

4 Cut the roll-ups on the diagonal for a pretty presentation. Place the slices on a bed of spinach or other green. For a more filling meal, serve Bean Roll-Ups with bowls of icy gazpacho or hot tomato soup.

BEANS

Bean Roll-Ups

PICTURED ON FACING PAGE

- 1 package (10 oz./285 g) frozen chopped spinach, thawed and squeezed dry
- 1 package (about 8 oz./230 g) Neufchâtel cheese, at room temperature
- ½ cup (about 1½ oz./40 g) grated Parmesan cheese
- 2 tablespoons (30 ml) reduced-fat mayonnaise
- 1 teaspoon prepared horseradish (or to taste)
- ⅛ teaspoon ground allspice (or to taste)
- 1 can (about 15 oz./425 g) cannellini (white kidney beans)
- 1 tablespoon (15 ml) seasoned rice vinegar (or 1 tablespoon/15 ml distilled white vinegar plus ½ teaspoon sugar)
- 2 teaspoons honey
- ¾ teaspoon chopped fresh thyme or ¼ teaspoon dried thyme
- ⅓ cup (35 g) thinly sliced green onions
- ⅓ cup (20 g) finely chopped parsley
- 6 reduced-fat flour tortillas (7-in./18-cm diameter)
  About 48 whole fresh spinach leaves, rinsed

In a medium-size bowl, combine chopped spinach, Neufchâtel cheese, Parmesan cheese, mayonnaise, horseradish, and allspice. Mix well; set aside.

Drain beans, reserving liquid. Rinse beans well, place in another medium-size bowl, and add vinegar, honey, and thyme. Coarsely mash beans with a fork; add enough of the reserved bean liquid to give mixture a spreadable consistency (do not make it too thin). Set aside. In a small bowl, combine onions and parsley; set aside.

To assemble sandwiches, divide spinach mixture equally among tortillas. With a spatula, spread spinach mixture to cover tortillas evenly. Then top tortillas equally with bean filling; carefully spread to cover spinach mixture. Sprinkle with onion mixture. Roll up each tortilla tightly to enclose filling. (At this point, you may cover tightly and refrigerate for up to 3 hours.)

Line 6 individual plates with spinach leaves. With a serrated knife, carefully cut each tortilla diagonally into 4 equal slices; arrange on spinach-lined plates.
Makes 6 servings

PER SERVING: *304 calories, 14 g total fat, 7 g saturated fat, 34 mg cholesterol, 942 mg sodium, 31 g carbohydrates, 7 g fiber, 14 g protein, 307 mg calcium, 3 mg iron*

Bean & Vegetable Chili

- 2 tablespoons (30 ml) olive oil
- 4 medium carrots, quartered lengthwise, and thinly sliced
- 1 large yellow onion, chopped
- 2 cloves garlic, minced
- 1 large red bell pepper (about 8 oz./230 g), diced
- 1 large green bell pepper (about 8 oz./230 g), diced
- 2 tablespoons chili powder
- 2 teaspoons ground cumin
- 1 teaspoon dried oregano
- 1 can (1 lb./455 g) tomatoes
- ¾ teaspoon salt
- 2 cans (about 1 lb. 3 oz./540 g each) kidney, pinto, or red beans, rinsed and drained
- ½ cup (120 ml) reduced-sodium vegetable broth or chicken broth, or water
- 2 green onions
- 1 small (about 8 oz./230 g) avocado
- 1 large lime
- ¼ cup (10 g) minced cilantro

Heat oil in a 5- to 6-quart (5- to 6-liter) nonstick pan over medium heat until hot but not smoking. Add carrots, yellow onion, and garlic; cook, stirring occasionally, for 5 minutes.

Add peppers and cook, stirring occasionally, until peppers are soft (3 to 4 more minutes). Stir in chili powder, cumin, and oregano. Add tomatoes (breaking them up with a spoon) and their liquid; add salt and bring to a boil. Add beans and broth, reduce heat, and simmer, covered, until richly flavored (about 20 minutes).

Meanwhile, cut green onions into thin slices. Pit and peel avocado (see page 125), then slice. Cut lime into eighths. Serve chili in bowls and garnish with green onions, avocado, lime wedges, and cilantro.
Makes 4 servings

PER SERVING: *448 calories, 16 g total fat, 2 g saturated fat, 0 mg cholesterol, 1,037 mg sodium, 63 g carbohydrates, 19 g fiber, 19 g protein, 177 mg calcium, 6 mg iron*

Cooking Dried Beans

Low in cost, high in nutrition, and rich in earthy, satisfying flavor, beans are one of the best food bargains available. No kitchen should be without an assortment of dried and canned varieties. Cooking dried beans is easy and requires little attention, but you do need to plan ahead because all dried beans require presoaking to rehydrate them before cooking.

Preparing the beans

Sort beans to remove debris, such as tiny pebbles. Rinse beans, then soak them in either of two ways:

Quick soaking. For each pound (455 g) of dried beans, bring 2 quarts (1.9 liters) water to a boil in a 6-quart (6-liter) pan. Add beans and boil for 2 minutes. Remove from heat, cover, and let stand for 1 hour. Drain and rinse.

Long soaking. For each pound (455 g) of dried beans, combine beans and 6 cups (1.4 liters) water in a 6-quart (6-liter) pan; soak for 6 to 8 hours, or overnight (in warm weather, refrigerate while soaking). Discard any beans that float. Drain and rinse.

Cooking the beans

Add 2 quarts (1.9 liters) fresh water to drained, soaked beans and bring to a boil. Salt and acidic ingredients, such as tomatoes and vinegar, tend to toughen beans and slow the cooking, so it's best to add such ingredients after the beans are soft. Reduce the heat and simmer, partially covered, until beans are tender to the bite (1 to 2 hours for most varieties). Cooking times for dried beans will increase with the age of the beans, the hardness of the water used, and the altitude. Test for doneness after the minimum suggested cooking time. Taste a bean; the skin should be tender and the flesh creamy enough to mash, but not mushy. Dried beans double in size when cooked; 1 pound (455 g) dried beans yields about 6 cups (1.1 kg) cooked beans.

Black Beans with Peppers & Dried Tomatoes

½ cup (60 g) oil-packed dried tomatoes, drained, with 1 tablespoon (15 ml) of the oil reserved

1 small red onion (about 4 oz./115 g), chopped

½ cup (about 3 oz./85 g) jarred roasted red peppers, drained and cut into thin strips

2 cans (about 15 oz./425 g each) black beans, rinsed and drained

¼ cup (10 g) minced cilantro
  Cilantro sprigs
  Lime wedges
  Sour cream

Coarsely chop tomatoes; set aside. Heat reserved tomato oil in a wide nonstick frying pan over medium-high heat. Add onion and cook, stirring frequently, until soft (about 5 minutes). Add reserved dried tomatoes and the peppers; cook, stirring frequently, until hot. Add beans and minced cilantro; stir gently until beans are hot. Pour into a bowl and garnish with cilantro sprigs. Serve with lime wedges and add sour cream to taste.   *Makes 4 to 6 servings*

PER SERVING: *262 calories, 16 g total fat, 2 g saturated fat, 0 mg cholesterol, 317 mg sodium, 25 g carbohydrates, 7 g fiber, 8 g protein, 50 mg calcium, 3 mg iron*

Rum Baked Beans

8 thick slices slab bacon (10 to 12 oz./285 to 340 g total), cut into ½-inch (1-cm) dice

1 large onion, chopped

2 cans (27 oz./765 g each) reduced-sodium dark red kidney beans

1 cup (220 g) firmly packed brown sugar

1 cup (240 ml) catsup

1 tablespoon (15 ml) red wine vinegar

½ teaspoon crushed dried mint
  About ½ cup (120 ml) dark rum

1 tablespoon mustard seeds

½ cup (120 ml) prepared mustard

½ teaspoon liquid hot pepper seasoning

In a 5- to 6-quart (5- to 6-liter) ovenproof pan, cook bacon over medium heat, stirring occasionally, until brown and crisp (8 to 10 minutes). With a slotted spoon, transfer bacon to paper towels to drain.

Discard all but 1 tablespoon (15 ml) of the bacon drippings. Add onion to pan and cook, stirring frequently, until soft and faintly browned (8 to 10 minutes). Stir in beans and their liquid, sugar, catsup, vinegar, mint, ½ cup (120 ml) of the rum, mustard seeds, prepared mustard, and hot pepper seasoning. Stir well and heat until bubbling. Stir in bacon and cover pan.

Bake beans in a 300°F (150°C) oven for about 2 hours. Stir well and continue to bake, uncovered, until beans are thick (about 30 minutes), or until they are the consistency you like. Add 1 to 3 tablespoons (15 to 45 ml) more rum to taste, if desired. *Makes 6 to 8 servings*

PER SERVING: *441 calories, 10 g total fat, 3 g saturated fat, 12 mg cholesterol, 1,248 mg sodium, 84 g carbohydrates, 11 g fiber, 18 g protein, 167 mg calcium, 4 mg iron*

Caribbean Baked Beans

2 cans (about 15 oz./425 g each) black beans
1 can (8 oz./230 g) crushed pineapple in unsweetened juice
½ cup (120 ml) tomato-based barbecue sauce
½ cup (50 g) chopped green onions
⅓ cup (70 g) firmly packed brown sugar
4 ounces (115 g) finely chopped cooked ham
2 tablespoons (30 ml) lime juice
1 tablespoon minced fresh ginger
2 teaspoons dry mustard

Rinse and drain beans; drain pineapple. In a 1- to 1½-quart (950-ml to 1.4-liter) shallow casserole, mix beans, pineapple, barbecue sauce, chopped onions, sugar, ham, lime juice, ginger, and mustard. (At this point, you may cover and chill for up to 2 days.)

Bake bean mixture, uncovered, in a 375°F (190°C) oven until bubbling in center (about 25 minutes or longer if chilled); stir occasionally.   *Makes 6 servings*

PER SERVING: *203 calories, 3 g total fat, 0.7 g saturated fat, 11 mg cholesterol, 690 mg sodium, 35 g carbohydrates, 4 g fiber, 10 g protein, 57 mg calcium, 3 mg iron*

Baked Curried Lentils

1 tablespoon (15 ml) olive oil
2 large onions, chopped
2 cloves garlic, minced or pressed
1 tablespoon curry powder
5 cups (1.2 liters) reduced-sodium chicken broth
1 pound (455 g) lentils
1 cup (about 4 oz./113 g) shredded white Cheddar cheese

Heat oil in a 5- to 6-quart (5- to 6-liter) pan over high heat until hot but not smoking. Add onions and garlic; cook, stirring, until onions are tinged with brown (about 8 minutes). Stir in curry powder. Add broth and bring to a boil.

Meanwhile, sort and discard debris from lentils. Rinse lentils, drain, and add to broth. Cover and simmer until lentils are tender to bite (30 to 35 minutes). If mixture is soupy, boil uncovered until liquid is just below surface of lentils; stir often.

Pour lentils into a shallow 2½- to 3-quart (2.4- to 2.8-liter) casserole. (At this point, you may cool, cover, and chill for up to 1 day.) Bake, covered, in a 350°F (175°C) oven until lentils absorb most of the liquid (about 30 minutes; if chilled, 1 to 1¼ hours). Uncover and sprinkle with Cheddar cheese. Bake until cheese melts (about 5 minutes). *Makes 8 to 10 servings*

PER SERVING: *271 calories, 7 g total fat, 3 g saturated fat, 13 mg cholesterol, 324 mg sodium, 35 g carbohydrates, 7 g fiber, 19 g protein, 131 mg calcium, 5 mg iron*

About Lentils

Mild in flavor and delicate in texture, lentils, like dried beans, are an excellent source of lowfat protein. They also supply good amounts of iron and calcium. Lentils require no presoaking, yet cook in about half an hour.

The lentils most commonly found in the supermarket are grayish brown; this type has its seed coat intact, and the lentils hold their shape nicely after cooking. Those stripped of their seed coats cook much faster, and can quickly turn mushy. Store lentils in a covered container in a cool place for up to two years. You can refrigerate leftover cooked lentils for about four days.

VEGETABLES

Few gustatory pleasures can match the treat of tiny peas in June, the luxury of ruby-red ripe tomatoes in July, or the miracle of midsummer corn. Those who grow their own vegetables enjoy produce at its peak, literally reaping the edible rewards of their labors.

For those of us who aren't so fortunate, a farmers' market or a well-stocked supermarket can yield a bounty of fresh-picked delights. It's prudent to buy vegetables when they are in season. Not only will they taste their best, but they'll also be at their lowest price. Frozen or canned vegetables will do in emergencies, but fresh produce should be on your table every day. Cook vegetables with care—briefly, to just the right degree of tenderness—in order to preserve flavor, color, texture, and nutritional value (you'll find cooking times and preparation information in the chart on pages 126–129). Vegetables don't need a lot of adornment. Add a drizzle of fine olive oil, a simple sauce, or a sprinkling of grated cheese so that the fabulous freshness is enhanced rather than obscured.

Storing to maintain freshness

Store the following vegetables, dry and unwashed, in plastic bags in the refrigerator: artichokes, asparagus, beets, broccoli, Brussels sprouts, cabbage, carrots, cauliflower, corn (in the husk), green beans, green peppers, parsnips, peas (in the pod), rutabagas, snow peas, summer squash, tomatoes, and turnips. Mushrooms keep better when stored in a paper bag, which allows air circulation.

Vegetables such as celery, green onions, leeks, and greens (such as lettuces, kale, spinach, and Swiss chard) need some moisture during storage, but they shouldn't be wet. Rinse them under cool running water and drain thoroughly. Wrap them in paper towels, place in plastic bags, and refrigerate.

Rinse watercress, and fresh herbs with tender leaves like cilantro, then stand in a container with the stems in water (like flowers in a vase). Slip a plastic bag over the tops, secure the bag to the container, and refrigerate. Put basil in water, but leave uncovered at room temperature.

Store yellow, white, and red onions; garlic; potatoes; sweet potatoes; and winter squash in a cool (about 50°F/10°C), dry, airy place out of the sun (refrigerating potatoes changes their flavor; refrigerated onions often spoil).

VEGETABLE CUTTING TECHNIQUES

A chef's knife (or French knife) is an indispensable tool for cutting vegetables. By learning to use it well, you can save a great deal of time and enjoy cooking more. Try the techniques illustrated on this page. It takes practice to chop and slice with speed, but once you learn the skills, you'll never forget them.

Chopping. Rock the knife handle up and down with one hand while the fingers of the other hand rest lightly on the tip of the blade. Scrape chopped vegetables into a heap, as necessary, with blade, and continue to chop to desired degree of fineness.

Chopping   Mincing

Mincing. Proceed as for chopping, but continue to cut until vegetables are very finely chopped.

Slicing. To slice a round vegetable, such as an onion or potato, cut it in half and lay halves, cut side down, on a cutting board. Gripping one half with your fingers, and curling your fingertips under toward your palm, cut straight down through vegetable at a right angle to board.

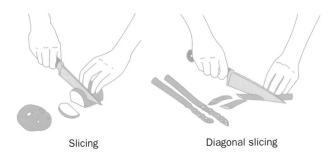

Slicing   Diagonal slicing

Diagonal slicing. Cut long vegetables crosswise on the diagonal. With long, slender vegetables, such as asparagus or green beans, you can diagonally slice several at a time.

Cutting into julienne strips. To cut vegetables such as zucchini, carrots, or potatoes into thin strips (similar in size to wooden matchsticks), first cut the vegetable, if necessary, into 2- to 3-inch (5- to 8-cm) lengths. Then cut a thin lengthwise strip off one side and lay vegetable on flat side. Cut into slices ⅛ inch (3 mm) thick, stack 2 or 3 slices at a time, and cut these into strips ⅛ inch (3 mm) thick.

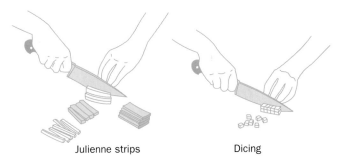

Julienne strips   Dicing

Dicing. Cut as directed for julienne strips, then cut strips, a handful at a time, crosswise into dice. For larger dice, start with slices ¼ to ½ inch (6 mm to 1 cm) thick, then cut crosswise to make ¼- to ½-inch (6-mm to 1-cm) cubes.

Why & How to Blanch Vegetables

The technique of blanching (parboiling) vegetables has many uses. You blanch tomatoes briefly to loosen their skins for peeling (see photo, page 124). Most vegetables are blanched before they're frozen to destroy enzymes that change texture, color, and flavor. And vegetables to be served cold, such as broccoli or asparagus, are generally blanched, then chilled at once to preserve their color.

To blanch vegetables, immerse them (whole or cut) in a large quantity of rapidly boiling water—6 quarts (6 liters) water for 2 pounds (905 g) vegetables. Boil, uncovered, for the minimum time suggested under "How to Cook and Test for Doneness" in the chart on pages 126–129 or until tender-crisp. Drain, plunge into a large quantity of ice-cold water to stop the cooking, then drain again. Spread on paper towels and pat dry.

PREPARING VEGETABLES: SPECIAL TECHNIQUES

1 To remove tough stalks from asparagus, hold stalk in both hands and bend the bottom toward you. Stalk should break off where the tough part begins.

2 To trim and string Chinese pea pods (snow peas), pinch off stem end, then pull string down front of pod toward tip; pinch off tip. Sugar snap pea pods require the same treatment, but have strings front and back.

3 To peel garlic easily, place cloves on a cutting board; lay blade of chef's knife on top. With heel of hand, strike blade gently to crack skins on cloves, then peel.

4 To peel tomatoes, loosen skin by blanching in boiling water for about 30 seconds (scoring tops first makes peeling easier). Skin is easily removed with a paring knife. Halve tomatoes; squeeze out seeds.

5 To handle chiles safely, wear rubber gloves—the oils in chiles can burn the skin and eyes. Halve chiles and remove seeds and spongy membranes, which is where the "heat" lies. For a hotter dish, leave in some seeds.

6 To roast bell peppers, halve and place on a flameproof pan; broil until skin is blistered and charred. Remove pan from broiler and cover with foil; let peppers steam for about 15 minutes. This loosens skins for easy peeling.

PREPARING VEGETABLES: SPECIAL TECHNIQUES

1 To chop or dice an onion quickly, cut off tip (not root end) and peel onion. Make two sets of perpendicular cuts toward root end. When cut crosswise, onion will fall into small, even bits.

2 To clean leeks, which tend to trap dirt in their tightly furled layers, cut off root ends, then halve lengthwise. Dunk leeks in basin of water, separating layers to rinse away grit. Wash under running water, too, if necessary.

3 To keep beets from "bleeding," leave the tops on, trimmed to about 1 inch (2.5 cm). After cooking, trim both ends and slip off skins with fingers or a paring knife (using a knife helps protect fingers from juice stains).

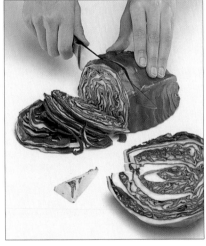

4 To prepare broccoli, first cut off very bottom of stalk. Then cut off flowerets about 1½ inches (3.5 cm) long. Peel lower part of stalks with a paring knife or vegetable peeler, then slice thinly or cut into julienne.

5 To shred cabbage, use chef's knife to cut the head in half through stem end. Remove triangular core. Lay cabbage half flat and slice downward; slices fall into shreds.

6 To pit an avocado, first halve avocado along its "beltline," sliding knife around pit. Cup avocado in both hands and twist the two halves apart. Steadying the half with pit, thrust the tip of the knife carefully into pit and twist out.

Preparing, Cooking & Serving Vegetables

The following chart provides an easy reference for preparing, cooking, and serving familiar vegetables as well as some types that may be new to you.

Use the information as a guide for boiling, steaming, and baking; to stir-fry vegetables, see page 137. Remember that uniform size and shape of whole or cut vegetables ensures even cooking. You will find that cooking times vary, depending on the size and freshness of the produce. The amounts of the vegetables listed are for 4 servings; you can adjust pan sizes for larger amounts.

To boil: Bring the designated amount of water to a boil over high heat, then add the vegetables. Begin timing. When the water returns to a boil, reduce the heat to keep the water boiling gently. Cover the pan, if specified.

To steam: Use a wide, deep frying pan. Add about 1 inch (2.5 cm) of water and a steaming rack. (There should be about ½ inch (1 cm) clearance between the water and the bottom of the rack.) Arrange vegetables on the rack. Keep water at a boil. Cover the pan and begin timing. (You may need to add more boiling water during cooking.)

To bake: Place vegetables in a 10- by 15-inch (25- to 38-cm) rimmed baking pan or on an oven rack, as directed in the recipe. Leave space between vegetables so heat can circulate.

When are vegetables done?

Test the vegetables after the minimum cooking time recommended in the chart—most will be tender-crisp when pierced (pierce vegetables such as artichokes, broccoli, Brussels sprouts, and cauliflower in the stem end or in the stalk). Potatoes should be tender throughout when pierced. Leafy greens should be wilted but still have their bright color.

The finishing touches

Drain the vegetables. Save the liquid for soup, broth, or sauces, if desired. Add one or more of the "compatible seasonings" suggested below (or for more information and recipes for sauces that go well with vegetables, see page 141); mix to coat. Spoon the vegetables into a serving bowl or onto plates.

(AMOUNT FOR 4 SERVINGS) Vegetable	Preparation	How to Cook and Test for Doneness*	Compatible Seasonings
ARTICHOKES—4			
Whole (3- to 4-in./ 8- to 10-cm diameter)	Cut off stem and top third of artichoke. Remove small coarse outer leaves. Using scissors, cut off thorny tips of remaining leaves. Rinse well. Plunge into vinegar-water or lemon-water.	**To boil:** in a 5- to 6-quart (5- to 6-liter) pan, cook, covered in 3 quarts (2.8 liters) water with 1 tablespoon (15 ml) vinegar per quart (950 ml) of water for 30 to 45 minutes. **To steam:** On a rack above boiling water, cook, covered, for 25 to 35 minutes.	Béarnaise sauce, melted butter, garlic butter, hollandaise sauce, lemon juice, mayonnaise, vinaigrette dressing
ASPARAGUS—1½ lbs. (680 g)			
Spears	Snap or cut off tough ends. If desired, peel stalks to remove scales. Rinse well.	**To boil:** In a wide frying pan, cook, covered, in 1 inch (2.5 cm) water for 3 to 10 minutes. **To steam:** On a rack above boiling water, cook, covered, for 4 to 12 minutes.	Melted butter, hollandaise sauce, lemon juice, tarragon, vinaigrette dressing
Slices	Same as above, then slice diagonally into ½- to 1-inch (1- to 2.5-cm) pieces.	**To boil:** In a wide frying pan, cook, covered, in ½ inch (1 cm) water for 1½ to 5 minutes. **To steam:** On a rack above boiling water, cook, covered, for 3 to 7 minutes.	Same as above
BEANS (green or wax)—1 lb. (455 g)			
Whole	Rinse well. Snap off ends.	**To boil:** In a 3-quart (2.8-liter) pan, cook, covered, in 1 inch (2.5 cm) water for 3 to 10 minutes. **To steam:** On a rack above boiling water, cook, covered, for 5 to 15 minutes.	Crumbled bacon, butter, cheese sauce, chives, dill sauce, dill weed, lemon juice
Slices	Same as above, then slice diagonally or crosswise into 1- to 2-inch (2.5- to 5-cm) pieces.	**To boil:** In a 3-quart (2.8-liter) pan, cook, covered, in 1 inch (2.5 cm) water for 4 to 7 minutes. **To steam:** On a rack above boiling water, cook, covered, for 5 to 12 minutes.	Same as above
BEETS—1 to 1½ lbs. (455 to 680 g)			
Whole (2- to 3-in./ 5- to 8-cm) diameter	Scrub well. Leave roots, 1 to 2 inches (2.5 to 5 cm) of stem, and skin intact. Do not peel before cooking. After cooking, trim off root and stem; slip off skins.	**To boil:** In a 4- to 5-quart (3.8- to 5-liter) pan, cook, covered, in water to cover for 20 to 45 minutes. **To bake:** Set beets in a pan and bake in a 375°F (190°C) oven for 1 to 1¼ hours.	Butter, mustard butter, dill weed, lemon or orange juice or peel, thyme, wine vinegar

For complete cooking instructions and doneness tests, refer to the text above.

(AMOUNT FOR **4 SERVINGS**) Vegetable	Preparation	How to Cook and Test for Doneness*	Compatible Seasonings
BROCCOLI—1 to 1½ lbs. (455 to 680 g)			
Flowerets or spears	Rinse. Cut off flowerets or cut into.spears. Trim bases of thick stalks, peel, then thinly slice.	**To boil:** In a wide frying pan, cook, covered, in 1 inch (2.5 cm) water for 5 to 12 minutes. **To steam:** On a rack above boiling water, cook, covered, for 8 to 20 minutes.	Butter, garlic, ginger, hollandaise or mornay sauce, lemon juice, olive oil, rosemary
BRUSSELS SPROUTS—1¼ to 1½ lbs. (565 to 680 g)			
Whole	Trim off stem ends and discolored leaves. Rinse well.	**To boil:** In a 3-quart (2.8-liter) pan, cook, uncovered, in 1 inch (2.5 cm) water for 3 to 5 minutes; cover and cook for 4 to 5 more minutes. **To steam:** On a rack above boiling water, cook, covered, for 10 to 25 minutes.	Butter, buttered bread crumbs, cheese sauce, nutmeg, grated Parmesan cheese
CABBAGE (all varieties)—1 to 1½ lbs. (455 to 680 g)			
Wedges	Discard any wilted outer leaves. Slice in half lengthwise and cut out core; rinse. Cut into 2-inch (5-cm) wedges.	**To boil:** In a wide frying pan, cook, uncovered, in 1 inch (2.5 cm) water for 2 minutes; cover and cook for 3 to 8 more minutes. **To steam:** On a rack above boiling water, cook, covered, for 4 to 12 minutes.	Butter, caraway seeds, dill weed, grated Parmesan cheese, sour cream
Shredded	Discard any wilted outer leaves. Halve lengthwise. Cut out core; rinse. Place cut side down on cutting board and thinly slice.	**To boil:** In a 4- to 5-quart (3.8- to 5-liter) pan, cook, uncovered, in 3 quarts (2.8 liters) water for 1 to 3 minutes. **To steam:** On a rack above boiling water, cook, covered, for 3 to 5 minutes.	Same as above
CARROTS—1 lb. (455 g)			
Whole medium-size	Scrub well or peel; cut off ends. Rinse.	**To boil:** In a wide frying pan, cook, covered, in 1 inch (2.5 cm) water for 10 to 20 minutes. **To steam:** On a rack above boiling water, cook, covered, for 12 to 20 minutes.	Butter, cinnamon, ginger, mint, nutmeg, parsley, thyme
Slices	Same as above; then slice diagonally or crosswise into ¼-inch (6-mm) pieces.	**To boil:** In a wide frying pan, cook, covered, in ½ inch (1 cm) water for 5 to 10 minutes. **To steam:** On a rack above boiling water, cook, covered, for 5 to 10 minutes.	Same as above
CAULIFLOWER—1¼ to 1½ lbs. (565 to 680 g)			
Whole	Remove outer leaves. Cut out core. Rinse.	**To boil:** In a 4- to 5-quart (3.8- to 5-liter) pan, cook, covered, in 1 inch (2.5 cm) water for 15 to 20 minutes. **To steam:** On a rack above boiling water, cook, covered, for 20 to 25 minutes.	Butter, chives, cheese sauce, curry sauce, dill weed, nutmeg, hollandaise sauce
Flowerets	Same as above, but break into flowerets.	**To boil:** In a wide frying pan, cook, covered, in ½ inch (1 cm) water for 5 to 9 minutes. **To steam:** On a rack above boiling water, cook, covered, for 8 to 18 minutes.	Same as above
CELERY (1 bunch)—1½ lbs. (680 g)			
Slices	Separate stalks. Trim off leaves and base. Pare off coarse strings. Rinse well, then slice into 1-inch (2.5-cm) pieces.	**To boil:** In a wide frying pan, cook, covered, in ½ inch (1 cm) water for 5 to 10 minutes. **To steam:** On a rack above boiling water, cook, covered, for 5 to 10 minutes.	Butter, grated Parmesan cheese, tarragon, thyme
CELERY ROOT OR CELERIAC—1 lb. (455 g)			
Slices	Peel and cut into ¼-inch (6-mm) slices. Immerse in vinegar-water or lemon-water. Blanch or cook.	**To boil:** In a wide frying pan, cook, covered, in ½ inch (1 cm) water for 8 to 15 minutes.	Garlic butter, lemon juice, mayonnaise
CORN ON THE COB (4 large or 8 small ears)			
Whole	Remove husks and silk; trim stem, if desired.	**To boil:** In a 4- to 5-quart (3.8- to 5-liter) pan, cook, covered, in 2 to 3 quarts (1.9 to 2.8 liters) water for 3 to 5 minutes.	Butter, lime juice, thyme
EGGPLANT (1 large or 2 small)—1½ lbs. (680 g)			
Slices	Trim off stem. Rinse and cut eggplant into ½-inch (1-cm) slices. Brush with vegetable oil.	**To bake:** Arrange in single layer in shallow baking pan. Bake, uncovered, in a 425° to 450°F (220° to 230°C) oven until soft (20 to 30 minutes).	Basil, garlic butter, oregano, grated Parmesan cheese

For complete cooking instructions and doneness tests, refer to the text on page 126.

Continued on next page

(AMOUNT FOR 4 SERVINGS) Vegetable	Preparation	How to Cook and Test for Doneness*	Compatible Seasonings
FENNEL—1½ lbs. (680 g)			
(3-in./8-cm diameter)	Remove tops and bruised outer parts. Slice ½ inch (1 cm) thick.	*To boil:* In a wide frying pan, cook, covered, in 1 inch (2.5 cm) water for 5 to 15 minutes.	Butter, chives, grated Parmesan cheese
GREENS (beet, collard, kale, mustard, turnip)—1 to 1½ lbs. (455 to 680 g)			
	Remove tough stems; rinse well in large quantity of water; drain. Coarsely chop leaves, if desired.	*To boil:* In a 4-quart (3.8-liter) pan, cook, covered, in 1 inch (2.5 cm) water for 5 to 9 minutes. *To steam:* On a rack above boiling water, cook, covered, for 7 to 9 minutes.	Crumbled bacon, butter, garlic, lemon juice, olive oil, sour cream, wine vinegar
JICAMA—1 lb. (455 g)			
Slices or shreds	Peel. Slice ¼ inch (6 mm) thick to cook; slice/shred for salads.	*To boil:* In a wide frying pan, cook, covered, in 1 inch (2.5 cm) water for 3 to 4 minutes.	Citrus juice, garlic, oregano
LEEKS—1½ lbs. (680 g)			
(1-in./2.5-cm diameter)	Cut off roots. Trim so that 1½ inches (3.5 cm) of dark green leaves remain; split lengthwise. Rinse well between layers.	*To boil:* In a wide frying pan, cook, covered, in ½ inch (1 cm) water for 5 to 8 minutes. *To steam:* On a rack above boiling water, cook, covered, for 5 to 8 minutes.	Crumbled bacon, ginger, lemon juice, grated Parmesan cheese
OKRA—1 lb. (455 g)			
Whole	Trim surface of stem ends. Rinse pods; leave whole.	*To boil:* In a 3-quart (2.8-liter) pan, cook, covered, in water to cover for 5 to 10 minutes.	Butter, chives, parsley
ONIONS—1 lb. (455 g)			
Whole (1- to 1½-in./ 2.5- to 3.5-cm diameter)	Cover with boiling water; let stand for 3 minutes, then drain. Trim ends and peel.	*To boil:* In a 3-quart (2.8-liter) pan, cook, uncovered, in 1½ inches (3.5 cm) water for 15 minutes. *To bake:* Place in baking dish; drizzle with butter. Bake, uncovered, in a 350°F (175°C) oven for 30 to 45 minutes, basting or shaking occasionally.	Butter, parsley, sage, brown or white sugar, thyme
PARSNIPS—1 lb. (455 g)			
Whole	Cut off ends, peel, and rinse.	*To boil:* In a wide frying pan, cook, covered, in 1 inch (2.5 cm) water for 10 to 20 minutes. *To steam:* On a rack above boiling water, cook, covered, for 15 to 20 minutes.	Butter, honey, lemon juice, brown sugar, Worcestershire
PEA PODS (Chinese, and sugar snap peas)—¾ lb. (340 g)			
Whole	Snap off both ends and pull off strings. Rinse.	*To boil:* In a 5-quart (5-liter) pan, cook, uncovered, in 3 quarts (2.8 liters) water for ½ to 2 minutes. *To steam:* On a rack above boiling water, cook, covered, for 2 to 5 minutes.	Butter, toasted sesame seeds, soy sauce
PEAS (green)—2½ lbs. (1.15 kg)			
	Shell peas (you should have 2½ to 3 cups/375 to 450 g shelled); rinse.	*To boil:* In a 3-quart (2.8-liter) pan, cook, covered, in ½ inch (1 cm) water for 3 to 10 minutes. *To steam:* On a rack above boiling water, cook, covered, for 4 to 12 minutes.	Butter, chives, mint, mornay sauce, rosemary, thyme
POTATOES (baking)—2 to 2½ lbs. (905 g to 1.15 kg)			
Whole (4 medium to large)	Scrub well. Rub with oil or butter, if desired, and pierce in several places with fork.	*To bake:* Place in a 10- by 15-inch (25- by 38-cm) rimmed baking pan or directly on oven rack; bake, uncovered, in a 400°F (205°C) oven for 1 hour.	Butter, chives, sour cream, paprika, grated cheese, dill sauce
Quartered	Peel, cut into quarters, and rinse.	*To boil:* In a 5-quart (5-liter) pan, cook, covered, in 1 inch (2.5 cm) water for about 20 minutes. *To steam:* On a rack above boiling water, cook, covered, for about 20 minutes.	Same as above
POTATOES (thin skinned, red or white)—1½ lbs. (680 g)			
Whole (3-in./8-cm diameter)	Scrub well.	*To boil:* In a 3-quart (2.8-liter) pan, cook, covered, in 2 inches (5 cm) water for 20 to 35 minutes. *To steam:* On a rack above boiling water, cook, covered, for 20 to 35 minutes.	Crumbled bacon, butter, dill weed, parsley, rosemary
Slices	Same as above; then slice into ½-inch (1-cm) pieces.	*To boil:* In a 3-quart pan (2.8-liter), cook, covered, in 1 inch (2.5 cm) water for 13 to 15 minutes. *To steam:* On a rack above boiling water, cook, covered, for 10 to 15 minutes.	Same as above

For complete cooking instructions and doneness tests, refer to the text on page 126.

(AMOUNT FOR 4 SERVINGS) Vegetable	Preparation	How to Cook and Test for Doneness*	Compatible Seasonings
POTATOES (sweet and yams) — 2 to 2½ lbs. (905 g to 1.15 kg)			
Whole (4 medium to large)	*For baking:* Scrub well. Rub with oil, if desired, and pierce in several places with fork.	*To bake:* Place in a 10- by 15-inch (25- by 38-cm) rimmed baking pan; bake, uncovered, in a 400°F (205°C) oven for 45 to 50 minutes.	Allspice, butter, cinnamon, maple syrup, brown sugar
	For boiling: Scrub well.	*To boil:* In a 3-quart (2.8-liter) pan, cook, covered, in 2 inches (5 cm) water for 20 to 40 minutes.	Same as above
RUTABAGAS — 1½ to 2 lbs. (680 to 905 g)			
Slices	Peel, rinse, and slice.	*To boil:* In a wide frying pan, cook, covered, in ½ to 1 inch (1 to 2.5 cm) water for 6 to 9 minutes. *To steam:* On a rack above boiling water, cook, covered, for 6 to 9 minutes.	Butter, cinnamon, dill weed, lemon juice, brown sugar
SPINACH — 1½ lbs. (680 g)			
Leaves	Discard wilted leaves and tough stems. Rinse well in large quantity of water; drain.	*To boil:* In a 4- to 5-quart (3.8- to 5-liter) pan, cook, covered, in water that clings to leaves, for 2 to 4 minutes; stir often.	Crumbled bacon, basil, butter, mint, nutmeg
SQUASH, SPAGHETTI — 2 lbs. (905 g)			
Whole	Rinse. Leave whole, but pierce all over with fork.	*To bake:* Place in a 10- by 15-inch (25- by 38-cm) rimmed baking pan; bake, uncovered, in a 350°F (175°C) oven for 1½ hours; turn over after 45 minutes. Halve cooked squash; remove seeds. Use a fork to separate spaghetti-like strands.	Butter, garlic, olive oil
SQUASH, SUMMER (crookneck, pattypan, zucchini) — 1 to 1½ lbs. (455 to 680 g)			
Whole (4 to 6)	Cut off ends; rinse. Do not peel.	*To boil:* In a 3-quart (2.8-liter) pan, cook, covered, in 1 inch (2.5 cm) water for 8 to 12 minutes. *To steam:* On a rack above boiling water, cook, covered, for 8 to 12 minutes.	Basil, butter, cheese sauce, dill weed, fines herbes, marjoram, onion
Slices	Same as above; then slice.	*To boil:* In a 3-quart (2.8-liter) pan, cook, covered, in ½ inch (1 cm) water for 3 to 7 minutes. *To steam:* On a rack above boiling water, cook, covered, for 3 to 7 minutes.	Same as above
SQUASH, WINTER (acorn, banana, butternut, Hubbard) — 1½ lbs. (680 g)			
Halves or serving-size pieces	*For boiling:* Rinse. Halve acorn or butternut squash lengthwise; cut banana or Hubbard squash into serving-size pieces. Remove seeds and stringy pulp. *For baking:* Same as above, then rub cut edges with butter.	*To boil:* In a wide frying pan, cook, covered, in 2 inches (5 cm) water for 10 to 15 minutes. *To bake:* Place, cut side down, in an oiled, 10- by 15-inch (25- by 38-cm) rimmed baking pan. Bake, uncovered, in a 400° to 450°F (205° to 230°C) oven for 30 to 40 minutes.	Allspice, crumbled bacon, butter, cinnamon, nutmeg, onion, brown sugar
Slices	Rinse, peel, and slice into ½-inch (1-cm) pieces.	*To boil:* In a wide frying pan, cook, covered, in ½ inch (1 cm) water for 7 to 9 minutes.	Same as above
SWISS CHARD — 1½ lbs. (680 g)			
Stems and leaves	Rinse well; drain. Slice stems into 1-inch (2.5-cm) pieces; slice leaves crosswise into 1-inch (2.5-cm) shreds.	*To boil:* In a wide frying pan, cook stems, covered, in ¼ inch (6 mm) water for 2 minutes, then add leaves and cook for 1 to 2 more minutes.	Crumbled bacon, butter, garlic, nutmeg, olive oil, onion
TURNIPS — 1½ to 2 lbs. (680 to 905 g)			
Whole (about 4 medium-size)	*For boiling:* Rinse and peel.	*To boil:* In a 4- to 5-quart (3.8- to 5-liter) pan, cook, covered, in 2 inches (5 cm) water for 20 to 35 minutes.	Crumbled bacon, butter, ginger, grated lemon peel, parsley, soy sauce
	For baking: Rinse; do not peel.	*To bake:* Place in single layer in an oiled, 10- by 15-inch (25- by 38-cm) rimmed baking pan. Sprinkle lightly with water. Bake, uncovered, in a 400°F (205°C) oven for 30 to 45 minutes. Peel.	
Slices	Rinse, peel, and slice into ¼-inch (6-mm) pieces.	*To boil:* In a wide frying pan, cook, covered, in ½ inch (1 cm) water for 6 to 9 minutes. *To steam:* On a rack above boiling water, cook, covered, for 6 to 9 minutes.	Same as above

*For complete cooking instructions and doneness tests, refer to the text on page 126.

Asparagus with Green Sauce

2 pounds (905 g) asparagus

½ cup (20 g) packed Italian parsley leaves

⅓ cup (35 g) sliced green onions

2 tablespoons (30 ml) reduced-sodium chicken broth

2 cloves garlic, sliced

¾ teaspoon dried tarragon, crumbled

½ cup (120 ml) plain lowfat yogurt

2 tablespoons (30 ml) olive oil

¼ teaspoon lemon peel

1 tablespoon (15 ml) lemon juice

½ teaspoon salt

¼ teaspoon pepper

Lemon wedges (optional)

Bring 1 inch (2.5 cm) of water to a boil in a wide nonstick frying pan. Lay the asparagus in the frying pan and cook, covered, turning occasionally, until tender (about 8 minutes).

Meanwhile, in a small nonstick frying pan, combine parsley, green onions, broth, garlic, and tarragon. Bring to a boil over high heat. Cover, reduce heat, and simmer, stirring occasionally, until onions are soft (3 to 4 minutes).

Transfer mixture to a food processor. Add yogurt, olive oil, lemon peel, lemon juice, salt, and pepper; whirl until smooth. Transfer sauce to a small bowl. Drain asparagus and serve with the green sauce on the side. Offer lemon wedges, if desired.
Makes 4 servings

PER SERVING: *140 calories, 8 g total fat, 1 g saturated fat, 2 mg cholesterol, 319 mg sodium, 13 g carbohydrates, 3 g fiber, 9 g protein, 136 mg calcium, 3 mg iron*

Herb Cheese Artichokes

4 artichokes (each about 3 in./8 cm wide with 2- to 3-in./ 5- to 8-cm stems)

White vinegar or lemon juice

5 or 6 black peppercorns

1 tablespoon (15 ml) extra-virgin olive oil

¼ cup (25 g) coarse dry bread crumbs

8 ounces (230 g) reduced-fat or regular garlic-and-herb Boursin or Rondelé cheese

Break off and discard outside artichoke leaves until you reach pale, tender inner ones. Slice off about the top third of the remaining leaves. Peel artichoke bottoms and stems to remove fibrous exteriors. Trim discolored ends of stems.

Fill an 8- to 10-quart (8- to 10-liter) pan halfway with water. Add 1 tablespoon (15 ml) vinegar for each quart water. Add peppercorns, cover, and bring to a boil over high heat. Add artichokes, cover, and simmer until bottoms pierce easily (25 to 30 minutes). Drain.

Cut artichokes in half lengthwise. Pull out sharp-tipped inner leaves. With a spoon, scrape out and discard fuzzy centers in bottoms. Rub stems lightly with 1 teaspoon of the oil.

In a small bowl, combine remaining 2 teaspoons oil with bread crumbs. Lay artichokes, cup sides up, on a baking sheet and fill cavities equally with cheese. Sprinkle cheese with bread crumb mixture.

Bake in a 400°F (205°C) oven until cheese is hot and crumbs are lightly browned (about 15 minutes). Transfer to a serving dish.   *Makes 4 servings*

PER SERVING: *207 calories, 10 g total fat, 5 g saturated fat, 20 mg cholesterol, 499 mg sodium, 20 g carbohydrates, 7 g fiber, 13 g protein, 72 mg calcium, 2 mg iron*

Stir-Fried Carrots & Peppers

4 medium-size carrots, cut into matchstick-size pieces

1 medium-size red bell pepper (about 6 oz./170 g), stemmed, seeded, and cut into matchstick-size pieces

1 medium-size fresh Anaheim (California) chile (about 1 oz./30 g), cut into matchstick-size pieces

2 tablespoons (30 ml) olive oil

2 teaspoons fresh rosemary leaves or 1 teaspoon dried rosemary

Salt and pepper

Heat oil in a wide nonstick frying pan over medium-high heat. Add carrots and stir-fry just until slightly browned (about 6 minutes). Add bell pepper, chile, and rosemary; stir-fry until pepper pieces are soft (about 2 minutes). Add salt and pepper to taste.   *Makes 6 servings*

PER SERVING: *69 calories, 5 g total fat, 0.6 g saturated fat, 0 mg cholesterol, 18 mg sodium, 7 g carbohydrates, 2 g fiber, 0.8 g protein, 18 mg calcium, 0.5 mg iron*

Broccoli & Bell Pepper Sauté with Toasted Pine Nuts

3 tablespoons pine nuts

4 cups (285 g) trimmed broccoli

1 tablespoon (15 ml) olive oil

1 small red bell pepper (about 4 oz./115 g), stemmed, seeded, and cut into thin slivers

Salt

In a wide, dry frying pan over medium-low heat, stir nuts until golden (6 to 8 minutes). Pour nuts into a small bowl to cool.

To the same pan, add broccoli pieces and ¼ cup (60 ml) water. Cover and cook over medium-high heat, stirring occasionally, until broccoli is tender-crisp (2 to 3 minutes). Drain and transfer to a serving bowl.

In the same pan, heat oil over medium-high heat. Add bell pepper, and cook, stirring frequently, until pepper is lightly browned (about 3 minutes). Pour pepper over broccoli; sprinkle with pine nuts. Add salt to taste.   *Makes 4 servings*

PER SERVING: *96 calories, 7 g total fat, 1 g saturated fat, 0 mg cholesterol, 25 mg sodium, 7 g carbohydrates, 4 g fiber, 4 g protein, 46 mg calcium, 2 mg iron*

Oven-Roasted Green Beans with Pasta

2 pounds (905 g) fresh slender green beans or 2 packages (10 oz./285 g each) thawed frozen French-cut green beans

⅔ cup (80 g) thinly sliced shallots

4 cloves garlic, minced

3 tablespoons (45 ml) olive oil or vegetable oil

2½ tablespoons grated lemon peel

2 teaspoons fresh thyme (optional)

Coarse salt

Pepper

⅓ cup (80 ml) lemon juice

1 pound (455 g) hot cooked fettuccine

½ cup (about 1½ oz./40 g) thinly shaved Parmesan cheese

If using fresh green beans, trim ends and cut into 2-inch (5-cm) lengths. Place beans, shallots, and garlic in an 11- by 17-inch (28- by 43-cm) baking pan. Drizzle with oil; sprinkle with lemon peel and thyme.

Gently mix to evenly coat with seasonings. Add salt and pepper to taste.

Roast beans in a 450°F (230°C) oven until edges are browned and beans are slightly blistered and crisp (about 30 minutes); stir after the first 10 minutes. Pour lemon juice evenly over beans; stir to coat.

Add beans to hot pasta, stir well to mix, and top with Parmesan cheese. Serve immediately.
Makes 4 servings

PER SERVING: *668 calories, 18 g total fat, 4 g saturated fat, 116 mg cholesterol, 232 mg sodium, 105 g carbohydrates, 7 g fiber, 25 g protein, 279 mg calcium, 8 mg iron*

Chilled Sugar Snap Peas with Mint Dressing & Bacon

1½ to 2 pounds (680 to 905 g) sugar snap peas or Chinese pea pods (snow peas)

1 tablespoon sugar

2 teaspoons cornstarch

½ cup (120 ml) reduced-sodium chicken broth

½ cup (120 ml) rice vinegar

4 thick slices bacon (about 6 oz./170 g)

2 tablespoons minced fresh mint

Pinch ends off peas and pull off strings (see page 124). In a 4- to 5-quart (3.8- to 5-liter) covered pan, bring about 3 quarts (2.8 ml) water to a boil over high heat. Add peas; cook, uncovered, until tender-crisp (about 1 minute). Drain and, at once, immerse peas in ice water until cold. Drain again. (At this point, you may wrap the peas airtight and chill up until next day.)

In a 1½- to 2-quart (1.4- to 1.9-liter) pan, combine sugar and cornstarch, then stir in broth and vinegar. Bring to boil over high heat, stirring. Remove from heat and let cool. (At this point, you may cover and chill up until next day; let come to room temperature and stir well before using.)

Just before serving, cook bacon in a wide nonstick, frying pan until crisp. Drain on paper towels and crumble.

To serve, arrange peas in a bowl; stir mint into dressing and pour over peas. Sprinkle with bacon.
Makes 8 servings

PER SERVING: *86 calories, 3 g total fat, 1 g saturated fat, 5 mg cholesterol, 126 mg sodium, 10 g carbohydrates, 2 g fiber, 5 g protein, 42 mg calcium, 2 mg iron*

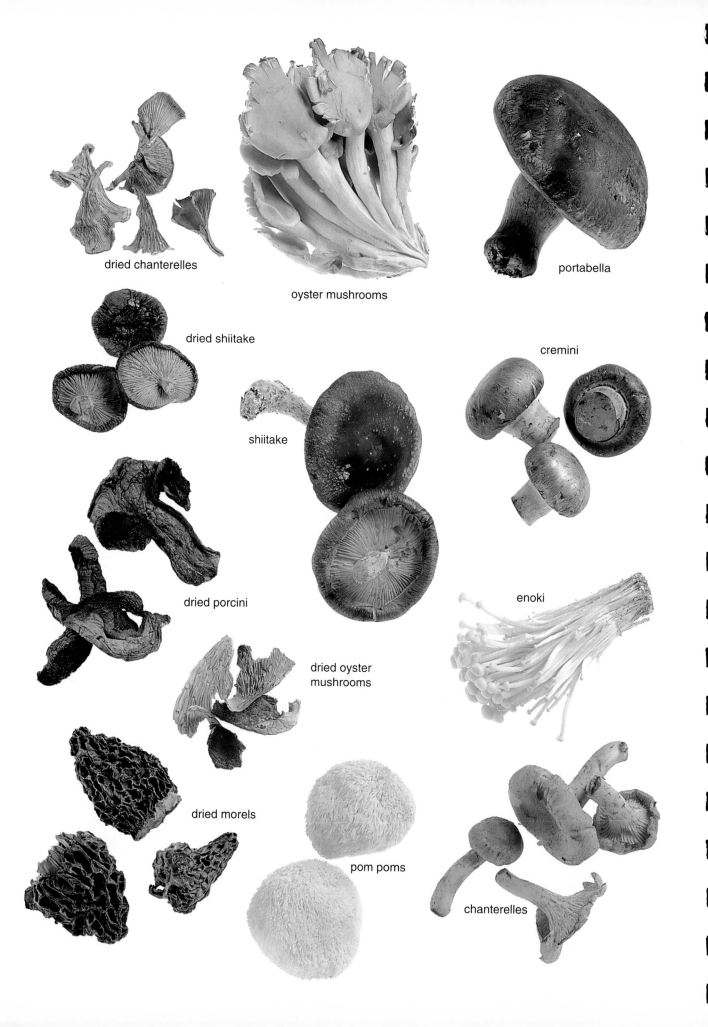

dried chanterelles

oyster mushrooms

portabella

dried shiitake

cremini

shiitake

dried porcini

enoki

dried oyster
mushrooms

dried morels

pom poms

chanterelles

Mixed Mushroom Sauté

1 pound (455 g) assorted fresh mushrooms, such as shiitake, cremini, and portabellas, cleaned, trimmed and cut lengthwise into thick slices

4 teaspoons (20 ml) olive oil

1 medium-size onion, finely chopped

2 cloves garlic, finely chopped

½ teaspoon dried rosemary

½ teaspoon salt

¼ teaspoon pepper

Heat oil in a wide nonstick frying pan over medium heat. Add onion and garlic; cook until soft (about 3 minutes). Add mushrooms, rosemary, salt, and pepper; stir to combine. Increase heat to high and cook, stirring, until liquid is nearly evaporated (about 5 minutes). Serve hot. *Makes 4 servings*

PER SERVING: *86 calories, 5 g total fat, 0.6 g saturated fat, 0 mg cholesterol, 275 mg sodium, 10 g carbohydrates, 2 g fiber, 3 g protein, 15 mg calcium, 2 mg iron*

Grilled Portabella Mushrooms with Greens

1 quart (950 ml) reduced-sodium beef broth

1 cup (240 ml) balsamic vinegar

8 ounces (230 g) red Swiss chard

12 ounces (340 g) broccoli rabe

4 large (4- to 5-in./10- to 12.5-cm diameter) portabella mushrooms (about 1 lb./455 g total)

1½ tablespoons (23 ml) olive oil

Salt and pepper

2 cloves garlic, cut lengthwise into paper-thin slices

12 ounces (340 g) spinach, stems removed

4 teaspoons chopped fresh chives

In a wide nonstick frying pan over high heat, bring broth and vinegar to a boil. Boil, stirring occasionally, until balsamic sauce is reduced to ⅓ cup/80 ml (15 to 20 minutes); set aside.

Trim stem ends from chard and broccoli rabe, then cut stems into ½-inch (1-cm) slices up to base of leaves. Stack leaves and cut into 1- to 2-inch (2.5- to 5-cm) strips. Set aside. Trim ends from mushrooms; clean caps. Lightly brush caps with 1½ teaspoons of the oil; sprinkle with salt and pepper.

Lay mushrooms, skin side up, on a grill above a solid bed of medium coals (you can hold your hand at grill level only 4 to 5 seconds). Cook, turning to brown evenly, until mushrooms are just tender when pierced through centers of stems (8 to 10 minutes). Set aside.

Heat remaining oil with garlic in an 8- to 10-quart (8- to 10-liter) pan over medium-high heat. When garlic begins to brown, add chard and broccoli rabe stems; stir until softened (about 3 minutes). Increase heat to high. Stir in sliced leaves and spinach; cover and cook just until wilted (2 to 3 minutes). Season to taste with salt and pepper.

With a slotted spoon, divide greens equally among 4 plates; top each with a mushroom. Spoon reserved balsamic sauce on top; sprinkle with chives. *Makes 4 servings*

PER SERVING: *138 calories, 5 g total fat, 0.7 g saturated fat, 0 mg cholesterol, 816 mg sodium, 16 g carbohydrates, 4 g fiber, 11 g protein, 113 mg calcium, 5 mg iron*

Roasting Garlic

For those who shy away from raw garlic's pungency, roasting opens the door to a new world of flavor. It tames garlic's harshness, leaving the bulb sweetly mellow.

If heads of garlic are baked whole, the cloves steam inside the skin and turn soft and mild. But if you cut the heads horizontally and bake them, cut side down, in a little oil, the cloves caramelize into a thick, savory-sweet paste ready to spread on bread or crackers, or on roasted or grilled meats, or to toss with hot pasta.

Allow ½ to 1 head of garlic per serving. For each head (choose firm ones), peel off the loose skin and cut in half horizontally. Line a roasting pan (preferably nonstick) with a very thin layer of olive oil (about 1 tablespoon/15 ml oil for each head). Place garlic heads in pan, cut sides down and ½ inch (1 cm) apart. Bake, uncovered, in the center of a 375°F (190°C) oven until cut sides are browned and oozing (35 to 40 minutes); lift garlic often to be sure it doesn't burn and add more oil as necessary.

◄ *A Selection of Fresh and Dried Mushrooms*

MAKING MASHED POTATO CASSEROLE

1 Any of these potato varieties may be used for making mashed potatoes. Clockwise from top left: Idaho baking potatoes, round white thin-skinned potatoes, Yukon golds (which have yellow flesh), and round red thin-skinned potatoes. For this recipe, peel and quarter the potatoes. If you like skins in your mashed potatoes, use the thin-skinned varieties.

2 When potatoes are tender, drain and return to cooking pan. Use a portable electric mixer or potato masher to mash potatoes until only a few lumps remain.

3 Add sour cream, cream cheese, salt, and pepper, and continue beating until potatoes are fluffy and smooth. Spoon into prepared flameproof casserole, dot with butter, and bake. To finish, place casserole under broiler and broil until top is browned.

4 A sprinkling of paprika and chives gives the finished casserole an appealing color. This side dish makes any meal a feast, and is ideal for holiday dinners.

Mashed Potato Casserole

PICTURED ON FACING PAGE

2½ to 3 pounds (1.15 to 1.35 kg) baking potatoes, or other variety

4 cloves garlic, peeled and left whole

½ cup (120 ml) reduced-fat sour cream

1 package (about 3 oz./85 g) cream cheese, softened

1 teaspoon salt

¼ teaspoon pepper

2 tablespoons butter or margarine
Paprika

1 tablespoon chopped fresh chives

Peel and quarter potatoes. Boil along with garlic cloves until potatoes are tender (see chart, page 128). Drain and return to pan.

While potatoes cook, in a medium-size bowl, combine sour cream, cream cheese, salt, and pepper. Stir until smooth; set aside.

Using a portable electric mixer or a potato masher, beat hot potatoes and garlic in pan until they are nearly smooth. Add sour cream mixture and continue beating until fluffy and smooth. Spoon potatoes into a well-buttered shallow 2-quart (1.9-liter) flameproof casserole; dot with butter. (At this point, you may cover and refrigerate until next day.)

Bake, covered, in a 400°F (205°C) oven for 25 minutes (50 minutes, if refrigerated). Uncover and broil about 6 inches (15 cm) below heat until top browns. Sprinkle with paprika and chives. *Makes 6 servings*

PER SERVING: 243 calories, 12 g total fat, 7 g saturated fat, 33 mg cholesterol, 468 mg sodium, 30 g carbohydrates, 3 g fiber, 6 g protein, 30 mg calcium, 1 mg iron

Stuffed Baked Potatoes

4 large baking potatoes (about 2¼ lbs./1 kg)

¼ cup (60 ml) 2% milk

3 tablespoons butter or margarine

½ teaspoon salt

½ cup (about 2 oz./55 g) shredded sharp Cheddar cheese

2 tablespoons minced green onion

½ teaspoon paprika

Prepare and bake potatoes (see chart, page 128). While potatoes are still warm, cut a thick slice off top of each potato. Using a spoon, scoop out pulp into a medium-size bowl, leaving potato shells ¼ inch (6 mm) thick. Using a hand-held electric mixer or a potato masher, beat potatoes until they are nearly smooth. Gradually beat in milk, butter, and salt; continue beating until smooth. Stir in Cheddar cheese and green onion.

Mound mixture into potato shells; sprinkle lightly with paprika. Place stuffed potatoes in a 10- by 15-inch (25- by 38-cm) rimmed baking pan. (At this point, you may cover and refrigerate up until next day.) Bake, uncovered, in a 375°F (190°C) oven until tops are golden brown and potatoes are piping hot (about 20 minutes). *Makes 4 servings*

PER SERVING: 328 calories, 14 g total fat, 9 g saturated fat, 39 mg cholesterol, 471 mg sodium, 44 g carbohydrates, 4 g fiber, 8 g protein, 145 mg calcium, 3 mg iron

Broccoli-Stuffed Baked Potatoes

Prepare *Stuffed Baked Potatoes*, but add 2 cups (145 g) small blanched *broccoli flowerets* to the stuffing.

Tex-Mex Stuffed Baked Potatoes

Prepare *Stuffed Baked Potatoes*, but substitute ½ cup (about 2 oz./55 g) *pepper jack cheese* for the Cheddar cheese. Stir in ½ cup (about 3 oz./85 g) minced *roasted red peppers* and ½ cup (83 g) *corn kernels*.

Rosemary Roasted Potatoes

2 tablespoons (30 ml) olive oil

4 cloves garlic, unpeeled

½ teaspoon dried rosemary

2 pounds (905 g) small, red, thin-skinned potatoes (1- to 2-in./2.5- to 5-cm diameter), quartered

2 green onions, thinly sliced

½ teaspoon salt

In a 9- by 13-inch (23- by 33-cm) baking dish, combine olive oil, garlic, and rosemary. Heat in a 400°F (205°C) oven until piping hot (about 5 minutes). Add potatoes, shaking pan to coat. Bake, uncovered, shaking pan occasionally, until potatoes are tender and golden brown (about 45 minutes). Sprinkle with green onions and salt; toss to combine. (Serve garlic in peel for squeezing onto potatoes.) *Makes 6 servings*

PER SERVING: 167 calories, 5 g total fat, 0.6 g saturated fat, 0 mg cholesterol, 195 mg sodium, 28 g carbohydrates, 3 g fiber, 3 g protein, 10 mg calcium, 1 mg iron

Roasted Beets with Balsamic Vinaigrette

    6   beets (about 6 oz./170 g each), stems cut to 1 inch (2.5 cm)
    2   tablespoons (30 ml) olive oil
    2   tablespoons (30 ml) balsamic vinegar
    2   teaspoons Dijon mustard
    ¾   teaspoon salt
    ¼   teaspoon pepper

Scrub beets but do not peel. Wrap each beet in foil and place in a 10- by 15-inch (25- by 38-cm) rimmed baking pan. Bake in a 400°F (205°C) oven until tender (1 to 2 hours). Unwrap beets and set aside to cool slightly. When cool enough to handle, peel beets with your fingers or a paring knife (the skins should slip off easily). Quarter beets and slice ½ inch (1 cm) thick.

While beets are baking, in a medium-size bowl, whisk together oil, vinegar, mustard, salt, and pepper. Add beets and toss to coat. Serve at room temperature or chill for up to 2 days. Bring to room temperature before serving.   *Makes 4 servings*

PER SERVING: *142 calories, 7g total fat, 0.9 g saturated fat, 0 mg cholesterol, 601 mg sodium, 18 g carbohydrates, 2 g fiber, 3 g protein, 32 mg calcium, 2 mg iron*

Roasted Root Vegetables

    1   pound (455 g) Yukon gold or baking potatoes
    2   tablespoons (30 ml) olive oil
    ¾   cup (about 4 oz./115 g) baby carrots
    1   large red onion (about 8 oz./230 g), coarsely chopped
    1   large beet (about 8 oz./230 g)
    1   large yam (about 8 oz./230 g)
        A few parsley sprigs or 2 tablespoons sliced green onion
        Salt and pepper

Scrub potatoes and cut into ¾-inch (2-cm) cubes.

In a 500°F (260°C) oven, heat oil in a 10- by 15-inch (25- by 38-cm) rimmed baking pan just until hot (about 1½ minutes). Add potatoes, carrots, and red onion. Cook for 15 minutes, stirring after 10 minutes.

Meanwhile, peel beet and yam; cut each into about ½-inch (1-cm) cubes. Add to pan after potatoes have cooked for 15 minutes. Cook, stirring every 10 minutes, until vegetables are golden brown (about 20 minutes).

Spoon vegetables onto a platter; garnish with parsley. Add salt and pepper to taste.
Makes 4 servings

PER SERVING: *258 calories, 7 g total fat, 0.9 g saturated fat, 0 mg cholesterol, 55 mg sodium, 45 g carbohydrates, 6 g fiber, 5 g protein, 37 mg calcium, 2 mg iron*

Candied Yams

    ⅓   cup (80 ml) apple juice
    3   tablespoons firmly packed brown sugar
    3   tablespoons (45 ml) maple syrup
    2   tablespoons (30 ml) dark molasses
    ⅛   teaspoon allspice
    ⅛   teaspoon ground cinnamon
    3   pounds (1.35 kg) yams or sweet potatoes, peeled and cut diagonally into slices ½ inch (1 cm) thick
        Salt and pepper

In a 10- by 15-inch (25- by 38-cm) rimmed baking pan, combine apple juice, brown sugar, syrup, molasses, allspice, and cinnamon. Turn yams in mixture to coat, then arrange in a single layer, overlapping slightly.

Cover tightly with foil and bake in a 375°F (190°C) oven for 20 minutes. Turn yams over, then continue to bake, covered, until very tender when pierced (about 25 more minutes).

Uncover yams and bake for 15 more minutes. Turn yams over and bake until only a thin layer of syrup remains in bottom of pan (about 5 more minutes).

Arrange yams in a serving dish; scrape syrup from pan and drizzle over yams. Season to taste with salt and pepper.   *Makes 8 servings*

PER SERVING: *229 calories, 0.3 g total fat, 0 g saturated fat, 0 mg cholesterol, 19 mg sodium, 55 g carbohydrates, 6 g fiber, 2 g protein, 80 mg calcium, 2 mg iron*

STIR-FRYING VEGETABLES

Of all the techniques for cooking vegetables, we think stir-frying is perhaps the most versatile—and the most fun. With this method, vegetables retain their crisp textures, bright colors, and natural flavors, and the cooking takes only a few minutes. You can stir-fry either in the traditional bowl-shaped wok (nonstick woks are also available) or in a wide nonstick frying pan.

Basic Stir-Fried Vegetables

1½ teaspoons cornstarch
⅓ cup (80 ml) reduced-sodium chicken broth
2 tablespoons (30 ml) olive oil
2 cloves garlic, minced
1 to 1½ pounds (455 to 680 g) cut vegetables (see box at right)
¾ teaspoon salt
¼ teaspoon pepper

In a cup, mix cornstarch with 1 tablespoon (15 ml) of the broth; set aside.

Heat oil in a wide nonstick frying pan or wok over medium-high heat until hot but not smoking. Add garlic and cook, stirring, until fragrant (30 to 60 seconds). Add vegetables, salt, and pepper; stir-fry for 3 minutes.

Add remaining broth and bring to a boil. Reduce heat to medium, cover, and cook according to the following timing until vegetables are tender-crisp: 6 to 7 minutes for hard vegetables, 4 to 6 minutes for medium-hard vegetables, and 3 to 5 minutes for soft or leafy vegetables. (See box at right for vegetable groupings.)

Stir cornstarch mixture to recombine, then add to vegetables; stir-fry until pan juices are thickened (30 to 60 seconds).   *Makes 4 servings*

PER SERVING: *112 calories, 7 g total fat, 1 g saturated fat, 0 mg cholesterol, 471 mg sodium, 11 g carbohydrates, 3 g fiber, 2 g protein, 40 mg calcium, 0.8 mg iron*

Oriental Stir-Fried Vegetables

Prepare *Basic Stir-fried Vegetables*, but add 1 tablespoon (15 ml) reduced-sodium *soy sauce* and ½ teaspoon *Oriental sesame oil* to the cornstarch mixture. Add 1 tablespoon each grated fresh *ginger* and *crushed red pepper flakes* to taste along with garlic. Reduce salt to ¼ teaspoon and omit pepper. Cook as directed.

What to Stir-Fry . . .

We have grouped the following vegetables by texture, since vegetables of the same texture cook at about the same rate. Follow the cutting suggestions below. For cooking times, see Basic Stir-Fried Vegetables, *at left.*

If you wish to cook several vegetables of different textures, add the hardest vegetables to the pan first and partially cook, then add the more tender vegetables.

Hard Vegetables

You will need about 1 pound (455 g) of one of these vegetables for 4 servings.

Broccoli: *Break into small flowerets; peel stalks and cut diagonally into slices ¼ inch (6 mm) thick*

Carrots: *Cut diagonally into slices ¼ inch (6 mm) thick*

Cauliflower: *Break into small flowerets*

Celery: *Cut diagonally into slices ¼ inch (6 mm) thick*

Medium-Hard Vegetables

You will need about 1½ pounds (680 g) of one of these vegetables for 4 servings.

Asparagus: *Cut diagonally into 2-inch (5-cm) pieces*

Bell peppers: *Cut into strips ¼ inch (6 mm) wide*

Green beans: *Cut diagonally into 1-inch (2.5-cm) pieces*

Mushrooms: *If small, leave whole; if large, cut into slices ¼ inch (6 mm) thick*

Onions: *Halve lengthwise and cut into slices ⅛ to ¼ inch (3 to 6 mm) thick*

Summer squash: *Halve lengthwise and cut diagonally crosswise into slices ¼ inch (6 mm) thick*

Soft or Leafy Vegetables

You will need about 1 pound (455 g) of one of these vegetables for 4 servings.

Bok choy: *Cut crosswise into slices 1 inch (2.5 cm) thick*

Broccoli rabe: *Remove tough stems; cut into 2-inch (5-cm) pieces*

Red or green cabbage: *Quarter and cut into 1-inch (2.5-cm) squares*

Tomatoes: *Cut into wedges ½ inch (1 cm) thick*

Chinese pea pods (snow peas): *Remove strings (see page 124) and use whole*

SAUCES & CONDIMENTS

The word "sauce" comes from *sal*, which is Latin for salt—the most basic of all seasonings. A simple pinch of salt would seem to have nothing in common with an elegant béarnaise sauce, but both serve the same purpose—to enhance food's flavor.

Indeed, sauces and condiments provide much more than a mere decorative touch. A sauce can mellow and blend diverse tastes and textures in a dish (as hollandaise does on eggs Benedict), while a condiment adds definite flavor to foods that are otherwise low-key (as cranberry sauce does for turkey). At the supermarket, you could easily fill a shopping cart with bottled sauces and condiments; but those you make at home will be fresher, and free of the preservatives that are almost unavoidable in store-bought sauces.

The cook's challenge is not only to use sauces and condiments artfully, but also to make them correctly. (Beginners will find the photographs in this chapter particularly helpful because each critical stage is explained in both words and pictures.) Technique and timing are important in sauce-making. For example, when preparing a white sauce—a culinary standby—you must be sure that the butter and flour are thoroughly blended before gradually whisking in the liquid. Rush, and the sauce may get lumpy. But once you've mastered the basic technique, you're ready to try any of our seven white-sauce variations—or to invent your own. Our recipe for hollandaise sauce—another classic—also comes with a number of variations.

Easy & elegant condiments

The highly flavorful, vibrantly colorful fruit and vegetable condiments on pages 144 and 145—guacamole, chutney, salsas—are a snap to make. Most can be mixed quickly in a bowl or a food processor, so you can serve them on the spur of the moment. Each condiment features fresh and sometimes unexpected flavorings—cilantro, vanilla, cinnamon, lime—that give it a unique appeal. You may want to share these condiments with friends; a jar of homemade cranberry sauce or spicy chutney is a great gift idea.

SAUCES

Hollandaise Sauce

This classic French emulsion sauce has an off-putting reputation: It's supposed to be tricky to prepare and easy to ruin. But, like mayonnaise (see page 25), it's not as temperamental as you might think.

In making hollandaise, one whole egg or three egg yolks can be used interchangeably. The all-yolk sauce simply has a more golden color and tends to be thicker.

Rich and elegant, hollandaise sauce pairs well with freshly cooked artichokes or asparagus; it's also a wonderful choice to crown poached fish or eggs Benedict.

    1 large whole egg or 3 large egg yolks
    1 tablespoon (15 ml) lemon juice or white wine vinegar
    ½ cup (4 oz./115 g) butter or margarine, melted and hot

Using a whisk or portable electric mixer, beat eggs, and lemon juice, off heat, in the top of a double boiler until thick and lemon-colored (about 5 minutes). Place pan over gently simmering water (water should not boil or touch bottom of pan). Beating constantly, add butter, a few drops at a time in the beginning, but increasing to a slow, steady stream as mixture begins to thicken. After all butter is added, continue to cook, beating, until sauce thickens (about 3 minutes). A cooked whole-egg sauce should look like cream that is just beginning to thicken when whipped; an all-yolk sauce should be thick enough to hold its shape briefly when dropped from a beater.

As soon as sauce has thickened, remove from heat and serve immediately. Or, if sauce is to be used within several hours, pour into a jar, cover, and let stand; then warm the sauce.

To warm hollandaise, bring sauce to room temperature and stir to soften. Place jar in water that's hot to touch; stir until sauce is warm, not hot.
Makes about ¾ cup (180 ml)

PER TABLESPOON: *74 calories, 8 g total fat, 5 g saturated fat, 38 mg cholesterol, 84 mg sodium, 0.1 g carbohydrates, 0 g fiber, 0.6 g protein, 4 mg calcium, 0.1 mg iron*

Mousseline Sauce

Prepare *Hollandaise Sauce*. Beat ⅓ cup (80 ml) *whipping cream* until stiff peaks form; fold into hollandaise (warm or at room temperature). Serve immediately over boiled or steamed vegetables or fish.

Béarnaise Sauce

In a small pan, combine 1 tablespoon minced *shallot* or onion, 1 teaspoon *dried tarragon*, and 3 tablespoons (45 ml) *white wine vinegar*. Simmer over medium heat until liquid is reduced to 2 teaspoons (about 1 minute.) Prepare *Hollandaise Sauce*, but stir shallot mixture (hot or cold) into egg mixture before adding butter. Good with green beans, salmon, beef, broiled chicken, lamb, and egg dishes.

Maltaise Sauce

Prepare *Hollandaise Sauce*, but stir 2 tablespoons (30 ml) *orange juice* and ½ teaspoon grated *orange peel* into egg mixture before adding butter. Good with asparagus, broccoli, and Brussels sprouts.

Fixing a Curdled Hollandaise

Don't give up if your hollandaise curdles and separates—here are three ways you can rescue it:

• *For ¾ cup (180 ml) curdled hollandaise, whisk curdled hollandaise into in 2 tablespoons (30 ml) water, whisking until smooth.*

• *If cooked sauce has just begun to separate, immediately set pan of sauce in a bowl of ice water to stop the cooking; beat until smooth. Gently reheat over simmering water.*

HOW TO MAKE A WHITE SAUCE

1 A white sauce begins with melted butter. Place 2 tablespoons butter in a 1½- to 2-quart (1.4- to 1.9-liter) pan and melt over medium heat; don't let butter brown.

2 After adding flour, whisk constantly to keep mixture smooth. Cook, whisking, until mixture bubbles and foams. This brief cooking eliminates the raw taste of the flour. Don't brown butter-flour mixture (roux) for a white sauce; it should be a very pale golden color.

3 Remove pan from heat and gradually add milk, whisking constantly so that lumps do not form.

4 With pan returned to heat, cook, whisking, until sauce thickens and comes to a boil. If properly made, White Sauce should be velvety smooth. If a thinner sauce is desired, whisk in ¼ cup (60 ml) more milk.

White Sauce

PICTURED ON FACING PAGE

Knowing how to prepare a white sauce is one of the hidden cornerstones of cooking, for the sauce is seldom an end in itself. Generally, it serves as part of another dish—the base for a soufflé, the binding agent for a casserole, the foundation for a "creamed" dish, or the final touch for an au gratin dish.

Our basic recipe for a medium-thick white sauce takes only about 5 minutes to prepare. The recipe and its variations will yield about 1 cup (240 ml) of sauce, but can easily be doubled.

> 2   tablespoons butter or margarine
> 2   tablespoons all-purpose flour
> 1   to 1¼ cups (240 to 300 ml) 2% milk
> ⅛   teaspoon salt
>   Pinch of pepper

Melt butter in a 1½- to 2-quart (1.4- to 1.9-liter) pan over medium heat. Add flour and cook, whisking, until butter-flour mixture (roux) is bubbling and foamy (about 1 minute). The flour must be cooked long enough to eliminate the raw flour taste, but not so long as to color beyond a light gold. Remove pan from heat and, using a whisk, gradually blend in 1 cup (240 ml) of the milk. Return pan to heat and cook, whisking constantly, until sauce is smooth, thick, and boiling (about 2 minutes). Add salt, and pepper to taste. For a thinner sauce, add ¼ cup (60 ml) more milk.   *Makes 1 cup (240 ml)*

PER TABLESPOON: *24 calories, 2 g total fat, 1 g saturated fat, 5 mg cholesterol, 40 mg sodium, 2 g carbohydrates, 0 g fiber, 0.6 g protein, 19 mg calcium, 0 mg iron*

Velouté Sauce

Prepare *White Sauce*, but use *reduced-sodium chicken broth* instead of milk. Good with any cooked vegetable or poultry.

Cheddar Cheese Sauce

Prepare *White Sauce*, but stir ½ cup (about 2 oz./55 g) shredded *Cheddar cheese* into finished sauce and simmer until cheese is melted (about 30 seconds). Good with broccoli, cauliflower, potatoes, or other vegetables.

Mornay Sauce

Prepare *White Sauce*, but stir ¼ cup (about ¾ oz./20 g) grated *Parmesan cheese* and a pinch of *ground nutmeg* into finished sauce and simmer for 1 minute. Good with broccoli, cauliflower, potatoes, crab, oysters, scallops, fish, poultry, pasta, and eggs.

Curry Sauce

Prepare *White Sauce*, but add 1½ teaspoons *curry powder* and ⅛ teaspoon *ground ginger* to butter along with the flour. Good with carrots, cauliflower, shrimp, lamb, poultry, and eggs.

Dill Sauce

Prepare *White Sauce*, but stir ¼ cup (15 g) chopped *fresh dill* and ½ teaspoon *lemon juice* into finished sauce. Good with green beans, carrots, potatoes, and fish.

Mustard Sauce

Prepare *White Sauce*, but stir 1 tablespoon (15 ml) *Dijon mustard* into finished sauce and simmer for 1 minute. Good with broccoli, Brussels sprouts, cabbage, potatoes, poached or baked fish, and poultry.

Mushroom Sauce

Melt butter for *White Sauce*. In it, cook 4 ounces (115 g) sliced *mushrooms* until soft. Add 1 tablespoon (15 ml) *dry sherry* and cook until evaporated (about 30 seconds). Stir in flour, then immediately add milk, and cook, stirring, until thickened (about 2 minutes). Stir in ¼ teaspoon each *salt* and *pepper*. Stir 2 teaspoons *lemon juice* into finished sauce. Good with green beans, potatoes, spinach (in creamed spinach), and hamburgers.

HOW TO MAKE A REDUCTION SAUCE

1 A full-flavored reduction sauce begins with pan drippings. To defat juices, pour into a gravy strainer. Fat will rise to top, allowing you to pour off juices from bottom through spout. If you don't have a gravy strainer, pour drippings into small bowl and spoon off fat. If you have time, chill drippings just until fat congeals on top, then lift it off.

2 Measure defatted drippings and add enough liquid (such as beef broth or chicken broth, wine, or sherry) to measure 1 cup (240 ml). Pour mixture into pan. Add herbs, mustard, or other seasonings, if desired.

3 Place roasting pan over heat and bring liquid to a boil, scraping browned particles from bottom of pan (this step is called deglazing the pan). Boil until reduced by half.

4 For a luxuriously rich sauce, stir in ⅓ to ½ cup (80 to 120 ml) whipping cream and return to a boil. Cook until large, shiny bubbles appear on the surface and sauce is reduced to ½ cup (120 ml). Serve immediately, or keep warm (see facing page for more information on keeping the sauce warm).

REDUCTION SAUCES MADE FROM PAN DRIPPINGS

Many a chef has built a reputation on deftly seasoned sauces that lend sophistication to simply cooked food. Perhaps the sauce that restaurateurs rely on most to embellish roasted and pan-broiled meats is a reduction sauce—and for good reason. It has a smooth texture, distinctive sheen, and rich flavor; yet it's surprisingly simple and quick to prepare.

The essential flavor comes from the liquid—generally broth or wine—used to deglaze the pan drippings from the meat or roast. Seasonings such as herbs, mustard, or shallots further enhance the flavor. (Salt is never added until the sauce is completed; always taste it first.) The deglazing liquid, along with drippings and seasonings, is reduced (boiled down) to about half the original volume to concentrate the flavor. You can then serve this simple reduction sauce (see Standing Rib Roast, page 69), or, to make a more elaborate version, continue with the steps that follow.

The texture of the more elaborate reduction sauces depends on whether you thicken them with whipping cream, or whipping cream and butter (or margarine), or just butter (or margarine). Cream alone makes a thick, satiny sauce; you just boil it down to reach the desired thickness. For an even thicker, silky-smooth sauce, add butter to the liquid-cream mixture, stirring constantly to force the liquid droplets apart and hold them in suspension. For a lighter, more sheer sauce, use only butter or margarine to thicken the reduced liquid.

Making reduction sauces

Lift pan-cooked or roasted meat or poultry from the pan; set aside and keep warm. Spoon off and discard most of the fat from pan drippings (or use a gravy strainer). Pour pan drippings into a glass measure, add enough liquid (suggestions follow) to make 1 cup (240 ml). Return liquid to roasting pan. Add seasonings (suggestions follow), if desired. Boil, uncovered, over high heat, scraping browned particles free from pan, until reduced to ½ cup (120 ml). At this point, you may serve sauce or, if desired, you can add cream, or cream and butter, or just butter.

To add cream: Pour in ⅓ to ½ cup (80 to 120 ml) whipping cream and boil again until big shiny bubbles form all over the surface, and sauce is again reduced to ½ cup (120 ml). You may serve sauce immediately, or keep warm, or add butter.

To add butter: To add butter to the reduced liquid or to the liquid-cream mixture, reduce heat to low or remove pan from heat to prevent liquid from evaporating too quickly. Add 2 to 6 tablespoons (1 to 3 oz./30 to 85 g) butter or margarine all at once (amount depends on consistency desired), stirring constantly to incorporate butter as it melts. The butter will thicken sauce. Serve immediately or keep warm as directed below.   *Makes 4 to 6 servings*

Suggested liquids: Use reduced-sodium beef broth or chicken broth; or use dry red or white wine, dry vermouth, dry sherry, Madeira, or port; or use half broth and half wine.

Suggested seasonings: Use about ½ teaspoon dried tarragon, dried basil, or dried thyme; or 1½ teaspoons fresh herbs, such as parsley or basil; and/or 1 or 2 teaspoons Dijon mustard; and/or 1 to 2 tablespoons minced shallots.

Keeping a reduction sauce warm

Since a reduction sauce can be made so quickly, there's little need to prepare it ahead. But if it's more convenient to hold the sauce for a time, set the serving container, uncovered, in a pan of hot-to-touch water. Stir occasionally, and if the water cools, replace it with more hot-to-touch water. (Reduction sauces tend to break down if reheated.)

Restoring a broken sauce

If you boil away too much of the liquid base before adding the cream or butter, the sauce will break down or separate, just as it will if you reheat the sauce over direct heat. To restore the sauce to the proper texture, heat 2 to 4 tablespoons (30 to 60 ml) of whipping cream or wine in a 1-quart (950-ml) pan over low heat. Beating constantly, whisk in the broken sauce, a few drops at a time, until all the sauce is incorporated.

CONDIMENTS

Guacamole

2 large avocados (about 12 oz./340 g each)
　About 2 tablespoons (30 ml) lime juice
⅔ cup (30 g) chopped cilantro
1 small tomato (about 4 oz./115 g), chopped
3 large green onions, minced
¾ teaspoon salt
6 drops liquid hot pepper seasoning (or to taste)

Halve and pit avocados. With a spoon, scoop out avocado pulp into a medium-size bowl. With a fork, mash pulp coarsely while blending in 2 tablespoons (30 ml) of the lime juice. Add cilantro, tomato, onions, salt, and hot pepper seasoning; stir to combine. Add more lime juice to taste, if desired.
Makes 2 cups/440 g (8 servings)

PER ¼ CUP (55 G): 108 calories, 10 g total fat, 2 g saturated fat, 0 mg cholesterol, 218 mg sodium, 6 g carbohydrates, 2 g fiber, 2 g protein, 16 mg calcium, 0.8 mg iron

Salsa Fresca

1 large tomato (about 8 oz./230 g), cored and chopped
2 large tomatillos (about 6 oz./170 g total), husked and chopped, or 1 small tomato (about 4 oz./115 g), chopped
¼ cup (10 g) chopped cilantro
⅓ cup (35 g) chopped yellow onion or green onions
2 tablespoons minced fresh or canned hot chiles (or to taste)
2 tablespoons (30 ml) lime juice
　Salt

In a medium-size bowl, combine tomato, tomatillos, cilantro, onion, chiles, lime juice, and salt to taste. Serve immediately or chill airtight for up to 3 days.
Makes 3 cups/720 g (8 servings)

PER ¼ CUP (60 G): 15 calories, 0.2 g total fat, 0 g saturated fat, 0 mg cholesterol, 3 mg sodium, 3 g carbohydrates, 0.5 g fiber, 0.6 g protein, 6 mg calcium, 0.1 mg iron

Dried Tomato Tapenade

1 jar (about 8 oz./230 g) oil-packed dried tomatoes, drained
½ cup (85 g) capers, rinsed and drained
1 can (2 oz./55 g) anchovy fillets, drained and chopped
1 tablespoon minced or pressed garlic
1 tablespoon chopped parsley
2 tablespoons (30 ml) extra-virgin olive oil
2 teaspoons brandy (optional)
1½ teaspoons Dijon mustard

In a food processor or blender, whirl tomatoes, capers, anchovies, garlic, parsley, olive oil, brandy (if using), and mustard until coarsely puréed. Serve immediately or cover and chill airtight for up to 1 week.　*Makes 1⅓ cups/280 g (16 to 18 servings)*

PER TABLESPOON: 78 calories, 7 g total fat, 1 g saturated fat, 2 mg cholesterol, 291 mg sodium, 3 g carbohydrates, 0.8 g fiber, 1 g protein, 12 mg calcium, 0.4 mg iron

Spicy Cocktail Sauce

1 cup (240 ml) chili sauce
½ cup (20 g) chopped cilantro
¼ cup (60 ml) lime juice
1 teaspoon ground cumin
¼ teaspoon salt
3 or 4 drops liquid hot pepper seasoning (or to taste)

In a medium-size bowl, combine chili sauce, cilantro, lime juice, cumin, salt, and hot pepper seasoning. Serve immediately or cover and chill for a few hours.　*Makes 1 cup/272 g (16 servings)*

PER TABLESPOON: 19 calories, 0.1 g total fat, 0 g saturated fat, 0 mg cholesterol, 264 mg sodium, 5 g carbohydrates, 0 g fiber, 0.5 g protein, 6 mg calcium, 0.2 mg iron

Peach & Honeydew Salsa

1½ cups (285 g) diced honeydew melon (¼-in./6-mm dice)

1½ cups (279 g) peeled, diced firm-ripe peaches (¼-in./ 6-mm dice)

2 tablespoons minced fresh mint

2 tablespoons (30 ml) seasoned rice vinegar (or 2 tablespoons/30 ml distilled white vinegar plus ½ teaspoon sugar)

1 tablespoon minced fresh tarragon or ½ teaspoon dried tarragon

1 tablespoon (15 ml) lemon juice

Salt

In a medium-size bowl, gently combine melon, peaches, mint, vinegar, tarragon, and lemon juice; add salt to taste.

Serve salsa immediately, or chill airtight for up to 2 hours.   *Makes 3 cups/720 g (6 servings)*

PER ½ CUP (120 G): *38 calories, 0.1 g total fat, 0 g saturated fat, 0 mg cholesterol, 104 mg sodium, 10 g carbohydrates, 1 g fiber, 0.5 g protein, 7 mg calcium, 0.1 mg iron*

Cranberry Sauce

2 bags (12 oz./340 g each) fresh or frozen cranberries

⅔ cup (150 g) firmly packed brown sugar

⅔ cup (135 g) granulated sugar

½ cup (120 ml) orange juice

1 tablespoon (15 ml) lemon juice

⅛ teaspoon ground cinnamon

1 tablespoon (15 ml) vanilla

In a 2- to 3-quart (1.9- to 2.8-liter) pan over high heat, bring cranberries, brown sugar, granulated sugar, orange juice, lemon juice, and cinnamon to a simmer. Reduce heat and continue to simmer, uncovered, stirring occasionally, until cranberries are tender when pierced (8 to 10 minutes).

Stir in vanilla; let cool. Serve, or chill airtight for up to 1 week.   *Makes 3½ cups/1.05 kg (14 servings)*

PER ¼ CUP (75 G): *107 calories, 0.1 g total fat, 0 g saturated fat, 0 mg cholesterol, 5 mg sodium, 27 g carbohydrates, 2 g fiber, 0.2 g protein, 14 mg calcium, 0.3 mg iron*

Dried Apricot Chutney

1 pound (455 g) dried apricots, finely chopped

2 medium-size firm-ripe pears (5 to 6 oz./140 to 170 g each), peeled, cored, and diced

1 medium-size apple (about 6 oz./170 g), peeled, cored, and diced

2½ cups (590 ml) white grape juice

1¼ cups (188 g) golden raisins

1 cup (220 g) firmly packed brown sugar

½ cup (120 ml) white wine vinegar

⅓ cup (80 ml) lemon juice

2 tablespoons diced candied ginger

1 tablespoon ground cinnamon

4 cinnamon sticks, each about 2 inches (5 cm) long

1 teaspoon mustard seeds

1 teaspoon ground nutmeg

½ teaspoon ground cloves

½ teaspoon ground red pepper (cayenne)

In a 5- to 6-quart (5- to 6-liter) pan, combine apricots, pears, apple, grape juice, raisins, sugar, vinegar, lemon juice, ginger, ground cinnamon, cinnamon sticks, mustard seeds, nutmeg, cloves, and ground red pepper. Place pan over high heat and stir until mixture begins to bubble. Reduce heat and simmer gently, stirring as needed to prevent sticking, until mixture is thickened and reduced to about 5 cups/1.2 liters (1¾ to 2 hours).

Let chutney cool. Discard cinnamon sticks and spoon chutney into 1- to 2-cup (240- to 470-ml) jars. Serve immediately, or chill airtight for up to 1 month; freeze to store longer.
Makes 5 cups/1.7 kg (20 servings)

PER ¼ CUP (85 G): *165 calories, 0.3 g total fat, 0 g saturated fat, 0 mg cholesterol, 12 mg sodium, 43 g carbohydrates, 3 g fiber, 1 g protein, 38 mg calcium, 2 mg iron*

BREADS & PIZZA

Crusty and fragrant, freshly baked bread adds a special warmth to any meal, and few foods are as rewarding to prepare. If you're accustomed to store-bought bread, the full flavors and marvelous textures of home-baked yeast breads and quick breads will provide unexpected pleasure. You'll also want to try your hand at our easy muffins, biscuits, scones, popovers, pancakes, waffles, and pizzas.

Don't let the thought of baking with yeast intimidate you. Yeast breads have the reputation of being chancy, but if you treat the yeast right (make sure the water in which it's dissolved isn't too hot), it will respond well. Yeast doughs do require kneading and rising; however, kneading is a relaxing activity, and the dough needs no attention while it's rising.

Quick breads, on the other hand, use baking powder or baking soda instead of yeast for leavening. They're assembled quickly, stirred only briefly, and baked immediately.

Bread-making machines and ready-to-bake bread doughs and pizza crusts eliminate most of the work and time involved in homemade methods. With them as backups,

you can set aside some time on weekends for baking with family or friends.

Both yeast breads and quick breads freeze well. Cool, wrap them airtight, and freeze for up to three months. Thaw at room temperature before placing them on a baking sheet. Cover soft-crusted breads loosely with foil; leave crusty breads uncovered. Reheat in a 350°F (175°C) oven for 10 to 15 minutes.

Baking bread in high country

Baking at altitudes above 3,000 feet requires recipe adjustments: Leavenings such as baking powder, baking soda, and yeast react faster, but foods cook more slowly. Experts suggest decreasing the baking powder and baking soda in standard recipes by one fourth. Yeast doughs will rise much more rapidly, so you may need to let the dough rise twice (punching it down after each rising) instead of once; don't let the dough rise beyond double its original size. Or, use less yeast.

Also, you may need to add more liquid. Popovers balloon faster at high elevations, so use an extra egg in standard recipes to strengthen the popovers' walls.

146

BREADS

YEAST BREAD

Home-baked yeast bread satisfies in every way—it's almost as much fun to make as it is to eat. Six basic ingredients interact to create this age-old food: yeast, liquid, sugar, salt, fat, and flour.

When yeast (a microscopic organism and therefore a biological, not chemical, leavening agent) is activated and "fed" with flour, it gives off bubbles of carbon dioxide. It is this gas that leavens the dough and makes it rise, just as baking powder and baking soda leaven quick breads. You will need at least ¼ cup (60 ml) of warm (110°F/43°C) water to dissolve 1 package (1¾ teaspoons) of active dry yeast granules. Here, temperature is crucial—if the water is too cool, the yeast action will be sluggish; if the water is too hot, it will kill the yeast and the dough will fail to rise. Use a thermometer until you learn to feel the right temperature with your hand.

Sugar provides food for the yeast, enabling it to grow; salt slows the action. The two together keep the dough on just the right leavening schedule for good texture and flavor. Fats make the bread tender, moist, and palatable. Flour provides structure and strength. There is no need to sift flour—on the other hand, do not pack it into cups or shake it down.

Three steps to a perfect loaf

The secret to a shapely, springy loaf of bread is the care and thoroughness given to mixing and kneading the dough. These steps develop the gluten in the flour. (Gluten is a protein that gives dough its elasticity and helps bread retain its shape when baked.)

Mixing. Dissolve the yeast first, then mix in other ingredients, adding flour last of all. A 4-quart (3.8-liter) bowl will hold the ingredients for most yeast breads. Yeast reacts well to a warm kitchen; in a cool kitchen, the dough will take a bit longer to rise. The most important thing is to keep dough away from drafts.

When adding the flour, sprinkle it, 1 cup (125 g) at a time, over the yeast mixture, stirring with a wooden spoon until evenly moistened. When enough flour has been stirred in to form a thick batter (usually two thirds of the total amount the recipe calls for), beat the batter very well with a wooden spoon or with a heavy-duty electric mixer on medium speed. After 5 minutes you can see the gluten developing—the batter becomes glossy and elastic, stretching with the motion of the spoon.

Kneading. Spread about ½ to ¾ cup (60 to 95 g) flour on a board, coating the center most heavily. Turn the dough out onto this area and sprinkle the dough lightly with flour. Now you're ready to start kneading, which will complete the gluten formation.

Your object is to shape the dough into a ball. As you knead, keep the dough lightly coated with flour and the underside smooth and unbroken. Develop a rhythm, and use a gentle touch. Brute force breaks the dough and allows too much flour to be incorporated. (Kneading instructions are on pages 148–149.)

Overkneading is virtually impossible; the longer you spend at it (perhaps 20 or 30 minutes), the higher and more evenly textured your finished loaf is likely to be. It's best to judge by feel. When dough is smooth and no longer sticky, and its surface is faintly pebbled with air bubbles, hold it to your cheek. If it has a firm bounce and velvety touch, you have probably kneaded it long enough.

Letting it rise. After the dough has been thoroughly kneaded, it almost takes care of itself. Your job is simply to provide a warm (about 80°F/27°C) draft-free place for the rising (sometimes called "proofing"). Most yeast breads rise twice: the first time until doubled, the second time until almost doubled.

Like so many aspects of bread-making, rising times are variable, depending mostly on temperature but also on the heaviness of the dough (whole grain breads rise more slowly than white breads) and the elevation at which the bread is being prepared.

. . . in a Warm Place

The most convenient warm place in which dough can rise is inside a switched-off oven with the oven light on. If your oven feels cool inside, turn it to the lowest setting for a minute or two, then switch it off before putting the dough inside. You can also place a pan of hot water on the oven shelf below the bowl of dough. Or place the bowl near a radiator, but not on it.

HOW TO MAKE FARMER'S BREAD

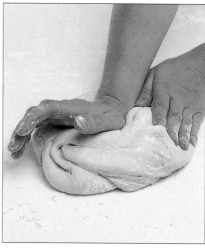

1 Dissolve yeast in water and set aside. In a large bowl, stir together 4 cups (500 g) of the flour and the salt. Then, using a pastry blender or 2 table knives, cut butter into dry ingredients until mixture is crumbly.

2 Pour in yeast mixture and stir—by hand or with a heavy-duty electric mixer—until dry ingredients are completely moistened. Gradually work in 1 cup (125 g) more flour; dough should hold together when lifted.

3 Place dough on a floured surface and dust your hands lightly with flour. Knead dough by alternately folding it over and gently pushing it away with the heels of your hands. Rotate dough a quarter turn after each kneading motion.

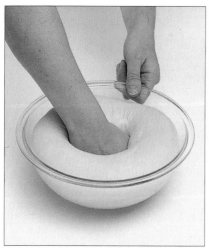

4 After kneading, dough should be a satiny-smooth ball. Place dough in large greased bowl and turn dough to grease top; cover and let rise until almost doubled. Then, with your fist, punch down dough to its original volume.

5 Make sure dough is placed on a large baking sheet to rise. After second rising, cut a deep "X" in top of loaf, using a floured sharp paring knife.

6 After its two-stage baking—first at 400°F (205°C) then at 350°F (175°C)—the loaf will have a tempting golden crust. To make sure it's done, rap the loaf with your knuckles; you should hear a hollow sound.

Farmer's Bread

PICTURED ON FACING PAGE

    2 packages active dry yeast
    2 cups (470 ml) warm water (about 110°F/43°C)
       About 6¼ cups (780 g) all-purpose flour
    1 teaspoon salt
    ⅓ cup (76 g) cold butter or margarine, cut into small pieces

In a 2-cup (470-ml) measure, dissolve yeast in water; stirring to mix. In a large bowl, combine 4 cups (500 g) of the flour and the salt. Cut in butter with a pastry blender or 2 table knives to make a crumbly mixture. Add yeast mixture; stir with a wooden spoon or a heavy-duty mixer until all flour is moistened. Work in 1 cup (125 g) more of the flour to make a stiff dough (dough should be stiff enough to hold together when lifted).

Turn dough out onto a floured board and sprinkle lightly with a little flour. Adding flour as needed to prevent sticking, knead the dough by reaching over the ball of dough and grasping the edge farthest from you. Then pull it toward you in a rolling motion and fold almost in half. With the heel of your hand, gently roll the ball away from you to lightly seal the fold. Rotate dough a quarter turn and continue this folding-rolling motion, making a quarter turn each time. Knead until the dough is smooth and satiny (about 10 minutes). Place in a butter-coated bowl and turn to coat top. Cover with plastic wrap and let rise in a warm place until doubled (1 to 1½ hours).

Lightly butter a large baking sheet (it must be large or bread will rise off sheet). Punch down dough in bowl. Transfer dough to a lightly floured board and knead briefly. Shape into an oval loaf (about 7 by 9 inches/18 by 23 cm); place on baking sheet, cover with plastic wrap, and let rise in a warm place until almost doubled (about 45 minutes).

With a floured sharp knife, cut a ½-inch- (1-cm-) deep cross in top of loaf; brush loaf lightly with water. Bake in a 400°F (205°C) oven for 25 minutes. Reduce heat to 350°F (175°C) and bake until loaf sounds hollow when tapped (about 15 more minutes). Let cool on a rack before slicing.
Makes 1 large loaf (18 to 20 servings)

PER SERVING: *187 calories, 4 g total fat, 2 g saturated fat, 9 mg cholesterol, 150 mg sodium, 32 g carbohydrates, 1 g fiber, 5 g protein, 8 mg calcium, 2 mg iron*

Super Simple Refrigerator Bread

    2 cups (470 ml) boiling water
    ⅓ cup (76 g) butter or margarine
    ⅓ cup (70 g) plus 1 tablespoon sugar
    2 teaspoons salt
    2 packages active dry yeast
    ¼ cup (60 ml) warm water (about 110°F/43°C)
    1 large egg, well beaten
       About 8 cups (1 kg) all-purpose flour

In a large bowl, combine the boiling water, butter, ⅓ cup (70 g) of the sugar, and the salt; let cool to lukewarm.

Meanwhile, dissolve yeast and remaining 1 tablespoon sugar in the ¼ cup (60 ml) warm water; let stand until bubbly (about 5 minutes).

Add yeast mixture to butter mixture and stir to combine; stir in egg. Stir in 4 cups (500 g) of the flour; then gradually stir in as much of the remaining flour as dough will absorb, mixing well. Place dough in a butter-coated bowl and turn to coat top; cover with plastic wrap, place in the refrigerator, and chill for at least 3 hours or up until next day.

To bake, divide dough in half. With buttered hands, shape each half into a smooth loaf. Place each loaf in a buttered 5- by 9-inch (12.5- by 23-cm) metal loaf pan; cover with plastic wrap and let rise in a warm place until almost doubled (about 2 hours).

Bake in a 375°F (190°C) oven until loaves sound hollow when tapped (30 to 35 minutes). Immediately turn loaves out onto a rack to cool completely.
Makes 2 loaves (12 slices each)

PER SLICE: *192 calories, 4 g total fat, 2 g saturated fat, 16 mg cholesterol, 213 mg sodium, 34 g carbohydrates, 1 g fiber, 5 g protein, 9 mg calcium, 2 mg iron*

If You Forget the Dough

What if you let dough rise too long? You'll find it has ballooned past double its original size; its "skin" is thin and transparent, with bubbles just beneath. Such "over-proofed" dough still makes excellent bread—just punch it down and let it rise again. Dough can over-rise two or three times without harm to the finished loaf. However, this doesn't suit breads baked at high altitudes.

PREPARING STICKY PECAN ROLLS

1 Brush dough rectangle with melted butter and sprinkle with cinnamon-brown sugar mixture. Starting at one long (15-inch/38-cm) side, roll up the dough rectangle, using the palms of your hands to put an even but gentle pressure on the roll. Make it as compact as possible without compressing it.

2 After cutting the dough cylinder into 12 equal slices, each about 1¼ inches (3.3 cm) wide, place them on top of the pecans in the bottom of the prepared muffin cups. If slices were flattened slightly when they were cut, gently reform them so they evenly fill the muffin cups.

3 Set the muffin pan aside in a warm place and let rolls rise, uncovered, until doubled (about 1½ hours). The rolls are now ready to bake.

4 After baking, place platter over muffin pan and invert, leaving muffin pan over the rolls briefly so all of the syrup can drizzle over them. Be sure to turn out rolls immediately after baking: If allowed to cool in the pan, the pecan mixture would harden and the rolls would be difficult to remove.

Sticky Pecan Rolls

PICTURED ON FACING PAGE

    1   cup (240 ml) 2% milk
    ¼   cup (50 g) plus 1 teaspoon granulated sugar
    3   tablespoons (45 ml) vegetable oil
    1   teaspoon salt
    1   package active dry yeast
    ¼   cup (60 ml) warm water (about 110°F/43°C)
    1   large egg
        About 3¼ cups (405 g) all-purpose flour
    6   tablespoons (83 g) butter or margarine, melted and cooled
    ¾   cup (160 g) firmly packed brown sugar
    2   tablespoons (30 ml) water
    ¾   cup (90 g) coarsely chopped pecans
    1   teaspoon ground cinnamon

In a 1-quart (950 ml) pan, combine milk, ¼ cup (50 g) of the granulated sugar, oil, and salt. Bring to a boil over medium heat; remove from heat and cool.

Meanwhile, in a large bowl, dissolve yeast and remaining 1 teaspoon granulated sugar in the ¼ cup (60 ml) warm water, stirring to mix; let sit until bubbly (about 5 minutes).

Add milk mixture, egg, and 2 cups (250 g) of the flour to yeast mixture; stir until well combined. Add about ¼ to ½ cup (30 to 60 g) of the remaining flour to make a sticky dough.

Turn dough out onto a floured surface and knead (see page 149) until dough is firm, smooth, and no longer sticky (about 10 minutes), adding more flour as needed. Let dough rest on board.

Butter a muffin pan with twelve cups 2½ inches (6 cm) in diameter. In a small bowl, combine 4 tablespoons (55 g) of the melted butter, ½ cup (110 g) of the brown sugar, and the 2 tablespoons (30 ml) water. Distribute mixture among coated muffin cups; top mixture evenly with pecans. Press mixture into bottom of each cup.

Roll dough into a 12- by 15-inch (30- by 38-cm) rectangle. Brush surface with the remaining 2 tablespoons butter. In a small bowl, combine cinnamon with the remaining ¼ cup (55 g) brown sugar; sprinkle evenly over buttered dough. Starting with one long side, roll rectangle into a cylinder, then cut into 12 equal slices (each about 1¼ inches/3.3 cm wide). Place, one cut side down, in muffin cups. Let rise, uncovered, in a warm place until doubled (about 1½ hours).

Place muffin pan on a baking sheet and bake in a 350°F (175°C) oven until tops are golden (about 25 minutes). Invert immediately onto a serving platter; let pan remain briefly on rolls so syrup can drizzle over them. Let cool for 10 minutes before serving. *Makes 1 dozen rolls*

PER ROLL: *347 calories, 16 g total fat, 5 g saturated fat, 35 mg cholesterol, 264 mg sodium, 47 g carbohydrates, 2 g fiber, 5 g protein, 52 mg calcium, 2 mg iron*

Bulgur Wheat Rolls

    ½   cup (88 g) bulgur (cracked wheat)
    ½   cup (120 ml) water
    1   package active dry yeast
    1   cup (240 ml) warm 2% milk (about 110°F/43°C)
    ¼   cup sugar
    1   teaspoon salt
    1   cup (120 g) whole wheat flour
    2   tablespoons butter or margarine, at room temperature
    1   large egg
        About 2¼ cups (280 g) all-purpose flour

In a medium-size bowl, combine bulgur and water; let stand until water is absorbed (about 45 minutes).

In a large bowl, sprinkle yeast over milk; let stand until dissolved (about 5 minutes). Add sugar, salt, whole wheat flour, butter, egg, and bulgur; stir to blend. Stir in 2 cups (250 g) of the all-purpose flour.

Turn dough out onto a lightly floured board and knead until smooth and springy (10 to 15 minutes), adding more all-purpose flour as needed to prevent sticking. Place in a butter-coated bowl and turn to coat top. Cover with plastic wrap and let rise in a warm place until doubled (about 50 minutes).

Punch dough down and knead briefly on a lightly floured board to release air. Cut into 12 equal pieces. Working with one piece at a time (keep remaining dough covered), gently knead each piece into a smooth ball. Place balls at least 2 inches (5 cm) apart on a buttered baking sheet. Cover lightly and let rise in a warm place until puffy (about 40 minutes).

Bake, uncovered, in a 400°F (205°C) oven until well browned (20 to 25 minutes). Transfer to racks and let cool. (At this point, you may wrap airtight and refrigerate for up to 5 days.) *Makes 12 rolls*

PER ROLL: *201 calories, 4 g total fat, 2 g saturated fat, 25 mg cholesterol, 221 mg sodium, 36 g carbohydrates, 3 g fiber, 6 g protein, 38 mg calcium, 2 mg iron*

Flour & Other Grain Products

The main ingredient of yeast bread is wheat, because it contains a protein called gluten. When wet and kneaded, gluten develops the strength and elasticity necessary to trap and hold the carbon dioxide produced by yeast—which is what makes the dough rise.

All-purpose flour (regular white flour) is a blend of refined wheat flours without the bran and germ. It is available bleached or unbleached. All-purpose flour may be combined with whole grain flours to keep whole grain breads from being too heavy and dense.

Whole wheat flour, ground from the entire wheat kernel, is heavier, richer in fiber, and more perishable than all-purpose flour. Unless you use it quickly, you should store it in the refrigerator or freezer to prevent it from becoming rancid. Many people prefer stone-ground flour, which is coarser and has a heartier flavor.

Unprocessed bran and wheat germ are, respectively, the outer coat and embryo portions of the wheat kernel. They are sometimes added to breads in small quantities for nutritional enrichment, heartiness, and special flavors. Both are much coarser than flour. Bran contributes dietary fiber; wheat germ is rich in food value (B and E vitamins as well as iron).

Cracked wheat, also much coarser than flour, results when wheat kernels or berries are cut into angular fragments. In small additions, it gives whole grain breads a nutty flavor and crunchy texture. If some of the bran has been removed and the kernels steamed before they are cracked and dried, the resulting grain is called bulgur.

Cornmeal and oatmeal come, respectively, from coarsely ground white or yellow corn and from rolled or steel-cut oats. Corn and oat flours, less widely available than the meals, can be found in health food stores.

Buttery Pan Rolls

  2 packages active dry yeast
  ¼ cup (50 g) plus 1 teaspoon sugar
  ½ cup (120 ml) warm water (about 110°F/43°C)
  4½ cups (560 g) all-purpose flour, unsifted
  1¼ teaspoons salt
  8 tablespoons (4 oz./115 g) butter or margarine, melted and cooled
  1 large egg
  1 cup (240 ml) warm 2% milk (about 110°F/43°C)

In a large bowl, dissolve yeast and 1 teaspoon of the sugar in warm water, stirring to mix; let stand until bubbly (about 5 minutes).

In a medium-size bowl, combine 2 cups (250 g) of the flour, the remaining ¼ cup (50 g) sugar, and the salt until well mixed. Beat flour mixture into yeast mixture, along with 6 tablespoons (90 ml) of the melted butter, the egg, and milk; beat for about 5 minutes to blend well (don't worry if mixture is a bit lumpy). Gradually beat in the remaining 2½ cups (310 g) flour. Cover with plastic wrap and let batter rise in a warm place until doubled (about 45 minutes).

Pour 1 tablespoon (15 ml) of the remaining melted butter into a 9- by 13-inch (23- by 33-cm) baking pan, tilting pan to coat bottom. Punch down batter and drop by handfuls into buttered pan, making about 15 rolls. Drizzle remaining 1 tablespoon (15 ml) butter over dough. Cover lightly with plastic wrap and let rise in a warm place until almost doubled (about 30 minutes).

Bake in a 375°F (190°C) oven until lightly browned (20 to 25 minutes). Serve hot.

Note: To bake in muffin cups, make batter as directed, but spoon about 1 teaspoon melted butter into each muffin cup. Fill cups about half full; let batter rise until almost doubled. Bake as directed.
Makes about 15 rolls

PER ROLL: *221 calories, 7 g total fat, 4 g saturated fat, 32 mg cholesterol, 259 mg sodium, 33 g carbohydrates, 1 g fiber, 5 g protein, 31 mg calcium, 2 mg iron*

BAKING POWDER BISCUITS

For tender, flaky biscuits with just enough moisture, be sure to measure ingredients precisely, and knead the dough for no longer than the recipe recommends. Sift dry ingredients together for a more even distribution of the baking powder; otherwise, tiny yellow and brown spots will appear on the surface of the baked biscuits. Once liquid is added to the dry ingredients, stir only until the flour is moist. Overzealous mixing or kneading may result in heavy biscuits that fail to rise completely.

   About 2 cups (250 g) all-purpose flour
 1 tablespoon baking powder
 ¾ teaspoon salt
 3 tablespoons cold butter or margarine, cut into pieces
 2 tablespoons solid vegetable shortening
 ¾ cup (180 ml) 2% milk

In a large bowl, sift together 2 cups (250 g) of the flour, the baking powder, and salt. Using a pastry blender or 2 table knives, cut butter and shortening into flour mixture until it resembles coarse cornmeal. Make a well in the center; pour in milk all at once and stir until dough cleans sides of bowl.

   Sprinkle a board lightly with flour. With your hands, gather dough into a ball. Turn dough out onto floured board and knead (see page 149) about 10 times (dough should feel light and soft, but not sticky). Roll out or pat dough into a round ½ inch (1 cm) thick. Using a floured 2-inch (5-cm) cutter and dipping the cutter in flour between cuts, cut biscuit rounds as close together as possible. Fit leftover bits of dough together, pat smooth, and cut (rerolling toughens dough). Place biscuits close together (for soft sides) or 1 inch (2.5 cm) apart (for crispy sides) on an unbuttered baking sheet.

   Bake in a 450°F (230°C) oven until tops are lightly browned (12 to 15 minutes).   *Makes 10 to 12 biscuits*

PER BISCUIT: *145 calories, 6 g total fat, 3 g saturated fat, 10 mg cholesterol, 323 mg sodium, 20 g carbohydrates, 0.6 g fiber, 3 g protein, 100 mg calcium, 1 mg iron*

Buttermilk Biscuits

Prepare *Baking Powder Biscuits*, but reduce baking powder to 2½ teaspoons and add ½ teaspoon *baking soda* and 1 tablespoon *sugar* to dry ingredients. Use ¾ cup (180 ml) *buttermilk* instead of 2% milk.

Drop Biscuits

Prepare *Baking Powder Biscuits*, but increase milk to 1 cup (240 ml). Do not knead or roll dough; instead, drop by tablespoons onto a greased baking sheet.

Old-Fashioned Cream Scones

   About 2 cups (250 g) all-purpose flour
 1 tablespoon baking powder
 3 tablespoons plus 2 teaspoons sugar
 ½ teaspoon salt
 ¼ cup (2 oz./55 g) butter or margarine
 2 large eggs
 ⅓ cup (80 ml) whipping cream

In a large bowl, sift together 2 cups (250 g) of the flour, the baking powder, 3 tablespoons of the sugar, and the salt. Using a pastry blender or 2 table knives, cut butter into flour mixture until it resembles coarse cornmeal; make a well in center. Separate 1 of the eggs; reserve egg white. Stir together egg yolk and remaining whole egg, then stir in whipping cream. Pour into well and stir with a fork until dough cleans sides of bowl.

   Sprinkle a board lightly with flour. With your hands, gather dough into a ball. Turn dough out onto board and knead (see page 149) about 10 times. Divide dough in half. Pat each portion of dough into a round about ½ inch (1 cm) thick and 6 inches (15 cm) in diameter. Place rounds on a buttered baking sheet about 1 inch (2.5 cm) apart. With a knife, score each round into 4 wedges. Brush tops with reserved egg white and sprinkle with the remaining 2 teaspoons sugar.

   Bake in a 400°F (205°C) oven until golden brown (about 12 minutes). Cut apart along scores and serve warm.   *Makes 8 scones*

PER SCONE: *243 calories, 11 g total fat, 6 g saturated fat, 80 mg cholesterol, 398 mg sodium, 31 g carbohydrates, 0.9 g fiber, 5 g protein, 122 mg calcium, 2 mg iron*

Orange Cream Scones

Prepare *Old-Fashioned Cream Scones*, but add 2 teaspoons grated *orange peel* and ½ teaspoon *vanilla* when you add liquid.

MUFFINS

Baking magnificent muffins is not only rewarding, but also surprisingly easy. The keys to perfection are careful measuring and just the right mixing technique. Follow the directions precisely, and you won't experience the classic pitfalls of muffin-making: tunnels, coarse texture, and toughness.

The following basic recipe creates a slightly sweet muffin that is tender but a bit coarse, with a pebbly, browned surface and a fairly symmetrical shape.

  2 *cups (250 g) all-purpose flour*
 ¼ *cup (50 g) plus 1 teaspoon sugar*
  1 *tablespoon baking powder*
 ¾ *teaspoon salt*
  1 *cup (240 ml) 2% milk*
  1 *large egg*
  3 *tablespoons butter or margarine, melted and cooled*

Butter a muffin pan with twelve cups, 2½ inches (6 cm) in diameter, or line cups with paper or foil baking cup liners; set aside.

In a large bowl, sift together flour, ¼ cup (50 g) of the sugar, the baking powder, and salt; make a well in center. Pour milk into a 2-cup (470-ml) measure and add egg and butter; beat with a fork to blend well. Pour liquid all at once into well. (This method allows you to mix the batter with fewer strokes, avoiding overstirring.) Making 12 to 15 full circular strokes that scrape bottom of bowl, stir just until dry ingredients are moistened. Batter should be lumpy. Fill each prepared muffin cup two thirds full with batter. Sprinkle remaining 1 teaspoon sugar evenly over the tops.

Bake in a 425°F (220°C) oven until tops are lightly browned (20 to 25 minutes). Remove muffins from pan immediately (otherwise moisture condenses on bottom of cups and muffins become soggy).
Makes 12 muffins

PER MUFFIN: *145 calories, 5 g total fat, 2 g saturated fat, 27 mg cholesterol, 304 mg sodium, 22 g carbohydrates, 0.6 g fiber, 3 g protein, 99 mg calcium, 1 mg iron*

Blueberry Muffins

PICTURED ON FACING PAGE

Prepare *Muffins*, but increase sugar to ⅓ cup (70 g) and stir 1¼ cups (180 g) fresh or frozen (unthawed) *blueberries* into flour mixture before making the well.

Bran Muffins

Prepare *Muffins*, but substitute 1 cup (2.2 oz./60 g) ready-to-eat *bran cereal* for 1 cup (125 g) of the flour.

Cinnamon-Raisin Muffins

Prepare *Muffins*, but stir ¾ cup (110 g) *raisins* (or currants or chopped dried cherries) and 1 teaspoon *cinnamon* into flour mixture before making the well.

Cornmeal Muffins

Prepare *Muffins*, but reduce flour to 1½ cups (185 g) and add 1 cup (135 g) *yellow cornmeal*.

Cornmeal-Cheddar-Jalapeño Muffins

Prepare *Muffins*, but reduce flour to 1½ cups (185 g), omit sugar, increase salt to 1 teaspoon, and add 1 cup (135 g) *cornmeal*. Stir ¾ cup (about 3 oz./85 g) shredded extra-sharp yellow *Cheddar cheese* and 1 teaspoon chopped fresh *jalapeño chile* into flour mixture before making the well.

Cranberry Muffins

Prepare *Muffins*, but increase sugar to ⅔ cup (135 g) and stir 1 cup (95 g) fresh or frozen (unthawed) *cranberries* into flour mixture before making the well.

Nut Muffins

Prepare *Muffins*, but increase sugar to ½ cup (100 g) and stir ¾ cup (94 g) chopped *nuts* into flour mixture before making the well.

Orange Muffins

Prepare *Muffins*, but increase sugar to ½ cup (100 g) and add 1 tablespoon grated *orange peel*. Substitute ½ cup (120 ml) fresh *orange juice* for ½ cup (120 ml) of the milk (you will need about 2 large oranges).

Whole Wheat Muffins

Prepare *Muffins*, but substitute 1 cup (125 g) *whole wheat flour* for 1 cup (120 g) of the all-purpose flour; reduce salt to ¾ teaspoon. Use ¼ cup (55 g) firmly packed *brown sugar* instead of granulated sugar and crumble with fingers to combine with flour mixture.

MAKING BLUEBERRY MUFFINS

1 For an even texture in muffins, baking powder needs to be evenly incorporated with the other dry ingredients. The best way to do this is to sift the dry ingredients together. If you don't have a sifter, use a fine-meshed strainer instead. Place the flour, sugar, baking powder, and salt in the strainer and hit it repeatedly with your hand until all of the flour mixture has sifted through.

2 Make a well in center of flour mixture and pour combined liquid ingredients all at once into the well. This method allows you to mix the batter with fewer strokes, which is essential in producing light, tender muffins.

3 Stirring muffin batter should be a quick affair—the idea is simply to moisten flour mixture, and no more. Start at the center where liquid ingredients are and make 12 to 15 circular stirs, scraping the bottom and sides of the bowl. The batter should look lumpy, not smooth and liquid.

4 Served hot from the oven, these golden, pebbly topped Blueberry Muffins are a delightful morning treat—not to mention mid-morning snack, lunch box dessert, or afternoon tea offering.

POPOVERS

PICTURED ON FACING PAGE

There's nothing to these fragile shells but crisp gold-en crust and a puff of fragrant steam. The egg batter puffs as it bakes, forming moist hollows that you can fill with butter or preserves, or something savory.

Popovers are easy to make, especially if you use a blender or food processor. Or you can mix the batter by hand. If you do so, however, be sure to get out all the lumps and beat in the eggs, one at a time, just until blended.

Once the popovers are in the oven, resist the temptation to peek: They will collapse if a draft of air reaches them just as they're swelling above the cup. You can bake popovers in your choice of containers: shiny, lightweight metal muffin pans; dark, heavy cast-iron popover pans; or ovenproof glass custard cups.

    1 cup (125 g) all-purpose flour
    ¼ teaspoon salt
    1 tablespoon butter or margarine, melted and cooled
    1 cup (240 ml) 2% milk
    2 large eggs

Butter containers generously. Place flour, salt, butter, and milk in a blender or food processor and whirl until smooth. Add eggs, one at a time, processing briefly after each addition just until blended. Pour batter into buttered containers, filling each about one third to half full. In ovenproof cups of ⅓-cup (80-ml) size, batter will yield 12 popovers; ½-cup (120-ml) size, 10 popovers; ¾-cup (180-ml) size, 6 or 7 popovers.

Bake in a 425°F (220°C) oven for 10 minutes; re-duce heat to 375°F (190°C) and bake until tops are richly browned (35 to 40 more minutes).

For drier popovers, loosen popovers from the con-tainers, but leave them sitting at an angle in the cups. Prick sides of each popover with a wooden pick and let stand in a turned-off oven, door slightly ajar, for 8 to 10 minutes. Remove from pans and serve hot.   *Makes 6 to 12 popovers*

PER ½-CUP (120-ML) POPOVER: *109 calories, 5 g total fat, 2 g saturated fat, 53 mg cholesterol, 101 mg sodium, 12 g carbohydrates, 0.4 g fiber, 4 g protein, 41 mg calcium, 0.8 mg iron*

Cheese Popovers

Prepare *Popovers*, but briefly process ½ cup (about 2 oz./55 g) finely shredded sharp *Cheddar cheese* or ½ cup (about 1½ oz./40 g) Parmesan cheese into bat-ter after processing milk and eggs.

Savory Herb Popovers

Prepare *Popovers*, but briefly process 1 small clove *garlic*, finely minced or pressed, and ¼ teaspoon *dried rosemary* or oregano into batter after processing milk and eggs.

Yorkshire Pudding

Yorkshire pudding is simply popover batter baked to a crisp golden puff in flavorful roast beef drippings. It's moister and tastes eggier than the hollow-shelled popovers—thus the name "pudding." You bake this side dish while the roast stands waiting to be carved, and you start carving the roast 5 minutes before the golden puff is done.

    1 cooked Standing Rib Roast (page 69)
    1 cup (125 g) all-purpose flour
    ½ teaspoon salt
    1 cup (240 ml) 2% milk
    2 large eggs

Remove roast from oven; keep warm. Turn oven up to 450°F (230°C). Pour pan drippings into a measur-ing cup. Measure out 3 tablespoons (45 ml) of the pan drippings and pour into a 9-inch (23-cm) square baking pan. Place pan in oven to keep warm while you prepare batter.

Place flour, salt, and milk in a blender or food processor and whirl until combined. Add eggs, one at a time, processing until very smooth. Remove pan from oven and pour in batter. Bake, uncovered, until puffy and well browned (about 20 minutes). Cut into squares and serve immediately.   *Makes 6 servings*

PER SERVING: *180 calories, 9 g total fat, 4 g saturated fat, 81 mg cholesterol, 224 mg sodium, 18 g carbohydrates, 0.6 g fiber, 6 g protein, 62 mg calcium, 1 mg iron*

HOW TO MAKE POPOVERS

1 Although popover batter could be mixed by hand, a blender makes the process quick and easy. The flour, butter, and milk all go in at once and are blended until smooth. Then the eggs are added, one at a time, with a brief blending after each addition. The batter should be blended as little as possible, but should have the consistency of whipping cream.

2 The pouring lip of a blender container makes it ideal for filling the custard cups. Fill each well-greased cup one third to half full. You'll find it easier to transport the cups to the oven if you place them on a baking sheet or pizza pan before filling them with batter—but do not bake them on the pan.

3 For drier popovers, loosen them from their cups and tilt them at an angle. Prick the sides of the popovers with a wooden pick or skewer (this will allow the steam to escape) and return them to the turned-off oven, with the door slightly ajar, for 8 to 10 minutes.

4 Inside the crisp baked popovers, thin, eggy walls form pockets for melted butter, jam, or honey.

QUICK BREADS

Quick breads require no rising time—and they are extremely versatile. You can lace them with fruit, nuts, spices—even chiles and cheese.

Banana Bread

  2   large ripe bananas (about 1 lb./455 g total)
  ¾   cup (150 g) sugar
  2   large eggs
  ¼   cup (2 oz./55 g) butter or margarine, melted and cooled
  1½ cups (185 g) all-purpose flour
  2   teaspoons baking powder
  ½   teaspoon baking soda
  ½   teaspoon salt

Lightly butter a 5- by 9-inch (12.5- by 23-cm) loaf pan; set aside.

In a large bowl, mash bananas; you should have 1 cup (225 g). Beat in sugar, then eggs and butter. In another large bowl, combine flour, baking powder, baking soda, and salt; add to banana mixture and stir just until all flour is moistened. Pour batter into prepared pan.

Bake in a 350°F (175°C) oven until bread begins to pull away from the sides of the pan and a wooden pick inserted in center comes out clean (55 to 60 minutes). Let loaf cool in pan on a rack for 10 minutes before turning out to cool completely.
Makes 1 loaf (about 12 slices)

PER SLICE: *178 calories, 5 g total fat, 3 g saturated fat, 46 mg cholesterol, 275 mg sodium, 31 g carbohydrates, 0.8 g fiber, 3 g protein, 55 mg calcium, 1 mg iron*

Quick Coffee Cake

  ¼   cup (55 g) firmly packed light brown sugar
  ¼   cup (33 g) chopped pecans or walnuts
  1¼ cups (155 g) plus 1 tablespoon all-purpose flour
  4   tablespoons (2 oz./55 g) butter or margarine
  1½ teaspoons ground cinnamon
  ½   cup (100 g) granulated sugar
  2   teaspoons baking powder
  ½   teaspoon salt
  ½   cup (120 ml) 2% milk
  1   large egg

Lightly butter an 8-inch (20-cm) square or round metal baking pan; set aside. In a small bowl, with your fingers, mix the brown sugar, nuts, the 1 tablespoon flour, 1 tablespoon of the butter, and the cinnamon until crumbly. Set aside.

Melt remaining 3 tablespoons butter in a 1-quart (950-ml) pan over low heat; cool.

Meanwhile, in a medium-size bowl, combine remaining 1¼ cups (155 g) flour, the granulated sugar, baking powder, and salt. Pour milk into a 1-cup (240-ml) measure; with a fork, stir in egg and cooled butter. Pour all at once into dry ingredients and stir just until flour is moistened. Spoon batter evenly into prepared pan. Sprinkle cinnamon-nut topping evenly over batter. Bake in a 350°F (175°C) oven until a wooden pick inserted in center comes out clean (35 to 40 minutes).   *Makes 6 servings*

PER SERVING: *327 calories, 13 g total fat, 6 g saturated fat, 58 mg cholesterol, 448 mg sodium, 49 g carbohydrates, 1 g fiber, 5 g protein, 143 mg calcium, 2 mg iron*

Mexican Cornbread

  ¼   cup (60 ml) vegetable oil
  1   large egg
  1   can (8½ oz./245 g) cream-style corn
  1   cup (about 4 oz./113 g) shredded pepper jack cheese
  ½   cup (120 ml) reduced-fat sour cream
  1   cup (135 g) yellow cornmeal
  1   cup (125 g) all-purpose flour
  1   tablespoon sugar
  2½ teaspoons baking powder
  ½   teaspoon salt

Lightly oil a 9-inch (23-cm) round or 8-inch (20-cm) square pan. In a medium-size bowl, beat oil and egg until well blended. Add corn, ¾ cup (about 3 oz./85 g) of the jack cheese, and the sour cream. Stir until well blended; set aside. In a large bowl, combine cornmeal, flour, sugar, baking powder, and salt. Add egg mixture and stir to combine. Scrape batter into the prepared pan and sprinkle remaining ¼ cup (about 1 oz./30 g) jack cheese over the top.

Bake in a 375°F (190°C) oven until crust is lightly browned and a wooden pick inserted in center comes out clean (25 to 30 minutes).   *Makes 8 servings*

PER SERVING: *303 calories, 15 g total fat, 5 g saturated fat, 47 mg cholesterol, 487 mg sodium, 34 g carbohydrates, 2 g fiber, 9 g protein, 193 mg calcium, 2 mg iron*

PANCAKES, WAFFLES & FRENCH TOAST

These breakfast favorites share one requirement: They all need to begin cooking at just the right temperature. Preheat your griddle or frying pan over medium heat, then sprinkle a few drops of water over the surface. When the drops begin to sizzle and jump about, it is ready to use. (If the water evaporates instantly, though, the griddle is too hot.) Follow manufacturers' directions for heating waffle irons.

Pancakes

   1½ cups (185 g) all-purpose flour
    1 tablespoon baking powder
    2 tablespoons sugar
   ½ teaspoon salt
    1 to 1¼ cups (240 to 300 ml) 2% milk
    2 large eggs
    3 tablespoons butter or margarine, melted

Preheat a large nonstick griddle or wide nonstick frying pan over medium heat. Coat lightly with butter—just enough to prevent pancakes from sticking.

In a medium-size bowl, combine flour, baking powder, sugar, and salt. Pour milk (use 1 cup/240 ml for thick pancakes or 1¼ cups/300 ml for thinner pancakes) into a 2-cup (470-ml) glass measure. Stir in eggs and butter; blend well. Pour liquid all at once into dry ingredients; stir just until flour is moistened.

Pour batter (about ¼ cup/60 ml for each pancake) onto hot griddle; spread batter out to make a 4-inch (10-cm) round. Cook until bubbles form and just start to pop on top surface and edges appear dry (3 to 4 minutes); turn pancake with a wide spatula to lightly brown other side. Turn pancakes only once. *Makes 10 pancakes*

PER PANCAKE: *149 calories, 6 g total fat, 3 g saturated fat, 54 mg cholesterol, 318 mg sodium, 19 g carbohydrates, 0.5 g fiber, 4 g protein, 124 mg calcium, 1 mg iron*

Light Whole Wheat Pancakes

Prepare *Pancakes*, but separate eggs. Add yolks to milk mixture; beat whites to stiff peaks, and fold in. Substitute up to ¾ cup (90 g) *whole wheat flour* for all-purpose flour.

Waffles

   1⅓ cups (165 g) all-purpose flour
    2 teaspoons baking powder
    4 teaspoons sugar
   ½ teaspoon salt
    2 large eggs, separated
   1¼ cups (300 ml) 2% milk
    3 tablespoons butter or margarine, melted

In a medium-size bowl, combine flour, baking powder, sugar, and salt; set aside.

In another medium-size bowl, beat egg whites just until stiff, moist peaks form. In another medium-size bowl, beat yolks lightly; stir in milk and butter, and blend well. Pour liquid all at once into dry ingredients; beat until smooth. Fold in beaten whites.

Bake in a waffle iron according to manufacturer's directions. *Makes 5 large waffles (20 sections)*

PER LARGE WAFFLE: *279 calories, 13 g total fat, 6 g saturated fat, 109 mg cholesterol, 541 mg sodium, 32 g carbohydrates, 0.9 g fiber, 8 g protein, 201 mg calcium, 2 mg iron*

French Toast

   ¾ cup (180 ml) 2% milk
    2 large eggs
    1 tablespoon sugar
    1 teaspoon vanilla (optional)
   ¼ teaspoon salt
    8 slices firm-textured day-old bread (about 8 oz./230 g total)
    2 tablespoons butter or margarine

In a medium-size bowl, beat together milk, eggs, sugar, vanilla (if using), and salt. Place bread on a 10- by 15-inch (25- by 38-cm) rimmed baking pan. Pour egg mixture over bread and let stand for 5 minutes. Turn slices over and let stand until all egg mixture is absorbed.

Melt a little of the butter on a nonstick griddle or in a wide nonstick frying pan over medium heat. Add bread, a few slices at a time, and cook until browned on one side; turn and brown other side (about 5 minutes total). Keep toast warm. Repeat with remaining butter and bread. *Makes 4 servings*

PER SERVING: *274 calories, 11 g total fat, 5 g saturated fat, 126 mg cholesterol, 553 mg sodium, 34 g carbohydrates, 1 g fiber, 9 g protein, 132 mg calcium, 2 mg iron*

PIZZA

Tomato-Cheese Pizza

 1 package active dry yeast

1½ cups (360 ml) warm water (about 110°F/43°C)

 About ½ teaspoon salt

 4 tablespoons (60 ml) olive oil

 About 3¾ cups (470 g) all-purpose flour

1½ pounds (680 g) Roma-type tomatoes, chopped, or 1 can (14½ oz./415 g) plum tomatoes

 1 pound (455 g) mozzarella cheese, thinly sliced

 ¼ cup (15 g) minced fresh oregano or 2 tablespoons dried oregano

 ¼ cup (about ¾ oz./20 g) grated Parmesan cheese

 Pepper

In a large bowl, stir yeast into water; let stand until dissolved (about 5 minutes).

Stir in ½ teaspoon of the salt and 1 tablespoon (15 ml) of the oil. Add 2¼ cups (280 g) of the flour; stir to blend. Beat with an electric mixer on high speed until dough is glossy and stretchy (3 to 5 minutes). Stir in 1⅓ cups (165 g) more flour.

To knead by hand: Scrape dough onto a lightly floured board and knead (see page 149) until smooth and springy (about 10 minutes), adding more flour as needed to prevent sticking.

To knead with a dough hook: Beat dough on medium speed until it pulls cleanly from sides of bowl and is springy (5 to 7 minutes); if dough is sticky, add more flour, 1 tablespoon at a time.

Place dough in a greased bowl; turn to coat. Cover bowl with plastic wrap; let dough rise in a warm place until doubled (about 45 minutes). Or let rise in refrigerator until next day.

While dough is rising, in a food processor or blender, whirl tomatoes (and their liquid, if using canned tomatoes) until coarsely puréed. Pour purée into a 3- to 4-quart (2.8- to 3.8-liter) pan and bring to a boil; reduce heat and simmer, uncovered, until sauce is reduced to about 1 cup/240 ml (about 30 minutes). Remove from heat. Lightly brush 3 large baking sheets with some of the remaining oil.

Punch pizza dough down, turn out onto a lightly floured board, and knead briefly. Divide dough into 6 equal balls. Roll each ball into a 7-inch (18-cm) round; place 2 rounds on each baking sheet. (If you have only one oven, shape only 4 pizzas—2 baking sheets—at a time; shape remaining 2 pizzas and let rise while first batch bakes.)

Brush rounds with some of the remaining oil. Let rise, uncovered, in a warm place until slightly puffy (15 to 30 minutes), then prick each round several times in center with a fork. Bake in a 450°F (230°C) oven for 5 minutes. Spread tomato sauce equally over each crust to within ½ inch (1 cm) of edges. Top each crust equally with mozzarella, oregano, and Parmesan cheese. Drizzle evenly with remaining oil.

Continue to bake pizzas until golden brown on top and crusty on the bottom (10 to 12 more minutes). Switch positions of baking sheets halfway through baking. Serve hot; season to taste with salt and pepper. *Makes 6 servings*

PER SERVING: *628 calories, 28 g total fat, 12 g saturated fat, 62 mg cholesterol, 538 mg sodium, 68 g carbohydrates, 4 g fiber, 26 g protein, 480 mg calcium, 5 mg iron*

Pizza in a Hurry

When you're in a rush, use a ready-made crust and a prepared sauce, then top with your favorite foods (see the box on the facing page for a few topping ideas). Don't overload the pizza, or the crust will become soggy. Bake in the lower half of a 450°F (230°C) oven until the crust is browned on the bottom and the toppings are hot (about 30 minutes).

Crust: Check supermarket bread shelves, refrigerator cases, and freezers for one of the following: baked bread shells or pizza crusts (plain or with cheese); focaccia (plain or with herbs); frozen bread dough (white or whole wheat—use 1 lb./455 g thawed dough to make a 3- to 6-serving pizza, or ½ lb./230 g to make a 1- to 2-serving pizza; pat out in an oiled pan and use at once); or refrigerated pizza dough—a 10-ounce (285-g) tube makes a 3- to 6-serving pizza.

Sauce: Select a prepared pizza sauce (canned or in a squeeze dispenser), a thick tomato pasta sauce (canned or from the deli section), or a canned salsa or taco sauce.

Whole Wheat Zucchini Pizza

  1 *package active dry yeast*

1½ *cups (360 ml) warm water (about 110°F/43°C)*

 ¼ *cup (24 g) wheat germ*

  4 *tablespoons (60 ml) vegetable oil*

  2 *teaspoons dried basil*

  2 *teaspoons dried oregano*

1½ *teaspoons salt*

  1 *teaspoon sugar*

     About 1½ cups (185 g) all-purpose flour

1½ *cups (180 g) whole wheat flour*

  1 *large yellow onion, chopped*

  1 *can (15 oz./425 g) tomato sauce*

  1 *can (6 oz./170 g) tomato paste*

 ½ *cup (120 ml) dry red wine*

  2 *medium-size zucchini (about 1½ lbs./680 g total), thinly sliced*

  1 *cup (about 4 oz./80 g) thinly sliced green or red bell pepper*

  4 *green onions (including tops), thinly sliced*

  1 *can (2¼ oz./63 g) sliced ripe olives, drained*

  1 *can (14 oz./400 g) artichoke hearts, drained and quartered*

  3 *cups (about 12 oz./340 g) shredded jack cheese*

 ¼ *cup (about ¾ oz./20 g) grated Parmesan cheese*

In a large bowl, stir yeast into water; let stand until dissolved (about 5 minutes). Add wheat germ, 2 tablespoons (30 ml) of the oil, 1 teaspoon each of the basil, oregano, and salt, the sugar, and 1½ cups (185 g) of the all-purpose flour. Beat until smooth (about 3 minutes if using an electric mixer). Using a heavy-duty mixer or wooden spoon, beat in whole wheat flour until dough holds together.

Turn dough out onto a lightly floured board and knead (see page 149) until smooth and elastic (about 5 minutes). Place dough in an oil-coated bowl; turn to coat. Cover with plastic wrap and let rise in a warm place until doubled (about 45 minutes).

Meanwhile, to prepare tomato sauce, heat remaining 2 tablespoons oil in a wide nonstick frying pan over medium heat. Cook chopped yellow onion until soft (about 5 minutes). Stir in tomato sauce, tomato paste, wine, remaining 1 teaspoon each oregano and basil, and remaining ½ teaspoon salt. Simmer, uncovered, for 10 minutes.

Punch dough down and divide in half. Roll out each half to form a 14-inch (35.5-cm) round, then transfer each round onto a oil-coated baking sheet or a 14-inch (35.5-cm) pizza pan. One at a time, bake on next-to-bottom rack of a 450°F (230°C) oven just until bottom of crust starts to brown (about 7 minutes). During baking, watch and prick any bubbles that form. Remove from oven; leave oven on.

To assemble pizza, spread tomato sauce over crust. Arrange zucchini, bell pepper, green onions, olives, and artichoke quarters over sauce. Sprinkle jack cheese and Parmesan cheese over all.

Continue to bake in a 450°F (230°C) oven until cheese melts (12 to 15 minutes). Cut hot pizzas into wedges to serve.   *Makes 2 pizzas (6 servings each)*

PER SERVING: *349 calories, 16 g total fat, 6 g saturated fat, 31 mg cholesterol, 836 mg sodium, 37 g carbohydrates, 5 g fiber, 15 g protein, 292 mg calcium, 4 mg iron*

Some Fun Pizza Toppings

Once you've mastered making a basic pizza crust, you can change the toppings to your heart's desire. Go beyond pepperoni and try lightly browned ground meat, thin sliced cooked ham, or chunks of chicken or turkey. Vegetable choices might include cooked broccoli flowerets, mushrooms, or drained and chopped oil-packed dried tomatoes. Choose a cheese that melts beautifully, such as shredded or thinly sliced jack (plain or flavored), mozzarella, provolone, Swiss, and teleme. Add a piquant accent with nonmelting cheeses such as freshly grated Parmesan or Romano or crumbled feta or cotija. Here are a few possible combos:

California pizza: *Top tomato-sauced pizza with fresh basil and oregano, yellow bell pepper slices, and mozzarella and Parmesan cheeses. Arrange cherry tomato halves on baked pizza .*

Greek pizza: *Top tomato-sauced pizza with onion slices, pitted calamata olives, and feta. Sprinkle baked pizza with chopped fresh mint.*

Mexican pizza: *Top tomato-sauced pizza with canned black beans, cumin-flavored jack cheese, tomato slices, crumbled feta, and shredded mozzarella. When baked, add avocado slices and a sprinkling of lime juice.*

DESSERTS

Sometimes creamy smooth and rich, sometimes light and fruity fresh, dessert gives any meal a happy ending. Take a moment and plan the dessert to fit the menu. It makes sense, for example, to serve a light dessert after a feast that's heavy or robust, a rich dessert after a lighter entrée.

Even if you don't have time to make dessert every day (it's hard to imagine who would), do treat your family to a special indulgence from time to time, and not just on the usual festive occasions. We like the idea of chocolate chip cookies on good-report-card days, apple crisp as a leaf-raker's reward, or warm gingerbread with a scoop of ice cream for no particular reason at all. If time is tight on weekdays, do a bit of baking on weekends. Cookies and cakes will keep for several days (or can be frozen for longer periods); some of the other desserts in this chapter can also be made hours or days in advance.

Dessert-making—particularly baking—requires more precision than other types of cooking. The proportion of baking powder to flour in a cake batter, for instance, is carefully calculated so that the cake will be lofty and light. So be sure to follow directions.

Tips for better baked goods

• If a recipe calls for butter or margarine at room temperature, it should be just that—not melted—or the baked product will have a different texture than expected or even desired.

• Start each batch of cookies on a cool baking sheet; otherwise the batter will begin to spread and cook before the cookies reach the oven. To make another batch on the same sheet, wash the sheet and rebutter it if the recipe specifies doing so.

• When freezing bar cookies, freeze them in one piece to keep them as moist as possible. After thawing, unwrap and cut into squares or bars.

• To ensure a light and tender cake, be sure to use cake flour if the recipe calls for it. Measure ingredients accurately, combine them in the order given, and beat for the precise length of time indicated.

• Pan size is also very important. In too large a pan, a cake will bake too quickly and turn out pale and flat. If the pan is too small, the batter may overflow, the center of the cake is likely to shrink, and the texture will be heavy and compact.

COOKIES

Cookies bring joy to the young-of-appetite. The recipes that follow feature simple-to-make drop and bar cookies, as well as biscotti, which are shaped into loaves, then baked twice.

Just as their name indicates, drop cookies are formed by dropping dough from a spoon, so that it falls in little mounds on the baking sheets. Bar cookies are easier still: You simply mix the batter or dough, spread it in the pan, and bake. Biscotti take a little more work, but the result is well worth the effort. All these cookies freeze and travel well. See the box on cooling and storing cookies, below.

Crisp Chocolate Chip Cookies

- 1 cup (125 g) all-purpose flour
- ¾ teaspoon baking soda
- ¼ teaspoon salt
- ½ cup (4 oz./115 g) butter or margarine, melted
- ½ cup (110 g) firmly packed brown sugar
- ⅓ cup (70 g) granulated sugar
- 3 tablespoons (45 ml) water
- ½ teaspoon vanilla
- 1 package (about 6 oz./170 g) semisweet chocolate chips
- ½ cup (65 g) chopped nuts (optional)

In a medium-size bowl, combine flour, baking soda, and salt.

In a large bowl, with an electric mixer on medium speed, blend butter, brown sugar, granulated sugar, water, and vanilla. Stir flour mixture into butter mixture, then beat until blended. Stir in chocolate chips, and nuts (if using).

Drop batter in 1-tablespoon (15-ml) portions about 2 inches (5 cm) apart on baking sheets.

Bake in a 300°F (150°C) oven until cookies are an even golden brown color all over (18 to 20 minutes). If using 2 baking sheets in 1 oven, switch positions halfway through baking.

Let cookies cool on baking sheets for about 3 minutes, then transfer to racks with a spatula. Serve warm or cool. Store airtight for up to 1 day or freeze for longer storage. *Makes 32 cookies*

PER COOKIE: *86 calories, 4 g total fat, 3 g saturated fat, 8 mg cholesterol, 77 mg sodium, 12 g carbohydrates, 0.1 g fiber, 0.6 g protein, 6 mg calcium, 0.4 mg iron*

Crisp, Chewy Chocolate Chip Cookies

Prepare *Crisp Chocolate Chip Cookies*, baking until the cookies are browned at edges but an area about 1 inch (2.5 cm) wide in the center is still pale (about 14 minutes).

Fudge Brownies

- ½ cup (4 oz./110 g) butter or margarine
- 4 ounces (115 g) unsweetened chocolate
- 2 cups (400 g) sugar
- ½ teaspoon salt
- 1½ teaspoons vanilla
- 3 large eggs, at room temperature
- 1 cup (125 g) all-purpose flour
- 1 cup (125 g) coarsely chopped walnuts
  Powdered sugar (optional)

Generously butter a 9- by 13-inch (23- by 33-cm) baking pan; set aside.

In a 2-quart (1.9-liter) pan, melt butter and chocolate over medium-low heat; stir until well blended. Remove from heat and stir in sugar, salt, and vanilla. Add eggs, one at a time, beating well after each addition. Stir in flour, then nuts. Pour into prepared pan.

Bake in a 350°F (175°C) oven until top springs back when pressed (20 to 25 minutes). Transfer pan to a rack. Let cool completely before cutting. Sprinkle with powdered sugar, if desired. *Makes 24 brownies*

PER BROWNIE: *187 calories, 11 g total fat, 5 g saturated fat, 37 mg cholesterol, 94 mg sodium, 23 g carbohydrates, 1 g fiber, 3 g protein, 14 mg calcium, 0.8 mg iron*

Cooling & Storing Cookies

Let cookies cool on a rack—in a single layer, never stacked or overlapped. Cool them completely before arranging them on a plate or storing them. To maintain freshness, keep cookies in an airtight tin, jar, or box, but do not store moist varieties in the same container with crisp ones.

Sturdy cookies can be frozen in heavy-duty plastic bags. Layer more delicate cookies in a food-storage box with sheets of wax paper between the layers.

MAKING LEMON POPPY SEED BISCOTTI

 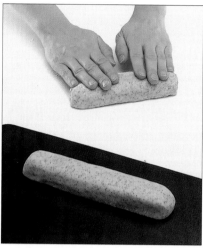 

1 Lemon, vanilla, and the nutlike flavor of poppy seeds make these biscotti unusually good. Blend butter, sugar, lemon peel, eggs, and vanilla, then add 2 tablespoons poppy seeds.

2 Working on a lightly floured board, shape each portion of dough into a log about 8 inches (20 cm) long and 1¼ inches (3.2 cm) in diameter. Place logs of dough on baking sheet.

3 Gently pat each log to flatten it into a loaf a scant 1 inch (2.5 cm) thick. Bake at 350°F (175°C) until loaves are firm to the touch.

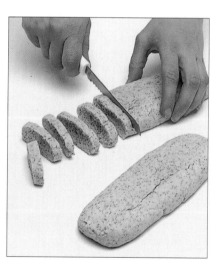  

4 Transfer baked loaves to cooling rack and let cool for 3 to 5 minutes. Then place on cutting board and cut with a serrated knife into slices a scant ½ inch (1 cm) thick. For longer biscotti, cut diagonally across loaf.

5 Lay slices, one cut side down, on baking sheet (use an additional baking sheet, if necessary). Return to oven and bake until biscotti are dry and lightly browned (about 10 minutes). Cool biscotti on racks before applying icing.

6 Spread lemon icing on half of each cookie. Return biscotti to rack and let stand until icing is firm.

Lemon Poppy Seed Biscotti

PICTURED ON FACING PAGE

½ cup (100 g) granulated sugar

5 tablespoons (70 g) butter or margarine, at room temperature

2 teaspoons grated lemon peel

2 large eggs

1 teaspoon vanilla

2 tablespoons poppy seeds

2 cups (250 g) all-purpose flour

2 teaspoons baking powder

1½ cups (150 g) sifted powdered sugar

About 5 teaspoons (25 ml) lemon juice

In a large bowl, beat granulated sugar, butter, and 1½ teaspoons of the lemon peel until well blended. Add eggs, one at a time, beating well after each addition. Stir in vanilla, then stir in poppy seeds. In a medium-size bowl, combine flour and baking powder; add to butter mixture and stir until well blended.

Divide dough in half. On a lightly floured board, shape each portion into a log about 8 inches (20 cm) long and 1¼ inches (3.2 cm) in diameter. Place logs on a large nonstick or regular butter-coated baking sheet, spacing them 3 inches (8 cm) apart. Flatten logs to make loaves a scant 1 inch (2.5 cm) thick. Bake in a 350°F (175°C) oven until loaves feel firm to the touch (about 15 minutes).

Remove baking sheet from oven and let loaves cool for 3 to 5 minutes; then cut crosswise into slices a scant ½ inch (1 cm) thick. Place slices, one cut side down, on baking sheet (you may need another sheet to bake biscotti all at once). Return to oven and continue to bake until biscotti look dry and are lightly browned (about 10 minutes); if using 2 baking sheets, switch their positions halfway through baking. Transfer biscotti to racks and let cool.

Meanwhile, in a small bowl, combine powdered sugar, remaining ½ teaspoon lemon peel, and 5 teaspoons (25 ml) of the lemon juice; stir until icing is easy to spread, adding a little more lemon juice, if needed.

Spread icing over about half of one end of each cooled cookie. Let stand until icing is firm before serving.   *Makes about 3½ dozen cookies*

PER COOKIE: *64 calories, 2 g total fat, 0.9 g saturated fat, 14 mg cholesterol, 41 mg sodium, 11 g carbohydrates, 0.2 g fiber, 1 g protein, 22 mg calcium, 0.4 mg iron*

Shortbread

1 cup (8 oz./230 g) butter or margarine, softened

½ cup (50 g) sifted powdered sugar

1 teaspoon vanilla

⅛ teaspoon salt

2 cups (250 g) all-purpose flour

Lightly butter a 9-inch (23-cm) square baking pan; set aside.

In a large bowl, combine butter, sugar, vanilla, and salt, stirring until light and fluffy. Stir in flour and blend well. With your hands, gather up dough and place it in the prepared pan. Lay a sheet of plastic wrap over dough and press dough evenly over bottom of prepared pan. Remove the plastic wrap.

Bake in a 325°F (165°C) oven until pale golden brown (40 to 50 minutes). Transfer pan to rack and cut into squares; let cool in pan.   *Makes 16 squares*

PER SQUARE: *174 calories, 12 g total fat, 7 g saturated fat, 31 mg cholesterol, 135 mg sodium, 15 g carbohydrates, 0.4 g fiber, 2 g protein, 6 mg calcium, 0.7 mg iron*

Buttery Lemon Shortbread

Prepare *Shortbread*, but press dough into a 9- by 13-inch (23- by 33-cm) baking pan. Bake in a 350°F (175°C) oven for only 20 minutes.

Meanwhile, in a bowl, beat 3 large *eggs* until light and frothy. Gradually add 1⅔ cups (335 g) granulated *sugar*, beating until thick. Add ½ cup (120 ml) *lemon juice*, ¼ cup (30 g) all-purpose *flour*, ¾ teaspoon *baking powder*, and 1 teaspoon grated *lemon peel*; beat until blended. Pour over hot baked crust, return to oven, and bake until pale golden (15 to 20 minutes). Remove from oven; sprinkle evenly with 3 tablespoons *powdered sugar*. Cut into squares; let cool in pan.   *Makes 2 dozen squares*

HOW TO MAKE FLAKY PASTRY

1. Form dough into a ball (or 2 balls if making a double-crust pie), then flatten into a 4-inch (10-cm) round. Wrap dough in plastic wrap and refrigerate for 1 hour. This makes dough easier to handle.

2. When rolling out dough, work from center outward with rolling pin, using light, even strokes. Work quickly and avoid overhandling dough. To transfer dough to pie pan, drape dough over rolling pin.

3. Ease dough into pie pan and, using your fingertips, gently push dough into bottom and corners of pan. Try not to stretch dough as you do this.

4. Place filling in bottom crust, then roll out top crust. If cutting design in top crust, do it now. Wrap dough loosely around rolling pin, then unroll over filling. Trim top and bottom crusts to 1-inch (2.5-cm) overhang.

5. Fold edge of top crust under bottom crust. Flute edges by pinching pastry between your thumbs and index fingers. If you have not cut design in crust, cut steam vents in top crust.

6. The top crust of this Apple Pie (see page 168) was brushed with milk for a lovely bronzed finish. The design was made with tiny canapé cutters, and the cutout pieces were placed on the crust as additional decoration.

PASTRY

The secret to blue-ribbon pie crust is careful measuring, mixing, and handling. Too much flour or too much handling toughens pastry. Too little liquid results in crumbly, unmanageable dough, and too much liquid makes it soggy and sticky.

There are two types of pie crust: flaky pastry and butter pastry. Flaky pastry, the usual choice for a double-crust pie, is made with solid vegetable shortening or lard; it can tolerate only minimal handling, and it must be rolled out. Butter pastry, ideal for recipes that require a richer crust, is made with butter. Because it can take a little more handling, you can roll it or press it into the pan with your fingers.

When rolling out dough, lift the rolling pin as it comes to the edge—otherwise the edge will be thinner than the middle. Lift and turn the dough a quarter turn after each roll, but avoid excessive handling and rolling. Ideal pastry dough is about ⅛ inch (3 mm) thick, though you may like it slightly thicker for the bottom crust of a fruit pie.

Baking a pastry shell without a filling is called "baking blind." Sometimes the crust is lined with foil and weighted down with uncooked beans or rice. See the information under Flaky Pastry and Butter Pastry for two ways to bake blind.

Flaky Pastry

PICTURED ON FACING PAGE

1¼ cups (155 g) all-purpose flour
¼ teaspoon salt
6 tablespoons (3 oz./85 g) solid vegetable shortening or lard
4 to 5 tablespoons (60 to 75 ml) ice water

In a large bowl, stir together flour and salt. With a pastry blender or 2 table knives, cut shortening into flour until particles are about the size of small peas.

Pour ice water into a cup. While stirring lightly and quickly with a fork, sprinkle water over flour mixture, 1 tablespoon (15 ml) at a time (up to 4 tablespoons/60 ml), just until all flour is moistened. If mixture seems dry and crumbly, sprinkle with another tablespoon (15 ml) of water; mixture should not be wet or sticky. Stir with a fork until dough forms a ball and almost cleans sides of bowl.

With your hands, gather up mixture into a ball and flatten into a 4-inch (10-cm) round. Wrap with plastic wrap and refrigerate for 1 hour.

On a lightly floured surface or on a pastry cloth, roll out dough until it is about ⅛ inch (3 mm) thick and 2 inches (5 cm) larger in diameter than pie pan. Wrap rolled-out dough loosely around rolling pin, then unroll onto pie pan. Fit pastry into pan.

For a single-crust pie or baked pastry shell. Leaving about a 1-inch (2.5-cm) overhang, trim edge of pastry with scissors. Fold edge under so it's even with rim. Flute edge (see photo 5, facing page). Prick bottom and sides of shell thoroughly with a fork and bake in a preheated 450°F (230°C) oven until lightly browned (about 10 minutes). Let cool before filling.

For a double-crust pie. Fill pie. Roll out top pastry (cut design, if desired) and place over filling; trim top and bottom pastry to 1-inch (2.5-cm) overhang. Fold edge of top pastry under bottom pastry, and flute. If no design has been made, cut steam vents.
Makes one 9-inch (23-cm) pie crust or pastry shell (6 to 8 servings)

PER SERVING: *178 calories, 11 g total fat, 3 g saturated fat, 0 mg cholesterol, 78 mg sodium, 17 g carbohydrates, 0.6 g fiber, 2 g protein, 4 mg calcium, 1 mg iron*

Butter Pastry

1 cup (125 g) all-purpose flour
¼ teaspoon salt
6 tablespoons (3 oz./85 g) cold butter, cut into chunks
3 to 4 tablespoons (45 to 60 ml) ice water

In a large bowl, combine flour and salt. Add butter chunks and stir to coat them. With a pastry blender or 2 table knives, cut butter into fine particles. Stir in ice water with a fork until dough holds together. With your hands, shape into a ball; wrap in plastic wrap and refrigerate for 1 hour.

On a lightly floured surface or on a pastry cloth, roll out dough to a 13-inch (33-cm) round and fit into pan; flute edge or press in dough.

To bake blind, place foil in crust and partially fill with uncooked beans or rice. Bake in a 450°F (230°C) oven for 10 minutes; lift off foil and beans. Bake empty crust for 5 more minutes.
Makes one 9-inch (23-cm) pie crust or pastry shell (6 to 8 servings)

PER SERVING: *152 calories, 10 g total fat, 6 g saturated fat, 27 mg cholesterol, 178 mg sodium, 14 g carbohydrates, 0.5 g fiber, 2 g protein, 6 mg calcium, 0.8 mg iron*

FRUIT PIES

A homemade fruit pie, with its tangy-sweet filling and flaky, fragile crust, is a wonderful way to please and impress family and friends.

Apple Pie

PICTURED ON PAGE 166

>   *Flaky Pastry (see page 167 and double recipe)*
> 8 cups (about 2 lbs./905 g) peeled, cored, and thinly sliced apples (Newtown Pippin or Granny Smith)
> 1 cup (200 g) sugar
> 3 tablespoons cornstarch or tapioca
> 1 tablespoon (15 ml) lemon juice
> 1½ teaspoons ground cinnamon
> ¼ teaspoon ground ginger
> 2 tablespoons butter or margarine
>   Milk

Prepare pastry and refrigerate while making filling. Place apple slices in a large bowl. Sprinkle apples with sugar, cornstarch, lemon juice, cinnamon, and ginger. Stir to blend well; set aside.

Roll out pastry for bottom crust (see page 167); place in pie pan. Place apples in pastry shell, mounding them in center. Pour in any remaining juice from bowl, then dot with butter. Roll out top crust (if cutting decorative design, do so before placing crust over filling). Place crust over filling and trim both crusts to 1-inch (2.5-cm) overhang; flute edge to seal. If no design has been made, cut steam vents in top crust, then brush top lightly with milk. To prevent excess browning of edge, wrap with foil. Set pie on a 10- by 15-inch (25- by 38-cm) rimmed baking pan.

Bake on lowest rack of oven in a 425°F (220°C) oven for 30 minutes. Remove foil and bake until apples are tender (20 to 30 more minutes). Let cool on a rack. Serve warm or at room temperature; or refrigerate. To reheat, warm pie, uncovered, in a 350°F (175°C) oven for 10 to 15 minutes.

Makes 6 to 8 servings

PER SERVING: *587 calories, 26 g total fat, 8 g saturated fat, 9 mg cholesterol, 191 mg sodium, 87 g carbohydrates, 4 g fiber, 5 g protein, 23 mg calcium, 2 mg iron*

Single-Crust Apple Pie

Bake a 9-inch (23-cm) *Flaky Pastry* shell (page 167). Following directions for *Apple Pie*, combine 6 cups (1½ lbs./680 g) sliced *apples*, 1 tablespoon (15 ml) *lemon juice*, ¾ cup (150 g) *sugar*, 2 tablespoons *cornstarch* or tapioca, 1½ teaspoons ground *cinnamon*, and ¼ teaspoon ground *ginger*. Place in baked shell. Sprinkle with streusel topping (recipe follows). Place pie pan in a 10- by 15-inch (25- by 38-cm) rimmed baking pan and bake in a 375°F (190°C) oven for 1 hour, checking pie after 15 to 20 minutes (if topping is browning too fast, cover loosely with foil).

Streusel topping

In a large bowl, combine 1 cup (125 g) all-purpose *flour*, ½ cup (110 g) firmly packed *brown sugar*, and ½ teaspoon ground *cinnamon*. With your fingers, work 6 tablespoons (3 oz./85 g) *butter* or margarine into flour until butter lumps are no longer distinguishable. Stir in ½ cup (65 g) chopped *nuts*, if desired. *Makes enough topping for a 9-inch (23-cm) pie.*

Blueberry Pie

>   *Flaky Pastry (see page 167)*
> 6 cups (870 g) fresh blueberries
> 2 tablespoons (30 ml) honey
> 1 cup (200 g) sugar
> ¼ cup (32 g) cornstarch or tapioca
> 1 tablespoon (15 ml) lemon juice
>   *Streusel topping (see above), made with ⅓ cup (70 g) sugar*

Prepare pastry and refrigerate while making filling. In a large bowl, toss blueberries with honey; sprinkle with sugar, cornstarch, and lemon juice. Gently stir to blend well; set aside. Prepare streusel topping.

Roll out pastry for single crust and place in pie pan (see page 167). Place berries and their juices in pastry shell and top with streusel topping. Place pie in a 10- by 15-inch (25- by 38-cm) rimmed baking pan.

Bake on lowest rack of oven in a 425°F (220°C) oven for 55 minutes (after about 20 minutes, check pie and cover topping with foil if it is browning too fast). Let pie cool on a rack. Serve warm or at room temperature; or refrigerate and serve cold. To reheat, warm pie, uncovered, in a 350°F (175°C) oven for 10 to 15 minutes. *Makes 6 to 8 servings*

PER SERVING: *584 calories, 22 g total fat, 9 g saturated fat, 27 mg cholesterol, 187 mg sodium, 96 g carbohydrates, 4 g fiber, 5 g protein, 20 mg calcium, 2 mg iron*

FRESH FRUIT TARTS

A fruit tart consists of a pastry shell, a shallow layer of filling and fruit, and a dusting of sugar or a glaze of melted jelly. Whether bite-size or party-size, tarts are pretty and simple to serve on short notice if you keep unbaked or baked tart shells in your freezer.

Tarts invite creativity—you can use just one fruit or a colorful combination. Pick your favorites from strawberries, raspberries, blueberries, loganberries, sectioned oranges, or sliced plums, kiwifruits, or figs. Peaches, nectarines, apricots, apples, and pears also make marvelous tarts, but these fruits darken when cut, so dip slices in lemon juice before using.

A ball of tart pastry, wrapped airtight, can be stored in the refrigerator for up to a week. Or you can press the dough into a pan, wrap airtight, then freeze. When it's frozen, remove the tart shell from the pan and wrap well; it can then be frozen for several months (do not thaw before baking). Unfilled baked tart shells, wrapped airtight, can be stored at room temperature for up to 4 days or frozen for up to 3 months, but they may lose a bit of their fresh flavor in freezing.

Short Paste for Tarts

- 2 cups (250 g) all-purpose flour
- ¼ cup (50 g) sugar
- ¾ cup (6 oz./170 g) cold butter or margarine, cut into chunks
- 2 large egg yolks or 1 large egg

In a large bowl, combine flour and sugar. Add butter and, with your fingers, work butter into flour mixture until well blended. With a fork, stir in egg yolks or whole egg. Stir until dough holds together. (Or whirl flour, sugar, and butter in a food processor until mixture resembles fine crumbs; add yolks or whole egg and whirl until dough holds together.)

With your hands, press dough firmly into a smooth shiny ball, kneading a bit to help bind the dough. (At this point, you may wrap dough with plastic wrap and refrigerate for at least 1 hour or up to 1 week; let come to room temperature before using.)

Note: If you use only egg yolks in this recipe, the dough will have a richer golden color.

Makes scant 2 cups (490 g) dough (8 servings)

PER SERVING: *305 calories, 19 g total fat, 11 g saturated fat, 100 mg cholesterol, 178 mg sodium, 30 g carbohydrates, 0.8 g fiber, 4 g protein, 16 mg calcium, 2 mg iron*

Assembling a Tart

One you've made the Short Paste for Tarts (at left), you can bake the shell (see below), then assemble the tart. Only the shell is baked, not the fruit or filling.

First, measure the tart pan (see page 7). Use 1 to 1¼ cups (260 to 325 g) dough for an 8- to 9-inch (20- to 21.5-cm) pan, a scant 2 cups (490 g) dough for an 11-inch (28-cm) pan. (To serve tart outside of pan, use a pan with removable bottom.) For small tarts, allow about 2 teaspoons dough for 2-inch (5-cm) pans, and ¼ cup (65 g) for 4½-inch (11-cm) pans.

To shape, press measured amount of pastry into pan, pushing dough firmly into bottom and sides to make an even layer; edge should be flush with pan rim. Bake in a 300°F (150°C) oven, uncovered, until lightly browned (30 to 40 minutes). Let cool in pan.

Invert small pans and tap lightly to free shells; then turn them cup side up. Leave large tart shell in pan.

To assemble a tart, fill the baked shell with your choice of filling, then top the filling with a layer of fruit. You can leave the fruit plain, sprinkle it with a little granulated or powdered sugar, or brush it with a glaze of marmalade or currant, apricot, or strawberry jelly, melted over low heat and then cooled.

Choices of filling include uncooked Lemon Cream Filling (page 170) or cooked French Pastry Cream (page 172). For an 11-inch (28-cm) tart, you'll use a full recipe of filling; for an 8- to 9-inch (20- to 23-cm) tart, about half of the filling.

Individual tarts can take a proportionately more generous amount of filling than large ones that must be cut. Allow about ¼ cup (60 ml) filling for each 4½-inch (11-cm) tart, and 2 to 3 tablespoons (30 to 45 ml) filling for each 2-inch (5-cm) tart.

Lemon Cream Filling

1 package (about 3 oz./85 g) cream cheese, softened
1 cup (240 ml) whipping cream
½ cup (50 g) sifted powdered sugar
½ teaspoon grated lemon peel
1 teaspoon lemon juice
½ teaspoon vanilla

Place cream cheese in a large, deep bowl and, with an electric mixer at high speed, beat until smooth. Beating constantly, pour in cream in a steady stream. (Mixture should have consistency of stiffly whipped cream at all times; if it looks soft, stop adding cream until mixture thickens. Do not overbeat or sauce will break down.)

Stir in powdered sugar, lemon peel, lemon juice, and vanilla. (At this point, you may cover and refrigerate until next day.)   *Makes about 2 cups (470 ml)*

PER TABLESPOON: *37 calories, 3 g total fat, 2 g saturated fat, 11 mg cholesterol, 11 mg sodium, 2 g carbohydrates, 0 g fiber, 0.4 g protein, 7 mg calcium, 0 mg iron*

CREAM PUFFS & ÉCLAIRS

These luxurious treats are made from a batter called choux paste—a simple mixture of butter, flour, and eggs. Shape it into cream puffs or éclairs and fill with pastry cream or whipped cream for dessert, or form the batter into bite-size pastries to serve with a savory filling as hors d'oeuvres.

The baked puff should have a hollow, moist interior and a crisp outer shell with a lightly browned, slightly pebbly surface.

Choux Paste

PICTURED ON FACING PAGE

1 cup (240 ml) water
½ cup (4 oz./110 g) butter or margarine
¼ teaspoon salt
1 teaspoon sugar (use only for dessert puffs)
1 cup (125 g) all-purpose flour
4 large eggs

Lightly coat a baking sheet with butter (or line a baking sheet with parchment paper) and set aside.

In a 3-quart (2.8-liter) pan over medium-high heat, bring water, butter, salt, and sugar (if using) to a boil.

When butter melts, remove pan from heat, add flour all at once, and beat with a wooden spoon until well blended. Reduce heat to medium. Return pan to heat and stir vigorously with a wooden spoon until mixture forms a ball and leaves sides of pan (about 1 to 2 minutes). Remove pan from heat and let mixture cool for 5 minutes. Transfer mixture to a food processor. Whirl in eggs, one at a time, processing briefly after each addition until smooth. (After each egg is added, mixture breaks apart into clumps and is slippery, but will return to a smooth paste after beating.) Let batter cool for 10 minutes before shaping.

Shaping and baking cream puffs. You need two spoons to shape cream puffs, or you can use a pastry bag without a tip or with a ½-inch (1-cm) plain tip. With one spoon, scoop up about 2 tablespoons batter for a large puff, 1 tablespoon for a medium-size puff, or 1½ teaspoons for a cocktail-size puff. With other spoon, push batter off first spoon and drop in a mound onto prepared baking sheet. Place mounds about 2 inches (5 cm) apart.

Bake in upper third of a 425°F (220°C) oven for 15 minutes. Reduce heat to 375°F (190°C).

Make a cut in lower side of each puff and continue baking until puffs are firm, dry, and golden brown (about 15 more minutes). Let cool on racks. Use within 24 hours, or wrap airtight and freeze. *Makes about 2 dozen large puffs, 3 dozen medium-size puffs, or 5 to 6 dozen cocktail-size puffs*

PER UNFILLED LARGE PUFF: *68 calories, 5 g total fat, 3 g saturated fat, 46 mg cholesterol, 72 mg sodium, 4 g carbohydrates, 0.1 g fiber, 2 g protein, 6 mg calcium, 0.4 mg iron*

Shaping and baking éclairs. Onto prepared baking sheet, drop about ¼ cup (50 g) batter for each éclair, placing mounds 2 to 3 inches (5 to 8 cm) apart. (Or put batter into a pastry bag and pipe out.) Using a small metal spatula, spread each mound into a strip 4½ inches (11 cm) long and 1½ inches (3.5 cm) wide. For mini éclairs, use scant 2 tablespoons for each éclair and spread 3 inches (8 cm) long by ¾ inch wide. Bake as for cream puffs. *Makes 12 large éclairs or 24 mini éclairs*

Serving dessert cream puffs or éclairs. With a knife, cut upper third from each puff or éclair and scoop out moist interior. Fill with French Pastry Cream (page 172), replace tops, and dust with powdered sugar. Drizzle with Chocolate Glaze (page 172).

MAKING CHOUX PASTE

1 Bring water, butter, and salt (sugar is optional) to a boil, then remove pan from heat and beat in flour. Return pan to heat and stir until mixture forms a ball and leaves sides of pan. Remove pan from heat and let mixture cool briefly.

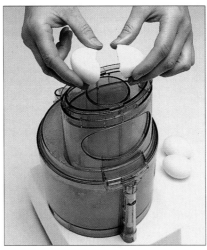

2 Transfer mixture to a food processor. Add eggs, one at a time, processing briefly after each addition. (If you don't have—or don't want to use—a food processor, leave flour mixture in pan and beat in eggs by hand.)

3 After all eggs are processed, finished choux paste will be thick and satiny smooth.

4 Using a large spoon, pick up a large dollop (about 2 tablespoons) of choux paste. With a second spoon, push choux paste onto prepared baking sheet. Or pipe choux paste onto baking sheet with pastry bag fitted with a plain tip.

5 When puffs are done, use a serrated knife to cut off a "cap" (top one third or so) from each one; set aside. With a teaspoon, scoop any moist, doughy portions from inside each puff.

6 Use a small spoon to fill puffs with pastry cream or whipped cream. Replace tops and dust with powdered sugar. For hors d'oeuvres, make cocktail-sized puffs and fill with chicken or tuna salad, or another savory mixture.

French Pastry Cream

½ cup (60 g) all-purpose flour
½ cup (100 g) sugar
4 beaten large egg yolks
   Pinch of salt
2 cups (470 ml) 2% milk, scalded (heated until small bubbles appear)
1 tablespoon butter
1 teaspoon vanilla

In a 3-quart (2.8-liter) pan off the heat, combine flour, sugar, egg yolks, and salt. Beating constantly with a spoon, gradually pour in scalded milk.

Place pan over medium heat and stir constantly with a whisk or spoon until mixture boils and thickens (2 to 3 minutes). Remove pan from heat and stir in butter and vanilla. Let cool, covered with plastic wrap, before using.
Makes 2⅓ cups/550 ml (fills 12 large cream puffs or éclairs)

PER TABLESPOON: *38 calories, 1 g total fat, 0.6 g saturated fat, 29 mg cholesterol, 16 mg sodium, 5 g carbohydrates, 0.1 g fiber, 1 g protein, 22 mg calcium, 0.2 mg iron*

Chocolate Glaze

4 ounces (115 g) semisweet chocolate chips, coarsely chopped
6 tablespoons (90 ml) whipping cream.

Place chocolate chips and cream in a 1-quart (950-ml) pan. Cook, stirring constantly, over medium heat, until chocolate is melted and well blended with cream.   *Makes about ⅔ cup (160 ml)*

PER TABLESPOON: *72 calories, 5 g total fat, 3 g saturated fat, 9 mg cholesterol, 3 mg sodium, 7 g carbohydrates, 0 g fiber, 0.6 g protein, 9 mg calcium, 0.3 mg iron*

CHEESECAKE & MOUSSE

Here we present some luscious and elegant desserts that make the ideal ending for a special meal. Standard cheesecake recipes call for as much as 2 pounds (905 g) of regular cream cheese—plus full-fat sour cream. Our recipes, while still rich, use yogurt cheese, Neufchâtel cheese, nonfat cream cheese, and nonfat sour cream to cut down on the fat.

Mousse, like cheesecake, takes a little extra time because it needs to chill before serving. But that's "hands off" time you can spend as you wish.

Elegant Cheesecake

3 quarts (2.8 liters) nonfat yogurt (made without gelatin) for yogurt cheese or 3 packages (about 8 oz./230 g each) cream cheese, softened
1½ cups (128 g) fine graham cracker crumbs (about 24 cracker squares)
⅓ cup (2.7 oz./76 g) butter or margarine, melted
1¼ cups (250 g) sugar
1 tablespoon (15 ml) vanilla
¼ teaspoon salt
4 large eggs, at room temperature

To prepare yogurt cheese, line a colander or a fine strainer with 2 layers of cheesecloth or 1 layer of muslin. Spoon yogurt into cloth, then fold cloth over it. Set a colander in a large pan or bowl; the bottom of the colander should be suspended at least 1 inch (2.5 cm) above the pan bottom. Enclose colander and pan with plastic wrap, making it reasonably airtight. Chill, pouring off whey as it accumulates so yogurt can drain freely. You will need 5 cups (1.25 kg) of yogurt cheese for this recipe, which will require about 24 hours of draining.

To make the graham cracker crust, in a large bowl, combine graham cracker crumbs, butter, and 2 tablespoons of the sugar. Press mixture firmly over bottom and 2 inches (5 cm) up sides of a 9-inch (23-cm) removable-rim pan. Bake crust in a 350°F (175°C) oven for 10 minutes, then set aside.

In a large bowl, combine 3 cups (750 g) of the yogurt cheese, the vanilla, and salt until soft and creamy. Add eggs, one at a time, beating well after each addition. Gradually beat in 1 cup (200 g) of the sugar until it is all incorporated. Pour batter into the prepared pan.

Bake for 45 minutes or until center jiggles slightly when pan is gently shaken (center will set upon standing). Remove cake from oven; let stand for 10 minutes. Increase oven temperature to 450°F (230°C).

In a small bowl, combine remaining 2 cups (500 g) yogurt cheese and 2 tablespoons sugar; spread over top of cake. Return cake to oven and bake until cream is set (about 10 more minutes). Transfer pan to a rack; let cool completely before removing pan rim. Then cover and refrigerate for at least 24 hours. Cut into wedges to serve.   *Makes 12 servings*

PER SERVING: *293 calories, 8 g total fat, 4 g saturated fat, 84 mg cholesterol, 288 mg sodium, 41 g carbohydrates, 0.5 g fiber, 12 g protein, 290 mg calcium, 0.6 mg iron*

Chocolate Cheesecake

   1   package (about 7¼ oz./208 g) butter cookies
   ¼ cup (2 oz./55 g) butter or margarine, melted
   1   package (about 12 oz./340 g) semisweet chocolate chips
   ⅔ cup (135 g) sugar
   1   tablespoon all-purpose flour
   2   packages (about 8 oz./230 g each) Neufchâtel cheese
   2   large eggs
   1   tablespoon (15 ml) sweet marsala or sweet sherry
   1   tablespoon (15 ml) vanilla

In a food processor or blender, whirl cookies to make fine crumbs. Pour into a 9-inch (23-cm) removable-rim pan. Add butter, mix well, then press crumbs evenly over pan bottom and about 1 inch (2.5 cm) up pan sides; set aside.

In a food processor or blender, whirl half the chocolate chips until ground. In food processor or bowl of an electric mixer, combine ground chocolate, sugar, and flour; whirl or stir to mix. Add cheese (cut into chunks), then eggs, marsala, and vanilla. Whirl or beat until well mixed.

Scatter half the remaining chocolate into crust, then pour cheesecake batter into pan; spread batter level. Sprinkle remaining chocolate over batter.

Bake in a 300°F (150°C) oven until cake jiggles only slightly in center when pan is shaken (1¼ to 1½ hours). Let cool; cover and chill for at least 4 hours or up to 2 days. Remove pan rim.   *Makes 16 servings*

PER SERVING: *305 calories, 18 g total fat, 11 g saturated fat, 66 mg cholesterol, 196 mg sodium, 33 g carbohydrates, 0.3 g fiber, 5 g protein, 36 mg calcium, 1 mg iron*

Cheesecake Tips

• *The top of a cheesecake can crack if it cooks too long and at too high a heat. This won't affect the flavor, just the appearance, and you can always cover it with a dollop of sour cream or a fruit garnish.*

• *For easy slicing, make sure the cheesecake is thoroughly chilled; refrigerate it for at least 4 hours. Cut into wedges with a long length of waxed dental floss stretched tightly across the cake—the slices will be neat and tidy.*

Espresso Cheesecake

   1   package (about 9 oz./255 g) chocolate wafer cookies
   ¼ cup (2 oz./55 g) butter or margarine, melted and cooled slightly
   1   tablespoon instant espresso powder
   ½ teaspoon vanilla
   4   large packages (about 8 oz./230 g each) nonfat cream cheese, at room temperature
   2   cups (470 ml) nonfat sour cream
   1   cup (200 g) plus 1 tablespoon sugar
   3   large eggs
   2   large egg whites
   3   tablespoons (45 ml) coffee-flavored liqueur
   1   tablespoon unsweetened cocoa powder
       Chocolate-covered espresso beans or mocha candy beans

In a food processor, whirl cookies to form fine crumbs. Add butter, instant espresso, and vanilla; whirl just until crumbs are evenly moistened. Press crumb mixture firmly over bottom and about 1 inch (2.5 cm) up sides of a 9-inch (23-cm) removable-rim pan. Bake in a 350°F (175°C) oven until crust feels slightly firmer when pressed (about 15 minutes).

In a clean food processor or in a large bowl, combine cream cheese, 1 cup (240 ml) of the sour cream, 1 cup (200 g) of the sugar, the whole eggs, egg whites, and liqueur. Whirl or beat with an electric mixer until smooth.

Pour cheese filling into baked crust. Return to oven and bake until filling is golden on top and jiggles only slightly in center when pan is gently shaken (1¼ to 1½ hours). Let cheesecake cool in pan on a rack for 30 minutes.

Meanwhile, in a small bowl, gently stir together remaining 1 cup (240 ml) sour cream and 1 tablespoon sugar; cover and refrigerate.

Spread cooled cheesecake with sour cream topping. Cover and refrigerate until cold (at least 4 hours) or until next day. Just before serving, sprinkle with cocoa; then remove pan rim. Garnish with chocolate-covered espresso beans.
Makes 12 to 16 servings

PER SERVING: *271 calories, 7 g total fat, 3 g saturated fat, 62 mg cholesterol, 492 mg sodium, 37 g carbohydrates, 0.7 g fiber, 15 g protein, 239 mg calcium, 0.9 mg iron*

HOW TO MAKE GIANDUIA MOUSSE

1 After toasting, pour hot hazelnuts into kitchen towel and rub between your hands. Most of brown skin will come off nuts. Don't worry if some of the skin remains.

2 Add chocolate to cream cheese mixture. It's easiest to use semisweet chocolate chips or chunks, but you can substitute good-quality semisweet chocolate bars. Buy three 3-ounce (85-g) bars and chop into ½-inch (1-cm) pieces.

3 Before adding beaten eggs to hot milk mixture, add a little of the milk mixture to the eggs and stir. This warms eggs so they do not cook when they hit the hot liquid.

4 Cool chocolate mixture in the refrigerator or, for quicker chilling, place bowl in a larger bowl half-filled with ice water. Stir often until cool (5 to 8 minutes).

5 With a rubber spatula, gently fold whipped crème fraîche into chocolate mixture until completely blended (no streaks should remain). Fold, don't stir, or you may deflate the whipped crème fraîche.

6 A dessert this special deserves a pretty dish, such as a footed goblet or a wine glass. Top the mousse with a dollop of whipped crème fraîche; sprinkle with cocoa powder; and tuck in a sprig of fresh mint, if desired.

Gianduia Mousse

PICTURED ON FACING PAGE

   1 *cup (125 g) shelled hazelnuts*
   1 *small package (about 3 oz./85 g) cream cheese, softened*
  ½ *cup (120 ml) hazelnut-flavor liqueur such as Frangelico*
1½ *cups (9 oz./255 g) semisweet chocolate chips or chunks*
   1 *cup (240 ml) 2% milk*
  ½ *cup (100 g) sugar*
   2 *large eggs*
   1 *cup (240 ml) crème fraîche or whipping cream*

To toast hazelnuts, place in a single layer in a 10- by 15-inch (25- by 38-cm) rimmed baking pan. Toast in a 350°F (175°C) oven, shaking pan occasionally, until golden under the skin (about 15 minutes). Pour hot nuts onto a towel and rub with cloth to remove the loose brown skin (some sticks). Lift nuts from cloth.

In a blender, whirl nuts to a smooth paste (3 to 5 minutes). Scrape container sides frequently.

In a large heatproof bowl, mash cream cheese, then gradually whisk in liqueur until smoothly blended. Add chocolate chips.

In a wide frying pan, heat milk with nut paste and sugar until steaming. In a small bowl, whisk eggs to blend, add some of the hot liquid, then return mixture to the pan. Stir over low heat until mixture is thick enough to mound (about 8 minutes).

Immediately remove pan from heat and add nut mixture to chocolate mixture. Stir until chocolate melts. Cover and chill until cool but still easy to stir (about 45 minutes). Or nest bowl in ice water and stir often until cool (5 to 8 minutes).

With an electric mixer, beat crème fraîche until it holds distinct peaks, then fold smoothly into chocolate mixture. Pour into individual dishes and serve, or cover and chill up until next day.
Makes 8 to 10 servings

PER SERVING: *454 calories, 31 g total fat, 14 g saturated fat, 82 mg cholesterol, 74 mg sodium, 38 g carbohydrates, 1 g fiber, 7 g protein, 132 mg calcium, 1 mg iron*

Strawberry-Rhubarb Mousse

   2 *cups (240 g) sliced rhubarb (¾ in./2 cm thick)*
  ¾ *cup (150 g) sugar*
   1 *tablespoon (15 ml) water*
   2 *envelopes unflavored gelatin*
  ½ *cup (120 ml) orange juice (preferably freshly squeezed)*
   2 *quarts (1.2 kg) strawberries, rinsed, hulled, and sliced lengthwise ¼ inch (6 mm) thick*
   2 *teaspoons grated orange peel*
1½ *cups (360 ml) whipping cream*
   2 *tablespoons powdered sugar*

In a 2- to 3-quart (1.9- to 2.8-liter) pan, combine rhubarb, ¼ cup (50 ml) of the sugar, and the water. Bring to a simmer over high heat, then reduce heat and simmer, covered, until rhubarb is very tender when pierced (8 to 10 minutes).

In a small bowl, stir gelatin into orange juice and let stand until softened (4 to 5 minutes); set aside.

Meanwhile, place 2 cups (240 g) of the strawberries and ½ cup (100 g) of the sugar in a wide nonstick frying pan over medium-low heat. Cook, occasionally shaking pan and stirring gently, until sugar dissolves (5 to 8 minutes). Remove pan from heat; gently stir in rhubarb and gelatin mixtures and orange peel. Let cool, then chill until mixture is cold to touch and flows slowly when tilted (30 to 40 minutes). Do not overchill.

In the large bowl of an electric mixer, beat whipping cream until thick. Beat in powdered sugar, then fold in rhubarb mixture until no streaks remain. Chill airtight until slightly firm to the touch (about 20 minutes).

If serving immediately, set aside about 6 of the prettiest berry slices for garnish. In a deep 2- to 2½-quart (1.9- to 2.4-liter) glass serving bowl, spread one fourth of the mousse in an even layer. Using half of the remaining strawberries, arrange them individually on top of the mousse in a very even double layer. Spread with half of remaining mousse. Repeat layering, ending with small mounds of mousse. Chill airtight until mousse is slightly firm to touch (at least 1 hour) or up until next day. Garnish with reserved berries before serving.   *Makes 10 to 12 servings*

PER SERVING: *202 calories, 11 g total fat, 6 g saturated fat, 36 mg cholesterol, 16 mg sodium, 26 g carbohydrates, 3 g fiber, 3 g protein, 61 mg calcium, 0.5 mg iron*

CUSTARDS

Exquisitely simple, custards are nothing more than sweetened, flavored egg-and-milk mixtures that are stirred over heat or baked. Crème anglaise is a soft custard sauce that glorifies plain cake or fresh fruit.

Crème Anglaise

    2 cups (470 ml) 2% milk
    ⅓ cup (70 g) sugar
    4 large egg yolks, lightly beaten
    1 teaspoon vanilla

In the top of a double boiler placed directly over medium heat, scald milk (heat until small bubbles appear); remove from heat and stir in sugar until dissolved. Whisk some of the hot milk mixture into the egg yolks until well combined, then whisk back into the milk mixture while stirring constantly.

Pour hot water into bottom of double boiler, being sure water will not touch bottom of top pan. Bring water to a boil over high heat, then reduce heat so water only simmers.

Put top of double boiler in place over simmering water. Stir milk mixture constantly (to prevent lumping) until custard has thickened and lightly coats a metal spoon (10 to 13 minutes); a finger drawn across spoon should leave a clean path. (Overcooking results in a grainy, curdled custard. If custard is slightly curdled, strain it into a bowl and beat with an electric mixer, or whirl in a blender or food processor for 1 minute until smooth. Excessively curdled custard cannot be corrected.) Stir in vanilla, then cool by placing pan in bowl of ice water. Stir often until cooled to room temperature; cover and refrigerate.   *Makes about 2 cups (470 ml)*

PER TABLESPOON: *23 calories, 0.9 g total fat, 0.4 g saturated fat, 28 mg cholesterol, 9 mg sodium, 3 g carbohydrates, 0 g fiber, 0.8 g protein, 22 mg calcium, 0.1 mg iron*

Double Caramel Flan

    ⅓ cup (70 g) sugar
    2 cups (470 ml) 2% milk
    ⅔ cup (135 g) Caramel Powder (recipe follows)
    6 large eggs
    1 teaspoon vanilla

In a wide nonstick frying pan, frequently shake sugar over medium heat until completely melted and deep amber in color (3 to 5 minutes). Immediately pour into an 8- to 9-inch (20- to 23-cm) straight-sided baking dish or pan (at least 1-quart/950-ml size). Rotate dish to coat bottom.

In a 1- to 1½-quart (950- to 1.4-liter) pan over medium-high heat, stir milk and Caramel Powder until all the caramel re-melts (about 7 minutes). In a medium-size bowl, whisk some of the hot liquid with eggs and vanilla; stir back into pan. Remove from heat.

Pour mixture into prepared baking dish. Set dish in a larger rimmed pan; pour boiling water into outer pan to a level of 1 inch (2.5 cm). Bake in a 350°F (175°C) oven until center of flan jiggles only slightly when gently shaken (35 to 45 minutes).

Remove baking dish from water. Let cool, then cover and chill for at least 4 hours or up to 2 days. To serve, run a thin knife between flan and dish. Invert platter over flan; holding together, invert. Lift off pan. Garnish with small chunks of caramel, if desired. Cut into wedges.   *Makes 8 servings*

PER SERVING: *217 calories, 5 g total fat, 2 g saturated fat, 164 mg cholesterol, 78 mg sodium, 37 g carbohydrates, 0 g fiber, 7 g protein, 93 mg calcium, 0.6 mg iron*

Caramel Powder

Line a 10- by 15-inch (25- by 38-cm) rimmed baking pan with a single sheet of foil, folding up at edges.

Pour 1 cup (200 g) sugar into a large nonstick frying pan; place over medium-high heat. Shake pan often until most of the sugar liquifies (about 10 minutes). Reduce heat to medium; tilt pan to mix hot caramel with sugar until completely melted and deep amber in color (3 to 5 minutes).

Immediately pour hot caramel into foil-lined pan. Using hot pads to protect hands, tilt pan to spread caramel in thin layer. Set aside until hard and completely cool (about 30 minutes).

When cool, lift foil from pan; peel foil from caramel. Break caramel into chunks. To make powder, whirl chunks in a blender or food processor fitted with metal blade (container must be completely dry). If you use a blender, you may need to make the powder in several batches. Use, or store airtight at room temperature for up to 1 month.
Makes ⅔ cup (135 g)

LAYER & SHEET CAKES

Everyone perks up at the mention of cake for dessert. Here you'll find a variety of layer and sheet cakes from classic Yellow Cake to spicy Gingerbread. For frosting ideas, see page 180.

Yellow Cake

About 2¼ cups (280 g) sifted cake flour

1¼ cups (250 g) sugar

1 tablespoon baking powder

½ teaspoon salt

½ cup (4 oz./110 g) butter or margarine, softened

1 cup (240 ml) 2% milk

2 large eggs

1 teaspoon vanilla

Butter and flour-dust two 8-inch (20-cm) cake pans or a 7- by 11-inch (18- by 28-cm) baking pan.

Sift 2¼ cups (280 g) of the flour, the sugar, baking powder, and salt into a medium-size mixing bowl; add butter and ⅔ cup (160 ml) of the milk. With an electric mixer at medium speed, beat for 2 minutes, scraping bowl often with a rubber spatula. Add remaining ⅓ cup (80 ml) milk, the eggs, and vanilla; continue beating for 2 more minutes. Pour batter into prepared pan(s). Bake in a 375°F (190°C) oven until top springs back when touched and the cake begins to pull away from the sides of the pan(s), 25 to 30 minutes for layers; 30 to 35 minutes for sheet cake. Cool layers in pans on a rack for 10 minutes, then turn layers out onto racks to cool completely before frosting. Cool sheet cake in pan on a rack. *Makes 12 servings*

PER SERVING WITHOUT FROSTING: *249 calories, 10 g total fat, 6 g saturated fat, 58 mg cholesterol, 312 mg sodium, 37 g carbohydrates, 0 g fiber, 3 g protein, 102 mg calcium, 2 mg iron*

White Cake

Prepare *Yellow Cake*, but substitute 4 *egg whites* for the 2 whole eggs.

Devil's Food Cake

Prepare *Yellow Cake*, but reduce flour to 2 cups (250 g), omit baking powder, and add 1¼ teaspoons *baking soda* instead; increase sugar to 2 cups. When adding egg mixture, add ½ cup (43 g) *unsweetened cocoa powder* blended with ½ cup (120 ml) *water*.

Carrot Cake

2 cups (400 g) sugar

1 cup (240 ml) vegetable oil

4 large eggs

1 teaspoon vanilla

2 cups (250 g) all-purpose flour

2 teaspoons ground cinnamon

1½ teaspoons baking powder

1½ teaspoons baking soda

2 cups (200 g) lightly packed shredded carrots

1 can (8 oz./230 g) juice-packed crushed pineapple, drained

½ cup (65 g) chopped walnuts

Cream Cheese Frosting or Orange Glaze (below)

Butter and flour-dust a 9- by 13-inch (23- by 33-cm) baking pan or a 10-inch (25-cm) fluted tube pan.

In a medium-size bowl, combine sugar and oil. Beat in eggs, one at a time, then stir in vanilla. Stir in flour, cinnamon, baking powder, and baking soda. Add carrots, pineapple, and nuts; stir just to blend. Pour batter into prepared pan.

Bake in a 350°F (175°C) oven until a wooden pick inserted in center comes out clean (45 minutes for sheet cake; 55 minutes for fluted tube cake). Place pan on a rack to cool; or, if using a fluted tube pan, let cake cool in pan for 15 minutes, then turn out and finish cooling on rack. Cool completely before frosting or glazing. *Makes 12 servings*

PER SERVING WITH CREAM CHEESE FROSTING: *599 calories, 34 g total fat, 10 g saturated fat, 102 mg cholesterol, 347 mg sodium, 69 g carbohydrates, 2 g fiber, 6 g protein, 75 mg calcium, 2 mg iron*

PER SERVING WITH ORANGE GLAZE: *516 calories, 24 g total fat, 3 g saturated fat, 71 mg cholesterol, 247 mg sodium, 73 g carbohydrates, 2 g fiber, 5 g protein, 63 mg calcium, 2 mg iron*

Cream Cheese Frosting

In a small bowl, blend 2 packages (about 3 oz./85 g each) *cream cheese*, softened; 6 tablespoons (3 oz./85 g) *butter* or margarine, softened; 1 teaspoon grated *orange peel* (optional); 1 teaspoon *vanilla*; and 1½ cups (150 g) sifted powdered sugar. *Makes 1⅔ cups (400 g)*

Orange Glaze

In a small bowl, stir together 2 cups (200 g) sifted *powdered sugar*, 3 tablespoons (45 ml) *orange juice*, 1 teaspoon grated *orange peel*, and 1 teaspoon *vanilla*. Drizzle over cooled tube cake. *Makes ⅔ cup (160 ml)*

Gingerbread

½ cup (100 g) sugar
3 tablespoons grated fresh ginger or 1 teaspoon ground ginger
½ teaspoon ground cinnamon
¼ teaspoon ground cloves
¼ teaspoon salt
½ cup (120 ml) vegetable oil
1 cup (240 ml) light molasses
1 cup (240 ml) boiling water
2 teaspoons baking soda
2½ cups (310 g) all-purpose flour
2 large eggs, well beaten

Lightly butter and flour-dust a 9-inch (23-cm) square baking pan; set aside.

In a medium-size bowl, combine sugar, ginger, cinnamon, cloves, and salt. Stir in oil, then molasses; blend well. In a cup, combine boiling water and baking soda and immediately stir into molasses mixture. Stir flour into liquid mixture gradually to prevent lumping. Stir in eggs, then pour into prepared pan.

Bake in a 350°F (175°C) oven until a wooden pick inserted in center comes out clean and cake starts to pull away from sides of pan (40 to 45 minutes). Place pan on a rack to cool.   *Makes 16 servings*

PER SERVING: *225 calories, 8 g total fat, 1 g saturated fat, 27 mg cholesterol, 208 mg sodium, 36 g carbohydrates, 0.5 g fiber, 3 g protein, 50 mg calcium, 2 mg iron*

SPONGE CAKES

Leavened by beaten egg whites, sponge cakes are characteristically light and delicate. Their main ingredients are eggs, sugar, and flour—sponge cakes never contain shortening. If made with whole eggs, the cake is called a sponge cake; if made with egg whites only, it is angel food cake—which, if unfrosted, is a virtually fat-free dessert.

The sponge cake for the Chocolate Cake Roll recipe is baked as a sheet cake, then rolled around a delectable chocolate-flecked cream filling. The Angel Food Cake is a basic recipe that's the perfect foil for fresh berries.

Perfectly beaten eggs are the key to success with these cakes. For sponge cake, the whole eggs should be beaten until thick and lemon colored. Adding a little cream of tartar to the egg whites for angel food cakes increases tenderness.

Chocolate Cake Roll

¾ cup (95 g) all-purpose flour

¼ cup (22 g) unsweetened cocoa powder

1 teaspoon baking powder

1 teaspoon ground cinnamon

¼ teaspoon salt

3 large eggs

½ cup (110 g) firmly packed brown sugar

½ cup (100 g) plus 3 tablespoons granulated sugar

⅓ cup (80 ml) water

1 teaspoon grated orange peel

1 teaspoon vanilla

   About ⅓ cup (40 g) powdered sugar

1 cup (240 ml) whipping cream

¾ teaspoon instant coffee granules

¾ cup (125 g) mini chocolate chips

   Fresh orange slices (optional)

Lightly butter a 10- by 15-inch (25- by 38-cm) rimmed baking pan. Line the bottom with wax paper, then butter paper; set aside. Sift together flour, cocoa, baking powder, ½ teaspoon of the cinnamon, and the salt; set aside.

In a medium-size bowl, beat eggs with an electric mixer at high speed until eggs are thick and lemon colored. Force brown sugar through a strainer to get rid of hard lumps. Gradually add brown sugar and ½ cup (100 g) of the granulated sugar to eggs, while beating egg mixture on high speed. Continue beating, scraping bowl often, until mixture is light and fluffy and falls in a thick ribbon. With a rubber spatula, mix in water, orange peel, and vanilla.

Sprinkle about one third of flour mixture over egg mixture and carefully fold together. Add another third of flour mixture and fold together. Repeat with final third of flour mixture, folding together until ingredients are well blended. Pour batter into prepared pan and spread evenly.

Bake in a 375°F (190°C) oven until top springs back when gently touched (12 to 15 minutes). Immediately invert cake onto a clean dish towel sprinkled with about ⅓ cup (40 g) powdered sugar. Remove wax paper and immediately roll cake and towel into a cylinder from one short end; let cool completely on a rack.

Meanwhile, to prepare chocolate chip filling, in a large bowl, beat cream with remaining 3 tablespoons sugar until soft peaks form. Add remaining

½ teaspoon cinnamon and the coffee granules, and beat until stiff. Fold in chocolate chips.

Unroll cake, spread with filling, then reroll. (At this point, you may wrap in plastic wrap and refrigerate for up to 24 hours.) To serve, let cake warm to room temperature. If desired, sift additional powdered sugar over cake and garnish with orange slices.
Makes 10 servings

PER SERVING: *311 calories, 14 g total fat, 8 g saturated fat, 90 mg cholesterol, 135 mg sodium, 46 g carbohydrates, 0.9 g fiber, 4 g protein, 72 mg calcium, 2 mg iron*

Angel Food Cake

1 cup (117 g) sifted cake flour

1¼ cups (250 g) sugar

1½ cups (360 ml) large egg whites (about 11 eggs)

¼ teaspoon salt

1 teaspoon cream of tartar

1 teaspoon vanilla

Sift together flour and ¼ cup (50 g) of the sugar; sift again and set aside. In a large bowl, beat egg whites with an electric mixer until frothy. Add salt and cream of tartar and continue beating until soft peaks form. Add the remaining 1 cup (200 g) sugar, 2 tablespoons at a time, beating well after each addition. Continue beating until stiff peaks form; add vanilla halfway through this process.

Sprinkle flour mixture, about ¼ cup (30 g) at a time, over stiff whites, each time gently folding in with a rubber spatula just until blended. Pour batter into an unbuttered 10-inch (25-cm) plain tube pan and gently smooth top. Slide spatula into batter and run it around pan to eliminate large air bubbles.

Bake in a 350°F (175°C) oven until crust looks golden and top springs back when gently touched (about 45 minutes). Remove pan from oven and immediately turn upside down over a funnel or soda bottle. (This prevents cake from shrinking and falling.) Leave cake in this position until completely cooled. Remove from pan and frost, if desired.
Makes 12 servings

PER SERVING: *126 calories, 0.1 g total fat, 0 g saturated fat, 0 mg cholesterol, 95 mg sodium, 28 g carbohydrates, 0 g fiber, 4 g protein, 4 mg calcium, 0.6 mg iron*

FROSTINGS: THE FINAL TOUCH

A crowning touch on any homemade cake, these luscious frostings are simple to mix, yet incomparably rich. The recipes on this page will be sufficient enough to frost a two-layer 8-inch (20-cm) cake, a two-layer 9-inch (23-cm) cake, or two 7- by 11-inch (18- by 28-cm) sheet cakes.

Fluffy Butter Frosting

    1 box (1 lb./455 g) powdered sugar
    ½ cup (4 oz./110 g) butter or margarine, melted and cooled
    4 to 6 tablespoons (60 to 90 ml) 2% milk
    1 teaspoon vanilla, almond, lemon, orange, or rum extract

Sift powdered sugar into a medium-size bowl. Add melted butter, 4 tablespoons (60 ml) of the milk, and extract of your choice; stir to blend. Beat with an electric mixer on high speed until frosting is light and fluffy and of spreading consistency (4 to 5 minutes). If it seems a little thick, beat in 1 or 2 more tablespoons (15 to 30 ml) of the milk.
Makes about 2¼ cups (595 g)

PER TABLESPOON: *73 calories, 3 g total fat, 2 g saturated fat, 7 mg cholesterol, 27 mg sodium, 13 g carbohydrates, 0 g fiber, 0.1 g protein, 4 mg calcium, 0 mg iron*

Chocolate Butter Frosting

Prepare *Fluffy Butter Frosting*, but sift ¼ cup (22 g) *unsweetened cocoa powder* into powdered sugar.

Mocha Butter Frosting

Prepare *Fluffy Butter Frosting*, but sift ¼ cup (22 g) *unsweetened cocoa powder* into powdered sugar, and stir 1 teaspoon *instant coffee granules* into melted butter.

Orange Butter Frosting

Prepare *Fluffy Butter Frosting*, but use ¼ cup (60 ml) *orange juice* instead of milk, and stir in 1 teaspoon grated *orange peel* with the powdered sugar.

Buttercream Frosting

    ½ cup (100 g) sugar
    ¼ cup (60 ml) water
    2 large egg yolks
   12 tablespoons (6 oz./170 g) butter, softened
    2 tablespoons (30 ml) 2% milk

In a small pan over medium-high heat, bring sugar and water to a boil, brushing down the sides of the pan with a damp pastry brush. Continue to boil without stirring, until mixture reaches the soft-ball stage (240°F/116°C on a candy thermometer).

Meanwhile, place egg yolks in a large bowl and beat with an electric mixer until light and lemon colored. With beaters going, add hot syrup to eggs by pouring it down the side of the bowl in a slow, steady stream (if sugar syrup hits beaters, it will form threads). Continue to beat, scraping bowl often, until mixture feels cool to the touch (about 5 minutes). Beat in butter, a tablespoon at a time, until light and fluffy. Stir in milk until mixture reaches desired spreading consistency. *Makes about 1⅓ cups (290 g)*

PER TABLESPOON: *83 calories, 7 g total fat, 4 g saturated fat, 38 mg cholesterol, 68 mg sodium, 5 g carbohydrates, 0 g fiber, 0.4 g protein, 6 mg calcium, 0.1 mg iron*

Frosting a Layer Cake

Completely cool cake layers before frosting them, and brush off all loose crumbs from the sides and bottom of each layer. To keep your cake plate clean, lay four narrow strips of wax paper around the plate's edge to form a square (the ends should overlap and extend beyond the plate). Pull the strips away when the cake is frosted.

Center one cake layer, top side down, on the plate. Spoon about ⅓ cup (72 g) frosting onto the center of the layer. Using a metal spatula, evenly spread frosting to the cake's edge. Place the second layer, top side up, on the frosted layer. Next, frost the sides. With a metal spatula held vertically, spread a thin layer of frosting around the sides of the cake. Then finish the sides with more frosting. Spoon the remaining frosting on top of the cake and spread it evenly from the center to the edges.

ABOUT FRUIT

Offering nutritional value that no other dessert can match, fruit also presents a nearly endless variety of taste and texture. Brimming with vitamins and minerals, fruits contain virtually no fat (avocados—more often eaten as a vegetable—are an exception). Packed with natural sugars, fruit is a good source of energy.

Fruit-lovers look forward to summer and the arrival of all their favorites—apricots, cherries, grapes, peaches, nectarines, and plums; watermelon and cantaloupe, as well as casaba, crenshaw, honeydew, and Persian melons; and a bounty of berries in shades of gold, red, purple, blue, and black.

In autumn you'll see more melons and grapes, but the glory of this season is a crop of crisp new apples and mellow pears. It's also time for two very special treats: persimmons and pomegranates.

With the winter months come tangerines, mandarins, oranges, and grapefruits. Then spring opens the show once again, as strawberries reappear among the apples, pears, and citrus fruits that have sustained us through the wintertime.

Thanks to modern transportation and storage, perishable fruits now travel year round to most parts of the country. But for best optimal flavor and texture—and best value for your money—it's still a good idea to buy fruits when they're in season. Better still, buy locally grown fruits when you can; that way you'll enjoy the crunchiest apples, juiciest peaches, and dewiest berries.

Choosing & storing fresh fruit

Fruit quality shows in degree of ripeness, color, firmness, and, of course, freedom from decay. Exceptionally large fruits are a risky choice—they often lack flavor and juice. The least expensive fruits in the bin may not prove to be bargains after all, if the price is low because they're bruised or past their prime.

Since fruit quality varies throughout a season and depends on the location of the harvest, only experience can guide you to wise choices. But a few general rules will help you select quality fruit. Choose loose fruit rather than fruit wrapped in cellophane, then store it in plastic bags in the refrigerator.

Bananas and pears, both picked when under-ripe, need some time to develop their natural sweetness. Ripen at room temperature, placing the fruit in a paper bag if you want to speed the process. Once it is ripe, eat the fruit as soon as possible; refrigeration damages the texture of both bananas and pears.

Melons, apricots, peaches, and plums, if purchased rock-hard and even slightly green, will never reach their ultimate sweetness and flavor; however, melons and stone fruits (those with a single large pit) will become softer and more fragrant if left at room temperature for a day or two. Look for melons that are well rounded and heavy for their size; avoid melons that have flat surfaces or peaked ends. Select watermelons with a yellowish streak on one side. Once ripe, melons should be refrigerated. Choose orange-yellow apricots and peaches that are firm but yield slightly to the touch. Plums should have rich, uniform color and be firm, yielding slightly to the touch.

Grapes should be plump and firmly attached to the stem; store grapes in the refrigerator. Berries are usually expensive, so it pays to be choosy when purchasing them. Check the basket or box for stains on the bottom, which indicate spoiled or crushed berries. When you take them home, pick through them, discarding any bruised, decayed, moldy berries—but don't wash them yet. Refrigerate, loosely covered, and use within a day or two.

Choose smooth-skinned citrus fruit that's fairly round, compact, and heavy for its size. In summer, refrigerate it if it's not to be eaten soon. If you're squeezing the fruit for juice, warm it under hot tap water and it will yield more juice.

Apples taste best when firm and crisp. If not refrigerated, they'll quickly lose their snappy taste and texture, turning bland and mushy. Sample different varieties rather than limiting yourself to the most familiar ones, such as McIntosh and Red Delicious. Try Jonathans for pie-baking, Gravensteins for making sauce, and Rome Beauties for baking whole.

Cheese with fruit

A natural dessert, fruit and cheese complement each other beautifully. Pass a basket of choice whole fruit with a tray of cheese wedges, and provide cheese cutters and small, sharp knives for informal feasting. Suggested below are some winning cheese and fruit partnerships—there are no rules, though, so experiment freely.

Try blue, Gorgonzola, and Roquefort with apples and pears; Brie with berries, papaya, mangoes, apples, and pears; Cheddar with pears and red-skinned apples; jarlsberg and Gouda with apples, pears, and apricots; provolone with pineapple; Swiss and Emmenthaler with pears; and jack or teleme with apricots, melons, and plums.

Apple Crisp

- ⅔ cup (85 g) all-purpose flour or whole wheat flour
- ¼ cup (55 g) firmly packed brown sugar
- ¼ cup (50 g) granulated sugar
- 2 teaspoons ground cinnamon
- 5 tablespoons (2.5 oz./71 g) butter or margarine
- 7 or 8 Golden Delicious apples (2 to 2½ lbs./905 g to 1.15 kg total)
- 1½ teaspoons grated lemon peel
- 1 tablespoon (15 ml) lemon juice

Lightly butter a 9-inch (23-cm) square baking pan; set aside.

In a small bowl, combine flour, brown sugar, granulated sugar, and 1 teaspoon of the cinnamon. With a pastry blender or your fingers, cut in butter until mixture is crumbly; set aside.

Peel and core apples; thinly slice into a medium-size bowl. Sprinkle with the remaining 1 teaspoon cinnamon, the lemon peel, and lemon juice; toss to coat apples. Spread apples in prepared baking pan. Sprinkle crumb mixture evenly over apples.

Bake in a 375°F (190°C) oven, uncovered, until apples are fork-tender and top crust is browned and crisp (about 45 minutes). Let cool for at least 30 minutes before serving, or let cool completely and serve at room temperature.   *Makes 6 to 8 servings*

PER SERVING: *252 calories, 9 g total fat, 5 g saturated fat, 22 mg cholesterol, 88 mg sodium, 43 g carbohydrates, 3 g fiber, 2 g protein, 25 mg calcium, 1 mg iron*

Pear Crisp

Prepare *Apple Crisp*, but substitute the same weight of d'Anjou or Bartlett *pears* for the apples.

Creative Crisps

You can easily vary the topping for a fruit crisp by substituting another ingredient for some of the flour. Rolled oats, chopped walnuts, pecans, or almonds, or crushed gingersnaps are some possibilities. You can also subtly alter the flavor of the filling by adding spices (nutmeg, allspice) or flavoring extracts (almond or vanilla).

Cherry-Blueberry Crisp

- 1 cup (80 g) quick-cooking rolled oats
- Generous ½ cup (110 g) firmly packed brown sugar
- ¾ teaspoon ground cinnamon
- ¼ teaspoon ground ginger
- 3 tablespoons (1½ oz./45 g) butter or margarine, melted
- 2 tablespoons all-purpose flour
- 3 cups (435 g) pitted sweet dark cherries
- 2 cups (290 g) blueberries, rinsed and drained
- 1 tablespoon (15 ml) lemon juice
- Vanilla lowfat frozen yogurt

To make oatmeal topping, in a large bowl, stir together rolled oats, ¼ cup (55 g) of the brown sugar, ½ teaspoon of the cinnamon, the ginger, and melted butter. Set aside.

In a shallow 8-inch (20-cm) round or square casserole, stir remaining brown sugar (gauge amount of sugar by sweetness of fruit) with flour and remaining ¼ teaspoon cinnamon. Add cherries, blueberries, and lemon juice; mix well. Spread fruit evenly in casserole and sprinkle evenly with oatmeal topping.

Bake in a 350°F (175°C) oven until fruit mixture bubbles and topping is golden brown (35 to 40 minutes). Serve hot, warm, or cool. Scoop into bowls and serve with frozen yogurt.   *Makes 6 servings*

PER SERVING: *276 calories, 8 g total fat, 4 g saturated fat, 16 mg cholesterol, 71 mg sodium, 52 g carbohydrates, 4 g fiber, 4 g protein, 45 mg calcium, 2 mg iron*

Peach Cobbler with Almond Topping

- 9 medium-size firm-ripe peaches (about 3 lbs./1.35 kg total)
- ½ cup (100 g) plus 2 tablespoons sugar
- 2 tablespoons (30 ml) lemon juice
- 4 tablespoons (32 g) cornstarch
- 1 cup (7oz./200 g) almond paste

Immerse peaches in boiling water to cover for 2 to 3 seconds. Lift out, cool briefly, then pull off skins with a knife. Pit and slice peaches into a shallow 1½- to 2-quart (1.4- to 1.9-liter) casserole.

Add the 2 tablespoons sugar, the lemon juice, and 2 tablespoons of the cornstarch to peaches; mix gently.

To make almond topping, crumble almond paste into a bowl. Add remaining ½ cup (100 g) sugar and 2 tablespoons cornstarch. Rub with your fingers until well blended. Squeeze mixture together, then break into about ½-inch (1-cm) chunks. Sprinkle fruit evenly with almond topping.

Bake in a 350°F (175°C) oven until topping is browned and center is bubbling (45 to 50 minutes). Serve hot or cool.   *Makes 8 servings*

PER SERVING: *259 calories, 8 g total fat, 0.7 g saturated fat, 0 mg cholesterol, 4 mg sodium, 46 g carbohydrates, 2 g fiber, 4 g protein, 72 mg calcium, 1 mg iron*

Strawberry Shortcake with Lemon-Ginger Cream

About 2 cups (250 g) all-purpose flour

About ⅓ cup (70 g) plus 4 tablespoons (50 g) sugar

3½ teaspoons grated lemon peel

2 teaspoons baking powder

½ teaspoon baking soda

½ teaspoon salt

½ cup (4 oz./115 g) butter or margarine, cut into chunks

⅔ cup (160 ml) buttermilk

2 large egg yolks

2 quarts (1.2 kg) strawberries, rinsed and hulled, at room temperature

1 cup (240 ml) crème fraîche or sour cream

⅓ cup (38 g) chopped crystallized ginger

½ cup (120 ml) whipping cream

In a large bowl, combine 2 cups (250 g) of the flour, ⅓ cup (70 g) of the sugar, 2 teaspoons of the lemon peel, the baking powder, baking soda, and salt. With a pastry blender or your fingers, cut in or rub in butter until mixture looks mealy. In a small bowl, combine buttermilk and egg yolks, then add to flour mixture and stir with a fork until dough holds together.

On a floured board, knead dough with floured hands just until smooth, 15 to 20 turns. Reflour board and pat out dough 1 inch (2.5 cm) thick. Cut into 6 rounds with a floured 2½- to 3-inch (6- to 8-cm) round cutter, gathering and repatting scraps as needed. Lift onto a 12- by 15-inch (30- by 38-cm) baking sheet and sprinkle with 1 teaspoon sugar.

Bake shortcakes in a 400°F (205°C) oven until deep golden (12 to 14 minutes). Transfer to a rack until cool (at least 30 minutes).

Set aside 6 whole berries. Slice remaining berries into a medium-size bowl. Add 2 tablespoons of the sugar and stir to coat; let stand for up to 1 hour.

Just before assembling, prepare lemon-ginger cream. In a small bowl, combine crème fraîche, crystallized ginger, 2 tablespoons of the sugar, and remaining 1½ teaspoons lemon peel. In the large bowl of an electric mixer, beat the whipping cream until thick. Fold in crème-fraîche mixture.

Split shortcakes horizontally and place each bottom on a plate. Cover bottom pieces with some lemon-ginger cream and sliced berries, then cover with the shortcake tops. Garnish each with a whole berry. Serve remaining lemon-ginger cream and sliced berries on the side.   *Makes 6 servings*

PER SERVING: *721 calories, 39 g total fat, 24 g saturated fat, 169 mg cholesterol, 682 mg sodium, 84 g carbohydrates, 7 g fiber, 10 g protein, 300 mg calcium, 6 mg iron*

Fruit Sauces

Try these sweet sauces drizzled sundae-style over scoops of your favorite ice cream or over fresh fruit.

Blueberry sauce. *In a pan, combine ⅓ cup (70 g) sugar and 1 tablespoon cornstarch. Add 2 cups (290 g) fresh or frozen (thawed) blueberries, 2 tablespoons (30 ml) lemon juice, and ⅓ cup (80 ml) water. Cook, stirring, over medium heat until mixture boils and thickens (4 to 5 minutes). Serve warm or cold. This sauce thickens as it cools.   Makes about 1⅔ cups (400 ml)*

Raspberry or strawberry sauce. *In a small pan, combine 1 package (about 10 oz./285 g) frozen (thawed) sweetened raspberries or strawberries, ½ teaspoon cornstarch, and 1 tablespoon (15 ml) light corn syrup. Bring to a rolling boil over medium-high heat; continue to boil, stirring constantly, for 2 minutes. Remove from heat; then cool, cover, and refrigerate. This sauce thickens as it cools. Serve cold.*
Makes about 1 cup (about 240 ml)

Red Wine Poached Pears

    4   medium-size firm pears (d'Anjou or Bosc), with stems
        (about 1½ lbs./680 g total)
    3   cups (710 ml) dry red wine
    ⅓   cup (70 g) sugar
   10   black peppercorns
    4   strips orange peel, about 1 by 3 inches (2.5 by 8 cm)
    ¼   teaspoon ground ginger

Using a vegetable peeler, peel pears; leave stems
With a melon baller or sharp paring knife, scoop out
and discard core and seeds, working from blossom
(bottom) end of each pear. Cut a thin slice from the
bottom of each pear so that the pears stand upright.

In a 2- to 3-quart (1.9- to 2.8-liter) nonstick pan,
combine wine, sugar, peppercorns, orange peel, and
ginger. Bring to a boil over medium-high heat. Stand
pears, stem up, in pan. Cover, reduce heat, and simmer until just fork-tender (15 to 20 minutes; time
will vary, depending on variety and ripeness of
pears).

With a slotted spoon, lift pears from spiced wine
to a bowl; set aside. Increase heat to high and boil
spiced wine, uncovered, stirring occasionally, until
reduced to about 1 cup (240 ml). Pour reduced wine
mixture over pears; cool, cover, and refrigerate for at
least 4 hours or until next day. To serve, place each
pear on a dessert plate and spoon some of the spiced
wine over each pear.   *Makes 4 servings*

PER SERVING: *179 calories, 0.7 g total fat, 0 g saturated fat, 0 mg
cholesterol, 9 mg sodium, 46 g carbohydrates, 4 g fiber, 1 g protein,
35 mg calcium, 1 mg iron*

Choosing Pears

*Whole pears poached in spiced wine make a beautiful and
sophisticated dessert. Boscs, with their elongated shape and
firm, crunchy flesh, hold their shape well, so they're especially good for poaching or baking. Plump d'Anjou pears
are nearly oval, have softer, blander flesh, but the assertive
spices in the recipe above will overcome any lack of flavor.
You could also use squat Comice pears, which are won-
derfully sweet, or Bartletts, which are extra-juicy.*

Tropical Fruit Platter with Strawberry Sauce

    2   cups (275 g) strawberries, hulled and rinsed
        About 2 tablespoons (30 ml) orange-flavor liqueur, such as
        Grand Marnier (optional)
        About 1 tablespoon sugar
    1   medium-size pineapple (about 3 lbs./1.35 kg), peeled, cored,
        quartered lengthwise, and cut crosswise into ¼-inch
        (6-mm) slices
    2   small firm-ripe papayas (about 2 lbs./905 g total), peeled,
        halved lengthwise, seeded, and cut crosswise into ¼-inch
        (6-mm) slices
    6   medium-size kiwifruit (about 1½ lbs./680 g total), peeled
        and cut crosswise into ¼-inch (6-mm) slices

In a blender or food processor, whirl strawberries
until smooth. Add orange-flavor liqueur, if using,
and sugar to taste. (At this point, you may cover
strawberry sauce and chill for up to 2 days.)

On a large platter, overlap slices of each fruit,
grouping each kind separately. Drizzle strawberry
sauce over fruit.   *Makes 12 servings*

PER SERVING: *91 calories, 0.6 g total fat, 0 g saturated fat, 0 mg cholesterol,
5 mg sodium, 23 g carbohydrates, 4 g fiber, 1 g protein, 33 mg calcium,
0.6 mg iron*

Berries with Herbs & Champagne

    1   quart (580 g) berries (raspberries, blackberries, or
        strawberries)
    1   tablespoon chopped fresh basil
    1   tablespoon chopped fresh mint
    1   bottle (750 ml) chilled champagne or sweet or
        dry sparkling wine
        Vanilla ice cream (optional)

Rinse and drain berries; hull and thinly slice strawberries (if using). Place equal portions of berries in
8 stemmed glasses. Scatter basil and mint over fruit.
Pour champagne over fruit. If desired, add a small
scoop of vanilla ice cream to each portion.
Makes 8 servings

PER SERVING: *94 calories, 0.3 g total fat, 0 g saturated fat, 0 mg cholesterol,
5 mg sodium, 8 g carbohydrates, 3 g fiber, 0.7 g protein, 23 mg calcium,
0.7 mg iron*

FROZEN FRUIT DESSERTS

Nothing is more refreshing on a hot day than a frozen fruit dessert. Only the Raspberry Sorbet recipe requires an ice cream maker.

Raspberry Sorbet

> 1¼ cups (250 g) sugar
> 1 cup (240 ml) water
> 1 quart (580 g) raspberries

In a 1- to 2-quart (950 ml- to 1.9-liter) nonstick pan over high heat, bring sugar and water to a boil, stirring until sugar dissolves. Let cool; chill until cold.

In a blender or food processor, whirl raspberries to a smooth purée. Press through a fine strainer set over a medium-size bowl, rubbing to extract all liquid; discard seeds. Blend in sugar syrup.

Freeze raspberry mixture in an ice cream maker according to manufacturer's directions until softly frozen. Place in freezer, airtight, until firm enough to scoop (2 to 3 hours). Before serving, let sorbet soften briefly at room temperature. *Makes 8 servings*

PER SERVING: *151 calories, 0.3 g total fat, 0 g saturated fat, 0 mg cholesterol, 0.3 mg sodium, 38 g carbohydrates, 3 g fiber, 0.6 g protein, 14 mg calcium, 0.4 mg iron*

Port Ice with Orange

> ½ cup (100 g) sugar
> 1½ cups (360 ml) water
> 1 cup (240 ml) port or cream sherry
> ¼ cup (60 ml) fresh orange juice
> 1 teaspoon aromatic bitters
> Orange slices and pomegranate seeds (optional)

In a 1- to 2-quart (950-ml to 1.9-liter) pan, combine sugar and water. Bring to a boil over high heat, stirring until sugar is dissolved. Remove from heat and let cool; then stir in port, orange juice, and bitters. Cover and refrigerate until cold (about 1 hour).

Pour port mixture into a 8- to 9-inch (20- to 23-cm) square metal pan; cover and freeze until solid (about 4 hours) or for up to 3 days.

To serve, break mixture into chunks with a heavy spoon, transfer to a blender or food processor, and whirl until slushy; then spoon into bowls and serve at once. Or pour cold port mixture into container of an ice cream machine and freeze according to manufacturer's directions. Garnish with orange slices and pomegranate seeds, if desired. *Makes 6 to 8 servings*

PER SERVING: *114 calories, 0 g total fat, 0 g saturated fat, 0 mg cholesterol, 3 mg sodium, 19 g carbohydrates, 0 g fiber, 0.1 g protein, 4 mg calcium, 0.1 mg iron*

Mango Granita

> 2 cups (372 g) chopped mango
> 1 cup (240 ml) guava juice
> ¼ cup (60 ml) fresh lime juice

In a food processor, whirl mango, guava juice, and lime juice to a smooth purée. Pour into ice cube trays and freeze for at least 2 hours. In food processor, with motor running, add slightly defrosted cubes and process until smooth. Serve, or freeze for up to 2 weeks. *Makes 4 to 6 servings*

PER SERVING: *82 calories, 0.2 g total fat, 0.1 g saturated fat, 0 mg cholesterol, 3 mg sodium, 21 g carbohydrates, 0.8 g fiber, 0.4 g protein, 11 mg calcium, 0.1 mg iron*

Ruby Grapefruit Sorbet

> 1 envelope unflavored gelatin
> 1½ cups (300 g) sugar
> 2 cups (470 ml) water
> 4 cups (950 ml) unstrained ruby grapefruit juice (takes about 4 lbs./1.8 kg of fruit)
> 2 tablespoons (30 ml) sweet vermouth (or grapefruit juice)
> 2 tablespoons (30 ml) grenadine syrup (or grapefruit juice)

In a 2- to 3-quart (1.9- to 2.8-liter) nonstick pan, combine gelatin and sugar; add water and bring to a boil over high heat. Stir until sugar dissolves. Let cool. Add grapefruit juice, vermouth, and grenadine syrup.

Pour mixture into a 9- by 13-inch (23- by 33-cm) metal pan; cover. Freeze until solid (at least 6 hours) or for up to 1 month. Break into small chunks and whirl in a food processor or beat with a mixer until a smooth slush forms. Return to freezer for 30 minutes.

Serve sorbet softly frozen. If stored, sorbet gets very hard; just beat again for smooth texture. Spoon into chilled dishes. *Makes 10 to 12 servings*

PER SERVING: *153 calories, 0.1 g total fat, 0 g saturated fat, 0 mg cholesterol, 3 mg sodium, 37 g carbohydrates, 0 g fiber, 1 g protein, 9 mg calcium, 0.2 mg iron*

HARD MERINGUE

Here, beaten egg whites are lightly sweetened, then transformed into crisp, delicate, baked meringues—irresistible with whipped cream or fresh fruit, or with scoops of ice cream, sherbet, sorbet, or granita drizzled with fresh fruit sauce.

Baked meringues should be white to faint amber in color, crisp, and very dry to the touch. Avoid making meringues on a very humid day because they won't be as crisp as they should. Meringues are baked at a very low temperature, then left in the turned-off oven to become crisp and completely dry. Because meringues absorb moisture readily, they shouldn't be filled or topped until just before serving. Store meringues in an airtight container.

Meringue Shells

 4 *large egg whites (about ½ cup/120 ml), at room temperature*
 ½ *teaspoon cream of tartar*
 1 *cup (200 g) sugar*
 1 *teaspoon vanilla*

Cover a baking sheet with parchment paper or plain ungreased brown paper (you can cut up a heavy brown paper bag, if you like). Trace eight 3½-inch (9-cm) circles on the brown paper, about 1½ inches (3.5 cm) apart. Set aside.

Using an electric mixer and a large bowl that holds at least 6 cups (1.4 liters) below top curve of beaters, combine egg whites and cream of tartar. Beat at highest speed until mixture is just frothy. Continue beating while gradually sprinkling about 1 tablespoon sugar a minute over the beaten whites, and scraping bowl frequently with a rubber spatula.

When all sugar is incorporated, add vanilla and beat for 1 more minute. When beaters are lifted out, whites should hold very stiff, sharp, unbending peaks. Spoon about ½ cup (55 g) of the beaten egg white mixture onto each circle on the prepared pan (or pipe the mixture onto the pan using a pastry tube with a large plain tip—or no tip). Using the back of the spoon, spread mixture to cover each circle, then form a hollow in each, building up a rim about ¾ inches (2 cm) high around the outside.

Position baking sheet just below oven center. Bake in a 250°F (120°C) oven for 1 hour; turn off heat and leave shells in closed oven for 3 to 4 hours to dry.

Remove from oven and cool completely; then carefully peel off paper backing. (At this point, you may store in an airtight container for up to 5 days.) *Makes 8 individual shells*

PER SHELL: *107 calories, 0 g total fat, 0 g saturated fat, 0 mg cholesterol, 28 mg sodium, 25 g carbohydrates, 0 g fiber, 2 g protein, 1 mg calcium, 0 mg iron*

Strawberry Clouds

 ⅓ *cup (42 g) slivered almonds*
 2 *large egg whites*
    About ⅔ cup (135 g) sugar
 ¾ *teaspoon almond extract*
 ¾ *cup (60 g) finely crushed vanilla cookie wafer crumbs (about 24 cookies)*
 2 *cups (240 g) strawberries, rinsed, hulled, and sliced*
    Vanilla nonfat frozen yogurt

Spread almonds in an 8- to 10-inch (20- to 25-cm) wide baking pan. Bake in a 350°F (175°C) oven until golden (5 to 8 minutes). Finely chop nuts.

In a large, deep bowl, beat egg whites with an electric mixer on high speed until they hold soft peaks. Continue beating at high speed, gradually adding ⅔ cup (135 g) of the sugar, 1 tablespoon at a time, until whites hold stiff peaks. Add extract and beat to blend, then fold in nuts and cookie crumbs.

Scrape meringue mixture into an oiled or buttered 8-inch (20-cm) removable-rim pan. Swirl mixture to make an even layer. Bake in a 350°F (175°C) oven until meringue feels dry and firm when touched and is a light golden brown (about 20 minutes).

Let meringue stand in pans to cool. (At this point, you may package airtight and let stand up until next day.) Remove pan rim and set meringue on a platter.

Mix strawberries with sugar to taste and spoon over the meringue. Cut dessert into wedges and serve with scoops of frozen yogurt.   *Makes 6 servings*

PER SERVING: *201 calories, 6 g total fat, 0.7 g saturated fat, 0 mg cholesterol, 53 mg sodium, 36 g carbohydrates, 2 g fiber, 4 g protein, 33 mg calcium, 0.7 mg iron*

INDEX